THE HIGH ACHIEVER'S GUIDE TO WEALTH

Second Edition

Also by

Palisades Hudson Financial Group LLC

Looking Ahead: Life, Family, Wealth and Business After 55

Also by

Palisades Hudson Financial Group founder Larry M. Elkin

Financial Self-Defense for Unmarried Couples:
How to Gain Financial Protection Denied by Law

SECOND EDITION

THE HIGH ACHIEVER'S GUIDE TO WEALTH

WRITTEN BY THE FINANCIAL ADVISERS OF

PALISADES HUDSON FINANCIAL GROUP LLC

EDITED BY AMY LABURDA

Edited by Amy Laburda

ISBN: 979-8-218-41893-9

Kindle Direct Publishing

Book Design by Iskon Book Design

ACKNOWLEDGMENTS

I've found that a hazard of working at a financial planning firm for many years is becoming a go-to source for advice — no matter how many times you explain to friends and family that you, yourself, are not a financial planner. I don't blame anyone who has asked me this sort of question. For one thing, after more than 14 years at Palisades Hudson Financial Group, I have learned a thing or two (though my experience has made me acutely aware of how much I still don't know). For another, my job is unusual. Not many financial firms have a dedicated, in-house editorial manager. Even fewer firms our size do. So I understand the confusion.

Luckily for me, when my friends ask for help these days, I can hand them a copy of this book. My name is on the cover as the editor, and I am very proud of it in that capacity. But the advice and expertise between the covers comes from 15 of my talented colleagues, the people who should be providing it. My friends feel like I helped them, and I know they are getting expert answers. Everyone wins.

This is the second edition of our book for adults in their 20s, 30s and 40s. When we wrote the first edition, we were loosely targeting my fellow millennials. Today, a solid portion of Generation Z has joined our intended audience, while the oldest millennials are inching their way out of it. That said, most generation labels are somewhat arbitrary. My colleagues have provided information and guidance on milestones including marrying, buying a home, welcoming children and assisting aging parents. Readers are likely to experience these events at a variety of times, if at all. This is why we have written each chapter to stand on its own, ready when it's needed.

In addition to the expertise of our 15 authors, I am indebted to the technical edit provided by Palisades Hudson's founder and president, Larry Elkin. Larry has been providing personal financial and tax counseling to clients since 1986. I deeply appreciated his experience when ensuring that the text was accurate and clear. Larry and I have worked together on all three editions of the firm's previous book, *Looking Ahead: Life, Family, Wealth and Business After 55*, as well as on the firm's *Sentinel* newsletter and (between 2010 and 2021) its "Current Commentary" blog. I continue to admire his eye for detail and his dedication to accessible writing.

As a writer and editor, I'm unapologetically a word person, but I know a book's look and feel matter too. Luckily, the expert help of Najdan Mancic of Iskon Design, Inc. means you have this attractive edition to read, whether you are holding a physical book or reading an e-book on your own device. He has my sincere thanks for his contributions.

While their names do not appear on any chapters, I would be remiss not to mention the rest of the Palisades Hudson staff. Our client service managers and associates benefit daily from the skilled support of our financial planning managers: Stephen Grady III, Ashley Luhmann and Kirstie Ward. They, along with financial planning associate Lesley Oberstadt, work in tandem with the rest of the client service team to provide the highest level of service to our clients.

Our authors also benefit from the varied skills of our administrative staff. My fellow administrative managers Pascale Bocchino, Melissa DiNapoli and Cristina Galante handle the firm's accounting, human resources and facilities functions, respectively. From experience, however, I can attest that these titles only scratch the surface of their many talents and responsibilities. We are supported by administrative associates Alyssa Drowne and Jake Luhmann, who answer the firm's phones, handle its mail, schedule staff travel and much more.

Most members of Palisades Hudson's executive team contributed to this book directly as authors, but the other two certainly contributed indirectly. Jeffrey Howard, our director of technology, coordinated the many tools and services we used to create this book (and that we use to do all of our other work). And Linda Field Elkin, our director of marketing and HR, was instrumental to hiring nearly everyone at Palisades Hudson — including me. Without her, there would be no one here to write or edit a book.

As with everything my colleagues and I create, this volume would not be possible without the ongoing support of our partners, spouses, parents, children, friends and other loved ones. They let us offer our best on the job and give our work meaning. My collaborators and I couldn't have created *The High Achiever's Guide* without them.

In every book I have edited for Palisades Hudson, I end my acknowledgements with our clients, and deservedly so. Some of them have given helpful feedback, formal or informal, on the first edition of *The High Achiever's Guide to Wealth*. Many of them are the "high achievers" who we wrote this book to help. And all of them have opened their homes, their lives and their families to our firm. Their trust means everything to us. As in everything we do at Palisades Hudson, this book is for them.

CONTENTS

CHAPTER 1

ANYONE CAN ACHIEVE WEALTH

Larry M. Elkin, CPA, CFP®

In entertainer Garrison Keillor's fictional town of Lake Wobegon, Minnesota, all the children are eternally above average. The humor works because the math doesn't.

When you add up all the wins and losses in Major League Baseball next year, they will balance out to a perfectly mediocre .500 winning percentage, just like last year and the year before that. Baseball does not award points for losing in extra innings, the way the National Hockey League gives credit to the team that loses in overtime. For every winner in baseball, there must be a loser. It is a zero-sum game.

When it comes to achieving success, however, life more closely resembles fictional Lake Wobegon than real-world baseball, because life is *not* a zero-sum game. Nobody must "lose" at life for someone else to win. Not everybody will be a winner, but practically anybody can be.

Most of us can do at least one thing better than most other people can do it. We might be able to run faster or hit a ball farther. We might excel at music or pottery, at singing or acting, at mastering science or math, at fixing things that are broken, or at dreaming up new ways to fill a niche in a marketplace that nobody even noticed before. We might be great at playing the latest video game, or at knitting, or at fantasy football. A high achiever is anyone who excels at anything. There are people who make at least a perfectly good living, and sometimes quite a bit more than that, at every single thing I just mentioned. In fact, there is almost nothing a high achiever can achieve that cannot be done for monetary gain. Some people make money by winning hot-dog-eating contests.

Of course, an individual's exceptional abilities in one area do not mean the individual excels when it comes to acquiring, investing, spending or even giving away money. These are different skill sets. Even people who start and run successful businesses, or earn fortunes on a field or a stage, can struggle with managing their taxes, saving for old age, or raising well-adjusted and productive children rather than proverbial "trust fund babies." Those who do inherit large sums can be overwhelmed by requests from relatives or friends, pleas from charities and offers of advice — for payment or otherwise — on what to do with the new wealth.

This is where my colleagues and I come in. For over 30 years, we have worked with all sorts of individuals and families at all stages of wealth-building. We have helped newly graduated professionals launch their careers, inventors form startup companies and teenage performers sign their first deal. We have also helped newly affluent business executives arrange their personal finances and "old money" families establish modern financial plans even when much of their wealth is held in structures that were created many decades ago.

Experience has taught us, and modern third-party research has affirmed, that "wealth" means different things to different people. To most Americans — in fact, to most people on Earth today — a million dollars is a considerable sum of money; the Federal Reserve reported in 2022 that the average U.S. household's net worth was $1,063,700. This figure is skewed higher by the vast fortunes of people with names like Bezos, Buffett, Musk, Zuckerberg and Gates, along with a small number of other billionaires who are less famous. The median household net worth reported in that survey was just $192,900, which means half the reporting households had net equity below that figure when you subtract their debts from their assets.

Yet a separate survey by Charles Schwab & Co. released in 2023 said most Americans would not describe a $1 million net worth as enough to be considered wealthy. The survey put the figure the average respondent considered worthy of the label at around $2.2 million.

But is being "wealthy" really a function purely of how much money or other material wealth an individual or household has accumulated? The same Schwab survey that produced the $2.2 million figure reported 72% of respondents who said their personal definition of wealth depends more upon how a person lives his or her life, rather than on net worth.

I would rephrase it this way: Net worth, or at least the appearance of net worth, is how we judge whether *someone else* is wealthy. We look at the houses they buy, the cars they drive, the clothes and jewelry they wear, and the vacations they post on social media, and we make assumptions about their personal balance sheets. Ostentatious displays of wealth can be misleading, but they are easy to see. Most of us are inclined to take mental shortcuts much of the time, especially when we don't have more reliable information to guide us. The converse is also true. Many people who have substantial wealth choose to live and dress so modestly that even some of their closest acquaintances may have no idea how financially well-off they are.

When it comes to judging whether we ourselves are wealthy, we look at other factors. We ask ourselves questions such as: Are our physical needs met? Do we find our work fulfilling and pleasant? Do we have access to companionship when we want it and solitude when we need it? Are our families well-provided for, healthy and content? Are we engaged and respected in our community? Do we have a sense of security that our situation may not abruptly take a turn for the worse? The more of these questions we answer affirmatively, the more likely we are to consider ourselves "wealthy," regardless of the exact level of our bank balance. If we were to encounter someone who possesses only money but none of these other attributes, we would probably be inclined more toward pity than envy.

Of course, while money alone may not buy happiness, it can help — a lot. Many of the other characteristics that give rise to a feeling of personal wealth require at least a certain amount of material comfort or professional success to achieve. A study by Harvard Business School researchers and several collaborators, published in 2017, surveyed 4,000 millionaires from countries around the globe. On balance, they were pretty happy, as we might expect. Those who created their wealth from their own efforts reported somewhat more happiness than those who inherited their money. It took a lot of money — a net worth greater than $8 million or so — before individuals reported themselves being significantly happier than their fellow millionaires of more relatively modest means. Genuine financial security is not the only driver of wealth, but it is an important component of it.

"Wealth" is a subjective and relative concept. In January 1941, with America still struggling to emerge from the Great Depression and Europe and the Far East already immersed in war, President Franklin D. Roosevelt made his famous "Four Freedoms" speech. It was his eighth State of the Union address to a joint session of Congress. In it, Roosevelt laid out a vision of what prosperity and security would mean in his place and time.

"In the future days, which we seek to make secure, we look forward to a world founded upon four essential human freedoms," Roosevelt declared. "The first is freedom of speech and expression everywhere in the world. The second is freedom of every person to worship God in his own way everywhere in the world. The third is freedom from want — which translated into world terms means economic understandings which will secure to every nation a healthy peace time life for its inhabitants everywhere in the world. The fourth is freedom from fear — which translated into world terms means a worldwide reduction of armaments to such a point and in such a thorough fashion that no nation will be in a position to commit an act of physical aggression against any neighbor anywhere in the world."

If having wealth is about having choices, achieving wealth is about making sound choices that bring you to that point.

An analysis by Max Roser published in 2019 on the website "Our World in Data" shows that even as Roosevelt spoke, the world was in the midst of a global explosion of economic growth that began with the Industrial Revolution and continued through the 20th century and into the 21st, lifting hundreds of millions of people out of physical poverty. The spread of freedom of expression has been a mixed bag at best, however. As for Roosevelt's pledge of global disarmament as a cornerstone of freedom from fear, we are probably further away from that position than ever. But most of us would agree that the world is, on balance, far wealthier now than was the case in 1941. We eat better and dress better. Virtually nobody would want to trade today's health care, communication or transportation options for what was available to Roosevelt's audience.

Psychologist Abraham Maslow provided a seminal definition of well-being in his 1943 paper "A Theory of Human Motivation." Maslow posited that there is a hierarchy of needs, beginning with physical needs, then security, then emotional needs, then the esteem of others, and finally that of "self-actualization," which I would call the achievement of one's own satisfaction and self-esteem. If you possess all of these things, you might consider yourself wealthy.

Another widely shared view of wealth, and one to which I subscribe, is that wealth gives us choices. You can choose (at least to a degree) how much to work, as well as how to work. Joseph P. Kennedy founded the family fortune that enabled multiple generations of his descendants to dedicate their careers to political, nonprofit or philanthropic endeavors they found personally or socially rewarding even if not especially remunerative. Warren Buffett told Fortune magazine in 1986 (when his fortune was a fraction of what it later became, but still measured in billions) that he viewed the perfect amount to leave his children as being "enough money so that they would feel they could do anything, but not so much that they could do nothing." Buffett is still alive and working in his early 90s as I write this, and his children ended up dedicating most of their work to philanthropy, using funds seeded by their family's wealth, but giving themselves a mission and purpose independent of their father's business career.

If having wealth is about having choices, achieving wealth is about making sound choices that bring you to that point. Most people who reach their own definition of wealth do not arrive there by accident. They make choices in a strategic manner, guided by their own priorities about which goals are most important to them, and about the timeline in which they want to achieve those goals. When we set out to write this book, my colleagues and I wanted to offer guidance and share our experience with people primarily in their 20s, 30s and 40s — the decades in which most schooling is finished and we make the decisions that direct our professional careers and personal finances for many years to come. Should we buy or lease a car, and if we buy, how much borrowing is appropriate? When is it time to consider purchasing, rather than renting, a home? How much money should we dedicate to paying down debt, building an emergency fund, and saving for our own retirement or our children's education? How should money best be directed toward those goals? What devices can we use to mitigate the friction of taxes in trying to reach our other financial goals?

We will answer these questions and many others in the chapters that follow. Or, rather, we will provide you with the information and perspective to answer these questions yourself, or with the help of a professional adviser if your situation warrants. There is no universal answer to any of these questions. It comes down to goals and priorities that are just as personal as the definition of wealth itself. Our views on these issues may be more broadly informed than most because of our extensive professional experience, but that does not make them better or more important than yours; quite the opposite is true. As professionals in our daily work and as authors of this book, our goal is to share our knowledge and experiences so you can apply them to your own situation. You already are, or expect to become, a high achiever in your field. Now let's make sure your achievements translate into real and durable wealth, however you define it.

CHAPTER 2

SPENDING VS. SAVING VS. DEBT REPAYMENT

Thomas Walsh, CFP®

Financial planning is not a one-time event. It is the process of meeting your goals through the proper management of your finances. This process should give direction and meaning to your financial decisions and allow you to understand how each decision affects all areas of your financial life. In the big picture, this sounds reasonable. But many people struggle with translating this broad idea into concrete action that allows them to reach their personal goals. How do you determine how much to spend and how much to save?

In a perfect world, you would start adulthood with a list of specific financial goals for each stage of your life, along with the precise level of savings required to meet each goal. You could then form a plan that would let you achieve those goals, one by one, and carry it out. But real life is more dynamic and complex. Your perspective, priorities and circumstances will change over the course of your lifetime. That does not mean you can't take steps early on to establish a strong foundation to help you navigate life's uncertainty, even as your goals change and grow. Learning to balance spending, saving and paying down any debt you have accrued will help you pursue your financial goals, no matter what they are.

SPENDING

When balancing spending, saving and paying down debt, spending has an unfair advantage for many of us. That's because it offers immediate gratification. Spending money is not inherently bad, of course. But the fact that it often feels good in the moment means you should be careful and approach spending with a plan in order to maintain balance.

The best way to do so thoughtfully is to create and maintain a budget. While Chapter 3 covers budgeting in more detail, an important consideration is that you budget with specific goals in mind. Those goals will likely involve plans to save and pay down debt, but those are means, not ends in themselves. Are you saving for a down payment on a home or a comfortable retirement? Are you paying down debt so that you can have more flexibility in your career or take more vacations? Your goals will be specific to you. But associating saving and paying down debt with positive goals, rather than just with the vague feeling that they are responsible things to do, will provide more motivation. That, in turn, is likely to help you stick to your budget.

Goal-setting can also help you weigh your various expenses and realistically measure how much they mean to you. If you find you are overspending and need to cut back, evaluating the importance of various expense categories can help you prioritize and identify areas where cutting back will cause less discomfort. Conversely, identifying areas that mean a lot to you can help you enjoy spending on nonessential items even more. When you determine the items or experiences you value most, you can make sure your spending is going toward what really matters.

A key component to effective budgeting is determining where your spending is now, if you do not already know. Gather your last few credit card and bank statements, add up your monthly income after tax and subtract your monthly purchases. If you don't have a surplus of cash at the end of the month, you are spending too much and it is time to cut back. Regardless of your financial goals, the most important reason to budget is to maintain control of your spending and avoid new debt. The key is to never spend beyond your means.

QUICK NOTES

Determining if you have a cash surplus

- ☑ Gather credit card and bank statements for the past few months
- ☑ Subtract monthly purchases from total after-tax income
- ☑ If you have no extra cash at all, or the total is negative, look for optional spending to cut (remember that big-ticket items will make more of a difference)

If you want or need to cut back on spending, it is important to take a big-picture look at your budget. While it can help to eliminate little things like your daily trip to Starbucks or eating lunch out, the greatest impact will come from bigger-ticket items. If you feel saving is difficult, consider giving up or postponing big discretionary spending, if any. Do you want to take that big international vacation in the next few years or save for a down payment on a house? That said, not everyone has such major discretionary spending to cut.

In that case, turn your attention to your fixed monthly expenses. Can you reduce the cost of your internet package? Give up cable or cut some streaming services? You might consider renting a cheaper apartment when your lease is up, trading in your car for one with a lower monthly payment or exploring alternatives to your gym membership. Balancing spending and saving is ultimately an exercise in priorities and trade-offs. The sooner you start, the easier this process will be.

If you haven't done so, open a credit card and a bank account as soon as possible. As income and expenses increase, financial situations grow more complicated and mistakes can have a larger impact. Mastering account management while your situation is relatively simple will set you up for success. A credit card can also help you to build your credit score. (For more on credit cards and credit, see Chapter 3.) If you are just starting out, take time to shop around and read the fine print before you commit to a particular credit card or bank, and make sure you are comfortable with all the terms and conditions. It is also important to know yourself. A credit card can help build your credit and provide flexibility in an emergency while you build your savings, but if you are prone to spend too much, be sure you set up roadblocks to impulsive behavior. For instance, don't routinely carry your credit card with you (physically or in your mobile wallet).

If you are part of a couple, don't stop with only your own financial goals and expenditures. Couples should create joint goals and assign responsibilities to improve spending habits. There is no right answer when it comes to how couples manage savings and spending. Some want to share everything, while others keep separate accounts. Some share their assets with a prenuptial agreement in place. (For more on blending finances and prenuptial agreements, see Chapter 11.) Be open to finding what works for you as a couple, even if it doesn't mirror your perception of how a couple "should" handle their money.

Regardless of how you divide your finances and financial chores, the most important point to remember is open communication.

SAVING

At the most basic level, savings are the excess of cash inflows over cash outflows after taxes. In other words, savings are any post-tax income that you don't spend right away. But effective saving isn't an end in itself — it's a way to pursue your financial goals.

Determining your ideal level of savings can be more complicated than it first appears. The percentage of income to set aside depends not only on your goals and preferences, but also on factors like the stability of your job, your budget's flexibility, and the cost of living and tax burden in your locale. You may encounter the rule of thumb that you should try to save between 10% and 20% of your gross (or pretax) income. If you can save 10% for retirement and 10% for other long-term goals, you are doing well. But a rule of thumb is only a broad suggestion; it may not be practical, or even best, for everyone. To find your right level, you will have to look at your goals, the practical constraints of your situation and your debt repayment priorities, among other factors.

Once you determine how much you want to save, the next step is to set up a plan. A proactive approach will help you make sure your savings don't accidentally become spending by the end of the month. You may have heard the advice to "pay yourself first." The idea behind this is to set aside money earmarked for savings right away, rather than putting any "leftover" money toward your goals at the end of the month or pay period. In other words, make savings a priority, not simply the destination for any money you didn't happen to spend. Transferring your money immediately after you get it to a savings or investment account can remove the temptation to overspend.

One strategy many people find helpful is automation. Most banks will let you set up an automatic transfer on a regular basis, so you don't need to rely on your own memory to fund a savings or investment account. Employer-based retirement plans often allow you to go one step further and set up automatic payroll deductions, so the money never reaches your checking account in the first place. Automating contributions is a hugely helpful tool for ensuring you meet your retirement saving goals each year. Many people find that when money is automatically deposited into a retirement account, they do not miss it. This is also the principle behind services that "round up" purchases and automatically transfer the difference to a linked savings account.

Emergency Funds

Your very first savings goal should be an emergency fund. Also sometimes called a "rainy day" fund, an emergency fund is meant to cover unforeseen expenses, which means you will need to dip into it from time to time. If you don't already have savings built up, an emergency fund should also be your first order of business. And if you do have a fund, be sure to prioritize replenishing it after you withdraw funds to deal with an emergency.

Building an emergency fund offers a few notable benefits. First, it promotes financial stability. Without such a fund, you might need to borrow at high interest rates to cover an unexpected expense. An emergency fund allows you to avoid the extra expense of carrying a credit card balance or other debt to meet an unanticipated financial need. Emergency funds can also combat frivolous spending. Keeping that money in a separate account can reduce the temptation to spend the funds on something inessential. Finally, an emergency fund can reduce stress and increase your confidence that you can handle the unexpected events that will inevitably crop up.

The exact amount you should save in your emergency fund will depend on your circumstances. You will likely encounter the rule of thumb that you should save three to six months of expenses. If you are married and both partners work, or if you are single but have multiple sources of income, three months may be a sufficient buffer. If you provide the sole income for your household, six months may be more prudent. Of course, every situation is different. When determining how much to save, try to understand how the various components of your financial life interact so you can better predict the impact different emergency scenarios might have. Consider the following questions: How secure is your job? Are you salaried or are your paychecks irregular? Do you have someone to cover the bills if you are out of work, such as a partner or family member? You should also factor in your own comfort, to some degree. Overfunding an emergency savings account involves an opportunity cost, in that you are tying up money that can't be used for other goals. But if it makes you sleep better at night, sometimes forgoing financial optimization is OK.

Your expenses will also be particular to you. Note that when you calculate your three-to-six-month figure, you should differentiate between critical and discretionary expenses. Critical ones such as housing, food, health care (including insurance), utilities, transportation and debt payments are relatively fixed. You will need to keep covering these bills indefinitely, so include them in your calculations. You do not need to include discretionary expenses that could be eliminated in case of a major financial emergency like job loss. These might include entertainment, eating out, nonessential shopping, vacations and long-term savings goals that you can pause until your situation improves. Take a detailed look at your spending, as well as your broader circumstances, to determine your savings target.

If six months, or even three months, of expenses looks daunting, remember that saving something is better than nothing. While an emergency fund is to help cover a temporary loss of income, many emergencies have a fixed duration, such as a major car or home repair. A 2021 study published in the journal SSRN found that the median size of an expense spike was equivalent to about three weeks' income. If you can set aside even $25 a week, or $50 from a biweekly paycheck, you could save $2,600 in two years, which would help defray or cover many smaller emergencies. Even a small emergency fund puts you ahead of many Americans. A 2023 survey from the Federal Reserve found that nearly two in five did not have enough saved to handle an unforeseen expense of $400.

QUICK NOTES

Benefits of an emergency fund

- ☑ Promote financial stability
- ☑ Avoid credit card or other high-interest debt
- ☑ Combat frivolous spending
- ☑ Reduce financial stress overall

An emergency fund should be reserved for true emergencies, ones that are sudden and unexpected, giving you little or no time to prepare. Common financial emergencies include unanticipated job loss, major medical problems, and home or car repairs. Create your own set of definitions or possible scenarios and consider writing them down. The clearer you are with yourself about how you plan to use the fund, the easier it will be to determine how much you should save. Being specific and having your own set of instructions also can help you avoid tapping into your fund for nonemergency purposes. Once you get in the habit of dipping into the fund for other reasons, it can be hard to stop. A weekend trip with your friends is not an emergency. Wanting a new car or new home appliance is usually not an emergency (though replacing older versions might be, depending on the circumstances). Don't dip into your emergency fund casually with the idea that you will replenish the money later. You never know when a true emergency will occur or how severe it will be.

Also bear in mind that an expense should not be considered an emergency just because it does not occur regularly. If the expense is something you can foresee, prepare for it by building funds into your regular budget. Say you anticipate your car will last about three more years and that it will cost approximately $15,000 to replace. If you ignore this future expense and wait until your car breaks down completely, it could become a true emergency. Instead, arrange your budget so that you can start setting aside $5,000 per year. Even if you do not set aside the full amount or your car fails sooner than expected, any amount you have saved will help you avoid raiding your emergency fund in a panic the day your car dies. If you can minimize the sudden need for cash occurring from irregular expenses, you will be better prepared to handle a true emergency.

Your emergency savings should be easy to access, so keep it somewhere you won't pay a fee to withdraw funds or lose value from selling at an inopportune time. Keep the emergency fund in cash, or other safe and liquid short-term investments. For example, while a two-year certificate of deposit is very safe, it is not very liquid. You may need the money before the two-year term ends, in which case you will incur early-surrender charges. On the other hand, you should keep your fund separate from your general checking account. For most people, a regular savings account or a money market account insured by the Federal Deposit Insurance Corporation is the best choice. These options will let you earn a bit of interest while giving you easy access to the funds. The yield on such accounts is relatively low, but the purpose of an emergency fund is not to generate income or have a good rate of return; it is to protect you and provide cash in an emergency. Still, online banks may offer better interest rates and lower fees than your local brick-and-mortar bank branch, with the same federal insurance coverage. It pays to shop around.

In general, build your emergency fund before you pursue other long-term savings goals. One major exception is if your employer matches contributions to your 401(k) or other retirement plan. In this case, try to build your emergency fund and your retirement plan at the same time. You want to secure the "free money" of the employer match in the 401(k) for as long as possible. If you're worried about job security or work in a particularly volatile industry, though, focus more on the emergency fund to the extent you have to choose between the two. And you will need an emergency fund even if you are dealing with debt; don't tap your emergency savings for routine debt payments or let eagerness to pay off debt keep you from building this form of savings.

Long-Term Savings Goals

Once you have a robust emergency fund, you can begin to think about how you want to invest your savings for long-term goals. As my colleague Ben Sullivan explains in Chapter 5, investing is key to making sure the money you save doesn't lose value to inflation over time. Beyond that, investing early is a great way to effectively pursue big financial goals. Yes, it involves risk. But as a young adult, time is on your side. If you were already setting aside a certain amount of savings for your emergency fund, you can now repurpose it toward other long-term goals such as retirement, future educational expenses, or big-ticket purchases like a home or a car. You may also want to save for periodic, nonemergency expenses such as routine health care or home upkeep.

One key to successfully saving for long-term goals is to avoid "lifestyle creep." In most cases, you can expect your income to rise as you grow more experienced and gain responsibility in your career. You may also experience a financial change when you blend finances with a higher-earning partner, or if you receive a lump sum as a lifetime gift or bequest. In any of these circumstances, try to maintain the same standard of living to the extent that you can. This will allow you to increase your contributions to retirement accounts and other long-term savings goals without substantially altering your spending habits.

What if you have debt? There is no one right answer to whether you should concentrate on paying off your debt first, or paying down debt while simultaneously building your savings. The right strategy will depend on your circumstances. For instance, paying off outstanding credit card balances before implementing a savings plan can be a good strategy, in part because credit card debt often carries a high interest rate. In contrast, if you are paying down federally subsidized student loans, which typically offer a low interest rate, a more balanced approach may make sense. That balance can shift even further if you have access to an employer match in a 401(k) or other workplace retirement plan; the benefits of securing the match contributions will typically offset the opportunity cost of not paying off your debt faster. If you are enrolled in an income-based repayment plan for federal student loans, reducing your take-home pay through payroll contributions to a retirement plan may even lower your monthly minimum payment amount. The rule of thumb is to prioritize saving over debt repayment when your anticipated investment return is materially higher than the interest you will pay on the debt. (And then, of course, be sure to invest that money, not spend it.)

DEBT REPAYMENT

Debt is a major problem in the United States, especially among young adults. In late 2023, the Federal Reserve reported that American households owed a collective $17.29 trillion. There is some good news; while young adults hold much of the more than $1.6 trillion in collective student loan debt, the U.S. Census Bureau's Survey of Income and Program Participation found in 2021 that millennials carried less credit card debt, on average, than their Gen X counterparts. But the median millennial respondent still carried a balance of $3,500.

Debt can create a vicious cycle, because compound interest can make the problem progressively worse if you cannot or choose not to deal with your debt aggressively. Not only is it costing you money, but debt can be a major roadblock to meeting your long-term financial goals. That said, debt can often trigger feelings of shame or appear to be an insurmountable problem. As much as you can, try to keep your debt in perspective and remember that you can take concrete steps toward paying it down.

Paying down debt from the highest interest rate to the lowest is wise. Compounding means you will pay much more on higher interest debt over time.

It is especially important to be honest and as objective as you can if you are dealing with outstanding debt as a couple. If only one partner is in debt, you should both express clear expectations as to who is responsible for repayment, and how. Ideally, the debt-free partner will agree to some short-term sacrifices to help the other one for the good of the couple's overall financial health. However, do not shy away from discussing future debt, too. If one of you is struggling with impulsive spending or other discretionary forms of debt-building behavior, consider jointly tracking your spending to gauge the problem areas. Budgeting together and talking about finances regularly are also key. However you decide to approach the process, couples should work as a team to pay off unproductive debt and avoid it going forward.

As a financial adviser, I typically recommend organizing existing debt by interest rate when you formulate a payment plan. You will want to pay down the debt in order of highest interest rate to lowest. This is because compounding means you will pay much more on higher interest debt over time. Credit card debt in particular can be difficult to dig out from, so you will likely want to knock this out before moving to other debts, such as your student loans. (I will discuss prioritizing types of debt more fully later in this chapter.) You should also prioritize paying down existing debt, if you can, before taking on a new mortgage or other ongoing financial commitments.

Becoming entirely debt-free has obvious advantages; you no longer accrue interest you will have to pay back, and you can devote money previously budgeted for debt to other priorities. But decreasing your debt has advantages even before you pay it off. For instance, when you apply for a mortgage or auto loan, lenders often consider your debt to income ratio. This figure is all of your monthly debt payments collectively divided by your gross income and is used to evaluate whether you can responsibly take on more debt. (For more details, see Chapter 8.) As a rule of thumb, your annual payments on all outstanding debt should not exceed 36% of your adjusted gross income (gross income minus specific federal tax deductions).

Types Of Debt

Not every sort of debt is created equal when it comes to your overall financial health. While being entirely debt-free has its advantages, you may hear financial professionals discuss "good" debt and "bad" debt.

The reality is slightly more nuanced, but this distinction does spring from a real difference.

Most advisers and commentators who talk about "good" debt mean low-interest debt that can help you increase your net worth in the long run. "Bad" debt is high-interest debt used to pay for discretionary or nonessential purchases. Some financial planners also advise favoring secured debt over unsecured debt. Secured debts, such as mortgages or auto loans, involve collateral. There is nothing inherently better about one sort of loan or the other, but lenders typically offer lower rates for secured loans. Some debts fall between "good" and "bad," while others start good and go bad as circumstances change. Still others don't fit this paradigm at all. For instance, medical debt is unusual in that it typically bears no interest and is not something you voluntarily choose to take on.

The most common form of so-called bad debt is consumer debt, which is any form of debt used to purchase consumable items or personal items that depreciate. This includes credit card debt, as well as personal loans used for discretionary purposes such as vacations or high-end electronics. In general, you should avoid this type of debt as much as possible and pay it off quickly if you can. Credit card debt is subject to high interest rates and unfavorable contract terms. After a steep rise in interest rates that was triggered by post-pandemic inflation, many credit cards set annual percentage rates (APRs) between 19% and 29%, with even higher rates for some borrowers with bad credit. Compounding means that carrying a balance can make even a small debt grow more quickly than you might expect.

Whether auto loans are considered good debt or bad depends, in part, on whom you ask. Since cars depreciate, it is usually better to buy them outright if you can. On the other hand, auto loans have characteristics that set them apart from other forms of consumer debt. Because the car itself is collateral, auto financing rates are usually low enough to make these loans less burdensome than credit card debt. Like mortgages, they can often be refinanced or renegotiated if necessary. In addition, in many parts of the country a car is a necessity to get to work, supporting your ability to earn an income. As long as you avoid going underwater — meaning that you owe more than the car is worth — you can always sell or trade in the car if payments become too burdensome. This is why it is important not to buy more car than you need, especially if you are financing your purchase. For more on financing a car, see Chapter 6.

A mortgage is the traditional example of so-called good debt. Many mortgages offer interest rates well below what you could earn through investing in a diversified portfolio, which means you may be in less of a hurry to pay it down. Mortgages are also designed to be paid back over years, rather than month to month. You can typically refinance to change the loan term or the interest rate, which offers other advantages. And while the housing crisis of the late 2000s was a vivid reminder that property does not appreciate in all circumstances, in most cases your home will gain value over the course of a 30-year mortgage. (For more on mortgages, see Chapter 8.) Small-business loans are also usually considered good debt. While starting a small business involves risk, securing a loan will mean creating a comprehensive business plan, making it unlikely you will take out this sort of loan carelessly. If you approach this debt prudently and methodically, a loan to get your business underway can ultimately prove a net positive for your financial outlook.

Educational debt may be either good or bad, depending on the circumstances. Loans to attend an accredited university are generally considered positive, especially if you take out an amount consistent with your expected ability to repay based on your future career. Student loans with oversized balances relative to future earning power, loans for a degree you did not finish or loans to attend a disreputable institution are more likely to become bad debt. It is also worth differentiating between federally subsidized student loans and private student loans. Loans from the government often have a low interest rate and mechanisms to help you handle payments. Private loans bear higher interest rates and lack many of these benefits. If you have both, it will often make sense to prioritize paying off private loans first. A particular hazard of student loans of either type is that they generally cannot be discharged in bankruptcy. For more information on student loans, see Chapter 4.

Debt is a reality for most people who own a home or a car, or who pay for their own or their children's education. But making sure you avoid unnecessary debt, especially consumer debt, as much as possible and that you approach secured debt in a thoughtful way can give you a better chance of staying on top of your repayment plan.

Paying Down Your Debt

When balancing saving and debt repayment, you should never neglect minimum payment amounts on any of your debt. The question is what you will do with available cash beyond that baseline. The overall goal when you decide to pay down your debt is to pay more than the minimum required. You want to not only pay off the interest each month, but slowly work down the principal balance as well. In general, it is best to focus on one debt at a time. Chip away at the principal payment by payment.

When you design a repayment plan, consider one that will naturally gain momentum the longer you stick with it. Two popular strategies are the "debt avalanche" and the "debt snowball" (described below). Both approaches have pros and cons. The debt avalanche strategy leads to paying less interest overall, but the debt snowball method can offer the encouragement to stick with your plan by overcoming common psychological barriers that hinder repayment. Researchers have found the debt snowball method works better for many people by keeping their motivation strong. Whichever method you choose, however, paying down one debt at a time has clear advantages. A study published in 2016 in the Journal of Consumer Research found that borrowers who concentrated on repaying one debt at a time repaid their overall debt 15% faster than borrowers who dispersed extra payments across accounts. Both the snowball and avalanche methods have their merits and, when implemented effectively, equally result in a clean financial slate.

QUICK NOTES

Avalanche	Snowball
PROS	**PROS**
► Pay less interest overall ► Become totally debt-free faster	► Overcomes common psychological barriers that can hinder repayment ► Quickly dealing with fewer outstanding balances
CONS	**CONS**
► Requires discipline and patience ► More loans to keep track of over time	► Pay more interest overall ► You may be in debt longer overall

In the debt avalanche method, you will prioritize your debts by interest rate, from highest to lowest. You will concentrate on tackling the highest interest rate first, while making minimum maintenance payments on any other debts. In the debt snowball method, you will also concentrate on paying off one debt at a time. But instead of ranking them by interest rate, you will rank them by the outstanding balance, from lowest to highest. The idea is that you get a positive psychological bump from successfully tackling an outstanding debt, no matter its size. Paying off small loans first gives you early wins and fewer overall loans to think about. This generates greater momentum as you turn toward larger, more burdensome debts.

Of course, certain types of debt should be top priority, regardless of interest rate or balance. For instance, payment of back taxes owed to the Internal Revenue Service should almost always be the first priority, regardless of balance or interest rate. You could face fines, or even jail time, if you fail to pay; short of that, the IRS can impose liens to make sure Uncle Sam gets his due.

Stay mindful, too, of any early repayment penalties. Some mortgages include provisions that trigger fees if you pay off too much of your loan early. Early repayment penalties are rarer on other types of loans, though some auto or personal loans also include them. Student loan lenders are not allowed to penalize borrowers who eliminate their debt early.

When considering which types of debt to pay down first, you should also pay attention to any associated tax benefits. For example, up to $2,500 of qualified student loan interest can be deducted against your taxable income per year (subject to an income phase-out), effectively reducing the actual interest paid on the loans. Mortgage interest is also deductible on loans up to $750,000, or up to $1 million if you purchased your home on or before Dec. 15, 2017. When you are ranking debt by interest rate, you may want to adjust that rate to reflect any associated tax benefits the debt offers.

Once you have satisfied your first debt in full, don't abandon the minimum maintenance payment you included in your monthly budget. Continue to earmark that amount for debt payment and apply it to the second debt on your list, so you are paying down even more of that debt's principal each month. Repeat this pattern and watch as the old minimums for the paid-off debt act to compound the rate at which you pay off your remaining debt. Treating the former minimum payments as if they never went away protects you from spending your extra income elsewhere, while helping you to build the momentum you need to become debt-free.

Depending on the types of debt you carry, you may find their sheer number and policy details overwhelming. In this case, debt consolidation may help. Assuming your outstanding debt hasn't drastically lowered your credit score (see Chapter 3), it's not uncommon for your bank to provide a loan so you can consolidate your credit card debt. Depending on your credit score, the interest rate on the bank loan often will be lower than your credit cards' APR. If you have several student loans, you may also want to consolidate these; see Chapter 4 for more on consolidating educational loans.

If you are close to paying off credit card debt but need a small boost, you may want to apply for a credit card offering a promotional balance transfer with a 0% interest rate. This method is best for those with a decent credit score and the ability to pay off their transferred balance quickly, since promotional offers tend to cover a relatively short time span before reverting to a high rate. Know yourself, however. If you feel that a fresh credit card could be too much temptation, avoid this method of consolidation.

Don't discount the possibility of negotiating directly with your debt issuers if you need to. If they suspect you are at high risk of default, or if you are contemplating the possibility of bankruptcy, issuers will often negotiate an interest rate or structure a repayment plan to avoid a total loss.

When paying down your debt, or trying to minimize future debt, the key is to be honest about your habits and inclinations. For many people, the inability to systematically pay down debt is much more a psychological issue than a financial one. Those who tend to max out their credit cards are prone to do the same once debts are repaid. It truly takes a shift in how you view debt to break the cycle of poor spending habits. You can find many success stories from individuals who paid off large amounts of debt, each using a different strategy, and many of them emphasize a change in perspective as much as a change in budget. It is important you look within and face your debt fears so you can begin to understand what caused you to get into that hole as well as what will get you out of it. Similarly, picking the debt avalanche repayment method does you no good if you get frustrated and give up paying more than the minimum after a few months because it doesn't feel like you are making progress. What may seem like the most effective strategy on paper may be unsuccessful in practice if psychological limitations keep you from sticking with a plan. Find the strategy that you can live with both financially and psychologically, then follow it.

Knowing yourself can also help you find a balance between long-term saving and debt repayment. For some people, the allure of becoming debt-free is a highly motivating factor; for others, the idea of saving enough for a down payment or an early retirement makes saving the more emotionally satisfying way forward. While there are certain steps you should take either way — keeping up with minimum payments or building an emergency fund, for instance — working with your natural inclinations rather than against them may help you stick to your plan, which is more important than pursuing perfect financial optimization.

Your financial awareness will likely grow sharper over time through experience. As you try to balance spending, saving and debt repayment, it is almost certain you will make some choices that are less than perfect. Everyone does — even financial professionals. While you are still gaining experience, though, you will benefit from turning elsewhere for advice. You can do your own research, ask a trusted mentor or consider a consultation with a professional financial planner. Picking up this book is, in itself, a great start. While experience will help you when it comes, attending to your financial well-being shouldn't wait. An imperfect plan is much better than no plan at all, and the best time to act is always now.

CHAPTER 3

BEING SMART ABOUT BUDGETS AND CREDIT

Rebecca Pavese, CPA

Budgeting and building credit are two of the foundational concepts of personal finance. At their cores, both are relatively simple. Budgeting is a tool to make sure that the way you spend your money is supporting your long-term goals, rather than undermining them. Building credit is a matter of showing that lenders should want to work with you on good terms because you have a track record of being financially responsible.

While these ideas can sound simple in the abstract, sitting down to break them into concrete steps can seem intimidating. Or perhaps you started with a "good enough" system as you began your career, but you aren't sure how to upgrade it as your life grows more complex with promotions, spouses, homeownership or kids. Before you get overwhelmed, it is worth getting back to the basics.

BUILDING YOUR BUDGET

A budget is the basis of all long-term financial planning. A budget can look many different ways and it may involve different steps. But the essential point of a budget is to make sure your spending and saving decisions are conscious and planned. In other words, you should be in control of your money, not the other way around. Budgeting is the first step in making confident financial choices.

Rather than thinking of budgeting as a task you do once, or even periodically, it may be helpful to think of budgeting as the ongoing give and take between your spending and your saving. Good budgeting is an ongoing process, because the balance between your needs, wants and goals will shift over time. Think of taking care of your financial health as similar to taking care of your physical health. It can be easy to ignore it until something goes wrong; then you are suddenly in disaster mode. If you take the time to pay attention to your health and make a habit of health-focused choices, those disasters will be much rarer — and you'll be in better shape to address them when they arise. The same holds true for your finances.

Everyone's financial life looks a bit different. But regardless of your situation, you need a budget. Even if you are lucky enough to live a financially comfortable life, budgeting has distinct advantages. First, it involves tracking your spending, so you will understand where your money is going every month. It will keep you from spending money you don't have out of ignorance or carelessness. Budgeting also allows you to make intentional choices about what is important to you and to prioritize those categories. People without budgets often overspend on discretionary items in the short term and don't save enough for future big-ticket purchases. Finally, budgeting involves accountability to yourself. Are your choices keeping you from reaching your goals? A good budget will help you answer that question, as well as identify changes you can make to get back on course if the answer is "yes."

Consider Jane. When she first began working, her earning power was relatively small. She had very little cash to save or spend on anything other than necessities. Several years later, Jane has succeeded at her job and gotten several raises. She can now treat herself to food delivery or a new pair of jeans without worrying about her monthly bills, which has improved her quality of life. But Jane still has no emergency fund to cover unexpected expenses, and she hasn't been able to save for a vacation despite her best efforts. Without a budget, Jane can't know where her money is going. That makes it hard to adjust her behavior.

QUICK NOTES

Advantages Of Budgeting

- ☑ Understand where your money is going each month
- ☑ Avoid careless overspending
- ☑ Make intentional choices about what is important to you
- ☑ Stay accountable to yourself over time

Everyone's circumstances are different, so not everyone will need the same type of budget. The first decision to make is whether you plan to set up a short-term budget to reach a specific goal, or a long-term budget to track your finances over time. Of course, a short-term budget that is working well can become a long-term budget. And even a well-constructed long-term budget will need to change if, for example, you get a raise or your rent goes up. But knowing whether you intend your budget to have a certain end date will likely shape how you approach it.

The level of detail in your budget will also vary based on your needs and your temperament. Some people find it helpful to "give every dollar a job," whether to pay a bill, fund some relaxation or head to savings.

A popular budgeting option of this type is the "envelope method." At the beginning of a month, you designate certain envelopes for different spending categories, such as groceries, clothing or expenses connected to a hobby. These envelopes can be physical, or they can be theoretical; how many and their categories are up to you. Once you've set up your envelopes, you divide your income into each of them, either by filling the real envelopes with cash or recording how much each theoretical envelope contains. Once an envelope runs out of money, no more spending in that category until next month. If you have any money left, you can roll it over or add to your savings.

For other people, this level of detail may be unhelpful or even overwhelming. In this case, it may work better to approach budgeting from a big-picture perspective. For example, your budget may involve only three categories: savings, fixed expenses and spending money. A popular approach is to devote 50% of your income to living expenses, 30% to nonessential spending and 20% to savings. Set aside your savings and fixed-expense amounts at the beginning of the month, and spend the other 30% as you like. For some people, this sort of simple, flexible approach is perfect.

Any given budget system has benefits and drawbacks. An envelope system can help if you tend to be an impulse shopper, but it involves tracking your cash flow in greater detail as you spend. Dividing your money into only a few broad categories relieves you of some day-to-day tracking, but it can leave you open to spending in ways you don't intend, even if you save toward your goals and pay for your necessary expenses. It may take some trial and error to find a system that works for you.

How To Make A Budget

Once you're ready to get started, you can settle on the tools you plan to use for budgeting. Luckily, you have many options.

Pen And Paper

You can write your budget out longhand if you want to, but when most financial professionals talk about a "pen and paper" budget today, they mean a spreadsheet like Microsoft Excel or Google Sheets. While you can build a more automated budget in these programs if you are a spreadsheet pro, there is no need to teach yourself to create macros just to set up your budget. You can create simple columns to track income, spending and saving, which should be plenty to get you started. You can also easily find free spreadsheet templates online. While a manual budget, either on paper or a spreadsheet, is a little more work than an automated alternative, it gives you a great deal of control. For some people, this hands-on approach is appealing.

Apps

There are plenty of apps to help you budget, and they come with a variety of features. Some are free, while others work on a subscription model. If you are new to budgeting, it may make sense to try out a free app first. If it works for you, great; if not, you'll have a better idea of what features matter to you before you invest in a premium tool. Take the time to research any app you choose to be sure the company behind it is reputable before you hand over personal financial information.

Once you decide on your tools, the next step in making a budget is to think about your goals. Most people have more than one, and not all of them will have the same timeline. You may want to pay off debt, save for a down payment on a home or plan a big vacation. It could be something as small as saving so that you don't have to put holiday gifts on your credit card, or as large as funding your retirement. Taking the time to really think about your goals will help you to prioritize and determine how much income you want to devote to those priorities. If you don't have anything particular in mind, a useful first goal is to create an emergency fund to cover unplanned expenses. As a rule of thumb, aim to save enough to cover three to six months of living expenses in case you lose your job or can't work.

Many younger adults must decide how to balance paying off debt, especially student loans, against saving for the future. Unfortunately, there is not a one-size-fits-all answer. Depending on your situation, it may make sense to balance both, especially if you benefit from tax breaks or other benefits related to your loans. (For more on paying down student loans, see Chapter 4.) In general, if you do not yet have an emergency fund, you should build a cushion before making more than your required monthly loan payment. On the other hand, if you are facing mainly credit card debt, you will want to pay it off as quickly as you can, since the interest rate is likely high. If your situation is complicated or you are not sure how to balance paying off debt with saving for the future, it may make sense to consult a financial adviser. Even if you are not ready to hire a professional for an ongoing relationship, many advisers are happy to set up a one-time consultation. Look for a fee-only Certified Financial Planner™; these professionals have passed a rigorous exam and are held to high fiduciary standards (that is, putting client needs first).

Setting goals can also allow you to save money in the long run by avoiding taking on new debt. Say you would like to travel to Spain in a little over a year. If you sit down and work out how much to set aside each month, you will be able to pay for plane tickets, hotels and other expenses outright. You can also decide in advance how much you plan to spend on meals, souvenirs and other day-to-day expenses while you are abroad. On the other hand, if you don't plan ahead and simply charge the entire trip on a credit card, you will have to pay additional interest while you pay down your balance after you are home.

If you have not budgeted before, or if you have gotten out of the habit, it will be helpful to monitor your regular spending for a month or two to establish your current baseline. This exercise will help you determine whether you are living beyond your means — that is, spending more than you earn. If you are, you will need to reduce your spending, increase your income or both. If you are already spending less than you earn, you can pat yourself on the back and move on to the next step: seeing how your choices are supporting or hindering your short-term and long-term goals.

Once you understand your spending, you can better evaluate how you are progressing toward the goals you identified earlier. You may be mostly on track, with only a few tweaks to make. Or you may be far from where you want to be, in which case you will need to decide on some bigger changes. The more you know about how you spend, the more control you have over spending decisions. The adage "knowledge is power" really is true when it comes to your money.

Many financial planners urge you to "pay yourself first" — that is, set aside savings as soon as you receive income. This is a sound idea, especially if you are an impulse shopper. Many people automate saving to make it a priority. If you automate transfers, you don't have to decide to take money out of your checking account every month. You may find that you don't miss what you don't see. Savings and brokerage accounts let you set up automatic transfers, and you can often time them to coincide with your paycheck. (For more on how to get started investing, see Chapter 5.) If you have a 401(k) plan, a health savings account or similar workplace benefits, setting up contributions to these accounts is another good way to automate savings. As with your other budgeting choices, the exact details will depend on your goals and overall situation.

You may also want to automate your bills and recurring payments, which can help you avoid late fees. Some student loan servicers even offer a reduced interest rate for borrowers who sign up for automatic payments. However, you should still keep an eye on these payments each month to make sure they go through, and so that you will notice if your bill goes up for any reason. (Or for no reason, as is often the case with cable, streaming and internet providers.) If any of your financial accounts charge an inactivity fee, you can also automate periodic transfers to keep the account active.

Many people think of budgeting as a practice of self-denial, but this does not have to be true. In fact, most budgets should include some room for indulgence. After all, you are living your life right now, even if you have your eye on a future prize. For many people, a well-structured budget can help them enjoy their monthly "fun" spending more, because they have removed any reason to feel guilty about a splurge. Unplanned spending can leave you scrambling to justify your purchase to yourself in hindsight. But if you know you have set aside a certain amount for tickets to concerts or sporting events, fancy dinners out or whatever other way you prefer to treat yourself, you can fully appreciate the experience without worrying about its impact on the rest of your financial life.

Your budget should have some flexibility. If it's too rigid, it is more likely you'll abandon your budget altogether. A budget you ignore does you no good.

As with any financial plan, it is important to revisit your budget from time to time. Even month to month, your budget should have some flexibility. If it's too rigid, it is more likely you'll abandon your budget altogether. A budget you ignore does you no good. Bigger life events, like an interstate move, marriage or career change, will mean revamping your budget more comprehensively. Marriage, or even blending your finances with a partner to whom you are not married, will make budgeting a partnered activity. A budget will also give you a starting point for a new financial plan if you receive a windfall — say, if you get a significant inheritance from a grandparent or if the tech startup you work for goes public. If you are in the habit of tracking and managing your cash flow, the basics of making a new plan will seem natural when you suddenly have much more income to manage.

MASTERING YOUR CREDIT

The first time you enter the world of credit scores can be intimidating. Even worse, if you have made mistakes that saddled you with a bad score, it can feel as if you have fallen into a hole you cannot climb out from. But whether you are starting from scratch or rebuilding after a disaster, you needn't feel overwhelmed. Yes, credit is very important — but you can do a lot to monitor and improve your credit over time.

A good credit score, along with the credit report the score is based on, has real consequences in your financial life. People with high credit scores typically have access to better rates on credit cards and loans. Scores can also affect insurance rates. Utility companies and cellphone providers may look at your score and require deposits if it is especially low. Some landlords consider your credit score when you apply to rent an apartment or a house, and certain employers consider credit histories in the hiring process.

Given the importance of your credit score, it is worth understanding what does — and does not — affect it. The most widely used is the basic FICO credit score, a three-digit number between 300 and 850. (This scale occasionally goes to 900 in industry-specific uses.) FICO breaks its score into five criteria. The most important is a history of paying bills on time. The longer and more consistently you make payments on your credit cards, student loans or other forms of debt, the better your score. The other factors include how much of your available credit you are using, the length of your overall credit history, the mix of accounts you have, and whether you have recently opened new accounts.

As with budgeting, understanding your credit is a key step in improving it. By law, the three major credit reporting agencies must provide you one free report per year. You can access these at AnnualCreditReport.com. Some people view all three at once; others space them out throughout a calendar year. Whichever strategy you choose, review each report annually to make sure there is no fraud or other suspicious activity. Look for addresses or accounts you don't recognize. If you spot anything suspicious, or any other errors, dispute the inaccuracy right away.

You will notice that one thing never appears on your credit report: your numerical FICO score. Unfortunately, you have to pay to get this number directly from the credit reporting agencies. There are ways around this roadblock, however. Some credit cards provide your FICO score as a member benefit. And various websites, such as Credit Karma (a service offered by the software company Intuit), offer you a rough idea of your credit score on demand. Many of these free scores are not one of your FICO scores. Instead, they may reflect your VantageScore (a competing but similar credit scoring model) or merely an estimation. You may see some small discrepancies depending on how they calculate their estimated score, but these services should give you a useful idea of where you stand.

Given the major data breach Equifax suffered in 2017 and the likelihood that hackers will continue to target credit reporting agencies, you may feel nervous knowing that these companies have so much of your personal information. While you do not have the option to opt out of credit reports, steps to deter fraud are available to you. You can place fraud alerts with each major credit agency or, even more effectively, request a credit freeze. Credit reporting agencies must allow you to freeze and unfreeze your report for free. A credit freeze does not affect your credit score, though you will need to remember to lift the freeze if someone, such as a mortgage lender or a potential employer, needs to access your credit history. You can also pay for credit monitoring services from a variety of companies. But for nearly everyone, regularly checking on your credit report or placing a freeze on your credit files protects you just as well without incurring extra costs.

In addition to keeping an eye on your credit, you can take steps to strengthen your score by keeping the criteria that determine it in mind. These steps can help whether you are building credit for the first time or repairing damage. Do everything you can to pay all your bills on time, month in and month out. Be aware that your score may take a temporary hit when you open a new account, or especially if you open multiple new accounts within a short time. Consider maintaining your oldest credit line if possible, to keep your history long. Even better, if your parents have a solid credit history and your relationship with them allows, ask if they would consider adding you as an authorized user on one of their cards, which can bolster your score. Keep an eye on your available credit and try not to use too much at a time. You might want to make multiple credit card payments in a month or spread your charges across multiple cards to keep your credit utilization low. Most experts suggest keeping it under 30% if possible.

Getting married does not automatically affect your credit score for good or ill. Each partner keeps his or her own score, and marriage alone will not create any particular change. However, if you open a joint account, your information will be shared going forward. And if you and your partner plan to purchase a home together, bear in mind that lenders will review both credit histories during the mortgage application process. This is one of the many reasons that it is important to have honest conversations with your partner about your financial history and your current situation before taking major steps together. If a couple knows that one partner needs to repair some credit mistakes, it can make sense to take time to boost that score before house hunting.

QUICK NOTES

How To Strengthen Your Credit

- ☑ Make sure your credit reports are accurate
- ☑ Do everything you can to consistently pay bills on time
- ☑ Maintain your oldest credit line, if possible
- ☑ Try to keep credit utilization under 30%

In today's largely cashless world, credit cards are a tool many people use daily. Of course, for some people, credit cards can do more harm than good. People who use credit cards without actively managing them can quickly run up high-interest debt that could break a budget. While you can get into trouble with credit cards quickly, undoing the damage often takes a long time. If you know you will be tempted to run up high balances you can't pay off each month, you may choose to rely on cash, debit cards and digital wallets alone. Credit cards typically charge high interest rates, which means carrying a balance can get costly very fast. If you don't think you will be in a position to pay the card off in full every month, or if you've already run into trouble with credit cards, you may want to remove the temptation to overspend. You should also be careful with cards that charge annual fees; if you consider them at all, make sure you're earning more in rewards than you're paying to carry the card.

However, despite the potential pitfalls, there are real benefits to credit cards if you use them responsibly. If you don't already have student loans or other forms of debt, regularly using credit cards and paying them off in full each month can help build your credit history. If you don't have a credit history, you may want to consider a secured credit card. These require a deposit, but as a result, they are much easier to get than unsecured cards. Assuming your credit is a bit more robust, rewards credit cards can earn you cash back, airline miles, hotel points and other perks for just using the cards for your regular spending. You may also find company-specific cards are worthwhile, depending on your lifestyle and interests. Disney superfans can save on merchandise and enjoy special perks at Disney parks with the company's branded Visa card; frequent travelers can avoid fees on checked bags and secure priority boarding with most of Delta Air Lines' card offerings.

Credit cards also routinely offer some useful features beyond their effect on your overall credit. Many cards offer purchase protection, which will allow you to make a claim if certain items are damaged or stolen shortly after you buy them. Credit cards also allow customers to dispute incorrect charges. If a company overcharges you or bills you for something you never receive, you can inform your credit card company. In many circumstances, you will be able to get your money back. Cards often extend other forms of coverage too, including rental-car collision insurance, protection for lost or delayed luggage, or travel insurance for trips canceled due to illness or injury. While claiming these benefits can require some legwork and documentation, they can add up to major savings if you need them. And if you travel internationally, cards without foreign transaction fees can be a much simpler and more economical payment method than changing large amounts of cash from one currency to another.

At its heart, your credit score is about allowing lenders to measure the risk of extending credit to you. When it works as intended, credit serves as a means to illustrate you will be responsible if a company issues you a card, a loan or some other form of credit. It becomes part of your identity, at least in financial and sometimes business settings. Monitoring your credit and taking steps to keep it strong allows you to present a trustworthy face to the world.

While making a budget and managing your credit may seem daunting, I hope this chapter has made clear that neither task needs to be intimidating. Instead, it's a matter of taking small, positive steps consistently over time. Once you master budgeting and credit, you will be in a strong position to pursue sound financial steps such as planning for retirement, building an investment portfolio or evaluating your insurance needs. It all starts with the basics.

CHAPTER 4

PAYING FOR EDUCATION AND PAYING IT OFF

Brianna Aviles and Amy Laburda

Whether you are considering making a career change, advancing your career with a second degree, returning to school for personal enrichment or planning for someone else's future education, understanding certain costs and strategies will help in achieving these goals. Perhaps you're paying off student loans and want to assess your progress and evaluate the options to better position yourself for repayment. This chapter will empower you to fund your educational ambitions, effectively pay down your debt or both.

The U.S. student debt crisis is well known. According to the Federal Reserve Bank of New York, as of early 2023 Americans collectively owed $1.6 trillion in such debt. This number was about $610 billion more than U.S. credit card debt. Federal student loan debt was spread among roughly 43 million borrowers.

These numbers are alarming, but the cost of postsecondary education only continues to rise. Between 2013 and 2023, the average cost of attendance rose 2.5% per year. While relatively cheaper, even flagship state universities can be expensive for in-state students after accounting for all the items that make up the total cost of attendance. According to research by the College Board, during the 2022-23 school year the average total cost of attending an in-state public college, out-of-state public college or private college was $27,940, $45,240 and $57,570, respectively. Keep in mind these figures are averages; it costs substantially more to attend certain universities. Out-of-state students paid $55,330 to attend the University of Michigan during the 2022-23 school year.

Prudent financial planning involves using available information to make decisions while acknowledging you can never eliminate all uncertainty. While some politicians have discussed forgiving student loan debt, significant obstacles stand in the way of this policy. For example, in August 2022, President Joe Biden announced his plan to relieve borrowers of federal student loan debt. Under this plan, borrowers who received a Pell Grant (a type of loan we will discuss later in this chapter) would have received up to $20,000 of debt forgiveness, and all others would have been relieved of debt up to $10,000. Although the plan was broad, it included strict limitations such as an annual earnings cap that would factor into the determination of who qualified for forgiveness. The plan faced several legal challenges, and the U.S. Supreme Court ultimately blocked it in a ruling issued in June 2023.

In January 2023, the White House proposed an income-based repayment plan for federal borrowers known as "Saving on a Valuable Education," or SAVE. In addition to controlling costs for borrowers, SAVE would cancel some debts after borrowers made at least 10 years of payments. The SAVE plan opened for enrollment in August 2023, but it is new enough at this writing that its wider effects are still unknown. In addition, the Education Department opened a rulemaking process in October 2023 designed to explore further options for borrower relief. At this writing, the outcome of that process is not yet known, but Biden has expressed an ongoing commitment to finding ways to help federal student loan borrowers.

In addition to forgiving existing debt, it is possible that future lawmakers could take action on either the national or state levels to control college costs. A sensible approach in the meantime is for students and their family members to assume that college is unlikely to get meaningfully cheaper in the immediate future. Therefore, it's important to rely on an organized and disciplined approach to manage the rising price tag of a college education.

PAYING OFF EXISTING STUDENT LOANS

Understanding Your Loans

If you're already one of the millions of borrowers paying off existing debt, the task can be overwhelming. Reminding yourself of the value in paying for your own education can be a significant motivator. Media coverage often discusses student loan debt as if it's inescapable, but you can take steps toward full repayment. First, make sure you understand the different types of loans you have.

Direct subsidized and unsubsidized loans are the two main types administered by the federal government. In some contexts, you may hear either described as Stafford Loans or Direct Stafford Loans. These are no longer the official names, but the loans are largely the same as these former offerings. The federal government pays the interest on subsidized loans while you're in college, meaning students aren't charged interest until after they leave school. Borrowers with these loans typically get an interest-free six-month grace period after either graduation or departure from school before they must begin repaying the loan. In some cases, falling below half-time attendance can trigger the beginning of this grace period. The interest on unsubsidized loans accrues while students are in school and during any grace or deferment period; the government isn't paying the interest. However, borrowers can pay the interest while in school or defer it until they begin repaying the loan's principal. If borrowers choose to defer, the interest is capitalized, which means it is added to the overall loan balance.

QUICK NOTES

Some Key Features Of Loans By Type

Subsidized Federal	Unsubsidized Federal	Private
► Lender is the federal government ► Fixed interest rate ► Government pays interest while student is in school	► Lender is the federal government ► Fixed interest rate ► Interest accrues while borrower is in school	► Nongovernment lender such as bank or financial service company ► Interest rate may be fixed or variable ► Interest accrues while borrower is in school (in most cases)

Since 2013, the government has set interest rates for student loans based on a formula using the yield of the 10-year Treasury note. These rates are set annually. Both subsidized and unsubsidized federal student loans are daily interest loans, meaning interest is added to the account balance every day. The loans charge different rates depending on your class standing. For the 2023-24 school year, the interest rate on both direct subsidized and unsubsidized loans for undergraduate borrowers was 5.5%. For graduate borrowers, it was 7.05%. The maximum annual amount that you can borrow is based on your year in school. For example, the 2023-24 cap was $7,500 for undergraduate juniors, of which up to $5,500 could be in subsidized loans.

Federal loans allow for a wide range of repayment plan options, including the following:

- The standard repayment plan, which uses a fixed monthly payment of equal installments for the term of the loan.
- The extended repayment plan, which stretches out the number of payments to reduce the size of each payment, but increases the total amount paid due to paying more in interest over the life of the loan.
- The graduated repayment plan, which starts with lower payments and gradually increases over time.
- The Saving on a Valuable Education (SAVE) Plan, which uses a percentage of your discretionary income. This is recalculated every year based on your income and family size. SAVE limits payments to a weighted average of between 5% and 10% of the borrower's income. (The SAVE plan replaces the Revised Pay As You Earn Repayment Plan, or REPAYE.)
- The Pay As You Earn Repayment Plan (PAYE), which is available to borrowers who took out loans after Oct. 1, 2007 and who received a disbursement on or after Oct. 1, 2011. This plan also sets payments at 10% of discretionary income, but adds a cap so monthly payments will never exceed what a borrower would have paid monthly with the standard repayment plan.
- The income-based repayment plan, which is similar to the SAVE plan, but payments can climb to 15% of income depending on when borrowers received their first loans.

- The income-contingent repayment plan, which sets the monthly payment at the lesser of 20% of a borrower's discretionary income or the amount a borrower would pay on a repayment plan with a fixed payment over 12 years, adjusted according to his or her income.

If you still fell short after borrowing the maximum federal amount and using your own money, scholarships, grants and work-study programs, you likely went to the private market to fill the gap. Private lenders such as banks and financial service companies can set their own terms and conditions for student loans. The loans usually require an established credit history or a co-signer, who is equally responsible for the terms of the loan contract. Private lenders may offer fixed or variable-rate loans. The interest rate on fixed-rate loans doesn't change over the life of the loan, while variable rates usually fluctuate alongside a particular rate index, commonly the Secured Overnight Financing Rate, or SOFR. Private lenders typically charge a higher interest rate than the government, a significant factor to consider when prioritizing your repayment plan. The interest rate can vary widely not only between servicers but between applicants, depending on their financial situations. Most private lenders don't subsidize their loans, and they make you responsible for paying the interest even before repayment of principal starts.

You should be sure to understand the type of repayment plan your loan agreement sets out. The loan provider generally determines the repayment plan, but don't hesitate to contact your lender to see if you have repayment options. When choosing a repayment plan, be mindful that the longer you take to pay, the more it will cost you overall. However, some of the plans above offer built-in forgiveness after a certain number of years. If you are choosing a repayment plan, sitting down with a financial professional could help you to weigh the pros and cons of the options available to you.

Repayment Strategies

Once you have begun a repayment plan, for either federal or private loans, be sure to make your minimum monthly payments. This will not only let you avoid penalties, but it will help your credit score. (For more on building credit, see Chapter 3.) Don't stop there, though. Outlining a detailed plan of action, with both short-term and long-term goals, can help accelerate repayment. Construct a realistic budget, which can help you find a balance between enjoying yourself responsibly in the present and pursuing your long-term objectives.

Your attitude about debt will be a significant driver in how you will pay down your loans. Some borrowers view their student loan payments as solely a monthly bill and do not feel immediate urgency about the outstanding balance. Borrowers with low interest rate loans, especially federal loans, often take this position, since the cost and burden of borrowing may be minimal. This outlook allows you to allocate some of your income to other financial priorities, such as investing for retirement, building an emergency fund or saving to travel. (See Chapter 2 for a broader discussion of balancing saving and debt repayment.)

If you are more debt-averse and want to pay off your loans as quickly as possible, you will want to aggressively assign as much of your monthly income as possible to your student loan payments. Unlike some other loan types, most education loans do not penalize you for early repayment. You should be mindful, however, that early repayment of student loans may temporarily lower your credit score. This temporary dip is because having a longer credit history enhances your score, and your student loan is likely to be one of your oldest credit accounts. Early repayment closes the account and, thus, can depress your score. While in general, paying off debt is still a net benefit to your financial outlook, if you're considering purchasing a larger asset that may require you to obtain a loan, such as a car or a home, you may want to consider the timing of your repayment.

In general, if you intend to pay more than the minimum, concentrate first on the loans with the highest interest rates. Let's look at how the numbers change according to the different types of strategies. Consider a borrower with a $58,000 principal balance and an average interest rate of 5.5%, paying $629 a month. According to this plan, the borrower will end up paying back a total of $75,534 in 10 years ($58,000 in principal and $17,534 in interest). If that same borrower were to pay $829 a month, the borrower would end up paying back a total of $70,106 ($58,000 in principal and $12,106 in interest) over eight years. Paying $200 extra each month saves the borrower $5,428 and about two years of payments. Whether this trade-off is worthwhile depends on a variety of factors, and there is no one right answer. Before you choose a payback plan, reflect seriously on what you are comfortable with and prioritize what is important to you.

Consolidating and refinancing are two options to ease the burden of paying off student debt. Consolidating the loans under one provider streamlines payment into one place and with one monthly bill. This involves combining multiple loans into one loan, with a single loan servicer, and often results in an extended payback period with a lower monthly payment. Lower payments usually result in lengthening your payment term, meaning you'll pay more in interest over the life of the loan. When considering consolidation, look at how the interest rate will be calculated and whether it results in a better or worse rate than your current one.

It's also imperative to know the differences between consolidating federal loans and private loans. A Direct Consolidation Loan is the governmental program for consolidating federal loans; private education loans are not eligible. This program offers only fixed interest rates and uses a weighted average of all the federal loans you are merging to offer a new loan with a new rate. In contrast, consolidating private loans usually means new interest rate terms based on current offerings and your personal information from your application, not the previous loan terms. Being proactive about acquiring and comparing quotes from different private loan companies is a good practice to identify the best deals.

If you have both federal and private loans, it is best to consolidate them separately.

A word of caution: While you can combine federal and private loans in a private consolidation, this is usually a bad idea. Federal loans offer various benefits and protections, such as options for postponement if you're having trouble making payments or forbearance, which lets you pause your payments for up to a year at a time. These features will not transfer to private lenders. If you have both federal and private loans, it is best to consolidate them separately.

Many people consolidate loans soon after leaving school. Refinancing is an approach you may want to take after you have been repaying your loans for a few years. When you refinance, the lender pays off your existing loans and replaces them with a new loan, with a new interest rate and repayment schedule. Going forward, you'll make monthly payments to the new lender. When you apply for refinancing, lenders will examine aspects of your finances, including your credit history. They may ask you to attach a copy of your most recent pay stub to your application, which is typically used to analyze your debt-to-income ratio. Lenders use this information to ensure that you have the means to fulfill your monthly obligation. Banks and national lending companies such as Education Loan Finance, Earnest,

SoFi and Laurel Road will compete for your business. Take the time to comparison shop. Several websites, including SimpleTuition, offer useful comparison tools.

A main benefit of refinancing is to potentially qualify for a lower interest rate. This can save significant money in the long term. Let's look at how the numbers change with different interest rates. Consider a borrower with a $65,000 principal balance, an average interest rate of 6.5% and a term of 10 years. With a minimum monthly payment of $738, the borrower will end up paying back a total of $88,567 ($65,000 in principal and $23,567 in interest). Consider the same borrower but with a 4.0% interest rate; the borrower's minimum monthly payment would be $658. With this new rate, from the time of the refinance until full repayment, the borrower will end up paying back a total of $78,971 ($60,000 in principal and $13,971 in interest). By lowering the interest rate from 6.5% to 4.0%, the borrower saves $9,596, even with a smaller monthly payment. Adjusting the timing of the decision to refinance could mean saving more (or less). This example reflects the benefits of a lower interest rate over the life of the loan. Deciding whether to consolidate, refinance or keep your original loans will depend on your specific situation. Consider whether you qualify to refinance at a lower rate or plan to take advantage of federal loan benefits.

Deferring your student loan payments allows you to reduce or temporarily postpone your payments if you cannot afford them due to unemployment or economic hardship. You can also defer your loans if you go back to school. While this option grants flexibility, interest will continue to grow while you defer payments (depending on the type of loan). This means that deferment can increase your total payback amount. Options for deferring private loans may be more limited than for federal loans, and deferring private loans will almost certainly increase your loan balance. However, you are still better off requesting deferment than defaulting on your loans entirely.

Your credit report will include deferred payments, but deferring won't hurt your credit score.

On the other hand, the government has the authority to defer student loan payments and interest accrual for an entire swath of borrowers. In March 2020, the government paused loan payments and interest accrual due to the COVID-19 pandemic. Repayments resumed more than three years later, beginning in September 2023. Many borrowers took advantage of this pause to pay down their debt. Others took advantage of the opportunity to keep more money in their pockets during a difficult time. While the circumstances were exceptional, this pause served as a reminder that if a lender opts for a deferral, you have options for how to best take advantage of it.

The U.S. government established the Public Service Loan Forgiveness (PSLF) program to offer borrowers with federal student loan debt another option for repayment. The program forgives the remaining balance on direct federal loans if you have made 120 qualifying payments while working full-time in public service. Qualifying employers include government organizations, tax-exempt organizations and private not-for-profit organizations that provide certain public services. Note that the 120 payments do not need to be consecutive. You should be prepared for the U.S. Department of Education to contact your employer to confirm the information you provided in your application if you pursue this option.

FUNDING FUTURE EDUCATION

Section 529 Accounts

If you plan to go back to school, or want to save for your child or another future student, one of the most effective ways to pay for educational expenses is a Section 529 plan account, legally referred to as Qualified Tuition Programs. (The "529" refers to a section of the Internal Revenue Code.) With their significant tax benefits, 529 accounts encourage individuals and families to contribute to an investment account for qualified educational expenses.

There are two main types of 529 accounts: prepaid tuition plans and college saving plans. A prepaid tuition plan, as the name suggests, allows you to pay for future college expenses at present rates. Some plans cover tuition and fees only; some also cover qualified educational expenses. A major benefit of these prepaid plans comes from knowing that regardless of the level of inflation, you've already purchased a certain number of course credits and can cash them in when needed. There are various types of prepaid 529 plans, whose rules are determined by the state or institution offering them. Contract plans allow you to prepay tuition for a set number of years or semesters at an in-state, public institution. In unit plans, you purchase fractional tuition units, typically 1% of one year's tuition. These units are redeemable based on average tuition rates at a target group of schools. Prepaid plans will often have different rules for participating colleges and nonparticipating colleges. Since most plans are aimed at in-state public tuition costs, they may not cover out-of-state or private college expenses. Currently, only a limited number of states offer prepaid tuition plans. These plans have become less prevalent as states struggle to fund various long-term obligations. If you are looking into prepaid plans, it is essential to find plans that put the credit of their state treasuries behind their prepaid 529 offerings. At Palisades Hudson, we recommend avoiding prepaid plans altogether. While they theoretically shift risk to the state, these plans rely on states to invest well enough to meet their financial obligations as tuition increases.

A 529 college savings plan is designed to encourage account holders to save for future qualified education costs. The account functions much like a Roth individual retirement account: Account owners make nondeductible contributions to an investment account that grows tax-free. The money invested in a 529 plan can be withdrawn tax-free if the beneficiary uses it for qualified expenses at eligible institutions. Qualified educational expenses vary from plan to plan, but usually include tuition and fees, books, supplies, computers, printers, and room and board. The Tax Cuts and Jobs Act, which Congress passed in late 2017, expanded qualified educational expenses to cover public, private or religious K-12 tuition expenses too, up to $10,000 per year, per beneficiary. Nonqualified withdrawals, such as transportation and travel costs, are subject to income taxes and a 10% penalty. However, account owners can withdraw original contributions for any purpose both tax- and penalty-free if desired.

If you plan to go back to school or if you are saving for future children, you can name yourself the account beneficiary. If your plans change and you won't need the funds, you can switch beneficiaries to a family member or roll over excess funds to a family member's plan without penalty. It's important to note that there is no penalty for changing the beneficiary to a family member in the same generation or older. On the other hand, if you change the beneficiary to a generation below the current account beneficiary, you may need to count the transfer as a gift for tax purposes. (To learn more about gift taxes, see Chapter 16.) If you're changing the beneficiary, you'll want to ensure that the account's asset allocation appropriately reflects the time horizon before the new beneficiary will need the funds. (See Chapter 5 for more details on asset allocation and investing time horizons.) Also, if your beneficiary is someone other than you, that beneficiary has no legal right to the funds in the 529 account. This provides assurance that any funds you save in the account will go toward the beneficiary's education.

QUICK NOTES

Pros And Cons Of Section 529 Plans

- Contributions build tax-free as long as withdrawals go toward approved educational expenses
- Many states offer resident account holders a tax break on contributions

529 Prepaid Tuition Plans

- Allow payer to cover future tuition expenses at present rates (plus a small premium)
- Many programs have struggled with funding, making these plans less common
- Plan may not fully cover cost of out-of-state or private college tuition
- Plans rely on states to invest well enough to meet future tuition costs

529 Savings Plans

- Owner can change beneficiary with no tax penalty, as long as new beneficiary is an extended family member of old beneficiary
- Qualified educational expenses include public, private or religious K-12 tuition expenses up to $10,000 per year, per beneficiary
- Limited investment options can only be changed a set number of times per year
- No guarantee savings will grow enough to fully cover tuition and associated costs

States administer 529 savings plans, and each plan offers different investment options. Depending on how the plan is set up, you can select investments yourself or choose a predetermined set of options. Most plans provide investment options that vary in their degrees of risk. In addition, 529 savings plans typically offer investment strategies that change based on the age of the beneficiary or the number of years until the expected educational start date. As the beneficiary approaches anticipated enrollment, the portfolio's risk decreases.

Even self-directed plans generally limit the number of times you can change your investment choices during a year. While the particular investment options vary by plan, no plans allow you to purchase individual stocks. Instead, they offer flexible mutual funds and exchange-traded funds (ETFs) to protect plan owners from overexposing their account to company-specific risk. Ensuring your account is properly invested across mutual funds, ETFs, bonds and cash-equivalent investments will give you the best chance to earn a return you anticipate, depending on the length of time you have to invest before you need the funds. That said, investments are always subject to market conditions. There is no guarantee that your savings will cover all costs associated with earning a postsecondary degree.

While contributing to a 529 gives no immediate federal tax benefit, some states offer a state tax break if you invest in their plan. New York, for example, offers its residents a $5,000 deduction ($10,000 for married taxpayers filing jointly) on their state income tax returns for New York plan contributions. While this is a nice perk, you are not required to participate in your state's plan, so shop around and compare. When choosing a 529 plan, focus on fees and available investment options. No annual maximum account contribution exists, except for the maximum account balance determined by the state, if you are the beneficiary of your own account. If your account is for a separate beneficiary, gifts up to $18,000 (in 2024) will qualify for the annual federal gift tax exclusion. Any amount over that must be reported on a gift tax return and will reduce your lifetime gift tax exclusion ($13.61 million as of 2024). (See Chapter 16 for more on gift and transfer taxes.) You can also contribute up to $90,000 without triggering gift tax by making a five-year election.

Each state caps contributions to 529 savings plans when the account grows to a certain threshold. You do not need to start with a large initial contribution, however, since initial minimum contribution amounts to 529 accounts are generally low. Adding a small amount to your account every month is a suitable plan. The earlier you start, the more time the funds will have to benefit from tax-free compounding. You may want to encourage your children to contribute to their own accounts, as a way to teach them about the value of a college education.

It is also important to consider your options for overfunding, especially if you're saving for a young beneficiary. If the beneficiary doesn't end up needing all of the saved funds, you can roll them over to another family member (with potential gift tax consequences in some cases). You can also opt to pay taxes and penalties on the earnings to withdraw the funds for nonqualified expenses. A relatively new option, created by the SECURE 2.0 Act that came into effect in December 2022, is to roll unused funds from a 529 plan into a Roth IRA for the 529 account's beneficiary. The law allows such rollovers up to $35,000 per beneficiary.

Other Funding Options

Aside from 529 accounts, Coverdell Education Savings Accounts (ESAs) and custodial accounts are also practical options to save for the educational expenses of your child or other young beneficiaries. A Coverdell ESA, similar to a 529 savings plan, is an account that grows tax-free. Contributions are not tax-deductible, but withdrawals are tax- and penalty-free for qualified educational expenses. Beneficiaries must be younger than 30; once the beneficiary reaches 18, you can no longer contribute to the account. Any funds remaining in the account when the beneficiary reaches 30 must be immediately distributed, subject to tax and a 10% penalty if there are no qualified educational expenses that year. The Coverdell ESA's main advantage is a wider range of investment choices than most 529 plans offer. The funds in these accounts can be invested in mutual funds, ETFs and individual securities. While annual contributions are essentially limitless for 529 plans in most cases, Coverdell ESAs have a $2,000 per year, per beneficiary contribution limit. Additionally, high earners face an income phase-out that doesn't apply for 529s. These income limits restrict your ability to contribute, with phase-outs between $95,000 and $110,000 of modified adjusted gross income for single taxpayers, and $190,000 and $220,000 for married taxpayers filing jointly in 2023. (For more on MAGI, see Chapter 15.) You can work around these limits by making a gift to the beneficiary and having the beneficiary make the contribution; however, federal gift tax concerns still apply. You can contribute to both a 529 and a Coverdell ESA to max out your annual college funding contributions.

Uniformed Transfer to Minors Act accounts (UTMAs) and Uniformed Gifts to Minors Act accounts (UGMAs) can also be useful options for education funding. These custodial accounts are investment accounts under a child's name that families can use for their children while they are minors. UTMA accounts allow minors to own property including real estate, art and intellectual property, as well as securities. UGMA accounts are limited to purely financial assets. For the purpose of this chapter, the two are similar enough to discuss together. Custodial accounts allow minors to own securities without the need for an attorney to prepare trust documents, or for the trust grantor or court to appoint a trustee. The custodian has an inherent fiduciary duty to manage the money prudently on the minor's behalf. The assets belong to the minor but are controlled by the custodian until the minor reaches the age of majority. This age varies by state and usually falls between 18 and 21. When beneficiaries reach the age of majority, they become the account owner. The major downside of custodial accounts for educational gifts is that these accounts are not tax-advantaged, so annual taxes will be due on any generated income or capital gains. Once the beneficiary reaches legal adulthood, the beneficiary will have complete control of the funds, and there is no requirement that the assets be used for educational expenses. College financial aid calculations consider these accounts the property of the child, which creates a substantial impact on need-based financial aid eligibility.

Financial Aid

When vetting different methods to pay for college, you should consider strategies to minimize and potentially avoid debt. The first step in the financial aid process is submitting a Free Application for Federal Student Aid (FAFSA) form, which is used to apply for federal aid, including grants, scholarships, work-study and federal loans. This form can be filled out only after Oct. 1 of the year before you or your student plans to enroll. For most incoming undergraduates, this will be the October of the student's senior year of high school. A new form is due each year thereafter while the student is enrolled to provide the college with the student's updated financial information. Whether you're completing the FASFA for yourself or helping your child or other dependent, you will likely need to have your most recent tax return readily available prior to preparing the form. Alternatively, applicants can use the IRS Data Retrieval Tool within the FAFSA application, which will automatically pull the necessary information from a previously filed U.S. tax return.

Whether pulled automatically or entered manually, this financial information will determine need-based aid and ultimately your expected family contribution (EFC), which is the difference between the financial aid package a school offers and the total cost of attendance. Total cost of attendance is the average expected annual amount needed to attend the school, including tuition and fees, room and board, books and supplies, transportation and other expenses directly related to a student's education during the enrollment period. Financial aid offices use a formula that deducts EFC from the total cost of attendance, resulting in the gap that a student will need to make up through grants, scholarships, work-study and loans. Annual loan limits restrict the amount that a student may borrow. These limits vary depending on whether the borrower is an undergraduate or a graduate student, the year of school the student is in, and whether someone else can claim the student as a dependent for tax purposes.

The College Scholarship Service ("CSS") Profile is an online form used to allow students to apply for financial aid from sources other than the federal government. The CSS Profile is similar to the FAFSA in the way it determines your eligibility for grants and scholarships. Certain schools ask students to provide the CSS Profile in order to create a more nuanced picture of their financial resources. You can find the schools that require the application on the CSS Profile website. The CSS Profile and FAFSA are separate; submitting one does not impact your ability to use the other. While the FAFSA is free, the CSS Profile involves an application fee for families with adjusted gross incomes above $100,000, as well as a fee to send the report to each additional institution.

The college's offer won't always match the amount you or your student needs, and so the remaining amount will need to be made up from outside sources. It is important to understand these different financing options to bridge that gap between what you can afford to pay versus the total cost of attendance of the school in question.

Grants can come from government or nongovernment sources. They don't need to be repaid, and are often need-based. As we mentioned previously, a student's eligibility for need-based aid is determined by the results of his or her FAFSA. The largest and most popular of the federal grants is the Federal Pell Grant, named after the late Sen. Claiborne Pell of Rhode Island. This grant is awarded to students with demonstrated financial need who have not earned a postsecondary degree. The maximum Federal Pell Grant award was $7,395 for the 2023-24 school year.

Scholarships also don't need to be paid back. In many cases colleges offer them to students directly, although outside organizations also award private scholarships. You should call the financial aid office or visit the financial aid website of the school you or your student is applying to identify available scholarships. Scholarships offered by institutions can generally be sorted into "need-based" and "merit-based" awards. (Often, need-based aid is called a grant and merit-based aid is called a scholarship, but this terminology varies from institution to institution.) Examples of merit funding include athletic scholarships, artistic and other talent-based scholarships, and academic achievement scholarships. Non-college sources of scholarships may include community organizations, religious groups, private companies and others.

Federal work-study is a form of need-based financial aid offered through the government and participating schools, which provide part-time jobs to students. The FAFSA will ask the applicant to opt into consideration for a work-study program. Even if an award letter includes work-study, the student must still apply and find an employer at the school to fill the hours corresponding to the amount of money allocated by the financial aid office to work-study. Most universities have student employment offices that assist students in finding a job that balances their income needs and school schedules. These jobs are usually on campus and have flexible work hours around a student's coursework. Depending on the particular work-study program, students may receive their pay in cash or in credit against their tuition bill.

Educational Loans

When making decisions about college funding, it is also important to consider the degree you or your student will earn. Especially if you are considering taking on debt, balance the degree's economic value against the amount of debt needed to earn it. Engineering and computer science are among the top-paying college majors, so a position in these fields is likely to bring in enough income to let you pay down the debt. Conversely, degrees like social work, while important, are toward the bottom in terms of pay scale. Taking on huge amounts in student loans to earn this degree could leave you struggling to repay your obligations. Considering future earnings potential is an important part of deciding whether to take out loans to fund a particular degree. Even for degrees where the average pay is high, if a student intends to go on to graduate school, it may not be worth taking out big loans for undergraduate study. Many undergraduate degrees are avenues to further schooling and not necessarily drivers for a successful career on their own. Majors such as business, medicine, law, science and mathematics often lead to graduate school for work on a master's degree or a doctorate.

Considering future earnings potential is an important part of deciding whether to take out loans to fund a particular degree.

Earning Credit Ahead Of Enrollment

If you are supporting a high schooler who is college-bound, consider encouraging the student to enroll in college-level classes and postsecondary coursework if it's consistent with their abilities. Many high schools in the U.S. offer college-level coursework such as Advanced Placement (AP) classes, the International Baccalaureate program, and the The Cambridge Advanced International Certificate of Education (AICE). Students who enroll in these courses can potentially earn credit toward their future college diploma. It's important to note that not every college or university accepts these courses for credit, even if the student passes a corresponding exam or receives the associated high school diploma. Some institutions allow students to skip certain prerequisites but will not issue actual credit for these courses, while others may only issue limited credits for even advanced work in high school. If you or your student have your eye on a particular college or university, it is worth taking the time to investigate its policies.

Another cost-effective approach a student can take is to participate in dual enrollment if it is available. Dual enrollment is an acceleration program that allows a student to enroll directly in postsecondary courses while attending high school. These courses will contribute to the student's high school degree as well as potentially transferring directly to their college or university. Access to this program varies by state.

Finally, if you are supporting a student who intends to get a degree but isn't yet sure of his or her ultimate career plans, attending community college for the first two years of an intended four-year degree can be a prudent decision. Students are likely to take general education classes before enrolling in coursework more directly related to their area of study, even at a four-year institution. Community colleges offer more affordable credit hours that are built to transfer seamlessly to four-year colleges. Even for students who know their ultimate career destination, starting at a community college can be a way to save money and add flexibility when desired.

As college costs continue to rise, even students who receive some financial aid through grants and scholarships often need to supplement it with savings, work-study, loans or some combination of these. While education is expensive, it is increasingly vital in many fields. If you want to extend your own education or help a young person in your life to obtain theirs, planning ahead is the best way to expand your options when weighing debt against the doors that a degree could open.

CHAPTER 5

INVESTMENTS: FUNDAMENTALS, TECHNIQUES AND PSYCHOLOGY

Benjamin C. Sullivan, CFP®, EA, CVA

Throughout your education, you likely focused on gaining skills that would help you earn an income. Assuming you have read this book's earlier chapters, you already know you should spend less than you earn over the long term and that you may need to balance saving with paying down debt. After you've built an emergency fund, it's time to invest.

Why invest, rather than just save?

You can accumulate wealth simply by earning more than you spend. But building your wealth is easier if you grow your savings, too. Also, the purchasing power of your saved assets declines by an average of 3% per year as a result of inflation. Sometimes inflation takes an even bigger bite, as we saw with inflation hitting a high of 9% in mid-2022. So if you're not investing aggressively enough, or not investing at all, your savings will effectively lose value even if the numbers on your statements don't decrease.

Investing is like having a team of dollar bills working to make you more money. Your team may be small at first, but as it grows, its impact on your life can grow, too. The earlier you start investing, the more time your money has to grow. As a result of your longer time horizon, you can also pursue investments with higher returns, a concept I'll discuss later in this chapter.

What sets investing apart from speculating or gambling is the goal. When you invest, you want to achieve your desired outcomes with a relatively high chance of reaching them. You can't control the markets. But you can control how you position your investments and how you react to changes in your portfolio. Learning and implementing the concepts discussed in this chapter should improve your chances of achieving your investing goals.

CLASSES OF INVESTMENTS

A portfolio's risk is determined by the type of assets it holds, so it's important to understand how different types of investments, or securities, impact a portfolio. The two most basic and fundamental asset classes are fixed income and equities. "Fixed income" generally refers to bonds and "equity" refers to stocks. In general, fixed income is safer than equities. Equity's increased risk leads to higher potential returns.

A bond is essentially an investment in debt. An investor lends money to a government or company for a defined period of time. In return, the investor expects to be repaid with interest. How the bond issuer repays the investor depends on the type of bond.

There are many different types of bonds and bond investment strategies; I will not go into all of them here. However, a common element to understand about most bonds is that the investor is guaranteed a fixed payment over a defined period of time. Of course, this guarantee is only reliable to the extent that the bond issuer can make the scheduled payments. The less likely an issuer is to follow through on its obligation, the higher the interest rate it must pay investors to make up for the risk. As with all investments, the riskier it is, the greater the expected return will be.

Equity is generally a stock or any other security that represents an ownership interest in a company. When an investor buys a share of a company's stock, the person becomes a part owner of that company. As owners, all shareholders have a right to the company's profits.

Equity investors receive compensation for the risk they take on in two ways: dividends and capital gains. When a company makes a profit, it must decide whether to reinvest that capital into the company or to pay it out to shareholders directly (a dividend). Not all companies pay dividends, however. Typically, companies that are growing quickly will reinvest profits, while more mature companies will pay dividends, especially if they lack attractive investment opportunities.

The other way shareholders earn money is through capital gains. As a company grows and increases in value, its stock price will rise. An investor can realize this increased value by selling the stock now that it is worth more than it was when the investor purchased the shares originally. The difference is called a capital gain. Investors expect capital gains from stocks, but such gains are certainly not guaranteed. While many stocks increase in value over time, some will not. A few may lose value or become worthless if the underlying business fails.

While fixed income and equity can be much more complex than the basics I've discussed above, the main point is that fixed income is generally safer and offers lower returns than equity. As I will discuss in more detail in this chapter, how you allocate your portfolio between these asset classes will largely determine your portfolio's overall expected return and risk.

RISK AND ITS RELATIONSHIP TO POTENTIAL RETURN

In general, there is a direct trade-off between risk and return. Be wary of anyone who tells you otherwise. If one company will pay you 8% to lend it money and another will only pay you 4%, there must be a reason for the difference. The law of supply and demand applies to stocks, too. If a given investment does not attract buyers, the price will drop. At the lower price, the potential future return goes up, which can entice new investors. All else being equal, a company's expected return goes up when its stock price goes down. In a properly functioning market, all investments should be priced so that the more risk embedded in the investment, the higher the expected return.

In valuation theory, there is a hierarchy of investment risk. Investors will demand to be paid a premium for each additional layer of risk they take on by holding an investment.

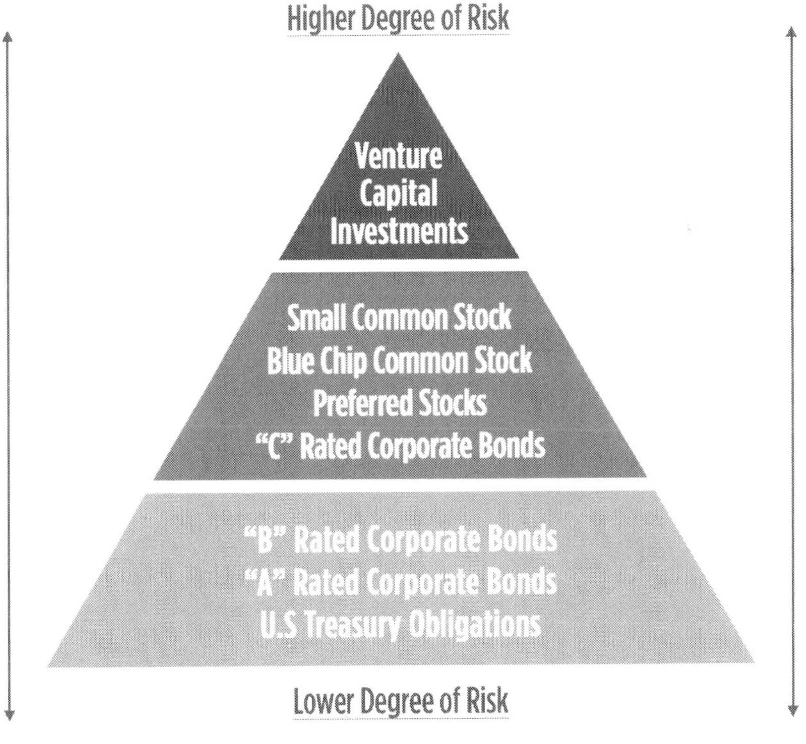

Figure 1: Order of Investment Risk

However, simply taking on the maximum amount of risk won't assure the highest long-term return. Higher rates of return are meant to reward risk takers in the event things go as planned, but higher risk also means a greater chance of failure. A risky investment means that you can face substantial downside, whether temporary or permanent.

In the 60 years ending Dec. 31, 2022, the average annual return of U.S. large-company stocks was 11.66.%. But in any given 12 months, the return ranged from negative 43.3% to positive 61.0%. If I offered you a chance of turning $100 into anywhere from $56.70 to $161 over a one-year period, you would rightly say that my offer sounded like gambling.

However, buying stocks is not like buying a lottery ticket. You're buying a share of a company's future income and growth, which has a positive rate of return in the long term in most cases. Over longer periods, the range of historical investment returns narrows to a tighter, more predictable range. This is why your odds of achieving a return close to the average increases over a longer time horizon. The chart opposite illustrates the broad historical range of returns over one-year periods and the narrower range of returns for longer time periods.

This is what financial professionals mean when they talk about stocks' volatility. Over short periods, stocks have a high degree of volatility, but as an investment class, they deliver more predictably positive returns over longer periods. The amount of risk that it is prudent to take on therefore varies based on the amount of time involved. Understanding that uncertainty and risk are higher over shorter periods is a major step toward being a good investor.

BEST AND WORST (MONTHLY: 01/01/1962 – 12/31/2022)

Average Annualized Rolling Returns (%)

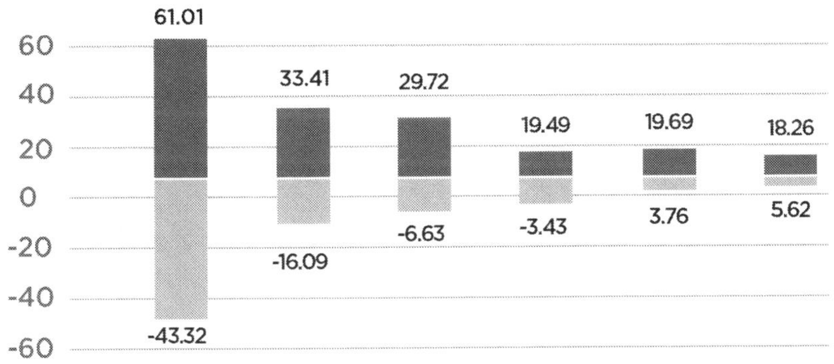

	1 Year	3 Years	5 Years	10 Years	15 Years	20 Years
S&P 500 Index	**11.66**	**10.71**	**10.46**	**10.34**	**10.38**	**10.79**
Best Return Start Date	**61.01** (7/1982)	**33.41** (8/1984)	**29.72** (8/1982)	**19.49** (9/1990)	**19.69** (8/1982)	**18.26** (4/1980)
Worst Return Start Date	**-43.32** (3/2008)	**-16.09** (4/2000)	**-6.63** (3/2004)	**-3.34** (3/1999)	**3.76** (9/2000)	**4.79** (4/2000)

Figure 2

Data Source: Dimensional Fund Advisors

THE BENEFITS OF DIVERSIFICATION

The two fundamental principles to keep in mind when investing are a long-term outlook and diversification. The previous section touched on the benefits of long-term investing, so now we can consider why diversification is important. Diversification is a risk-management technique that mixes a wide variety of investments within a portfolio. Buying and holding a diversified portfolio that includes various individual investments, different types of assets, and investments reflecting different geographic regions, company sizes and investment styles can all minimize your exposure to any particular investment's risks.

There are two main types of investment risk. "Firm-specific risk" refers to attributes unique to the particular investment. For example, a CEO who is integral to the success of a company could die unexpectedly. Although this could have a disastrous effect on the company in question, other companies will be unaffected. "Market risk" refers to factors that affect a wide range of securities. For example, during the recession of 2008-09, nearly all stocks and many bonds lost value at the same time.

Diversification can eliminate or greatly reduce firm-specific risk, but it does not protect investors from market risk. If your investment portfolio held stock in only one company and that company declared bankruptcy, the announcement would be disastrous for your portfolio. On the other hand, if you invested in 500 companies, one of them going bankrupt is unlikely to have a major effect on your portfolio.

Investors should be mindful of various types of diversification, too. If all the companies you invest in are based in the same region of the same country, a natural disaster such as an earthquake or a hurricane could create heavy losses for you. In a geographically diversified portfolio, losses caused by the same hurricane might be offset by gains in other regions. The more diversification and the more types of diversification you can build into your portfolio, the less specific risk you must bear. This is why diversification leads to more consistent, and often higher, long-term investment returns.

INVESTING GOALS AND RISK TOLERANCE

Before investing, you need to establish and understand both your goals and your risk tolerance. These will shape any sensible investment plan, no matter what philosophy you employ. Your goals are your destination; your risk tolerance dictates how many highs and lows you're willing to endure to get there.

Most people have multiple investment goals of varying levels of importance. Are you investing to meet an immediate need, such as purchasing a home or managing debt? Are you saving for your children's educational expenses? Do you want to grow your wealth to secure a comfortable retirement income? Knowing why you're investing will help you make better investment choices and keep you motivated to stick to your long-term investment plan when things get difficult. Goals also help you time your investments.

Pinpointing your risk tolerance is harder for most people, because it is more abstract. But it is no less essential to your investment plan. Your risk tolerance refers to the amount of short-term uncertainty you are willing to accept in pursuit of long-term gains. There is no one "right" amount of risk. Each investor's relationship with risk is different, depending on an individual's cash-flow needs and temperament.

Since the odds of a positive stock market return increase as your investment time horizon extends, you should invest funds that you'll need to withdraw within the next several years in safer investments, such as cash or short-term bonds. Beyond this reserve, try to determine how much short-term volatility you can comfortably tolerate in the pursuit of the higher expected returns associated with stocks. Don't be overconfident. Overinvesting in stocks often leads to costly mistakes. If you don't need the money within the next several years, the real risk is not fluctuations in the value of your investments, but that volatility could make you nervous enough to abandon your long-term strategy.

There is no shame in recognizing that you are not comfortable with risky investments. But it is important to remember that all investing carries some risk. Even fairly conservative portfolios may suffer the effects of major financial events, such as the housing bubble and credit crisis in 2008. Although the ensuing recession hurt nearly everyone, what made the most difference was not necessarily the original portfolio but investor behavior. Investors who pulled out of the market at the bottom missed the subsequent rebound and locked in their losses. Those who remained invested experienced a steady recovery in asset prices after the market's bottom in early 2009. Within a few years, these investors had made up what they lost. This is why it is so important to cultivate a long-term mindset.

Some people will follow the market's daily moves and stress over every downswing, no matter how small. These people typically have a high aversion to risk and may want to seek steadier investments, even if it means forgoing a higher long-term return. On the other hand, investors with a higher risk tolerance may be comfortable with larger and more frequent downturns, as long as their investments ultimately rise over many years. Realistically assessing how you will deal with short-term volatility is essential in crafting an investment strategy that will work for you over the long haul.

Remember: Risk isn't the enemy. Calculated risk is an investor's best friend, since it is the principal driver of returns. Even if you are comfortable with risk, however, you should take on risk with discipline and within limits. You may find it easier to cope with risk by dividing your portfolio into "buckets." You can assign each bucket a different risk threshold and a different time horizon. If you are hungry for risk, setting aside a bucket for high-risk investments will let you pursue long-term goals responsibly. On the other hand, if you are more risk-averse, knowing that you have covered your short-term needs with relatively safe investments can provide you with the fortitude to pursue higher returns with money you're investing for the long term.

SETTING AN ASSET ALLOCATION AND REBALANCING

Once you understand your goals and risk tolerance, you should create a long-term plan and stick to it. An investment adviser can help you translate your goals into a plan that will work for you, keeping in mind the principles of diversification and long-term perspective.

The first step in creating any diversified portfolio is to determine the asset allocation — the mix of investments — that will satisfy your financial goals and risk tolerance. Asset allocation is the most important factor in overall portfolio performance, which means the allocation you settle on will have a profound effect on your portfolio's returns over time.

Asset allocation is the most important factor in overall portfolio performance, which means the allocation you settle on will have a profound effect on your portfolio's returns over time.

Although asset allocation generally refers to a selected mix of stocks and bonds, advisers and investors can also talk about sub-asset classes. For example, you may break down fixed income allocations for government bonds and corporate bonds, or short-term bonds and long-term bonds. You can break down stocks by investment style, economic industry, firm size, geographic region, and so on. Constructing your portfolio's asset allocation is the primary way to ensure diversification.

One way to diversify is by geographic region, including a mixture of U.S. and foreign securities. Although companies in the United States operate globally, it still does not make sense to limit your investment universe to U.S. companies. Companies headquartered and predominantly operating abroad experience different conditions and can perform differently than U.S. companies. It's possible for one region of the world to grow rapidly while another is undergoing a major economic slump. Owning a globally diversified portfolio provides you with the opportunity to share in global growth.

QUICK NOTES

Some Types Of Portfolio Diversification

General

- Asset class (and subclass)

Fixed Income (Bonds)

- Government vs. corporate bonds
- Long-term vs. short-term bonds

Equities (Stocks)

- Investment style
- Industry
- Business size
- Country/region

Another good way to diversify is by market capitalization, or "market cap." A company's market cap is the total value of its outstanding shares. In investing, it is used as a measure of a company's relative size. You should consider investing in equities that represent both large companies — sometimes called "large-cap" equities — and smaller or medium companies ("small-cap" or "mid-cap"). Small-cap stocks represent more growth potential than larger capitalization stocks, and thus provide a greater expected rate of return. They are appropriate additions to a long-term portfolio for someone who is financially secure. Based on data going back to 1926, the expected one-year total return for small-cap stocks is about 16%, compared with approximately 12% for the S&P 500 (an index of 500 top companies in major U.S. industries). The higher expected return of U.S. small-cap stocks is attractive, but as with all investments, higher returns and higher volatility go hand-in-hand.

Your stock allocation can — and often should — also include allocations to publicly traded real estate investments and stocks operating in the natural resources markets. These allocations can counteract general downward shifts in the broader stock and bond markets. They also generally perform well during periods of high inflation. Some investors buy pure commodities, such as oil and precious metals, to offset inflation risk. At Palisades Hudson, we generally forgo direct exposure to commodities in favor of investing in enterprises that sell or extract them. These businesses can generate profit even if commodity prices decline, by cutting costs or investing in research and development to find alternative products.

Asset allocation is not deciding that one asset class is superior to another. Instead, it's about developing an appropriate balance of various asset classes. That balance lets you build a diversified portfolio with an acceptable level of risk and potential return. A healthy portfolio shouldn't necessarily include every type of asset in equal portions; that's where the "allocation" part comes in.

Once you have selected a reasonable asset allocation, it is essential to stick with it unless your financial situation or objectives materially change. This means you should always avoid attempting to time the markets. Do not try to predict which individual investments or asset classes will perform well or poorly over short periods and shift your asset allocation in an attempt to profit. Market timing often leads to emotional decisions based on short-term market movements, a poor investment strategy.

The consequence of inaccurately timing the stock market can be significant. Consider the effect of missing the best single day in the market. Between 1990 and 2022, according to Standard & Poor's, the S&P 500 returned 9.75% on an annualized compounded rate. When you subtract the single best performance day, this return drops to 9.39%. Subtracting the best five days, the return drops even further, to 8.23%. If you missed the best 25 days, your return would have been 4.72%, which is only 2.19% greater than you would have earned investing in a one-month U.S. Treasury bill (or bond) over the same period. For reference, one-month T-bills are considered one of the safest investments. As such, they offer a very low expected return compared with equities.

The lesson is that you must remain in the market to succeed as a long-term investor. Attempting to time market upturns and downturns is not only nearly impossible; the consequence of timing incorrectly can be devastating to a portfolio's return.

Sticking with your asset allocation doesn't mean leaving your portfolio alone. In fact, it means the opposite. Over time, your investments will grow, but not all of them will grow at the same rate. When rising markets lead to an over-concentration in one asset class, you should reduce your stake in it. Conversely, when falling markets leave a segment of your allocation underrepresented, you should increase your investments in that sector. This process is called rebalancing.

Different financial planners approach rebalancing differently. At Palisades Hudson, we generally rebalance a portfolio when its asset allocation deviates outside a predetermined acceptable range. This is called a "banded" approach. A banded approach ties rebalancing directly to a portfolio's changing asset allocation, rather than to a set period of time. In this method, a portfolio's asset allocation is banded within a certain threshold of the ideal balance (often within 5% and 15%). If an asset class rises above or drops below this range, this signals a rebalance is warranted. While frequent rebalancing can increase transaction costs and income tax liability, a methodical and disciplined approach to rebalancing will lead to superior long-term investment results.

IMPLEMENTING YOUR PORTFOLIO

Until now we have talked about how to successfully manage your investments and stick to a long-term investment strategy. But how exactly should you get started as a new investor? In general, you have two options. You can either hand-pick individual securities, such as stocks and bonds, or you can buy diversified vehicles, such as mutual funds.

Although some investors pick individual stocks and bonds, at Palisades Hudson we rely mainly on mutual funds and exchange-traded funds (ETFs). A mutual fund pools capital from many investors and invests it in stocks, bonds or other securities. Mutual funds issue shares to investors. The price investors pay for these shares depends on the fund's net asset value (NAV) per share, which is the value of all of the fund's underlying holdings divided by the total number of shares outstanding. A mutual fund's NAV updates once per day after the market closes, based on the change in value of all its holdings. Some mutual funds have a broad, go-anywhere investment strategy, while others maintain a more focused investment mandate, such as investing only in U.S. small-cap stocks.

Mutual funds can be either passively or actively managed. A passively managed fund typically tries to replicate a benchmark index, such as the S&P 500. In an actively managed fund, fund managers will pick individual securities they think will outperform the benchmark index. Actively managed funds will typically have higher costs in the form of fees and expenses, since investors are paying for the managers' expertise.

Like passively managed mutual funds, nearly all ETFs try to mimic a benchmark index. Unlike mutual funds, which only trade at the end of the day, ETFs can be traded throughout the day based on a market price. In this way, they function more like stocks. An ETF's market price changes throughout the day, just as a stock's price does. Mutual funds and ETFs can both play a role in a portfolio. We select which type of fund to use in each case based on their tax efficiency, cost and investment strategy.

Broadly, passive management (or "indexing") is more appropriate for large-company stocks in efficient markets, such as the U.S. and Western Europe. Active management, where fund managers have the opportunity to profit from market inefficiencies, is more appropriate in less efficient markets. These may include small companies in emerging markets, such as Latin America or China. When selecting an actively managed fund, be sure to keep an eye on both the fund's long-term performance record and its fees, which can quickly eat away at your returns.

As I discussed earlier in the chapter, the goal in investing is to pursue your desired outcomes in a way that is highly likely to succeed. If you're picking a handful of individual stocks, you're unlikely to achieve predictable returns. Using index funds ensures that your portfolio will achieve returns close to what that market delivers, which is reasonably predictable over long periods. Even actively managed mutual funds are a much more predictable means of accessing the market's overall return than picking stocks on your own. Mutual fund managers will carefully consider portfolio construction and allocation decisions when picking the stocks. In this way, mutual funds and ETFs build in extra diversification for you.

While we mainly use mutual funds and ETFs, at Palisades Hudson we sometimes also consider alternative investments, such as private equity, venture capital and hedge funds. These investments are not appropriate for all investors. They can be especially risky, because they are less diversified and often rely on leverage strategies that may not ultimately pay off. (Leverage strategies involve borrowing capital in order to try to increase potential returns.) Alternative investments also tend to be illiquid, meaning it can be hard to retrieve invested capital if you need it. However, despite these drawbacks, such investments offer the potential for high returns. While alternative investments can be a worthwhile addition to a diversified portfolio in some cases, it is wise to limit your total commitment to these investments to a relatively small percentage of your overall wealth.

I have mentioned fees a few times in the discussion above. At this point, it's worth pausing to discuss expenses in a bit more detail. As you select investment products, it is important to pay attention to the fees, commissions and other costs that may be attached to a particular investment vehicle.

Some charges are intuitive and easy to grasp, such as a fee for the fund manager or a commission when you buy or sell a certain fund. Other fees are less clear and can require some digging to understand. For example, annuities usually set restrictions on when and how much money you can withdraw. If you have to withdraw your funds in a different way or at a different time, you may incur surrender charges. When evaluating a certain investment vehicle, it's important to factor in all the fees, both certain and potential.

Assuming you hire a professional to help you manage your investments, you should also understand the distinction between fee-only and commission-based investment advisers. Fee-only advisers are only paid by their clients. Their fee is usually based on a fixed percentage of the assets they manage on a client's behalf. Commission-based advisers charge a certain amount for every trade they execute or each product they sell. Fee-only advisers are better for most investors because their interests are better aligned with those of their clients. Commissions set up potential conflicts of interest between adviser and client that are best avoided.

Taxes are an equally important consideration. Some accounts — such as 401(k) plans, traditional IRAs and Roth IRAs — are tax-free or tax-deferred. If you invest through multiple accounts, you should consider the tax consequences of your investments. Different types of income are taxed differently; for example, long-term capital gains are taxed at a lower rate than regular income. (For more details, see Chapter 15.) You should consider not the pure return you expect from an investment, but how much of that return you will keep after taxes. A good investment for a taxable account might not make as much sense in a Roth IRA and vice versa. Setting up an investment strategy for a nonprofit organization will likely look very different from setting up a strategy for an individual investor. Be sure to take your investments' tax consequences into account when you decide how to implement your overall strategy.

INVESTMENT PSYCHOLOGY

While understanding the technical aspects of investing is important, the emotional and behavioral aspects are sometimes the harder ones to get right. One of the biggest risks to investors' long-term wealth is their own behavior. Investment professionals and laypeople alike are prone to biases that lead them to make subpar financial decisions. Becoming a good investor requires education and experience, but these alone are not enough to overcome the way human brains are wired to avoid immediate perceived threats. Subconscious thought patterns that are deeply ingrained can trip up even experienced investors.

Behavioral economics is an entire field of study devoted to understanding how and why people make financial decisions. Nobel Prize-winning researcher Daniel Kahneman wrote extensively about the subject in his book *Thinking Fast and Slow*, which I highly recommend if you want to learn more.

All of us constantly use mental shortcuts and emotional cues to simplify decisions in our day-to-day lives. In many cases, such habits are beneficial, but when it comes to investing, they can lead to trouble. Although it's incredibly hard to prevent yourself from succumbing to these natural biases, especially as many of them are subconscious, you can still improve your decisions. Acknowledge these potential weaknesses, plan ahead using data, and avoid putting yourself in the position to make important decisions at emotional times. With a better awareness of the following common investor biases, ideally you will come to appreciate the need to stick to a long-term investment plan when euphoria, panic or hype try to take control.

Investor Biases

Experts in behavioral finance have identified some emotional shortcuts that investors unconsciously rely on as they make financial decisions. These biases can lead people to over- or undervalue the information available to them in a variety of predictable ways. Some of these biases are cognitive, or logical, in nature. Cognitive biases include logical fallacies, errors in interpreting statistics and errors of memory. Other biases are emotional, springing from impulse or intuition rather than from calculation. Both logical and emotional errors can have devastating impacts on a portfolio if given free rein.

It may be helpful to think of these biases as techniques your brain has evolved to save time and energy. If you had to fully and deeply process every decision you make, you would quickly become exhausted and unable to make any decisions at all. However, the cost of these shortcuts is that they can warp your perception of reality. The following are some common biases that you should anticipate when making financial decisions.

Overconfidence

Most people believe they are better at many things than they actually are, from driving to investing. Compounding the problem, we don't notice this talent inflation in ourselves, because people also generally tend to believe they are less overconfident than others.

This is why many people think that they can beat the market by picking a few great stocks. It is easy to believe that a hot tip or insightful article should give someone an edge in the stock market — why not you? Unfortunately, the facts don't back up this hypothesis. A study published by S&P Dow Jones Indices found that not a single actively managed mutual fund, of more than 2,000 studied, consistently outperformed its benchmark in the five years between 2017 and 2022. The results are similar over different time periods and in different markets. Although the jury may still be out on whether professional stock pickers can sometimes outperform index funds, the casual investor is sure to be at a disadvantage against the professionals. Financial analysts, who have access to sophisticated research and data, spend their entire careers trying to determine the appropriate value of certain stocks. Many of these well-trained analysts focus on only one sector and still regularly underperform the market. Even if some individual traders do well due to pure luck, the typical trader is ultimately worse off after accounting for the taxes and trading costs incurred by frequent trades.

Whether in picking stocks or frequent trading, overconfidence leaves investors focusing on games they can't win. Instead, investors are better served by focusing on what they can control — their own behavior, including their overall asset allocation, as well as their spending and saving habits.

Familiarity

People tend to stick with what they know because familiar things are comfortable. This is why people return to the same few restaurants again and again, or read books by authors they already like. However, in investing a bias toward the familiar leads many people to invest most of their money in areas they feel they know best, rather than in a properly diversified portfolio. The known feels safe; the unknown feels risky.

A bias in favor of the familiar can show up in a portfolio in several ways. A banker might create a "diversified" portfolio of five large bank stocks. A Ford assembly line employee might invest predominantly in company stock. A 401(k) investor might allocate his portfolio over a variety of funds that all focus on the U.S. market. Whether it means holding too much of your employer's stock or investing too heavily in your own geographic region, familiarity is the enemy of well-balanced investing.

Sticking with one type of investment concentrates risk. The market doesn't reward investors for risks that they can, and should, remove from their portfolios through proper diversification. Investors who give in to their bias toward the familiar create portfolios with higher risk or lower expected rates of return than a properly diversified portfolio.

Anchoring

While there are complex models that can help calculate the value of an investment, our brains usually want an easier answer. This desire leads many people to default to either the original cost of an investment or to some other benchmark, such as the value they saw on the prior quarter's statement. Although both measures might provide a framework for determining value, much of the time the past is irrelevant to the current situation. This tendency to fixate on a point of reference may seem like an easy mistake to spot, but in practice it can be hard to dislodge a perception anchored this way. Investment values are ephemeral and situationally dependent.

Some investors also become overly focused on the dollar value of their account statements and may anchor to a certain value. This becomes a problem because obsessively checking on your portfolio or investments can make you hyperaware of fluctuations, leading to greater (and unnecessary) anxiety. In addition, if you have a long time horizon, price declines early in your investing career can wind up being great opportunities to buy low.

Loss Aversion

Not only do we tend to cling to what we know and anchor to historical prices, but we generally avoid facing the truth of a financial loss. An investor who makes a speculative trade that performs poorly often continues to hold the investment, even if new developments have made the investment's prospects increasingly dismal.

In Economics 101, students learn about "sunk costs" — costs that have already been incurred. Students also learn that they should typically ignore such costs in decisions about future actions, since no action can recover them. Only the potential future return on the investment, and the associated risk, should matter. Yet knowing this theory and applying it are two different things. Sunk costs can lead investors to hold on to losers too long so they can avoid acknowledging mistakes, hoping to recoup their original loss.

In most cases, people who are averse to risk when it comes to gains are willing to take much larger risks to prevent possible losses. This is because most of us place different emotional weights on gains and losses of equivalent size. The pain of losing $10,000 is generally much larger than the happiness of winning $10,000. Unwillingness to accept this pain is what often leads investors to hold on to failing investments too long.

When deciding on an asset allocation, you should focus on both the expected return and the potential losses the portfolio could incur in a market downturn. At the same time, you must not allow loss aversion to prevent you from taking appropriate risks. While losses are never pleasant, investors should not focus obsessively on avoiding them. Understanding the magnitude of potential losses in a particular investment or portfolio of investments may help you stick with your plan when markets drop.

Recency

In the years that immediately followed the financial crisis of 2008-09, many investors focused on defending themselves against another market free fall, rather than on seeking opportunities to profit from the recovery as conditions stabilized. This is a great example of the recency bias, which is the assumption that conditions created by a recent event will persist or recur far into the future. After the market had recovered for several years, people kept expecting a market crash, because they thought a crash would inevitably arrive a few years into a bull market.

We are prone to pay undue attention to recent news, either good or bad. As a result, we may underemphasize long-term averages or trends. It's an adage in financial planning that past performance is no guarantee of future results. In fact, performance in the recent past is arguably the least useful information about an investment to consider in isolation. Yet recent performance data is easy to access and remember, so it exerts an outsize influence on many investors' decisions.

The human brain's tendency to identify patterns can be helpful in a variety of areas, but it also leads us to interpret events as if they are part of a pattern even when they are random. If you do not stop to consider the reasons behind the pattern you perceive, it can be easy to buy into an illusory meaning. This can lead you to make choices based on data that is ultimately irrelevant. Seeking patterns can also lead you to chase "hot" funds or stocks, which will actually tend to hurt returns as you trail behind the market. Similarly, if you remember hearing a recent news report about startups that made a lot of money, you may feel as if venture capital is a sure thing. But how well other companies have done in the past is more or less irrelevant to a particular investment you might consider. Here again, data can help you, while emotion will lead you astray.

Herd Mentality

Investing can sound easy in theory. Don't chase the latest hot idea or protect against yesterday's disaster seems like common-sense advice. Yet it is still hard not to get caught up in hype when the crucial moment arrives.

It isn't that investors consciously decide to follow an irrational trend. A belief begins to seem plausible when enough people buy into it. It is easy to accept the theory that if many people are doing something, it must be a good idea. In the long term, though, this sort of thinking can burn investors.

A stock or an asset class usually begins to appreciate based on some valid, fundamental cause, such as the arrival of a promising new product or a technological advance. As the asset's price increases, more and more people hear about the idea and buy in, causing further appreciation. Finally, every news channel and website proclaims that gold, Apple stock, emerging markets, cryptocurrency or the investment du jour is the place all smart investors should put their money. By this time, you don't want to miss out, so you take the plunge and buy.

Unfortunately, all streaks come to an end. The cycle of positive news takes a turn and transforms into a negative feedback loop. Yesterday's market darling becomes today's burst bubble. From the tech bubble of the 1990s to the real estate bubble of the 2000s and the "meme stocks" of the 2020s, bubbles grow because the people who believe the growth is not a bubble generally reap rewards in the short term.

By the time the bubble's inevitable pop arrives, many investors' fear of missing out has trumped their self-control, leaving them to suffer the consequences. They may buy a security after the gains have already been earned, or stay in too long and take the brunt of the downswing. Conversely, following the crowd can lead investors to wait too long to invest in a down market. Waiting until signs of recovery arrive can lead investors to buy at higher prices than they should; waiting for signs of trouble can mean investors miss opportunities to sell at the market's height.

To avoid getting caught up in hype, you should be sure to base your investment decisions on quantifiable data that you understand, not simply headlines or news reports. Basing your financial strategy on the emotions of a crowd is no wiser than basing it on your own emotions.

Confirmation Bias

The conclusion you seek often determines the data that you find. We tend to hear what we want to hear — or, put another way, we tend to make a decision and then search for data to back it up, ignoring any evidence that doesn't support it. This tendency is aggravated by both herd mentality and overemphasized recent information. Investors' optimism or pessimism can thus be amplified, as the market responds with price increases or decreases. Investors see these shifts as evidence their original confidence or fear was justified, leading them to double down on their conclusions and encouraging others to follow suit.

On a smaller scale, if you are convinced that a certain sector is a sure bet, you will be inclined to find and remember any news that suggests it is growing strong, and ignore or write off as flukes those reports that should trigger you to act more cautiously. Remember to research both sides of an issue equally and to honestly consider any potential bias inherent to the news source. On the internet, you can find data supporting any conclusion.

Action Bias

Inaction is a powerful choice that is generally undervalued. It feels better to do something, especially when the market is in turmoil.

This psychological effect holds even if the action you take is not particularly wise.

If you are losing money, you may find it easier to believe that you are doing something wrong than that the market is experiencing short-term volatility. It can be hard to accept that our financial fate is partially beyond our control. Yet if you follow a long-term investment plan with a portfolio appropriate for your risk tolerance, that plan should already account for the possibility of down markets. At Palisades Hudson, we generally recommend that clients keep five years of expected portfolio withdrawals in safe investments that aren't subject to the stock market's fluctuations. This precaution can give people added comfort and can help them to recognize that changing course during a volatile period is unnecessary.

Inaction can feel neglectful or foolish, especially if everyone else is furiously taking action. In reality, however, rash decisions can do active harm by locking in your portfolio's losses. Choosing not to act is itself a choice. Sometimes it's the right one.

Mental Accounting

How easy it is to stay the course in a crisis may depend, for some, on the source of the money in question. One of the most prevalent and illogical of our emotional financial biases is treating dollars differently depending on their origins and their destinations. This mental accounting can lead to decisions that seem very sound on the surface. Sometimes they are: Setting aside money for retirement may prevent us from spending it too early, for example. Many people budget by either figuratively or literally putting money into different "envelopes."

This sort of division becomes a problem, though, when we categorize our funds without stepping back to look at the bigger picture. Money you earned through work is no different than money you inherited, as far as your portfolio is concerned. Yet many investors are more willing to take risks with one category than the other. On the spending side, it is possible to become overly focused on one goal at the expense of another. Maintaining an easily accessible emergency fund can distract from retirement planning; you may be reluctant to spend money that you set aside for a vacation or a major unexpected health expense. It's essential to take stock of your assets as a whole, both incoming and outgoing. Don't let your mental assignments keep you from rearranging if necessary.

Avoiding Bad Investing Behavior

All of these fears and biases may make it seem like the deck is stacked against you when you make investment decisions. It is true that mental shortcuts can be hard to notice in yourself, even when you know what to look for, because many of them operate on an unconscious level. We can convince ourselves that, in the moment, we are making perfectly sound choices. It's only when you try to evaluate the actions under the lens of the tendencies discussed in the previous section that you begin to see the emotional or illogical forces driving your decisions. You typically will not see a bias as it influences your decision, but you might notice it in retrospect.

Setting up an investment plan will remove the temptation to rely on yourself to remain unbiased and unemotional in any circumstances.

Knowing your own tendencies is vital, but it doesn't mean you can expect to rewire yourself. You, like your family, friends and yes, even your financial adviser, are only human. Since these biases generally work on your unconscious mind, being aware of them may help, but it won't eliminate their influence. So how can you avoid falling into traps created by your own mental shortcuts?

The most effective tool for combating bad mental habits is a written investment plan and the commitment to stick to it. An investment policy statement puts forth a prudent philosophy for a given investor and describes the types of investments, investment-management procedures and goals that will define the portfolio. The plan should focus on long-term results and should include contingencies for such events as a market downturn or the failure of a major investment. By considering such problems in advance as hypothetical situations, you can avoid the temptation to react emotionally. In essence, you will sign an "investment contract" with yourself, agreeing that you won't let market conditions or outside influences cause you to abandon your original plan.

Further, creating a detailed plan will allow you — perhaps with a financial adviser's help — to set benchmarks for your portfolio. These might include what an appropriate amount of spending looks like, how much of a loss to expect in a market downturn, or what conditions should trigger rebalancing. Keeping your asset allocation in line with your risk tolerance will help you weather turbulent markets much more effectively than trying to react in the moment as volatile situations arise. By setting up an investment plan, you will remove the temptation to rely on yourself to remain unbiased and unemotional in any circumstances.

For example, a classic piece of investing advice is to "buy when there's blood in the streets" — that is, when there is panic in financial markets. Panics are the time to make money, as long as you avoid emotional reactions and stick to your plan. The market is effectively on sale, and yet people typically buy less, not more. A plan can help you avoid this tendency without forcing you to rewire your own natural responses. Similarly, sticking to an investment plan can prevent you from acting on overconfidence borne of a market boom. Your plan will allow you to avoid impulsive action.

Investor biases are one form of the human brain's adaptations for dealing with a complex world through patterns and shortcuts. The inclinations to focus too much on just a few factors or to answer an easy question rather than a hard one are quite natural. Such mental biases are a part of us, and none of us can get rid of them completely. Yet that doesn't mean investors are powerless. Though we cannot eliminate our biases, we can recognize them and respond in ways that help us avoid self-defeating behavior.

Planning and discipline are the keys. Think critically about your investment processes from start to finish, rather than letting your subconscious drive your actions. Make plans calmly over time, when you are well-rested and well-informed. Once you have a plan, stick to it diligently. Adhering to a long-term investment plan will limit the extent to which fears and biases can influence your behavior as an investor. We all make mistakes, but a plan that accounts for such foreseeable temptations can help protect you from avoidable missteps.

Hiring a financial adviser can help mitigate emotional responses and make sticking to your plan easier. Many experts believe that we are blind to our own biases in practice, even when we are aware of them in theory. An adviser can also be useful for those without the time or skill to manage their own investments properly. A professional has the resources necessary to perform sufficient due diligence for your investments, replacing emotion and guesswork with data. The adviser can also provide moral support or coaching in rough times when you begin to doubt the wisdom of your own plan.

Beginning to invest is a major step forward in your financial life. But investing well does not need to be overly complicated. While avoiding individual biases and counterproductive behaviors does matter, the best way forward is to make a plan based on your long-term goals and your risk tolerance. Then stick to that plan in whatever way you need to. If you keep these simple principles in mind, your portfolio will work for you for years to come.

CHAPTER 6

SHOULD I BUY OR LEASE A VEHICLE?

ReKeithen Miller, CFP®, EA

In most parts of the United States, you need a car to get around. According to statistics from the Federal Highway Administration, about 85% of American adults are licensed drivers. While changes in the way we travel have begun to affect vehicle-ownership habits, for now odds are good that you will find yourself shopping for a car at some point in your working life. Whether your old car has finally called it quits, you are looking for better gas mileage (or to go all-electric) or you have moved from an area with extensive public transit to one without, you should proceed methodically to make sure your new car is one that serves you well without leaving your monthly budget in shambles.

DECIDING TO BUY OR LEASE

Deciding to acquire a new car is a major financial decision, regardless of how you proceed, but one of the biggest choices you will face is whether you will lease or buy your vehicle. The most commonly used comparison for this decision is whether to rent or buy your own home. Renting generally requires less of a financial commitment, while purchasing allows the buyer more control over the asset and offers the ability to build equity. (For more about buying a home, see Chapter 8.) The same holds true when acquiring a car. As with most financial decisions, the option that is right for you will depend on your wants and needs, and what trade-offs you are willing to make to meet them.

If you can afford to buy the car you want outright, a purchase is almost certainly the least expensive option over the long run. You will save money by avoiding interest and other finance charges. Most people, however, do not have the savings to buy a brand-new car outright. This means that, in practice, buying a car usually means selecting a used vehicle or securing financing, or both.

Used cars often get a bad rap that's undeserved. For many people, they are the thriftiest option and may have fewer drawbacks than expected. A dealer-certified, pre-owned vehicle often comes with a strong warranty, so you are unlikely to be stuck with a huge repair bill in the first year or two. In fact, most modern cars can make it to around 100,000 miles before drivers notice any substantial problems, which means buying a "like new" car and a new car will feel the same for quite a while. With a used car, the previous owner has already shouldered the heaviest depreciation load, even if the car is only a year or two old. While estimates on the amount of depreciation vary based on the source, most data providers estimate that a car's value depreciates between 20% and 30% within the first year. That means if you look for a late-model car with low mileage, you can secure significant value for a much lower price than buying new.

Some people, however, want the peace of mind of a new car's warranty or are just fond of that "new car smell." If you are set on a new car, you will likely finance your purchase in some way. If you are financing, why should you buy a new car rather than lease it? If you are the type to hang on to a car for the long haul, buying will still be the more economical approach. The longer you own a vehicle, the more you will save over leasing an equivalent one. Assuming you drive a well-made car and avoid major accidents, you can look forward to years with no car payments once you pay it off. If you lease, you will always have a car payment. Leasing can also involve extra costs when it comes to insurance. To protect their interest in the vehicle, leasing companies typically set their own standards for "acceptable insurance," which means you could end up paying for more coverage than you would select for yourself.

In addition to the savings, buying a car offers you the freedom to sell or trade in your car when you want. If you sell a car you own, you can use the cash as you like, giving you additional flexibility. Say you lose your job and need to cut expenses. You can trade in your car for a cheaper one to cut down on your costs, or sell your car and rely on cheaper ways to get around, such as a bike or public transit. Should you need cash or no longer need a car, you can't just sell a leased vehicle whenever you like. When you factor in early termination fees, breaking the lease may cost you more than continuing to make monthly payments. You can look into transferring the lease to another party if your contract allows it, but that approach has its own drawbacks. There will likely be transfer fees, and if the new lease owner is unable to make the payments, you are generally still on the hook.

The longer you own a vehicle, the more you will save over leasing an equivalent one. Assuming you drive a well-made car and avoid major accidents, you can look forward to years with no car payments once you pay it off.

Leases also include various provisions that can trigger fees. Car buyers do not have to worry about driving over certain annual mile thresholds, for example. While traditional leases allow for 12,000 to 15,000 miles per year, some newer lease agreements go as low as 10,000 miles. When signing a lease, the mileage limits may not be a problem. However, things can easily change if, for example, you get a new job and your daily commute suddenly quadruples in length. Paying for extra miles, whether upfront or in penalties at the end of the lease, can quickly become expensive. Most lease agreements specify overage rates between 10 and 25 cents per mile. If you own your car, mileage will still contribute to depreciation. However, you won't have to pull out a calculator if someone suggests a spur-of-the-moment road trip.

Buying is generally a better option if you tend to be rough on your car. Wear and tear on a car you own may affect its resale value or your driving comfort but, unlike with a lease, a few scratches and dings will not trigger financial penalties. If you have kids or pets, this can be especially comforting. While lease contracts generally allow for "average" wear and tear, you may be unpleasantly surprised at what auto companies consider to be average. You can also customize a car you own. In general, you must return a leased vehicle looking the same way it did when you drove it off the lot. This means any modifications will need to be reversible, and some will be out of the question.

On the other hand, for a select group of drivers, leasing can make more sense than buying. When you lease a car, you borrow the car's full value, less any down payment or the trade-in value of a previous car. You are still charged interest, but you only pay back the car's depreciation over the course of the lease term, not its full cost. Once the lease ends, you return the car; its value makes up the rest of the loaned amount. Some leases include an option to purchase the car, but even in these cases, your lease payments do not build equity. In a "lease to own" arrangement, you lease first, then you buy.

If you tend to want a new car every two or three years, the financial upside of buying tends to decrease. Maybe you have a job in which a nice car is expected, or maybe you just have automotive FOMO. If you know yourself well enough to expect you won't keep a car more than three years, the financial balance can tip in favor of leasing. Buying often involves greater upfront costs, since most dealerships require higher down payments for financed purchases than for leases. In some cases, drivers who lease can even start with $0 down. This is also why you typically need excellent credit to lease at all; in contrast, buyers with bad credit pay higher interest rates, but generally still qualify for a loan in all but the most extreme cases.

Monthly payments for an equivalent car are generally higher for financed purchases than for leases, since you are paying off the entire purchase price plus interest. If your primary goal is to keep your monthly expenses down, a lease might be the best option. Furthermore, when you factor in a car's depreciation, a person who finances a car may still be "upside down" — owe more on the loan than the vehicle is worth — when they go to trade it after two or three years. This means they will have to either pay the difference out of pocket or roll it into the new car's loan, which will mean higher finance costs. This is not an issue for a person who leases. If you only plan to hold on to the car for a year or two, leasing can end up being more cost-effective in the short term.

Buying a car also means gambling on its eventual resale value. Most people know that, unlike homes or many other major purchases, cars begin to depreciate as soon as you drive them off the lot. The speed of that depreciation and the car's condition over time become your problems when you own the car. With a lease, the dealer has agreed to take back the car at the end of the agreement. You hand over the keys and walk away. Deprecation is not your problem. Similarly, long-term upkeep is not a worry if you lease. Most lease agreements stipulate that the factory warranty will cover repairs for all or most of the lease period. If you buy, you will take on full responsibility for any necessary repairs or upkeep once your warranty expires.

Bear in mind, too, that the points I raised in this section reflect normal market conditions, but occasionally market abnormalities will change the equation. In the early 2020s, the U.S. auto market faced a noticeable shortage of new vehicles. This was driven by shutdowns during the early months of the COVID-19 pandemic and exacerbated by supply chain problems, especially problems with obtaining computer chips. In practice, fewer cars available meant that cars often sold for prices well above the manufacturer's suggestion. The market got so distorted that, for some models, used car prices exceeded new car prices. This occurred because buyers were willing to pay more to get a car immediately, in the color and with the features they wanted, rather than waiting several months for a new car to arrive. It also meant that some people who leased cars in early 2020 made money upon discovering their car's trade-in value exceeded the original estimated residual value. This let them buy out the lease and, if they liked, turn around and sell the car at a profit. Meanwhile, since automakers usually earn more from sales than leases, they pulled back from attractive lease terms; by early 2023, the number of Americans who lease had fallen significantly. The personal vehicle market will doubtless find a new equilibrium, but it is worth remembering that short-term distortions can undercut conventional wisdom now and then.

Determining How Much Your New Car Will Cost

Before you set foot on a dealer's lot, it pays to take the time to do your research. Many people rely on the Kelley Blue Book, or KBB, a long-standing resource for automotive pricing. These days, the Kelley Blue Book is no longer a physical reference. However, the website of the same name covers the information that the hard copy once did:

kbb.com draws information from real-world car prices, historical trends and overall economic conditions. The company's algorithm also adjusts outputs for your location and the time of year. The resulting values are not perfect, of course. Valuation is an imprecise art, and there can be a delay between market changes and the Blue Book's information. Overall, the KBB is a useful starting point to determine what you can expect to pay for a new or used car.

While the KBB is a well-known tool, it is not the only resource available. Edmunds, the National Automobile Dealers Association, and TrueCar are other prominent pricing guides aimed at consumers. Since these providers all use different methods to calculate value, it is wise to consult all of them to get a sense of an average price among them. You may also want to visit consumer review sites such as J.D. Power or Consumer Reports, which offer general pricing information as well as reviews. You may also find it useful to review websites that help you to calculate costs of car loans and leases. For example, Bankrate offers a variety of auto calculators that can help you compare different options in advance.

Using these tools, start plugging in real numbers based on your preferences and circumstances. For example, you may want to compare one six-year auto loan to a pair of three-year leases on the same make of car. Be brutally honest about factors such as how much you drive, how careful you are with your cars and how restless you will get three years into ownership.

Don't just stop at comparing the monthly payment of different cars, or at comparing a lease to a loan. You should also factor in your down payment or cash due at signing, including taxes and fees; your likely interest rate and total interest paid over time; and your likely resale value if you buy the vehicle. If you are considering a used car, remember to budget more for regular upkeep and maintenance. In other words, you want to estimate what the car will cost overall, not just how much your monthly payment will be.

Remember to calculate the potential costs of insurance too, especially since you may need more comprehensive coverage for a lease. If you have a specific car make and model in mind, you can call your insurance agent and ask them to provide you with an estimate of your monthly insurance premium based on the coverage you need. If your car is stolen or totaled in an accident before the loan is paid off or the lease ends, you may be liable for any additional costs that your auto insurance does not cover. Guaranteed asset protection insurance, often called "gap" insurance, is designed to pay the difference between the car's value at the time it is totaled or stolen and the balance remaining on the auto loan or lease.

For car owners, gap insurance is most helpful if they purchase a new car with a relatively small down payment or if the term of the loan is longer than average (60 months or more). In those cases, the likelihood that you will be upside down on the car if it is deemed a total loss in the early years is much higher. This makes gap insurance more valuable. As for a leased vehicle, obtaining gap insurance is often a requirement. You may get gap insurance from your dealership or directly through your auto insurance company. Note that, as with any sort of insurance, you should take the time to understand the specifics of what you are paying for when you commit to a policy. When estimating the cost of gap insurance ahead of time, know that it may either come in the form of a flat fee or an annual payment, and that it is not a substitute for comprehensive or collision coverage.

Doing your homework can help you decide between buying and leasing, and can ensure that you end up with a vehicle that fits your budget.

QUICK NOTES

Buying	Leasing
PROS	**PROS**
► Ownership of vehicle ► Equity that can be used for a trade-in or tapped via sale ► No mileage restrictions ► Freedom to customize vehicle ► Lower long-term cost of ownership	► Lower monthly payments ► New car every few years ► Vehicle warranty generally covers major repairs and maintenance ► No worries about resale value of vehicle
CONS	**CONS**
► Higher monthly payments ► Possible higher repair and maintenance costs ► Potential for vehicle obsolescence	► No ownership rights ► Mileage restrictions ► Restrictions on customizing vehicle ► Cost of insurance might be higher ► End of lease charges can increase cost (such as for unusual wear and tear)

Alternatives To Buying And Leasing

Even if you live in a place where public transit is limited or unavailable, it is worth considering whether you really need your own car. In addition to car payments, insurance, gas and maintenance, a car of your own means registration fees and costs. Depending on where you live, it could also mean paying for a parking place or garage access. You will need to invest time in cleaning and maintaining the car. Depending on how you feel about driving, that may feel like one more chore.

In the age of ride hailing and online services that will deliver everything from home furnishings to groceries to your door, it can pay to ask whether you need a car at all. Instead, you could consider relying on a ride-hailing service such as Uber or Lyft, potentially in combination with biking or public transit.

For most people, it is still cheaper to own a car than to take an Uber everywhere, but in certain circumstances, it can be a financially sound decision. Say your commute is very short, but it is dangerous or impractical to walk or bike. That said, AAA released a study in 2018 comparing the cost of using ride-hailing to the cost of car ownership in 20 urban areas. The study found the annual cost of ride-hailing services was twice as much as owning a car — $20,118 compared with $10,049 — even when factoring in the cost of insurance and parking. The AAA study assumed annual mileage of 10,841, which was the average mileage for drivers in the subject areas. If you need to travel many miles by car, using ride-hailing services as your primary mode of transportation might not be cost effective.

However, if you do not use your car very often, ride-hailing can be a viable option. For example, say your partner usually drops you off at work, and you only drive on the occasional morning when your partner has an early meeting. You may not need to remain a two-car household if you use Uber or Lyft to fill in those gaps. The calculation of whether to keep a car of your own may also shift if you have high insurance rates due to your driving history or if you live in a city where ride-hailing rates are especially low and drivers are plentiful. On the other hand, if you live in a rural area, the lower density of drivers may make this plan impractical as well as prohibitively expensive. Online calculators can help you compare the financial impact of ride-hailing and driving. Both Uber and Lyft offer calculators that provide fare estimates between addresses. You can use these estimates as a baseline for your expected commuting cost between destinations you travel to frequently.

If you need a car every now and then, you could also consider a car-sharing service such as Zipcar. Members pay a flat monthly fee for access to the service, then can reserve a car by the day, the hour or sometimes the minute when they need a vehicle. Depending on how often you drive, this could end up a cheaper solution than buying or leasing a car. However, you will likely secure these savings at the cost of convenience. A car may not be available when you need it, or you may have to rush to return the car on time if your plans take longer than you intend. In addition, in suburban or rural areas, getting to the lot where the car is waiting may prove challenging, assuming the service is available at all.

Ride hailing and car sharing have their uses but also limits. Neither is practical for long-distance trips. These options can also leave you at the mercy of the law of supply and demand. However, if you dislike driving or only need a car now and then, it is worth considering whether the benefits are worth these potential drawbacks.

Depending on your needs and your location, you may find it useful to consider subscription services offered by vehicle manufacturers. Companies including Porsche and Volvo offer subscriptions in which you pay a monthly fee for access to several models in the carmaker's lineup. The fee is usually substantial but also covers insurance, maintenance and roadside assistance. These services are often restricted to only a few cities and tend to be expensive, but for customers who need or prefer the ability to swap vehicles more than every few years, they can be worth considering.

HOW TO SHOP FOR A CAR

Once you have decided to buy or lease a car, how do you go about shopping for one?

Online shopping has revolutionized the experience of buying a car. Companies such as Carvana and Vroom allow you to search for, finance and purchase a car entirely online. The only thing you have to do in person is pick it up — if that, as many services will deliver your new car to you. Services like AAA and Consumer Reports also offer tools to connect buyers with local dealerships online. Manufacturers won't sell you a car directly, but their websites will often point you toward dealers in your area. You can even initiate the sales process on the website of a particular dealership.

There is no right or wrong choice when it comes to shopping online versus in person. The internet option can involve less time and make it easier to resist attempts at a "hard sell." You may not even need to resist pushy tactics, as internet sales teams are often trained differently and may have different incentives than traditional salespeople. Internet sales representatives also generally understand that online shoppers are likely to do their homework and may not be ready to buy the same day they begin the conversation. Some commentators have suggested that these factors mean an online sale often results in a better deal. However, a knowledgeable sales representative can sometimes guide you through the buying process in person more easily, and some people are still more comfortable seeing a car in real life. The best approach for you may be a hybrid method, in which you do research online but still conduct some parts of the process in person. For example, you can arrange a test drive, even if you shop online.

QUICK NOTES

Shopping Online	Shopping In Person
► Can be less time-consuming ► Often easier to avoid a hard sell ► Less pressure to make a same-day decision	► Knowledgeable salesperson can guide you through the process ► Option to see and evaluate vehicle in person ► Test drive availability

Regardless of how you shop, do your research and come prepared to negotiate. While some dealerships are experimenting with a "no haggle" model, in most places negotiating on price is still an expected part of buying a car.

Negotiating

The first step in negotiating a car purchase is to know what you want to spend. Earlier in this chapter, I discussed how to compare the costs of buying and leasing. Even if you know what method you prefer, take the time to get a clear-eyed picture of your budget. Focus on the total cost of the lease or purchase, rather than just the monthly payment amount. When you research the cost of a particular car, remember that the manufacturer's suggested retail price is just that — suggested. Don't assume that amount is what you should actually pay. (Tesla and some other electric-vehicle manufacturers are a notable exception. They sell directly to consumers, usually online or through showrooms in states where they are legally allowed to bypass traditional franchised dealers, and they typically sell at a nonnegotiable fixed price.)

Of course, price isn't the only thing that matters when you are comparing potential makes and models. If you have a car, list things you like and dislike about it. These might be fundamentals like fuel economy or comfort features such as seat warmers. You may need a car with plenty of cargo space or one suitable for transporting clients. Make a list of must-have and nice-to-have features and hold firm to which is which. This can help you narrow your selection and avoid certain types of sales pressure.

If you are trading in an old car, know your vehicle's trade-in value before you start talking to a dealer. This will help you set expectations when it comes to your budget and how you plan to finance your new vehicle. Consult the KBB, Edmunds or both to get a good baseline figure. When you do, be honest about your car's condition to get a realistic estimate. While you generally will not mention your trade-in until much later in the purchase, it is helpful to have a value in mind early.

You can also ask a used-car retailer such as CarMax to make you an offer, then ask the dealership to meet or beat it. If the dealer declines, you can sell the car to the third party for cash instead. Even if the dealer offers you less for your trade-in than a third party would, it might still make sense to go with the dealer's offer when you factor in potential sales tax savings from the trade-in tax exemption you receive on the purchase of a new vehicle. Note that, as of this writing, California, Hawaii, Kentucky, Virginia and the District of Columbia don't offer a trade-in exemption. In Michigan, the exemption from sales tax is capped at $9,000 of trade-in value at this writing.

Once you have identified your top candidates, schedule a test drive. Don't be afraid to take the time to see how the car handles on a variety of roads and in different conditions. If you plan to connect your phone via Bluetooth or if you have car seats for your kids, ask to see how the car seat fits or the Bluetooth connects. Resist the allure of the new (or "like new," if you're buying used) and be ruthlessly honest with yourself about the pros and cons of the test drive. Considering the amount of money you will spend on your car and the amount of time you will spend inside it, you should be sure you are pleased before you proceed.

Assuming you identified a price for your new vehicle online, be sure to ask the dealer if the model you are driving includes any dealer-installed options, such as nitrogen in the tires or theft-protection features. If so, ask about the cost and whether you can request a car without these modifications. Add-ons can add hundreds of dollars to a car's price, and they may not be especially important to you. Be clear on what you are paying for.

It always pays to get quotes from more than one dealer when you are car shopping, whether you are buying outright, financing or leasing.

If you buy a used car, whether outright or with financing, don't neglect an additional step: Pull a vehicle history report on the car you are considering. To do so, you will often need the car's vehicle identification number, or VIN. In some cases, you may only need the license plate number. Services including AutoCheck and CARFAX will let you run a search for a vehicle history report, which can alert you if the odometer has been rolled back or if an insurer has previously declared the vehicle a total loss. Most of the time, such checks will show nothing to worry about, but it is best to be sure early in the process. You should also consider asking a third-party mechanic to inspect the car before you agree to buy. Reputable sellers will not object, though you will need to pay for the examination (typically $100 or $200, depending on your area). If the car is certified pre-owned, this step is usually unnecessary.

When you have settled on a vehicle, it is time to get some quotes. The plural is deliberate. It always pays to get quotes from more than one dealer when you are car shopping, whether you are buying outright, financing or leasing. Especially in the age of online car purchases, there is no reason to settle for your first offer, even if the first dealer you talk to is the one you eventually choose. Use email or online forms to contact other salespeople, and don't be shy in mentioning any competing offers. The salesperson you are talking to may be able to match or beat it. Make sure you fully understand any services that will be included, such as prepaid maintenance or an extended warranty. Salespeople often will not mention these until later in the process, but you can and should ask for this information proactively.

When considering financing offers, take the time to dig into the specifics. Don't just consider the interest rate. Identify and understand other details such as the loan term and potential fees, like prepayment penalties. If high monthly payments are a concern, you can consider opting for a longer loan term to bring individual payments down. Use this strategy with caution, however. Cars depreciate over time, so your risk of going upside down is much higher with a longer loan term. In addition, a longer loan often means you will pay more interest overall. The particulars will vary, so take time to consider the pros and cons of this approach. A reputable dealer will give you time to read and consider the offer and to propose any changes before you sign.

Some drivers prefer to be preapproved for a loan from a third-party lender before they even start talking to a salesperson. Doing so will give you a good idea of what you can afford and give you a reference point for the interest rate the dealer offers you. However, if you go this route, plan to shop within about two weeks of preapproval. This will reduce the effect of multiple "hard" inquiries into your credit history. (For more about credit, see Chapter 3.)

Once you say yes to an offer, it is important to read everything carefully before you sign the paperwork. Not only should you look to be sure the numbers reflect your expectations, but keep an eye out for any unexpected fees or terms. Ideally, there should be no surprises, but better to spot them before you sign on the dotted line. A good finance manager will be happy to take the time to explain any forms or terms you do not understand. If you feel pressured, do not be afraid to walk away. You can always take your business elsewhere.

If you are leasing, there are a few other specifics to consider. Some experts claim that you will get a better deal if you negotiate as if you plan to buy, then tell the dealer you want to lease after you have agreed on a price and trade-in value. In the age of more transparent online pricing, this may be changing, but it is still not a bad idea. Just as with financing, fully read and understand the lease's terms before committing to it. Be especially mindful of the residual value or optional purchase price. You may also want to consider asking for a higher mileage limit or other changes; even if the dealer does not agree, it can't hurt to ask. On a lease, you can generally offer to make a down payment if one is not already required. Doing so can lower your monthly payment. However, it usually does not pay to make a substantial down payment, since the money won't provide you equity in the vehicle.

DEFRAYING THE COST OF OWNERSHIP

However well you negotiate, owning or leasing a car is not cheap. Some drivers choose to defray the costs of car ownership by driving for a ride-hailing company like Uber or Lyft. If you are not interested in a part-time job, there is also a more hands-off option for making money with your car.

Turo is to vehicles what Airbnb is to houses and apartments. The service connects car owners with drivers who temporarily need a vehicle. Potential earnings vary by market and the type of vehicle.

As of August 2023, Turo estimates that a Ford Fiesta owner in metro Atlanta could earn about $655 monthly, while a Tesla Model 3 owner in Los Angeles could earn roughly $1,295. Like Airbnb, Turo is a peer-to-peer service, which means you will do the handing off to the person using your car. However, Turo's contract with its "hosts" in the United States provides physical damage reimbursement as well as liability protection. To participate, you must (at this writing) have a car no more than 12 years old and with no more than 130,000 miles. If you have a lease, be sure to check the lease agreement to make sure participation would not violate its terms. Turo and its peer-to-peer competitors will not be right for everyone, but these services can offer a way to make car ownership more affordable for some.

After where you choose to live, the choice of whether to own a car or not and how to pay for it is arguably one of the most significant expenses of your overall lifestyle. Taking the time to put thought and research into the decision will pay dividends in reduced costs, increased reliability and additional peace of mind. Once you have done that work, sit back and enjoy the ride.

CHAPTER 7

APARTMENT LEASES

Victoria Dubuc and Amy Laburda

Homeownership has long been considered a pillar of the American dream. Owning allows the potential for greater privacy and deeper ties to a community, in addition to tax benefits every April. Most notably, it provides the opportunity to build equity in your home, creating a nest egg for you and even future generations. Historically, home-price appreciation has been the cornerstone to build wealth in the United States. And while it can't be quantified, many people feel a strong sense of pride associated with owning their home. So why would anyone rent?

Renting offers the flexibility to relocate and adapt to changing circumstances, advantages that are especially useful for young adults in the process of establishing a career and, potentially, starting a family. Renting also keeps young professionals free from the financial burdens that accompany homeownership, such as accumulating a down payment before a purchase, or paying for routine maintenance and unexpected repairs afterwards. If homeownership is your eventual goal, renting lets you save for a larger down payment and build a financial cushion for these costs. (See Chapter 8 for more on buying a home.) But while many people once considered renting a transitional step toward ownership, increasing numbers of Americans are drawn to renting long-term. There were more renters in the United States in 2021 than a decade ago, according to a 2021 report by the Pew Research Center. Renters account for nearly 35% of American heads of household at this writing.

You may already know that renting makes practical sense for you, but you still face many important decisions before you will be ready to officially settle into your new place. When you approach these considerations diligently, renting can make terrific financial and social sense, whether or not it serves as a bridge to eventual homeownership.

HOW MUCH CAN I AFFORD?

The logical first step for anyone looking to rent is to establish affordability parameters. While you may dream of living your early professional years in a luxury apartment in midtown Manhattan, it is unlikely you'll be able to shell out the $5,000 a month needed to live there. A great starting place when considering what you can afford is the 30% rule. Ideally, no more than 30% of your gross (pretax) income should go toward rent. However, in reality, calculating what you should spend isn't quite that simple. Most landlords charge upfront costs before you move in. These may include an application fee, a security deposit and the first month's rent. Some places may require the last month's rent as well. Bear in mind, too, the cost of furnishing an apartment, if you are renting your first apartment or moving into a larger space. If you already have furnishings, factor in the cost of movers or renting a truck.

In addition to one-time costs, you should consider monthly housing expenses beyond your rent. Many apartments do not include utilities, internet or cable in the rent. (For utilities that are not included, you can factor in more upfront setup costs, too.) Almost all buildings assess an extra fee for pets. Some may also charge a monthly fee for parking. It is important to have a full understanding of what is and isn't included in the monthly rent payment before you sign on the dotted line. If possible, it's best to approach all of the costs collectively when budgeting, and to limit all your apartment expenses to 30% of your gross income or less.

However, as with all budgeting decisions, the 30% "rule" is really just a guideline. Your needs, your income and the cost of housing in your market may make it impractical to limit your housing costs to this level, or you might simply be willing to limit other forms of spending in order to have the living arrangements you want. Local conditions can also be factors in your decision-making. New York City residents can face combined state and city income tax rates of nearly 14.8% at this writing, while residents of Miami (and the rest of Florida) have no state or local income tax. All else being equal, the Miami resident can probably afford to spend more on rent.

When you are budgeting, you should also do a bit of research about the particular market where you are looking for an apartment. Sometimes, though not always, a market may involve extra expenses or procedures that do not apply universally. For example, in New York City, renters who use brokers typically pay the broker's fee. In most other parts of the country, the property owner is responsible for this cost.

Let's look at an example:

As a recent graduate, Sam has taken a job at a marketing firm in New York City. His pretax gross income is $60,000. He commutes from his childhood home in Connecticut every day, but he is getting sick of taking the Metro North commuter rail to and from work. He has decided to move into the city and needs to determine how much he can spend on an apartment.

Our 30% rule applied without nuance tells us that Sam should spend no more than $1,500 a month on rent. (30% of $60,000 is $18,000; $18,000 spread over 12 months is $1,500.) Yet if we were advising Sam, we would suggest he not stop there. Instead, we would recommend that he work backward from this number and incorporate estimates for utilities, cable, internet and other outside expenses related to the rent before arriving at the "high end" of his affordability parameter. The chart below illustrates a very basic example of how this might work. If Sam spends no more than $1,225 on rent every month, he should be able to stay under the 30% rule, even when factoring in other costs. (In Manhattan, this will almost certainly mean looking for a roommate.) Sam should also be prepared for the upfront costs that accompany moving into a new place.

THE TRUE COST OF RENTING AN APARTMENT	
UPFRONT COST	
Application Fee	$100.00
Security Deposit	$1,225.00
First Month's Rent	$1,225.00
TOTAL	**$2,550.00**
MONTHLY COST	
Rent	$1,225.00
Utilities	$180.00
Cable and Internet	$95.00
TOTAL	**$1,500.00**

Figure 3

What Factors Dictate Whether An Apartment Is Affordable For Me?

Once you've established the high end of your affordability parameter, it's time to start narrowing your search. It can be daunting to try to find a place that strikes the right balance between comfort and affordability, but having a clear understanding of what drives pricing will help point you in the right direction. Off the bat, you are likely to assume that an apartment's location and amenities are the main factors in its price. You'd mostly be right, but there are other factors to consider.

It doesn't take a genius to deduce that an apartment in Los Angeles would cost substantially more than one of similar size in Atlanta. In fact, at this writing the average cost of an apartment in Los Angeles was $3,198, compared with $1,562 a month in Atlanta — more than $1,600 more every month. The cost of living in the market you are looking at will be one of the primary restrictions on your apartment search. How much do you value being close to family and friends, or in the heart of a city? Is it important to have a short commute to work? Depending on how you answer these questions, you may be willing to pay more or less for your apartment.

Do not forget to consider the logistical and financial impact of location. A long commute may also mean higher costs in the form of gas and tolls. If you live near public transit, on the other hand, you may be able to save money by relying on it some or all of the time. You may also want to consider how walkable your neighborhood is. If you are able to go to the grocery store, pharmacy or other shops without transport costs at all, it could potentially offset some of the costs of living somewhere more centrally located.

The amenities associated with your apartment will affect your monthly rent, too. Some typical examples include a gym, on-site parking, a pool, an in-unit washer and dryer, or a residents' lounge. You may also want to consider more practical factors, such as whether the building has an elevator or a built-in sprinkler system. Ultimately, the decisions you make regarding these aspects of a building come down to opportunity cost: Do you value having a nicer apartment in a prime location more than the potential alternative uses for the money? Spending more money on your apartment means you will have less money available for other things. If you are willing to deal with making sacrifices in other areas of your life, you can be comfortable proceeding even if you find yourself on the higher end of your affordability range.

Roommates are one of the best ways to help defray the costs of renting. Living with other people may make it possible to live in areas or developments you would otherwise be unable to afford. Of course, roommates have potential drawbacks. We would be willing to wager that more than a few of the people reading this book have a roommate horror story or two. All the savings in the world may not justify the misery of having to live with an awful roommate. Compatibility is at least as important as finances when you consider moving in with someone. Remember that good friends don't necessarily make good roommates. For those moving to a completely different area on their own, there are apps and websites that can be used to meet new people and potential roommates. Just keep in mind it is always a good idea to meet up, multiple times if possible, before making any sort of living commitment. Getting a feel for someone's habits, schedule and personality can go a long way in determining whether you are a good fit. Common interests are an added bonus.

The length of the lease you decide to sign will also play a role in determining your monthly rent. While some landlords offer strictly one-year leases, others are more flexible. Some leases can be as short as six months or even just month to month; others may go as long as two years. Shorter leases are typically more expensive on a monthly basis, while longer leases are often less expensive (though this can vary by market). If you are starting a new job or have just moved to a new location, a year-long lease might be the best compromise between the monthly rent rate and the length of the lease. When it comes time to renew the lease, you can consider signing for a longer term if you are pleased with the situation and have stability at work or in other areas of life.

Typically, the landlord will offer a new lease to a renewing tenant at a modest increase in monthly rent from your old one, or may even maintain that current rate. It's also worth remembering that, in extraordinary circumstances, the economic environment can impact rental prices more dramatically. For instance, the Pew Research Center reported that during the COVID-19 pandemic, eight out of the 15 largest cities in the United States experienced average monthly rent increases of 10% or higher (specifically between 2019 and 2021). A longer lease can lock you in at a lower rate, but it can also limit your flexibility.

Of course, many young professionals find that even after carefully considering all of the above, the costs of renting in a certain place are beyond their reach — especially right out of school. You should not look at the expenses associated with renting an apartment in a vacuum. If you have other significant debts — for instance, credit card debt or student loan debt — affording an apartment may be close to impossible early in your career. That's OK. Those who find themselves in this situation should know that they are not alone. According to the U.S. Census Bureau, the number of adults aged 25 to 34 staying or returning home to their parents has risen noticeably since 2000. At this writing, 19% of men and 12% of women between ages 25 and 34 are living with their parents. Spending extra time at home can be a prudent financial move that allows you to accumulate savings, which can jump-start you on your path to renting an apartment in a few years.

UNDERSTANDING THE LEASE

Let's fast-forward a tiny bit. You have done everything right up to this point. You were diligent in your search and have found a great place that makes sense in light of all that we have discussed. Soon after your application gets approved, you will likely meet with a leasing agent or landlord, who will provide a lease agreement for you to review. Reading a lease can be overwhelming, and often a renter's first impulse is to just go ahead and sign it rather than wade through all the details. But closely reviewing the lease is an important part of the process. After all, a lease is a legally enforceable contract, and you could find yourself in trouble later if you fail to abide by its terms.

Your lease is likely to include a lot of information. Exact details may vary depending on the management, and any caveats that accompany a specific complex or unit. However, the major details of every leasing agreement should be similar.

The lease should include information about who manages the property, and the address and contact information (phone numbers or email addresses) of the landlord or any staff, if applicable. It should clearly specify which property you are renting, the monthly rent amount and the amount of the security deposit. Most leases allow a grace period for paying the rent every month, but check the lease for exactly how long it is. A typical apartment may require rent due on the first of every month, but give you until the 10th before imposing any penalties, for instance. The lease should also specify the penalty amount for late payment. This may be a set fee, such as $25 or $50, or a percentage of the total rent payment. That being said, most states limit the amount a landlord can charge as a penalty. Setting automated monthly reminders is a quick and easy way to make sure you don't forget to make a payment.

The lease will also dictate how long you will rent the property and how far in advance you will need to notify the landlord regarding lease renewal. Some contracts default to a month-to-month agreement after the original term runs out, or may include an automatic renewal clause — meaning the lease will renew unless you give notice by a certain date. If you do not plan to remain in your unit beyond your current lease, many landlords require notice at least 30 days in advance, and sometimes longer. Failure to give sufficient notice will likely mean, at a minimum, losing your security deposit.

Some leases may also include an escalation clause, so be sure to look out for this. This is a provision in the lease in which the landlord will require you to pay a higher rent by adjusting the annual base rent by an agreed-upon method. The clause is typically tied to a fixed dollar amount, a percentage of the first year's rent, or cost of living increases. As noted earlier in the chapter, signing a longer lease may help mitigate any increase in rent.

One benefit of renting an apartment compared with homeownership is that the landlord typically handles major repairs, such as issues with plumbing, heating or electricity. That being said, minor repairs will often remain the tenant's responsibility. These might include projects like patching a tiny hole left in a wall from a picture. There may also be stipulations about the maintenance of an outside area or yard, if necessary. Some landlords also require tenants to buy some amount of renters insurance; if so, the lease should specify how much. (For more on renters insurance, see the next section of this chapter.)

When it comes to modifications, most lease agreements will require you to get the landlord's permission before making changes to the property. This could include something as simple as painting a room. If you were to make changes to the unit without prior consent, the landlord could use the security deposit to pay for the costs of returning the property to its original condition.

In addition to a monthly pet fee, the lease may specify breed or size restrictions. For instance, some apartments may allow most dogs, but not pit bulls. If you are planning to move with a pet, calling the landlord or apartment complex to get their pet policy upfront may save you the inconvenience of looking at a place where you ultimately won't be able to live. Information may also be available on the apartment building's website.

QUICK NOTES

Lease Review Checklist

- ☑ Do the details of the specific property you are renting, the monthly rent and the security deposit amount match what you expect?
- ☑ Who manages the property? How can you contact the landlord and any other management staff?
- ☑ What is the grace period for paying rent? What is the penalty for late payment?
- ☑ How long is your lease? How far in advance do you need to renew or give notice you're moving out?
- ☑ Can you sublet?
- ☑ Are you required to buy renters insurance? If so, how much?
- ☑ What modifications to the property are allowed? Which repairs are your responsibility? Which utilities are covered, if any?
- ☑ What are the rules for pets?

The lease will also detail what is and isn't covered with respect to utilities and fixtures. Most apartments will provide water, sewer and garbage at a minimum, but may require the tenant to cover electricity, gas, internet and cable. Permanent kitchen appliances, such as a stove or refrigerator, are typically included in your rent. However, if you viewed a unit with removable fixtures, such as a microwave or toaster oven, double-check your lease to see exactly what the landlord will provide. In some instances, you may be able to rent furniture for an extra fee, or you can coordinate with the previous tenant if they are leaving anything behind.

Additional information detailed in the lease could include rules on maximum occupancy and overnight guest policies. Many cities have fire codes that limit the number of people allowed to sleep in a room, and many rental agreements will restrict how many days someone can stay at the property if the person isn't on the lease. This restriction could apply to your personal guests, but also to any plans you have to offer your apartment on Airbnb or similar services. Another detail to look out for in the lease is whether you are allowed to sublet; some apartments and landlords will allow it, others won't. The lease should also clarify information about parking, smoking on the property, trash collection, landlord right of entry and eviction. Landlords of apartment buildings with shared spaces, like a patio or meeting room, will typically include language in the lease about how and when residents can use, reserve or rent those spaces.

If you do not see something in the lease that you expect, or you are unsure about any of the terms, the easiest solution is to ask for clarification. You may also want to talk to someone who has experience or expertise in this area, just to ensure everything stipulated in the lease is legal.

Once you've read through the lease in its entirety and are sure you understand it, you are ready to sign. You and any roommates are all required to sign the lease. Many young adults may require a co-signer, such as a parent or guardian, for their first apartment, since they often have little credit history. Keep in mind that under a lease's legal terms, the co-signer and the person who is signing the lease are equally and fully responsible for payments and are on the hook for damages or potential lawsuits.

RENTERS INSURANCE

Once you have signed the lease, you'll be ready to move in and begin a new chapter of your life. It's an exciting and busy time — moving furniture, setting up the cable and decorating, all while potentially adjusting to the new job that led you to move in the first place. Many people think the work is done after the dust settles. But that isn't necessarily true. There is something else you should think about before you sink into the sofa: renters insurance.

Most people are aware of the importance of homeowners insurance. When it comes to renting, that isn't the case. A 2020 Insurance Information Institute poll conducted by ORC International found that while 93% of homeowners report having homeowners insurance, only 57% of renters say they have comparable coverage. This disparity is notable but probably unsurprising. Many people remain confused about renters insurance policies and their cost and coverage. In addition, most mortgage lenders require borrowers to carry a certain amount of insurance, but landlords don't consistently require tenants to buy renters insurance. Some do, but no U.S. state requires the coverage by law. It is very likely that renters insurance will be optional for you. But this doesn't mean you should overlook it.

You may assume that renters insurance is not necessary, since the landlord's insurance coverage on the building would extend to your personal belongings. This is a common misconception. A landlord's property insurance only covers structural damage to the building as a result of fire or inclement weather. It does not cover your personal property. Another common misconception, especially relevant for new graduates just beginning their careers and often facing high student loan payments, is that renters insurance policies are expensive. In reality, most basic policies are quite affordable, running about $180 annually. Even optional additional coverage seldom raises the cost above $200 for the year. If you live in a building with certain features, such as on-site security or sprinkler systems, your policy may cost even less. Bundling renters insurance with other policies, such as car insurance, can further reduce the price — in some instances by as much as 10%.

Renters insurance is affordable for most people, but as with any insurance product, it is important to understand what it actually covers. Many people think of it first and foremost as a way to protect their personal belongings from damage or theft. Renters insurance does meet this need, but it also protects you against liability. If a visitor sustains a serious injury in your apartment and that injury is found to be your fault (rather than, say, the landlord's), the visitor can file a claim and your insurer may partially cover the costs of his or her medical care. If that visitor sues you, renters insurance can also cover part or all of the cost of your legal defense or settlement.

Renters coverage, like any insurance policy, is subject to limitations. A typical policy covers $20,000 to $30,000 worth of personal property. Most provide at least $100,000 of protection against liability claims or lawsuits. This coverage includes injuries caused by anything that occurs in your apartment, such as injuries caused by your children or pets. With regard to hospital bills, even the cheapest plans typically offer coverage of no less than $1,000.

Not everyone should have, or will need, the same type of coverage when it comes to renters insurance. The best way to find out how much coverage you need is to make a detailed inventory of your personal possessions, creating itemized lists that include purchase prices and replacement costs. After you account for personal items including electronic equipment, clothes, tools and kitchen gadgets, you may be surprised at how the value of your personal property adds up. Industry estimates suggest that the average person's belongings are worth about $20,000, though this figure can vary widely.

Most standard policies determine payouts on an "actual cash value" basis, often abbreviated ACV. This means that the insurance company will base your payment on the current value of an item, factoring in depreciation. If you bought a laptop five years ago for $2,000, the insurer will pay out the value of a used, five-year-old laptop, not the $2,000 you originally paid. Most companies also provide the option to purchase "replacement cost" coverage, which pays what it costs to replace the item. In the example above, you would receive the full $2,000 for a new laptop, regardless of when you purchased it. Since replacement cost policies typically pay higher amounts for claims, their premiums will be higher than an actual cash value policy.

A landlord's property insurance only covers structural damage to the building as a result of fire or inclement weather. It does not cover your personal property.

Choosing between a high deductible and a low deductible plan is another important consideration. A deductible is a specified amount of money that you must pay before the insurance company will pay your claim. The higher the deductible, the more you must pay out-of-pocket before coverage kicks in. The trade-off is that higher deductible plans offer lower monthly premiums. A low deductible plan will not require you to fork over as much in the event of a claim, but you will pay higher monthly premiums for that privilege.

A renters insurance policy obviously covers personal belongings inside your apartment, but many people forget or don't realize that coverage often extends to your possessions while they are physically outside of the residence, too. If property is stolen from your car, for instance, the policy still covers it in most cases.

Almost all policies will cover displacement costs if your living quarters become uninhabitable, though usually only for a limited period of time and up to a maximum dollar amount. You should read policy documents carefully to understand what counts as "uninhabitable," since there is no strict legal definition. A missing window, a leaking ceiling, a broken air conditioner, or a persistent and overwhelming bad smell may qualify; ugly wallpaper or worn carpet will not. Nearly all policies offer coverage if your apartment is uninhabitable because of a fire or storm damage.

It is possible, especially early on, that you will inhabit your apartment with nonfamily members, such as romantic partners or roommates. Most insurers allow roommates to share a policy, but doing so will not necessarily save money. Sharing can also create complications. If you move in with a partner whom you plan to marry in the future, filing a claim that ends up on both people's insurance records may not be a major concern. However, if you live with friends and plan to go your separate ways after a year or two, this may matter more. If you choose to share a policy, make sure each tenant is listed on the policy, since insurers may ask who owned what property when processing a claim.

Standard renters policies do not cover everything. Depending on your needs, it may make sense to consider purchasing additional coverage or a policy rider. A rider is an optional add-on to the primary policy, which provides additional coverage without the need to purchase an entirely separate policy. Many renters fail to take advantage of the coverage plans and riders they can bundle.

Expensive items — such as jewelry, antiques, collectibles or premium electronics — are typically covered under a renters insurance policy, but only up to a certain dollar amount. For example, $1,500 of coverage is standard for all jewelry; to assure coverage for a $3,000 ring, you may need to purchase an additional rider. Similar considerations apply for a prized baseball card collection, high-end musical instruments or any other especially valuable or hard-to-replace items.

Riders may serve specific purposes in addition to covering valuables. In most cases, renters with an existing ACV policy can add replacement-cost coverage with a rider, though certain property specified within the original policy may only qualify for payout under actual cash value. If you work out of your home, most insurance companies offer incidental business liability protection or home business endorsement riders. These will protect business-related property beyond the policy's baseline limits. Some policies even have the option to add riders for pets. This is because certain policies may not cover liability related to particular dog breeds, such as German shepherds or rottweilers. A rider can provide liability coverage in the event your pet bites a guest in your apartment.

In addition to riders, you may want to consider additional policies, especially if you live in an area prone to natural disasters such as floods, earthquakes or hurricanes, which are not covered by standard policies. Gaps in your insurance coverage could lead to substantial financial damages, which is important to consider if you're going to live near a fault line or in a flood plain. For the particularly worry-prone, note that most policies will cover losses due to a volcanic eruption, however.

All in all, there is no "one size fits all" answer when it comes to renters insurance, but you should have some form of coverage. In all likelihood, you can sufficiently protect yourself and your property for a year for less than the price of a fancy steak dinner in New York City.

CONCLUSION

Renting an apartment is no small matter. For many, moving out on your own signifies a giant step toward adulthood and an independent life. As one of the first major life choices you may make after school, choosing an apartment can set you on the right course if done correctly. Establishing good financial habits early in life will serve you well when other potentially expensive decisions and delicate trade-offs arise. But for now, enjoy the benefits that renting will provide you as a young professional. The freedom, flexibility and potential social benefits that come from renting are invaluable during this stage of your life. We began the chapter suggesting that homeownership is a pillar of the American dream. We'll end it by saying that, today, so too is renting.

CHAPTER 8

BUYING A HOME

Eric Meermann, CFP®, CVA, EA

Buying a home is among the largest purchases most people will ever make. It can represent the achievement of a long-term financial goal, the beginning of a new life chapter, or an external sign that you are ready to put down roots. Especially for first-time homeowners, the process may seem daunting. But if you approach the path to homeownership as a series of achievable steps, there is no reason you can't take this financial step forward with confidence.

DECIDING TO BUY

Before you start down the path to homeownership, it is important to take time to really evaluate whether you want — or need — to purchase a home. Many people consider homeownership a mandatory life milestone, a sign you've "made it." But the truth is homeownership isn't right for everyone. Demographic patterns suggest Americans are taking a more nuanced view of homeownership these days, especially in the wake of the housing crisis of the late 2000s. According to the

Pew Research Center analysis of U.S. Census Bureau data from 2021 (the latest figures available at this writing), nearly 46 million American households were renting that year, accounting for more than a third of all U.S. households. There are a variety of reasons for this trend, including — in recent years — a mismatch between housing supply and demand. More broadly, owning a home involves a lot of work and expense, even if you do not stretch beyond your means. While homeownership can be rewarding, you should not let simple inertia carry you toward it without some initial reflection.

Conventional wisdom has long said that buying a home is more frugal than renting. This is sometimes true, since building equity in your home is a form of forced savings. (More on this later in this chapter.) That said, a lot of specific factors mean individual cases can vary widely. The assumptions you use to compare the financial impact of buying and renting will be shaped by your local housing market. Variables such as the rate at which the property will appreciate, property tax levels (and prospective future tax increases), maintenance costs and the demand for rental property in your area can all affect the conclusions you draw. You should also factor in the strength of your credit, along with your partner's credit if you are buying a house together, and how much you can afford to put down toward your purchase. Online calculators can help you in comparing the cost of renting and buying under a variety of circumstances. Whatever tools you use, be sure to think carefully about your assumptions. Consider using more than one calculator so you can compare the outputs, too.

Of course, financial considerations are not the only ones that matter when you consider whether you want to become a homeowner. If you plan to stay in the same place for a while, homeownership can provide a sense of stability and security. You may want to put down roots in a community; families with young children may want them to have the continuity of the same schools from year to year. Owning a home also may be among your financial goals just because it is something that matters to you. On the other hand, if you prioritize flexibility, renting may serve you better. If you anticipate major life changes in the short term, such as changing careers, going back to school or having children, it may make sense to wait until you have settled the related details before committing to buy a home.

There is not necessarily any right or wrong answer to whether you should buy a home. The decision ultimately comes down to a mix of personal, lifestyle and financial reasons. Only you can answer whether buying is important to you.

HOW MUCH HOME CAN YOU AFFORD?

Once you decide to buy a home, the next step is settling on a price range. This process should happen well before you start attending open houses and talking to real estate agents, especially if you want to take some time to build up your savings for a down payment.

Typically, you should expect to put about 20% down when you purchase a home. In years past, you might not be able to secure a mortgage at all without 20% down (or more). These days, many lenders have relaxed this standard. That said, even when it isn't required, a substantial down payment has advantages. A bigger down payment means borrowing less, which in turn means paying less interest. Some lenders compound this advantage by offering a lower interest rate to borrowers who put a full 20% down. A larger down payment also means a lower monthly payment. You will also start out with more equity in your home, lowering the chance you could owe more than your home is worth if property values decline. (See the next section for more on equity.)

Keeping your down payment at or above 20% also means avoiding private mortgage insurance, often abbreviated PMI. Many lenders require borrowers to pay for PMI if their down payment is smaller than the standard amount. This is bad news for borrowers, since PMI will increase monthly payment amounts and protects the lender, rather than the borrower. PMI premiums range from 0.5% to as much as 5% of the mortgage loan. Usually the lender will require you to keep paying PMI until your mortgage's principal balance is less than 80% of your home's original appraised value or its current market value, whichever is less. Some borrowers take out "piggyback" loans to avoid the PMI requirement. These secondary mortgages allow borrowers to cover some portion of their down payment, so they can avoid taking out more than 80% of the home's value with their primary mortgage. However, while avoiding PMI this way, borrowers are typically subject to higher interest rates than they can expect from single mortgages.

Borrowers who meet certain criteria may be able to borrow with less than 20% down through the Federal Housing Administration. These criteria are strict, and borrowers should expect more paperwork and a higher interest rate than a traditional mortgage (with a larger down payment) would entail. These loans are also generally more expensive over the course of the entire term, especially for buyers with relatively strong credit. However, for those who qualify, an FHA-insured loan can facilitate homeownership with a down payment as small as 3.5%.

In addition to the size of your down payment, you should consider your ongoing monthly costs when determining a budget for your new home. Depending on where you live, you may have heard an estimate that your overall monthly housing costs should not exceed either 25% or 30% of your gross, or pretax, income. Mortgage lenders will also look at your debt compared to your income when evaluating whether you will be able to afford the home you want. Lenders may consider the "front-end ratio," which includes mortgage principal, interest, insurance and taxes, as well as the "back-end ratio," which adds in any other recurring debt obligations, such as student loans or car payments. Historically, lenders looked for a front-end ratio of 28% or less and a back-end ratio of 36% or less. While these are not hard-and-fast rules, they still serve as a useful guideline for evaluating whether you are realistically budgeting for your housing costs.

QUICK NOTES

Advantages Of A Large Down Payment

- ☑ Borrow less and pay less in interest overall
- ☑ Potentially secure a lower interest rate
- ☑ Pay less each month
- ☑ Start out with more equity
- ☑ Avoid private mortgage insurance (PMI)

Don't forget to budget for one-time closing expenses, too. These may include paying for a home inspection or getting quotes from contractors for any necessary repairs. You will also need to pay mortgage origination fees, escrow fees, and fees charged by the realtors and lawyers involved in setting up your mortgage. You can expect closing costs to be around 2% to 5% of the home's value. When you decide on a down payment amount, don't forget you will need to cover these obligations at the same time.

Many homebuyers feel pressure to get prequalified for a mortgage before they proceed. Note that prequalification is different from preapproval. Prequalification is essentially an estimate of how much you may be able to borrow based on a credit check and other financial information. Preapproval is a more formal process, in which you complete a full mortgage application; if you are preapproved, the lender will issue a letter that serves as an offer — though not a formal commitment — to lend you a specific amount within a short period, often 90 days. Preapproval is often wise, because it can make a seller or agent more inclined to accept an offer, especially in tight housing markets.

Prequalification, on the other hand, is designed to give you an idea of how much you are able to borrow. However, be wary of letting prequalification lure you into exceeding your budget. Just because you qualify to borrow a given amount does not mean you should look for a home priced accordingly. Many buyers fall into the trap of borrowing as much as they can without determining whether a home at that price point is affordable in the long run. It is important to stay realistic in the budgeting stage. Don't buy more house than you need simply because you can stretch your finances to make it work. You certainly should not cut into your general emergency fund when budgeting for housing. You want to leave room in your budget for other financial goals, too, such as saving for retirement or for your children's education.

It was once true that most homebuyers were married couples. During the past few decades, though, the pool of buyers has become more diverse. Today it is common not only for single adults to buy homes, but for unmarried partners or even groups of friends to consider sharing a home. If you are buying a home with a spouse, or anyone else, you should work with them on the calculations above. Bear in mind that your co-owner's credit history could affect your ability to secure a loan and overall mortgage costs. Couples should also look into state laws regarding joint property ownership. (For more on this topic, see Chapter 11.) If you are single or buying with someone who isn't your spouse, be aware that lenders cannot discriminate against you based on marital status. However, everyone on the mortgage is legally on the hook for the entire amount. In the absence of a marriage license, you may want to have an attorney help you draw up a simple contract to protect you both, specifying each person's responsibilities and setting clear consequences for failing to meet them. The contract should also outline the process if one of you eventually wants to leave.

BUILDING EQUITY

One of the most significant advantages of buying over renting is building equity in your home. Assuming that, like most people, you finance your home's purchase, you will build equity gradually over time. Home equity is the difference between your property's fair market value — the price it would sell for in the open market — and the remaining principal balance on your mortgage.

Each month, a portion of your monthly mortgage payment goes toward paying back the loan's principal. When you hear homeownership described as a means of forced savings, equity is the mechanism in question. The portion of your monthly payment that goes toward the principal is, essentially, you paying yourself each month. In addition to repayment, property appreciation can build your home equity. If property values rise in your area, the difference between the property's value and the principal balance will grow. Even though you owe the same dollar amount on your loan, your equity has increased. That said, there is no guarantee that real estate in a particular location will gain value at a rate outpacing inflation, especially if you consider a time horizon of only a few years. You should think of your home primarily as a purchase, not an investment. The belief that real estate values can only appreciate was a major contributor to the housing crisis of the late 2000s.

One of the benefits of homeownership is that it can simplify your monthly budget. If you lock in a long-term fixed-rate mortgage, you will know that your housing cost is essentially set for years or decades to come. ("Essentially" because insurance premiums and property taxes may increase, though your mortgage payment will not.) Even if you do not succeed in setting any money aside for savings in a particular month, you have still improved your overall net worth by increasing your equity with your monthly mortgage payment. In most mortgages, the amount of your monthly payment applied to principal increases over time, so you will build equity at an increasing rate each year.

You should think of your home primarily as a purchase, not an investment.

Later in life, you may want to tap the equity you have built in your home. The most direct way to do this is to sell the property. After you sell, you can downsize and pocket the difference. It may even make sense to return to the flexibility of renting, depending on your situation.

Many people also access their home equity while staying put. This may take the form of a home equity loan (sometimes called a second mortgage); a home equity line of credit (a HELOC); cash-out refinancing; or a reverse mortgage. Reverse mortgages are restricted to homeowners age 62 and older, but you may want to use one of the other strategies sooner.

In either a home equity loan or a HELOC, you will use your home equity as collateral. A home equity loan is a lump-sum loan, meaning you designate an amount and get all of it at once if you're approved. You repay the loan with interest via monthly installments over a set amount of time, usually between five and 15 years. In most cases, your interest rate will be fixed, though it will likely be higher than the interest rate on your first mortgage. The amount you can borrow varies by lender, but can rise as high as 80% of your home's value. A HELOC, on the other hand, is a line of credit rather than a one-time loan. You can withdraw the amount of equity you need when you need it for as long as the line of credit remains open, which is typically five to 10 years. During that time (called the "draw period"), you will need to make modest payments on your debt. Once the draw period ends, you will pay off the rest of the debt on a more aggressive schedule, usually 15 to 20 years. Unlike home equity loans, HELOCs are typically structured with a variable interest rate.

Some homeowners choose to refinance their primary mortgage, setting a principal amount higher than their current principal balance and taking the difference in cash. Not all lenders will allow such strategies, with good reason. Cash-out refinancing means effectively using your home as an ATM in exchange for extending the term of your original mortgage, increasing your monthly payments or both. Worse, if the home's value suddenly falls, you could end up in a very uncomfortable spot. Widespread use of this technique was another major contributor to the 2008 financial crisis.

While any of these borrowing methods can have legitimate uses, you should be careful when using your equity this way. You are using your home as collateral, which means you could risk losing it if something goes wrong. If you cannot make payments, the lender has the right to foreclose on your home. You can also seriously mar your credit history if you default. (For more information about credit, see Chapter 3.) Given these risks, avoid drawing on home equity for vacations, luxury cars or other nonessential spending.

MORTGAGES

The majority of homebuyers finance their purchases. According to a report from the National Association of Realtors, 78% of buyers financed their home purchases in 2022. While this number has fallen somewhat in the early 2020s, it still represents a major share of purchasers overall. This means that most of the time, buying a home means taking on a mortgage. But not every mortgage works the same way, and it is important to understand your options before you choose which is right for you.

Types Of Mortgages

Fixed-Rate Mortgages

As the name implies, fixed-rate mortgages lock in an interest rate over a relatively long period. Generally, these mortgages are available in two sizes: 15-year mortgages or 30-year mortgages.

If you are interested in rapidly building equity, a 15-year fixed-rate mortgage is an attractive option. While monthly payments will be higher than many alternatives, you will build your equity faster and will be done with monthly mortgage payments sooner. Buyers who are able to afford higher monthly payments may find the prospect of owning their home outright earlier an attractive incentive.

Yet for many — if not most — buyers, a traditional 30-year fixed-rate mortgage remains the gold standard. If you are buying your "forever home," or at least the home in which you plan to raise your children or otherwise stay put for a long time, a 30-year fixed-rate mortgage locks in an interest rate for decades. Since the loan term is longer, monthly payments are typically lower than in 15-year fixed-rate mortgages. With both 15- and 30-year mortgages, you can usually make additional principal payments at any time without prepayment penalties if you decide you wish to build equity or repay the loan faster than scheduled.

Even if you do not plan to stay in your home for decades, bear in mind that life does not always go as planned. Simple inertia can easily keep people in homes much longer than they originally intended. So can changed circumstances. A financial setback may require that you rethink plans to grow into a larger space or to move to a trendier neighborhood. Even if you do move to a larger home, you may also decide to keep your starter property. If you start out in an urban condo and move to a free-standing home in the suburbs, you may find it convenient to keep a place to stay downtown, offering short- or long-term rentals to defray the costs.

The major drawback of a 30-year fixed-rate mortgage compared with a 15-year loan is that you will pay more interest. A 15-year fixed-rate mortgage means higher payments, but less interest paid overall. In both cases, however, you know your housing costs will be relatively fixed over the course of your loan (or until you refinance, if you choose to do so).

Adjustable-Rate Mortgages

Adjustable-rate mortgages, sometimes called variable-rate mortgages or floating-rate mortgages, offer relatively low interest rates for a fixed term. After this period, often five or 10 years, the interest rate becomes variable. Buyers who know they plan to sell before the end of the fixed term may find these mortgages especially attractive, since the initial monthly payments are usually lower than a fixed-term mortgage. Buyers can also refinance when the term ends, though there is no guarantee that interest rates will not rise — perhaps significantly — over time. Some adjustable-rate mortgages offer rate caps that will limit either the amount a rate can change from year to year or the amount the rate can increase over the life of the mortgage. Others include a payment cap that restricts the monthly mortgage payment amount to a certain maximum dollar value.

You will usually see an adjustable-rate mortgage expressed as two numbers, such as 3/27 or 5/5. In most cases, the first number is the number of years that the fixed interest rate applies, but the second number can indicate a variety of information depending on how the loan is structured. For example, a 3/27 ARM offers a fixed rate for three years and a floating rate for the remaining 27 years of a 30-year loan. Yet the 5/5 ARM starts with a five-year fixed interest rate and then adjusts the variable rate every five years. A common adjustable-rate mortgage setup is a 10/1 ARM, in which the interest rate is fixed for 10 years and then adjusts annually.

Interest-Only Mortgages

In an interest-only mortgage, the borrower pays only interest for a certain amount of time. During this period, often five or 10 years, none of your mortgage payments go toward the loan principal. As a result, early payments are substantially lower than later ones.

Most borrowers should avoid interest-only mortgages. They involve taking on substantial risk, since you are not building any equity in the first years of the loan term. A decline in the property's value can therefore quickly become a disaster. If you owe more on your mortgage than your property is worth — called "going underwater" or "going upside-down" on your mortgage — then selling or refinancing can become difficult or impossible.

Borrowers should also be wary of loans that include a large lump sum at the end, often called a "balloon payment." In this sort of loan, the monthly payments are lower because the loan's full value isn't amortized over its term. But unless you save carefully, the final balloon payment can sneak up on you. If you are unable to pay it in cash, you will need to sell your home (assuming property values have not dropped significantly) or refinance at what could be a higher interest rate.

Which mortgage is right for you depends primarily on how long you intend to own the property. You may also want to factor in other financial goals, such as becoming debt-free by a certain age or saving the most money over the life of your mortgage. As with budgeting for your overall home price, you should not choose a mortgage based solely on how much you want to pay each month.

How To Get A Mortgage

When you are ready to start the mortgage process, the first step is to find a lender. You may want to borrow from a local bank or credit union, but they are not your only options. Many companies specialize in mortgage lending, including some companies that are online-only. Given the sheer number of available lenders, many buyers are initially overwhelmed. If you already do business with a bank, check out its offerings. Ask friends and family for recommendations. If you are using a real estate agent you like, he or she may also have suggestions. Some buyers choose to hire mortgage brokers, who specialize in helping borrowers find the best mortgage. Some brokers are paid by the lender and others by the borrower; whether this service is worth the fee will depend on your situation.

Most borrowers should avoid interest-only mortgages. They involve taking on substantial risk, since you are not building any equity in the first years of the loan term.

Whether you use a broker or go it alone, it is wise to talk to more than one lender to compare offers. After researching various companies, narrow it down to your top three and apply for preapproval at all of them. This will allow you to compare offers directly. When you do, be sure you are clear on the difference between an interest rate and the annual percentage rate, or APR. APR is the rate, as a percentage, that you will pay each year for borrowing, including fees or additional costs. APR essentially controls for differences in upfront and annual fees between lenders, which means it is a more useful way to compare offers than relying on interest rate alone.

The rates lenders offer will depend largely on your credit score and your debt-to-income ratio. Before you apply for a mortgage, check your credit reports for errors and promptly correct any you find. You should also generally avoid applying for new credit cards or auto loans just before applying for a mortgage, as recent credit inquiries from other lenders can temporarily bring down your score. Even relatively small differences in credit scores can make a big difference in your mortgage terms.

Preapproval is not approval, so once you have selected the offer you prefer, you will need to go through the application process. Even though preapproval will speed things up, expect to dedicate some time to shepherding your paperwork through the steps your lender requires. Before you sign, make sure you understand all your mortgage's provisions. For example, be sure your loan does not include penalties for prepayment. There should be no surprises for anyone at closing.

Lenders sometimes offer borrowers the option of paying "points" at closing. The homebuyer pays fees upfront, and in exchange the lender lowers the interest rate. Each point costs 1% of your total mortgage amount. In most cases, you should avoid the temptation to pay points. Even though points will lower your monthly payments, they transform interest into a sunk cost. If you sell your property before the mortgage ends, you cannot recover any money you paid in points.

PROPERTY TAXES

As a homeowner, you can expect to pay property taxes. Most mortgage lenders require borrowers to include property tax (and homeowners insurance) in their monthly mortgage payments. Since the city, county and state governments assessing these taxes do not require payments each month, the lender places these funds in escrow until payment is due. (Escrow is an arrangement where a third party — in this case, the mortgage lender — receives and disburses money for two parties in a particular transaction.)

If you paid for your home in cash, or if you have paid off your mortgage, you will need to remember to pay property tax yourself. Depending on where you live, these taxes may be due quarterly, semiannually or annually. Some mortgage lenders also allow borrowers to waive the escrow requirement for a fee. While most borrowers find it more convenient to let the lender take care of taxes, some prefer the control of handling their own tax payments. In addition, most states let lenders keep any interest earnings on a borrower's escrow account, so some borrowers prefer to invest and receive this income themselves. Note, however, that the upfront fees involved in forgoing escrow mean borrowers won't necessarily come out ahead by much.

Remember to budget for increases in property taxes. At a minimum, you can expect taxes to rise along with inflation. But depending on the local housing market and your local government's financial situation, property taxes may rise more sharply. Municipalities arrange tax assessments on a regular basis to adjust property tax to reflect any change in the property's value. If you disagree with a tax assessment, you can take steps to have it reviewed. The particulars will depend on where you live, so you will need to research the requirements of your city or town. Note, however, that you cannot contest your property tax rate; you can only contest the assessed value of your home.

OTHER TAX CONSIDERATIONS FOR HOMEOWNERS

A major historical benefit to American homeownership has been the mortgage interest deduction. If you itemize your deductions on your federal income tax return, this deduction can reduce your out-of-pocket interest costs, especially early in your mortgage's term. This is because in most mortgages, more of the borrower's monthly payments are devoted to interest in the earliest years of the loan. However, the tax-reform package that passed in late 2017 substantially raised the standard deduction, which means that fewer taxpayers find it worthwhile to itemize deductions. This, in turn, means that fewer people benefit directly from the mortgage interest deduction. (For more about the standard deduction and itemizing, see Chapter 15.)

Taxpayers who do itemize can also benefit from the state and local tax (SALT) deduction. However, the 2017 tax-reform package capped the total SALT deduction at $10,000 annually. This amount includes both property taxes and state income taxes, if any. High earners in high-tax states may already be using their entire SALT deduction on income taxes, which means property taxes will provide them no benefit on their federal income taxes.

On the other hand, if you live in a state with no income tax, you may end up taking the standard deduction even if you could deduct your housing-related expenses. Unless your property tax, mortgage interest and any other itemized deductions together exceed the standard deduction — $14,600 for individuals and $29,200 for married couples filing jointly in 2024 — you should continue taking the standard deduction as a homeowner. Note that many provisions of the 2017 legislation, including the currently high standard deduction and the current limit on SALT deductions, will automatically end in 2026 unless Congress takes action to extend them.

If you do itemize your deductions and adding mortgage interest and property taxes increases those deductions significantly, you may end up entitled to a large federal refund. In this case, you should reduce the withholding on your wages, assuming you are an employee rather than a freelancer. Reducing your withholding means taking home a bigger paycheck every month, reducing or eliminating your annual refund. With more cash in your pocket, you can better fund your — likely higher — monthly housing costs. Keep this possibility in mind when you are budgeting for your original purchase.

HOAS, CONDO ASSOCIATIONS AND CO-OP BOARDS

Many residential neighborhoods have a homeowners association, or HOA, to maintain a cohesive atmosphere. If your new home is a condominium, a townhouse or part of a planned development, you will likely encounter a homeowners association. (Note that in a condominium building, this may be called a "condo association." In this section, I will largely use "homeowners association" or "HOA" to cover both unless otherwise specified.)

Belonging to an HOA involves both obligations and benefits. If you choose to live in a property covered by an HOA, you will gain access to shared amenities, security and other potential perks. The precise benefits vary, so it is important to understand what you are getting before you commit to buy a home. You may have access to a community pool or clubhouse, or your HOA fees may cover utilities or internet service. Condo-association fees often cover upkeep of common areas and exterior maintenance, as well as insuring the building's common property. There is no standardized package that you should expect.

Bear in mind that living in a home that's part of an HOA can be costly. Expect to pay monthly membership fees that can range widely depending on your location and the type of home you buy. A 2017 survey from Trulia found median HOA fees ranged from $218 per month in Warren, Michigan, to as high as $571 per month in New York City. Inflation has pushed many of these fees higher in the past few years. Buildings and communities that are older, include more units or offer more amenities also usually impose higher fees. Some associations also charge special assessments outside the monthly fee to cover major repairs that exceed the funds in reserve, such as replacing a roof or an elevator unexpectedly. Depending on your circumstances, HOA membership fees could make up a significant portion of your overall monthly housing costs.

QUICK NOTES

Pros And Cons Of Living With An HOA

PROS

- Access to shared amenities (pools, clubhouses)
- Association covers upkeep of common areas and exterior maintenance, and possibility utilities or internet for residents
- Security
- Involvement in an association can be a way to get to know neighbors

CONS

- Often costly
- Potential for additional "special assessments" to cover major repairs
- May need to comply with restrictions on matters such as exterior decorations or street parking
- Potential interpersonal politics with neighbors

If you live in the New York City region, or a few communities elsewhere in the U.S., you may encounter a property that is part of a co-op. Unlike purchasing a condo, securing a co-op unit does not technically involve a real estate purchase at all. Instead, buyers become shareholders in a corporation that owns the building. Share ownership includes what amounts to a perpetual lease on a particular unit, giving the shareholder the right to live there. Because of this ownership structure, co-op boards have a great deal of power over residents, including restricting when and to whom they can buy and sell. Boards may also impose restrictions similar to those imposed by HOAs or condo associations.

As part of a co-op, condo or other community governed by an HOA, you give up some freedom regarding your property in exchange for the offered amenities. For example, a particular association may require you to remove your garbage cans from the curb at a certain time or may forbid all holiday decorations other than lights of a certain color. Communities with free-standing homes may restrict the sorts of vehicles you can park in driveways or on the street. In some situations, you may also run afoul of interpersonal politics or nitpicking that can cause major headaches. On the other hand, active involvement with your HOA or co-op board can be a rewarding way to get to know your neighbors, since most are run by residents. A reasonable, well-run HOA can also help you to mediate disputes you may have with a neighbor in a structured, nonconfrontational way.

Whether you find the prospect of living in one of these communities appealing or stifling largely depends on your temperament and priorities. If you don't think you can happily live with the association's covenants, conditions and restrictions, you may decide it is better to live elsewhere.

INSURANCE

Most people know that homeowners insurance is a necessity. Not only does it protect your property, but most mortgage lenders require borrowers to keep their homes sufficiently insured as a condition of making the loan. "Sufficient" in this case generally means holding insurance for the property's full or fair value — often the purchase price.

What new homeowners may not know is that there are a variety of types of homeowners insurance to navigate. Insurers offer eight main types of coverage, abbreviated "HO1" through "HO8." The types of coverage are:

- **HO1** is "basic" homeowners insurance, which covers 10 major causes of damage including fire, lightning strikes and theft. For the most part, it only covers the home itself, not personal belongings within it. Any damage caused by something other than the 10 major causes specified is also not covered. Mortgage companies often find these policies insufficient coverage, making them relatively rare. Many insurers no longer offer these policies at all.
- **HO2** offers a broader scope of coverage than HO1. It covers the home and its contents from a variety of disasters and accidents. As a "named peril" policy, it still does not cover any events beyond those specified in the policy document.
- **HO3** is the most common type of homeowners insurance. Instead of naming the perils it covers, an HO3 policy covers all perils except any specifically mentioned as exclusions. This policy protects your home and belongings, as well as any attached structures like a shed or garage. It also provides personal liability protection if someone is injured on your property. When you hear someone mention homeowners insurance in a general way, they are often talking about an HO3 policy.
    - In some coastal areas, you may run across HOB coverage. This is essentially the same as HO3 coverage except that it offers additional coverage against certain types of water damage.
- **HO4** is renters insurance.
- **HO5** is comprehensive insurance. It is structured similarly to an HO3 policy, but usually covers more perils and offers broader liability coverage. In turn, premiums will be more expensive.

- **HO6** is insurance designed for condo owners. It includes the unit and its contents, typically including the walls, floors and ceiling. The rest of the building is usually covered by the condo association. Co-op residents also generally buy an HO6 policy.
- **HO7** is similar to an HO3, but designed for owners of mobile homes.
- **HO8** policies specifically address concerns that apply to older homes. The basic format is similar to an HO3 policy, but with adapted coverage for buildings with historic significance or registered landmarks. These policies are usually used for buildings where certain modernizations are impractical or forbidden.

If you own a condo, co-op or mobile home, your choice will be obvious, at least as far as insurance type. Otherwise, you will have to decide how much coverage you need and can afford while still meeting your mortgage lender's requirements. Most homeowners find HO3 policies the best balance between cost and coverage, but your needs may vary, so take the time to do some research. Specifics also vary by insurer, so be sure to read the details of the policy you are considering before you commit.

Homebuyers who financed their purchase generally will include homeowners insurance premiums with their monthly mortgage payments. Lenders hold funds in escrow, as with property taxes, and make premium payments on the homeowner's behalf. The cost of these premiums will vary widely depending on your property's value. For example, if you own a condo, you are only insuring property from "the walls in." As a result, insurance will likely be quite cheap. However, remember that you are also indirectly funding the building's overall insurance policy through your HOA fee. As with property taxes, once you pay off your home, you will need to take over the responsibility of paying insurance premiums directly.

Like other forms of insurance, homeowners insurance will offer premiums that reflect perceived risk. If the previous owner of your property filed several claims within a short period, it can bump your pricing to a higher tier. The home's building materials and the crime rate in the neighborhood will also contribute to an insurer's perceived risk. Conversely, you can sometimes secure discounts by taking steps such as installing a security system or certain sorts of weatherproofing.

Costs will also vary depending on the amount of coverage you need. If you have dealt with renters insurance in the past, you may already be familiar with the difference between "actual cash value" coverage and replacement coverage. Actual cash value means the insurance company reimburses you for the current value of your home and its contents, factoring in depreciation. Replacement cost coverage does not factor in depreciation. Most HO3 policies offer actual cash value, while some HO5 policies offer replacement value. Homeowners policies also sometimes offer guaranteed (or extended) replacement-value coverage. This type of coverage builds in inflation, paying whatever it costs to repair or rebuild your home (sometimes up to a predetermined ceiling). This coverage is the most comprehensive option, though typically also the most expensive.

In addition to the value of the home itself, you will need to consider the value of the possessions within your home. Most policies cover your possessions — to a point. In many policies, insurers will cover possessions equal to 50% to 70% of the overall value of your home's structure. If you collect art, own valuable pieces of jewelry, or have other possessions that ordinary homeowners insurance will not cover sufficiently, you may want to add more coverage. You can investigate adding an insurance rider, also known as an endorsement or scheduled personal property, to your policy for any particularly valuable items.

If you live somewhere prone to flooding, you may need to secure separate flood insurance for your home. Homeowners insurance typically does not cover flood damage. The National Flood Insurance Program regulates the price of flood-insurance policies, so these costs will not vary between agents. If your home is in a flood-prone area, note that your mortgage lender may require you to obtain flood insurance in addition to your homeowners insurance.

MAINTENANCE AND IMPROVEMENTS

As a homeowner, most work you do on your property falls under the umbrella of general maintenance. While such projects improve your quality of life and may improve "curb appeal" when you sell, they do not offer you any tax benefits. However, if you make what the Internal Revenue Service calls "capital improvements," you can add to your residence's cost basis.

Cost basis is the starting point for determining whether you recognize a gain or a loss on your home when you sell it. If you buy (or build) your home, basis starts as what you paid, including your down payment and your mortgage. Capital improvements can be added to your home's cost basis, reducing the potential for gain — and thus taxes — when you sell. (For more details about taxes on capital gains, see Chapter 15.) If your gain on a primary residence is less than $250,000 for a single taxpayer, or $500,000 for a married couple, you may be able to exclude it from tax entirely.

Homeowners may not always find it easy to distinguish capital improvements from repairs and maintenance. In general, the IRS recognizes capital improvements as changes to a home that last for more than one year. These projects should also prolong the life of the home, add to its value or adapt it to new uses. For example, mowing your lawn is maintenance; modernizing your kitchen is likely a capital improvement. The IRS provides a list of examples in Publication 523, "Selling Your Home," although it is not comprehensive. If you plan to claim a project as a capital improvement, be sure to keep documents tracking your associated costs. You may want to consult a tax professional, who can help you evaluate your project and guide you toward proper documentation.

Even though maintenance does not offer tax rewards, it is a necessary component of homeownership. When you budget monthly housing costs, don't forget to build in maintenance expenses. If your air conditioning unit dies or you unexpectedly need to retile a flooded kitchen, you can and should have dedicated funds available to cover these sporadic costs. Even in cases where insurance will eventually reimburse you, it can often take months to navigate your insurer's requirements. Being able to fix your home in the meantime will keep it livable and potentially prevent more extensive damage. A common rule of thumb is to save a certain percentage of your home's cost, say 1.5% or 2% each year, to deal with common maintenance tasks. You may need to set aside more if your home is older, or if you live someplace where regular storms or other weather events are likely to damage your property. You may also want to save more upfront for your first home, as you will need to make one-time purchases like lawn mowers that more seasoned owners may bring from a previous home.

Owning a home is a big commitment. But there is a reason why it has traditionally served as a cornerstone of the stereotypical "American dream." If you decide to purchase a home and approach the process sensibly, your home can potentially serve as one of your greatest assets — as well as a place to call your own.

CHAPTER 9

MEDICAL AND DISABILITY INSURANCE

Rebecca Pavese, CPA

Many young adults find it easy not to think about insurance. Maybe you are still on your parents' health insurance plan, or you signed up for an employer-provided medical plan without thinking much about it. Maybe you have even considered going uninsured. It is very likely that, if you are like most Americans, you have not considered disability insurance at all.

All this is understandable. If you are lucky enough to be in good health, it is easy to imagine you will stay healthy forever, or at least for years to come. And no one enjoys shopping for insurance policies.

But serious illness or injury can strike without warning. As with any insurance, you buy coverage with the hope you will never need to test its limits. Taking the time to review and secure adequate medical and disability coverage is one of the smartest financial moves you can make. In a worst-case scenario, it can make the difference between a temporary financial setback and a major financial crisis.

MEDICAL INSURANCE

Health care insurance is a necessity largely because of two factors: Anyone can be unexpectedly injured or become seriously ill, and the cost of health care in the United States is quite high. Still, many Americans go without coverage for a variety of reasons. They may experience a gap in coverage due to job loss or may choose to go without because of cost. However, while circumstances may make it difficult to access or afford medical insurance, it should remain a priority whenever possible.

Even if you are in good health and have no dependents, medical insurance is critical. Say you are in your mid-twenties, with a family history free of major health concerns and a healthy lifestyle. You devote very little of your budget — or your mental energy — to medical costs. But then you miss a step on a staircase and break your ankle. Without insurance, medical bills could climb into the thousands or tens of thousands of dollars, especially if you need physical therapy or surgery. Even with insurance, these costs could be burdensome, but insurance provides the knowledge that there is a cap on what you will be expected to pay. Around 67% of personal bankruptcies in the U.S. are tied to medical bills or time missed from work because of medical issues, according to a study published in the American Journal of Public Health.

Medical insurance can cover costs, or reduce the cost through negotiated rates, for preventative health services, emergency services and prescription drugs. Many plans also allow you to access preventative care at little or no cost, even before meeting your deductible, which can help avoid additional health care costs down the road. These covered services may include physicals, screenings, vaccinations and certain types of counseling. The deductible is the amount you must pay each year before your plan pays for your health care costs in full or up to the policy limits, less any coinsurance (your share of the covered costs).

Between 2014 and 2018, having some form of medical insurance was legally required for most Americans. The Affordable Care Act's individual mandate stipulated that, in most cases, individuals had to pay a fine if they could not demonstrate satisfactory coverage. Congress has since removed this stipulation from the law, and failing to secure coverage no longer triggers a penalty. Note that some states have passed their own mandates, so you may face a state-level penalty if you go uninsured.

Types Of Medical Insurance

In the U.S., private health insurance is among the most common options for coverage. According to the Centers for Disease Control and Prevention, as of 2022 nearly 68% of adults between the ages of 18 and 64 had private health insurance. Public health insurance — programs such as Medicare, Medicaid and the Veterans Health Administration — covered 22% of that group. But private and public are not the only way to differentiate types of insurance plans. You can also define plans by the way they interact with doctors, hospitals and other health care providers.

Managed Care Plans

Health maintenance organizations, or HMOs, are usually the cheapest option among managed care plans but offer the least freedom to choose your providers. When participating in an HMO, you will designate a dedicated primary care physician from the plan's network of providers. That doctor will coordinate all of your necessary care, and usually only treatment referred by this doctor is covered. The HMO negotiates fees with various providers for each medical service to minimize costs. If you see a provider outside the network, you will likely have to pay the full cost yourself. The major exception is for emergency care. An exclusive provider organization, or EPO, is very similar to an HMO but does not require a referral for a specialist visit.

QUICK NOTES

Managed Care Insurance Plans

	Must designate a primary care physician?	Need a referral to see a specialist?	Benefits cover out-of-network care?
HMO	Yes	Yes	Emergency care only
EPO	Usually	No	Emergency care only
PPO	No	No	Yes
POS	Yes	Sometimes	Yes

A preferred provider organization, or PPO, allows you to visit any doctor you like. The plan, like an HMO, offers a network of providers with which the insurer has negotiated costs. In general, out-of-pocket costs for in-network care will be lower than for out-of-network care. You may need to pay all costs upfront and submit paperwork for reimbursement if you go outside your network. But in contrast to an HMO, in a PPO the insurer generally will pay for treatment outside the network to a point. Patients with a PPO can also self-refer to specialists without having to visit a primary care physician first.

The point-of-service, or POS, plan is a hybrid policy that blends features of HMOs and PPOs. Like an HMO, you select a primary care provider to help coordinate your care. Like a PPO, you can choose to see specialists in and out of your network. Depending on the details of your plan, you may or may not need a referral to see a specialist, or you may need a referral only for a specialist outside your network. Like a PPO, if you go out of your network, you will need to pay the bill upfront and then submit a claim for your insurer to reimburse you. You can also expect less coverage for out-of-network care.

Other Plans

Managed care plans are the most common, but they are not the only options. **Indemnity**, or traditional, plans stand in contrast to the managed care plans I have just discussed. They are also sometimes called "fee-for-service" plans. In an indemnity plan, the insurer does not have a network of providers at all. You can go to any provider you like, but you can expect higher out-of-pocket expenses, a relatively high deductible and only partial coverage of any remaining bills once you have met your deductible. For instance, you may be expected to pay 20% coinsurance on expenses after you meet your deductible, unless you reach the plan's maximum payable amount. Also, the insurer may limit the amount of any charges it will cover to a level it considers reasonable and customary in the provider's area. If the provider's bill is for an amount above that limit, you are usually responsible for the balance.

High-deductible health plans offer much lower premiums than most other options. However, you will be responsible for the entire cost of your care until you satisfy the large deductible. If and when you meet the deductible, your insurer picks up the rest of your medical bills. The way these plans are structured means you should expect to pay for most, if not all, routine care. There are a few exceptions; for example, certain types of preventative services are covered even before you meet your deductible, including blood pressure screenings and certain immunizations like the flu shot. Ideally, in this sort of plan, you would set aside money each month to cover potential medical bills up to your deductible.

Catastrophic plans, as defined by the Affordable Care Act, are a similar option available to individuals under age 30. (Certain people over 30 may qualify for a hardship exemption that allows them to access these plans too.) These plans also typically involve high deductibles and relatively lower premiums. Even in a catastrophic plan, preventative care and three primary care visits a year are covered, regardless of whether you have met your deductible. However, enrolling in a catastrophic plan means you cannot use a health savings account (which I will discuss in the next section). This means these plans are not automatically the most cost-effective option even for people who qualify. Both catastrophic and high-deductible health plans may be managed care plans as well.

You may also encounter **critical illness insurance**, but this is not traditional health insurance coverage. These plans are meant to supplement other plans, or to substitute for disability insurance in very specific circumstances. Critical illness insurance provides a lump sum to those who develop one of the diseases or conditions specified in the policy. While premiums tend to be modest compared with other forms of medical or disability insurance, qualifying illnesses are narrowly defined. Because of these plans' limitations, most people would do better to cover these costs through disability insurance, increased health savings or both.

How To Choose A Health Insurance Plan

Before you pick a plan, it is important to go beyond simply comparing the cost of monthly premiums. You will want to balance the different types of costs you may be asked to cover. In most insurance plans, costs are divided three ways: premiums, deductibles, and copays or coinsurance. Premiums are the fixed monthly cost of your insurance and are easy to anticipate. You may or may not pay your full deductible in a given year. But many plans also require copays or coinsurance. A copay is a flat fee you pay each time you get care — $15 for an office visit, for example. With coinsurance, you pay a set percentage of the charges for care.

When comparing plans, consider not only how much care you needed in the past year or two, but a variety of scenarios that could arise in the future. For example, if you are in good health, you could still experience a serious accident. If you are someone who could become pregnant, you may experience an unplanned pregnancy. Or you may develop a chronic condition due to genetic or environmental factors. For especially catastrophic scenarios, you will also want to consider a plan's out-of-pocket maximum for an individual or a family. In many plans, you will still owe coinsurance even after you meet your annual deductible. Your out-of-pocket maximum is the most you will have to pay in any given year. This amount is usually high enough that you are unlikely to reach it unless you or someone in your family becomes very ill or suffers a serious injury. In some plans, you may have separate out-of-pocket maximums for in-network and out-of-network care.

The Affordable Care Act established tiers of coverage. ACA marketplace plans, and some others, now fall into one of four categories: bronze, silver, gold or platinum. These plans are not sorted by the quality of offered care, but rather the way the plan and the insured split costs. Bronze plans offer the lowest monthly premiums but highest annual deductibles; platinum plans have the highest premiums but lowest deductibles. Silver and gold fall in between. The metal ratings are meant to help consumers compare plans from different insurers.

Before you pick a health insurance plan, it is important to go beyond simply comparing the cost of monthly premiums.

In addition to costs, you should consider whether you already have providers that you like. If so, check to see if they are in-network for any managed plans you are considering. You should also check the regional footprint of a managed care network, especially if you travel often or split your time between several states. A POS or EPO plan often covers a larger geographical area than an HMO or PPO plan. On the other hand, if you live in a remote area, a PPO plan's freedom to go out of network may give you necessary flexibility.

If you take prescription medication, you should also investigate the details of a plan's drug coverage. This may take some additional legwork on your part, but it is important information about the plan. Most insurance plans divide the list of covered prescription medications, called a formulary, into cost tiers. The number of tiers varies but usually falls between three and five. Drugs in the lowest tier are "preferred" and will cost the least, or sometimes nothing at all. In the highest tier, you will shoulder much of the cost yourself — though what you pay may still be less than what someone without insurance would be charged. While generic prescriptions are generally cheaper than brand-name medications, knowing which tier a particular drug occupies is critical in anticipating roughly how much you will need to pay. Your out-of-pocket costs may be wildly different depending on the tier your prescription occupies. This information varies not only between plans, but within the same plan from year to year. Also note that in some plans, you will have a separate deductible just for prescriptions.

Health Savings Accounts (HSAs)

Since 2003, individuals who participate in high-deductible plans have had the option to open a health savings account, or HSA. Note that, for HSA purposes, a high-deductible plan is one in which the deductible is at least $1,600 for individuals or $3,200 for families (in 2024). Catastrophic plans are excluded. An HSA offers the ability to reap income tax benefits from saving for medical expenses. A wide range of expenses are eligible, including dental and vision-related expenses, and all withdrawals to pay for qualified expenses are tax-free. Some employers offer HSAs as employee benefits, in which case account holders can make pretax contributions. Funds your employer deposits directly, such as a contribution match, are not taxed. If you make contributions to an HSA with after-tax dollars, you can deduct them from your gross income on your federal income tax return. (For more information on gross income, see Chapter 15.) Any accrued interest or investment earnings within your HSA are tax-free as well.

Anyone can contribute to an HSA on your behalf, including family members or your employer. However, the IRS limits annual contributions. For 2024, this limit is $4,150 if you are covered by an individual health care plan and $8,300 if you are covered by a family plan. This limit is per account, not per contributor. That means that if your employer contributes $500 for the year, you can only contribute $3,650 (under the 2024 limits). Account holders over age 55 as of the end of the tax year may make an additional $1,000 "catch up" contribution. You can contribute to an HSA for a given tax year until April 15 of the next year; for example, for tax year 2024, you can make contributions until April 15, 2025 as long as they don't exceed the overall contribution cap.

Using an HSA can make a high-deductible health plan more practical in some circumstances. And unlike flexible spending accounts, HSAs do not require account holders to use the full balance by the end of the year. The account is yours, even if you later enroll in a plan without a high deductible or go to work for a new employer. For HSAs that you set up through an employer, you have the option to roll over to a new administrator if you prefer, much like an individual retirement account. If you do not use your HSA account balance for medical expenses by age 65, you can make withdrawals for any purpose without penalty, though such withdrawals are only tax-free if you use them for medical expenses. Before age 65, withdrawals for nonqualified expenses carry a 20% penalty in addition to taxes, so it's important to remember to save receipts and other documents to prove that you used your withdrawals for qualified expenses.

Where To Buy Insurance

About half of Americans get health care coverage through their employers — roughly 49%, according to 2021 data from the Kaiser Family Foundation. If your employer offers a health insurance plan, this will likely be your best bet for affordable coverage, even if the company does not fully cover the plan premiums. If you must pay some or all of the premiums yourself, you still can generally do so with pretax dollars in an employer-provided plan, which lowers your individual taxable income. Group plans also offer better rates than individual plans, especially if you earn too much to be eligible for income-based subsidies. Married couples should spend some time estimating whether a family plan makes sense and, if both spouses' employers offer health insurance, which plan better fits your needs. Getting married typically triggers a special enrollment period that lets you make changes outside the annual enrollment window. If you are 26 or younger, you also have the option to remain on your parent's plan; some states allow unmarried individuals to stay on their parents' plan even longer.

If you don't have access to care through your employer — and you are not eligible for Medicaid, extended employer-based coverage under COBRA, or another program — you will need to shop for a plan yourself. The Affordable Care Act created the Health Insurance Marketplace, a website that lets individuals without coverage shop for health insurance. You may also hear this system referred to as the "health care exchanges." Depending on your income, you may qualify for a premium tax credit to offset your policy's cost. (Individuals who have access to qualified health insurance plans through their employers can opt to shop through the Marketplace too, but they will pay full price for their plans regardless of their income.) Because health insurance is regulated at the state level, the Marketplace will look different depending on where you live. In some places, the exchanges are run by the state, and in others they are run by the federal Department of Health and Human Services. The plans offered vary widely by region, and in some places your choices may be limited.

You can also shop for policies beyond the exchanges if you choose. This may involve going directly to insurers, working with an insurance agent or using websites like eHealth that offer comparison shopping tools. If you are not shopping through an exchange, you should bear in mind the difference between Affordable Care Act-compliant and noncompliant offerings. Noncompliant plans do not meet all of the law's requirements, such as covering certain essential services. Short-term insurance plans are a common type of noncompliant plan. These generally offer dramatically lower premiums than alternative options, but may make it harder to file claims, or could include annual or lifetime benefit caps. Noncompliant plans may also deny coverage to customers with preexisting conditions, something compliant plans cannot do. However, some customers may find short-term plans suitable as temporary stopgaps. Regardless of the type of plan you choose, take care to understand what you are buying when you select a plan.

As you compare your options, a plan's summary of benefits and coverage (SBC) will illuminate the trade-offs the plan offers.

This is, of course, easier said than done. The world of medical insurance is complex, and even careful research can sometimes yield confusing results. For some people, working with an insurance broker is a worthwhile investment. Brokers can help you compare different quotes more effectively. Unlike a health insurance agent, who works for a particular company, brokers can direct you to a range of companies. Brokers generally earn a basic commission that is built into the standard premium, so you will not pay more for your policy if you go through a broker. However, some brokers also charge customers separate service fees, so be sure to understand these potential fees in advance. As with any financial professional, ask around for recommendations from people you know and trust, including your accountant or attorney if you have one.

Whether you work with a broker or go it alone, you should expect to spend time going over a plan's summary of benefits and coverage, or SBC, before you sign up. This document will include information such as your deductible, copayment and coinsurance responsibilities. It can also specify whether a particular type of care is covered, such as mental health services or fertility treatment As you compare your options, a plan's SBC will illuminate the trade-offs the plan offers. In general, high premiums mean a low deductible and low copays, and vice versa. But the specifics of each plan can vary quite a bit. You should also make sure to look closely at a plan's network of providers, especially if you are considering an HMO or EPO. Most insurers allow you to search their network online, and you can also reach out to your current providers directly to see if they participate in the plan you are considering.

In addition to the type of plan you select, your insurance costs will depend largely on where you live and how old you are. Other factors that can affect costs include whether you are on an individual or a family plan, and whether you use tobacco. And while the Affordable Care Act specifies that compliant plans cannot deny coverage altogether due to a chronic illness or other preexisting condition, noncompliant plans may still do so.

Unlike most forms of insurance, you can't shop for health insurance whenever you choose. In most cases, you need to shop during open enrollment each year. The dates can change, but are usually toward year-end. For example, open enrollment for the exchanges' 2024 coverage options ran between Nov. 1, 2023 and Jan. 15, 2024. (Employer enrollment periods may vary.) However, certain life events can qualify you to enroll at other times of the year. As I mentioned, marriage is one such event, as is changing jobs. Other special circumstances include getting a divorce, having a baby, experiencing a death in the family, or moving to a new county or state. In most cases, you have 60 days after a qualifying event to secure a new health insurance plan.

Dental And Vision Coverage

Many medical insurance plans for adults do not cover expenses related to dental and vision care, though such expenses are often qualified for HSA purposes. Some employers offer dental or vision coverage as benefits to employees, either as add-ons to health insurance or as stand-alone plans. But most Americans who want such coverage need to purchase it on their own.

As with health insurance, going it alone is apt to be more expensive than participating in an employer-provided plan. Unlike health insurance, however, it is not self-evident that most people will benefit from paying for dental or vision coverage. Even in a worst-case scenario, you are unlikely to rack up bills in the tens of thousands of dollars if you go uninsured. This is not to say you should neglect dental or optical care, which are both important to your overall health. But there are other financial approaches that may make more sense.

Most dental plans, including employer-provided options, limit annual coverage amounts. According to the National Association of Dental Plans, most dental insurance offers a deductible between $50 and $100, and nearly 40% of dental PPOs cap coverage at $1,500 or less. This means that if you need extensive dental work, such as a crown or a root canal, you could easily still pay a lot out of pocket even with insurance. If you need only basic checkups and the occasional cavity filled, you could pay more in premiums than a couple of appointments would cost out-of-pocket. And, like health insurance, many dental plans have a preferred provider network, which may make finding a dentist in your area more difficult.

If you do choose to shop for dental insurance, you can use the health insurance exchanges for stand-alone policies, or see if your health insurance provider offers an add-on to your existing policy. You can also shop directly with other insurers. As with any insurance option, dental insurance is largely a question of balancing benefits and drawbacks. Look at a particular plan's specifics and consider your oral health and recent history. Also bear in mind that dental insurance is much less standardized than medical insurance, so pay close attention to what a plan does and does not cover. Many, if not most, people are likely to come out ahead putting the money they would have spent on premiums aside in a savings account, or an HSA if they have access to one. However, if an employer-offered plan costs you little or nothing, there is no reason not to take advantage of it.

The situation is very similar for vision insurance. Most vision insurance covers basic preventative care, eyeglasses and contact lenses, but not medical issues related to your eyes. If an issue requires your optometrist to refer you to an ophthalmologist — a medical eye doctor — it's likely that vision insurance won't cover that issue, though your existing medical insurance may. Most vision plans also do not cover LASIK eye surgery, though some may offer a discount on the procedure. You can shop for vision coverage the same way you would for dental coverage; in fact, many insurers offer the two as a combination plan. As with dental insurance, if your employer offers vision coverage for free or little cost to you, there is no reason not to take advantage of the benefit. But if you are going it alone, you may do better to set aside what you would spend on premiums in a savings account or HSA to cover services out-of-pocket.

DISABILITY INSURANCE

Young professionals often undervalue their most valuable financial resource: their ability to make a living. You may not have become a homeowner, and you may not have children or other dependents, so it is easy to imagine your insurance needs are restricted to health insurance, renters insurance and auto insurance (if you have a car). But this neglects the reality that for adults who support themselves, losing the ability to work is one of the greatest risks to their financial stability.

Generally speaking, a healthy 20-year-old is more likely to be disabled at some point in life than to die prematurely. The Social Security Administration has found that just over one in four of today's 20-year-olds will experience sufficient disability to qualify for Social Security benefits before age 67. Of course, not every disability means your working life is over. Your illness or injury may be temporary, or you may adjust to your new level of ability over time in a way that allows you to return to work. But depending on the sort of work you do and the challenges you face, you may need to work part time, change careers, or take one or more years away from the workforce. Even a robust emergency fund generally covers three to six months of living expenses, and many people have much less than that saved, especially when they are starting out.

Who Should Have Disability Insurance?

Anyone supporting himself or herself should at least consider disability insurance. Most disability insurance claims are related to illness, though some are the results of accidents. In either case, you may have little or no warning before your life substantially changes. And while medical insurance will help you to bear the cost of hospital stays, physical therapy and other treatment, there are many expenses it will not cover. First and foremost, medical insurance does not replace your income if you must spend an extended period away from the workforce.

Without disability insurance, the expenses of daily living can quickly eat through any savings cushion you may have. Those expenses may even rise because of your condition. If you are unable to cook, clean, drive or handle routine errands, you may need to pay others to help you, or rely on relatively expensive services as a replacement. Without disability insurance, this financial burden may fall on your family or friends if you run out of savings. Alternatively, you may accrue burdensome credit card debt to stay afloat. Neither option is ideal.

QUICK NOTES

Short-Term vs. Long-Term Disability Coverage

Short-Term	Long-Term
► Generally provides benefits up to six months, though occasionally up to two years	► Provides benefits up to a certain age or for life, depending on the policy
► Common as employee benefits, rare as individual policies	► More useful option for young professionals in most cases

If you support a spouse or young children, disability insurance gives you peace of mind that your partner won't need to juggle caring for you and finding a more lucrative job (or a second job) to help offset your loss of income. And if you are a freelancer or run a small business, disability insurance can provide a critical safety net if you are unable to work due to injury or illness. You may even have access to a discounted group plan through an organization such as the Freelancers Union.

Do not assume that you are not eligible for disability insurance if you have a preexisting health issue. Depending on the issue in question, it may not affect coverage at all. In other cases, it may result in modified coverage or an extra premium because of increased risk of future disability. Often, your preexisting condition is exempted, but you can still get coverage for any disability that does not result from that condition. If you are supporting yourself fully through your work, it is still worth looking into your coverage options even if you are not in perfect health. You can make a more informed decision once you know what sort of coverage is available to you.

It is easier to acknowledge that disability insurance is important in theory than to decide that you, personally, should purchase it. A 2022 survey by LIMRA, an association of financial services companies, found that 61% of respondents said they would experience financial hardship within one year if their household's primary wage earner was injured or became seriously ill. Yet, in that same group, only 11% of respondents said they would turn to an individual disability insurance policy in such circumstances. The survey also found that 38% of respondents were "very/extremely concerned" about being able to support themselves if they became disabled. Recognizing that disability insurance is important is good; just make sure you translate that recognition into action.

Types Of Disability Insurance

Disability insurance is sorted into two major categories: short-term and long-term disability. Short-term coverage generally lasts for up to six months, though occasionally a policy will last as long as two years. The monthly premiums are sometimes a bit lower than long-term policies, although in general the difference is not substantial. These policies are relatively common as employer benefits, but rarely as individual policies. If you aren't already getting disability insurance at work, buying a long-term policy will likely be more straightforward.

Long-term disability coverage can provide benefits for life or until the insured reaches a certain age. Common cut-offs include ages 65 and 70. While long-term coverage is more expensive, it is also the more useful option for young professionals. Researchers at the U.S. Census Bureau estimated that a person with a bachelor's degree can expect to earn an average of $2.4 million over the course of a career. For master's degree holders, this figure goes up to $2.8 million and for those with a doctorate, it reaches $3.5 million. Obviously, this outlook may significantly over- or understate the case for a particular individual, but however you look at it, losing the ability to earn a living early on can have a huge effect on your lifetime financial outlook.

Disability insurance policies usually pay between 50% and 70% of your lost monthly gross wages, though some policies may go as high as 80%. Short-term policies typically replace a higher percentage of income than long-term policies do. Insurers do not provide full income replacement because they want to give the policyholder an incentive to return to work if possible. According to data the Council for Disability Awareness cited in 2016, the average duration of a long-term disability claim is a little less than three years.

For either short-term or long-term policies, benefit payments may be taxable or tax-free. The difference isn't the type of policy, but rather the way you paid your premiums. If you used pretax funds, or if your employer paid for your coverage, benefit payments are taxable income. If you paid your premiums with after-tax dollars, insurance proceeds are not subject to income tax.

Getting A Disability Insurance Policy

As with medical insurance, disability insurance is usually easiest to get through your employer if that route is available to you. According to LIMRA, 47% of employers offer short-term disability insurance as a benefit. Some employers have even adopted a process of automatic enrollment unless workers opt out. If your employer covers some or all of your premiums, you are likely to get the most value participating in this plan. Even if you are responsible for most or all of the costs, however, you may get a better deal at work through a group plan than by shopping as an individual. Participating at work also means you are likely to have the option to pay premiums using pretax dollars, reducing your taxable income. If your employer offers short-term disability coverage at low or no cost, you may want to consider it as a complement to an individual long-term policy.

In some cases, you may have access to a group plan through a membership organization or association. Common examples include labor unions and medical or legal associations. These policies are generally very similar to an employer-provided group plan and are therefore more affordable on average than individual disability insurance. As with an employer-provided plan, take care to determine what the group plan does and does not provide. Despite lower premiums, it may not offer as much coverage as you want or need. For instance, some group plans impose monthly or annual benefit caps.

Even if your employer offers disability insurance, you may wind up looking for a private policy, either because your employer only offers short-term coverage or because you want to be sure you can take your long-term coverage if you change jobs. You may also end up shopping on your own because you don't have access to a workplace or other group plan. For more on shopping for an individual policy, keep reading.

Depending on where you live, you may have access to state disability insurance. As of this writing, five states — California, Hawaii, New Jersey, New York and Rhode Island — offer state disability insurance. Benefits are funded by paycheck withholdings, and all five states require workers to have contributed to the fund for some set amount of time before they are eligible for benefits. These programs are generally short-term, ranging from 26 to 52 weeks of benefits. If you live in one of these states, look into the details of your particular program. Social Security also offers disability benefits in certain circumstances. However, these can be hard to successfully claim, and benefits are relatively small even for individuals who are approved. In most cases, you should use state programs and Social Security to supplement other disability coverage, not replace it.

If you are shopping for individual coverage or want to compare your group plan to other options, third-party websites such as Disability Insurance Quotes or Policygenius can provide information for comparison shopping. You may also want to work with a professional who can help you compare various quotes. You can work with a fee-only financial adviser, an independent broker or an online insurance agent, depending on your needs.

What To Look For In A Disability Policy

When shopping for disability coverage, make sure the policy covers both accidents and sickness. Accident-only policies exist, and their premiums are usually cheaper than more comprehensive options. But for most workers, they do not provide enough coverage.

You should also make sure you understand the policy's definition of disability, since the particulars can vary. Common disability definitions include:

- **Social Security**: This uses the Social Security Administration's definition, which is relatively restrictive. To qualify for benefits, the insured cannot engage in any substantial gainful employment. In addition, the disability must have lasted for five months, and it must be expected to last at least 12 months or result in the insured's death.

- **Any Occupation:** Under these policies, the insured receives benefits if he or she cannot engage in any reasonable occupation for which he or she might be suited based on education, experience, training, age, etc. In other words, even if you can't work at your previous job, if you have the ability to perform a different job you are likely not disabled under the plan's definition. (The specifics vary from plan to plan.)

- **Own Occupation:** This definition of disability hinges on the insured's ability to engage in the occupation he or she had before becoming disabled. This policy is the most expensive, but can make sense depending on the insured's career. For example, a neurosurgeon who injures her hands and can no longer perform surgery may be able to work as a teacher in a medical school or in some other adjacent profession, but she has still lost a significant portion of her previous earning power. An "own occupation" policy would likely pay benefits in this scenario, while an "any occupation" policy would not.

Certain policies provide benefits for partial, as well as total, disability. (These may also be called "residual benefits.") The definition for partial disability, like full disability, will depend on the insurer. It may also vary depending on the insured's occupation. This option is often attractive, since it will support a transition to part-time work or to a less lucrative career after illness or accident. But make sure you understand the details of the particular policy when evaluating the benefit compared to the expense of higher premiums.

If you are shopping for a long-term policy, you should take note of its duration. A policy that provides benefits until retirement offers maximum protection, at the expense of higher premiums. In most cases, you should look for a benefit period of at least five years. Less than this will leave you at risk for running out of benefits during even an average length of illness or injury recovery. Whether five years of coverage is enough will depend on your financial circumstances, your family health history and how much you value the peace of mind a longer benefit period offers. Take special care to note any distinction your policy may apply to disabilities based on mental illness, since many policies limit benefit payments for these claims to a shorter period (often two years).

Each policy will also specify a particular waiting period, called the "elimination period," before the insurer starts to pay benefits. Common elimination periods are 30, 60, 90 or 180 days. Long-term disability insurance usually involves a longer elimination period than short-term insurance, but particulars can vary. Longer elimination periods usually also translate into lower premiums but mean that you will need sufficient funds to cover the period while you wait. Note that when you do this calculation, you should add an extra 30 days to whatever elimination period you consider. Most insurers pay benefits at the end of the month after the elimination period ends. On the other hand, if you have short-term coverage through your employer, you may not need to pay extra for a shorter elimination period on your long-term policy, since the short-term plan could cover the gap.

Especially as a younger shopper, you may want to look for a policy that guarantees noncancelable coverage. This feature ensures that a carrier will not raise rates or cancel your policy unless you stop paying premiums. If it is available, this sort of policy will allow you to lock in a reasonable rate over the long term. A guaranteed renewable option is a lesser form of this feature; an insurer cannot change or cancel a policy as long as you stay current with premiums, though the insurer can raise rates when you renew.

You should also look for any cost-of-living adjustment (COLA) and to see whether the policy offers an additional purchase benefit. These are features that may especially appeal to young professionals. As the name suggests, a COLA feature increases monthly benefits by an amount based on inflation. Especially in a long-term policy, this can ensure that inflation doesn't eat away at the real value of benefit payments over time. An additional purchase benefit lets you purchase more insurance at certain intervals without having to prove your insurability again. It is likely that your earning power will grow as you progress through your career, so this benefit makes sure your coverage keeps up with a potentially greater cost of living over time.

These benefits may be built in for some policies, and in others they may be available to add as riders.

As a good rule of thumb, look for a disability insurance policy with annual premiums between 1% and 3% of your gross income

---

Certain policies have provisions that coordinate between the insurer and Social Security or workers' compensation. In this case, any benefits the policy will pay are offset by any benefits received under the other program. These provisions do not render disability insurance a bad idea, however. As mentioned earlier, Social Security's definition of disability is restrictive, so you may qualify for insurance benefits but not Social Security. Workers' compensation only covers injuries that happen at work; accidents that happen elsewhere and illnesses of any kind are not covered.

For most consumers, cost will be a major factor in selecting a policy. The type of coverage you choose and the policy's features will affect your total premiums. So will the particulars of your occupation, along with your age, sex and general state of health. As with medical insurance, smokers can expect to pay more. Prices will also vary depending on where you live. As a good rule of thumb, look for a policy with annual premiums between 1% and 3% of your gross income. Note that prices for disability policies are fixed by law and filed with state regulators. For consumers, this means that buying a policy through an independent broker will not cost more than buying a policy directly from an insurer.

It is also worth looking into the operations and stability of the insurers you are considering. Ratings agencies such as Standard & Poor's or Moody's rank insurance companies reflecting how financially stable a given company is, which is an important consideration, especially for long-term policies. Note that each ratings agency has its own system. In general, you should look for a carrier with at least a rating of AA- from Standard & Poor's, or Aa3 from Moody's. You may also want to check your state's department of insurance to see if customers have filed complaints against the insurer. An independent financial adviser can also help you to evaluate both insurers and their offerings.

After all of this research, it will eventually be time to decide on a policy. Before you make a final selection, make sure you have evaluated and understood all of the products available to you. Also be sure you can articulate your needs and wants, so you can wisely decide on the trade-off between a policy's features and its costs. There is no single answer to what amount of income you need to replace, how long you want benefits to last or how broadly you want your policy to define "disability." But you should think carefully about all of these questions before you decide what is right for you. If you did not work with a financial adviser or broker during your research, have an expert look over your policy before you sign. Having a financial adviser, disability claims consultant or attorney review the policy at this point can help you spot any irregularities or provisions that might trip you up when making a claim.

Like any insurance product, disability insurance is not something you should "set and forget." Even if you choose a long-term policy that lasts until you reach retirement age, your needs and circumstances will change over time. At a minimum, your income is likely to increase. Plan to revisit your coverage periodically, as well as when you experience significant life events such as the birth of a child, a move to a new city or state, a major promotion or a change of career path.

I hope this chapter has convinced you of the importance of both medical and disability insurance. Even if you are lucky enough to get comprehensive insurance through your employer, you will benefit from better understanding how these forms of insurance work and how to get your own coverage if your job or other life circumstances change. While not everyone's needs are the same, everyone benefits from suitable coverage. Understanding what you are looking for is a major step toward finding the insurance coverage that's right for you.

CHAPTER 10

LIFE INSURANCE

Anthony D. Criscuolo, CFP®, EA

You may feel a variety of emotions as you approach particular aspects of your financial life for the first time. Your first investing experience may be exciting. Maybe you'll feel pride at paying off debts and mastering your budget. If nothing else, finishing your income tax return can offer a sense of relief (at least until next year). But it is the rare individual who wants to think about life insurance long enough to feel anything. After all, few of us enjoy contemplating our mortality. Even fewer like spending time dealing with insurance companies. Under the circumstances, it is easy to see why many young professionals delay getting life insurance as long as possible.

This attitude, while understandable, is misguided.

Professionals in their 20s and 30s may first think about life insurance when someone they know suggests it, or they may have a vague sense that buying it is a responsible thing to do. But why? Like all financial planning decisions, there is no one-size-fits-all approach to life insurance. Understanding the real and concrete reasons to get insurance can motivate you to start your search for the right coverage.

The most traditional reason to buy life insurance is for personal income protection. If you die prematurely, life insurance provides support for a spouse, children or other dependents you leave behind. Like other forms of insurance, it is a way to protect against risk. But life insurance can serve other financial planning purposes, too. Depending on the type of insurance you buy and the way you structure your policy, it can also be part of your long-term investment plan. Policies that accumulate cash value can serve as a form of forced savings. And life insurance can be a useful estate planning tool. When you look at life insurance as part of your overall financial plan, it can play a role in your wealth management strategy and the pursuit of other financial goals.

Many young adults put off getting life insurance because they overestimate its cost. A 2022 study from Life Happens (a nonprofit supported by insurers and brokerages) and LIMRA (a global life insurance research and consulting group) found that a large portion of survey respondents estimated higher costs for life insurance than they would actually face. Among respondents identified as millennials, 43% estimated the monthly cost of a term-life policy for a healthy 30-year-old was $1,000 or more per year, when the actual cost for the policy in question was $170 annually. The same survey found that nearly half of responts between ages 24 and 40 said they either needed to secure life insurance or felt they needed additional coverage.

Buying life insurance while you are young is generally a smart financial move, because it is often cheaper than waiting. Your rates are unlikely to ever be lower than when you are a young, healthy adult. Even if you need little coverage right away, you can look for a policy that allows you to convert it from one type to another without a new medical exam, or one that includes an option to expand coverage later. Note, however, that certain policies require periodic physicals, usually every five or 10 years. Beware of these policies; while they may offer comparatively attractive rates in the beginning, they shift the risk of future health changes from the insurer back to you. This reduces or eliminates the benefits of buying coverage early.

You may have access to life insurance as an employer-provided benefit. While better than nothing, this coverage is often insufficient for someone supporting a spouse or children. Most employers provide the equivalent of one or two years of salary, which may fall short of your dependents' needs. You may be able to buy additional coverage through your workplace, but bear in mind that such add-on coverage may or may not follow you if you leave your job. Fully employer-paid coverage almost certainly will not. Buying additional coverage through a group plan may also be more expensive than buying a stand-alone policy if you are young and in relatively good health. Be sure to read and understand the details of the particular coverage available to you.

Almost everyone should consider at least some life insurance coverage. Even if your income is relatively low or you have no dependents, you may not want to leave your family with debts or funeral costs. For example, while federal student loans are discharged if the borrower dies, private student loans may or may not be discharged. If your loan documents indicate your co-signer must take on any remaining debt, your parents could be left with any remaining student loan balance. Life insurance can help cushion such a financial blow.

It is common for young adults to think of life insurance as a way to protect their children. But don't forget that you may also become a caregiver to your aging parents or grandparents. If you become their primary source of support, you should consider the consequences if you should unexpectedly predecease them. Even if your spouse or kids have access to other resources, you may need life insurance for your parents' sake. (For more general information on caring for aging parents, see Chapter 19.)

WHAT KIND, HOW MUCH AND FOR HOW LONG

Once you have decided you need life insurance, you may be tempted to start plugging in numbers right away. You can find many insurance calculators online that will allow you to scratch this itch. But it is impossible to calculate your needs accurately if you start there. Instead, first answer the most important question: What do you need the insurance to do — in other words, what is its purpose?

In general, life insurance has four main purposes.

1. **Personal income protection.** This is the most traditional use for life insurance. Using it this way means you are mainly concerned with protecting and supporting your dependents, whether young children, aging parents or a partner who can't easily shoulder existing expenses alone. For example, if you and your spouse own a home together, a mortgage payment that is comfortable with two incomes may become burdensome on one.

2. **Business or partnership income protection.** If you run your own business or are a partner in an enterprise, life insurance can serve the same function for your business that it can for a family. The unexpected or premature death of a key employee, such as a founder or other principal, can throw a small business into turmoil. Life insurance can help to ease a difficult transition, at least financially.

3. **Wealth transfers.** Life insurance can be a useful tool in estate planning. If you set up a policy properly, proceeds are generally free of both income and estate tax, maximizing the value you pass to your heirs. In addition to avoiding tax, a well-structured life insurance policy lets you transfer funds outside of probate. (For more information on probate, see Chapter 12; for more on estate taxes, see Chapter 16.)

4. **Liquidity.** If your major assets are things like real estate or a small business, an insurance policy can help your heirs avoid having to sell an asset below market value to meet immediate needs. If estate tax is a concern, you may want to use life insurance to make sure your estate will have enough cash to pay any transfer taxes. With a life insurance policy in the proper amount in place, your beneficiaries can keep these assets in the family or sell them at a more advantageous time in the future.

Once you determine what purpose you want your insurance policy to serve, the questions of when to get it, how much insurance you will need and how long you intend to hold it all become much easier to answer. For example, if you plan to use life insurance to protect your personal income, you will need enough to take the place of that income, and only for as long as your family would rely on it.

It is also worth noting that not everyone needs life insurance. If you do not have family members or a business relying on your income, you have sufficient liquid assets to cover funeral expenses and are unlikely to be subject to estate tax, you may not need life insurance — at least for now. But your situation can always change, and you are the best judge of your likely future. You may be single with no dependents but plan to get married and start a family in the near future. Or you may be an employee now but plan to start your own business with a partner. You may still want to consider life insurance before you need it, because it will be less expensive if purchased when you are younger and healthier rather than waiting until illness- or age-related risk factors emerge. Sometimes those later-developing risk factors can prevent you from getting insurance at all.

	LIFE INSURANCE BY PURPOSE			
	Personal Income Protection	Business Income Protection	Wealth Transfer	Liquidity
Do you need life insurance?	Do you have dependents who would struggle without your income?	Do you own a business that would struggle without the income or sales that you generate?	Do you want to guarantee a certain amount will pass to your heirs? Does a life insurance policy fit into your overall estate plan?	Are you likely to be subject to estate tax? If so, will your heirs need liquid assets to meet the estate's tax obligations?
How much?	Enough to replace your income for as long as your dependents will rely on it.	Enough to replace your earning power for as long as the business needs it.	As much as fits with your overall estate plan or investment strategy, or as much as you need to guarantee for your heirs.	Enough to pay likely estate tax obligations on nonliquid assets, like business interests or real estate.
For how long?	As long as your dependents rely on your income.	As long as the business relies on the income or sales you generated.	As long as a life insurance policy remains part of your overall estate plan.	As long as you expect your estate will be subject to estate tax and may pose liquidity challenges for your heirs.

Figure 4

Types Of Life Insurance Policies

Assuming you need life insurance, you must decide what type you want. The insurance market is full of policies with varied provisions, but we can break available policies into a few main types. The two major categories are term insurance and permanent insurance; as their names suggest, the difference involves how long the policies last.

Term Insurance

Term insurance provides coverage for a set period of time. This may be just one year in an "annual renewal policy," or a span between five and 30 years in a "level term policy." In either case, premiums typically remain set throughout the term. Most term policies give the insured the option to renew, but you can expect premiums to increase with each renewal. This is because the chance of premature death rises as the insured ages. After a certain age — usually between 70 and 80 — some term policies can't be renewed at all.

Term life insurance can work on a "pure" insurance model, much like homeowners or auto insurance. Risk of an unlikely but catastrophic event is spread among a pool of insured individuals, and only a small percentage of them will ever collect benefits. For a relatively low but certain cost, you can protect yourself against the consequences of an unlikely but expensive event. While death is certain for all of us, death within a particular time frame is not. This is what allows insurers to offer reasonable premiums, especially to younger and healthier customers whose risk of death in the short term is low.

Term insurance is often a great fit for working professionals who want to use life insurance to protect against the loss of income for their dependents, their business or both. You can protect against income loss for a particular span — say, until your children reach adulthood or until you pay off your mortgage — after which you will not need to worry about rising premiums. Some term policies also offer decreasing benefits, rather than increasing premiums, at renewal. These arrangements can keep your premiums level as your coverage needs decrease, due to paying off a mortgage or expanding the revenue streams for your business.

Permanent Insurance

Permanent insurance is designed to last until it pays out. Because every policy can eventually be redeemed, permanent insurance is structured differently than term insurance. Permanent policies typically build cash value over time, and that value is used to pay death benefits. The insurer takes on more risk early in the policy, when the policyholder's death is less likely. Over time, as the policy's cash value grows, the insurer's risk decreases. You can think of a permanent life insurance policy as a combination of a term life insurance policy and a tax-sheltered investment or savings account.

When you are young, a permanent insurance policy generally costs significantly more than a term insurance policy with the same death benefit. The insurer invests the excess on the policyholder's behalf, building the policy's cash value. Once the cash value equals the policy's promised death benefit, that policy has "endowed." After a policy endows, there is no more risk for the insurer. The policy essentially becomes a pure savings or investment product, rather than a hybrid. In most cases, policyholders can take loans or withdrawals from their policies' cash balances. (Note, however, that the cash value of a policy is typically lower than the sum of premiums paid plus interest. This is because the insurer puts some portion of premiums toward sales commissions and other expenses, and toward paying benefits in cases where an insured person dies before a policy endows.)

Since a permanent policy is guaranteed to pay out if you keep up with premiums, it works well as part of an estate plan. If you intend to use life insurance as a means to pass assets to your heirs or a way to help your heirs pay estate taxes, the increased costs of permanent policies can be worthwhile in the long run. On the other hand, if you are concerned mainly with income protection, a term policy is usually a more economical choice.

There are two major types of permanent insurance: whole life and universal life. When selecting a permanent insurance policy, you will need to balance the expense of the policy with the amount of risk you take on for the investment component of the policy.

Traditional whole life insurance usually guarantees both your premium levels and your benefit levels. This makes it the least risky option, but also the most expensive. The insurance company takes on the risk of investing premiums to balance the probability of early mortality against expected investment returns. In addition to the added expense, whole life policies are generally inflexible. Policyholders cannot expect to change coverage levels or to adjust their premiums (whether higher or lower). Insurers offer several ways to structure payment, however:

- *Whole (Ordinary) Life:* You will pay a level premium for life or until a high cut-off age (such as 100).
- *Limited Pay Life*: You will pay premiums at a level rate until a certain age, such as 65, or for a certain number of years after buying the policy. Coverage extends past this premium cut-off point.
- *Graded Premium Whole Life/Modified Life*: You will pay lower premiums at first. They will increase until they eventually level off at a designated point.

	TYPES OF LIFE INSURANCE			
	TERM	PERMANENT		
		Traditional Whole Life	Universal Life	Variable Universal Life
Purpose	Personal or business income protection	Personal or business income protection; estate tax liquidity; wealth transfer	Personal or business income protection; estate tax liquidity; wealth transfer	Personal or business income protection; estate tax liquidity; wealth transfer
Pros	Most cost-effective within a limited time frame	Guarantees premium levels and death benefits	Offers the ability to adjust premiums and death benefits with a guaranteed interest rate	Maximum flexibility: adjust premiums, benefits and investment choices
Cons	Premiums increase with age; if the insured is still alive when the policy ends, beneficiaries do not receive a death benefit	Most expensive option; limited flexibility	No ability to direct investments; earnings may be relatively low	Highest risk; no guaranteed rate of return

Figure 5

Universal life insurance shifts some of the investment risk from the insurer to the insured. This creates added flexibility. For example, you can choose to apply the policy's investment earnings to premium payments if necessary. If you need to reduce or eliminate your out-of-pocket premium costs for a time, a universal policy will allow you to maintain your coverage. You can also typically adjust your death benefit if you choose. In **variable universal life insurance**, the flexibility goes even further, as policyholders can decide how their insurer should invest the policy's cash balance. Usually this takes the form of choosing investments, such as mutual funds, from a set menu the insurer provides. However, this control means taking on the highest degree of risk. If your policy's cash value drops dramatically, you may need to make additional premium payments to keep the insurance portion of the contract in force.

A word of caution when it comes to universal life insurance. Many of these policies have struggled in recent years, largely because insurers wrongly assumed that interest rates would not drop significantly. When the product first arrived in the 1980s, projected interest rates of 10% to 13% annually were the norm. After a prolonged stretch of historically low interest rates in the early 21st century, many policyholders found that the investment component of their policies had grown much more slowly than expected, leaving them to choose between paying dramatically higher premiums or letting their policies lapse. While traditional whole life is significantly more expensive than universal or variable universal policies, the risks involved in the latter two products are very real.

BUYING AND MONITORING LIFE INSURANCE

Once you have decided why you need insurance and what type of policy best fits your needs, it is time to shop. Many people are eager to help you in this process. Two of the most common sources are insurance agents and independent financial advisers.

Life insurance agents get a sometimes undeserved bad rap. While the perception of a pushy salesperson trying to lure you into a needlessly expensive and complicated policy did not arise out of nowhere, there are plenty of reputable agents who adhere to high ethical standards. Agents do generally work on commission, so it pays to be mindful of how their recommendations affect their compensation. But trustworthy agents can add real value by helping you navigate a complex marketplace. Consider asking friends and family for referrals, or talk to several agents before settling on one who makes you comfortable.

You may also want to involve a third-party adviser in your shopping process. An objective professional can give you the assurance that someone has your financial interests front and center. Look for an adviser who is compensated with a flat fee, which will remove commission considerations. In addition to an objective but experienced perspective, an adviser can help you review policy documents and compare various policies. Ideally, if you already work with a financial planner, that person can help you to consider life insurance's place in your overall financial situation.

How To Pick An Insurer

When you look for a policy, you aren't only evaluating the details of the particular contract. You are also evaluating the company issuing it. After all, you are considering entering an agreement that could last decades (a term policy) or for as long as the rest of your life (a permanent policy). You should feel confident that an insurer will be willing and able to hold up its end of the bargain when the time comes, and that you will not face any unpleasant surprises in the meantime.

When evaluating any company, look for an organization with a management team that has a solid track record of building value for both owners and policyholders. Most insurers are organized as either mutual companies or stock insurance companies. Some people prefer mutual companies, in which the policyholders are also the company's owners. Profits return to policyholders as either dividends or decreased premiums, and the interests of the company and policyholders are intrinsically aligned. A stock insurance company has outside investors it must consider. However, managers of a well-run stock insurance company will recognize that building value for policyholders ultimately leads to higher value for shareholders. If you find a stock insurance company and your research supports the conclusion its leaders run it well, there is no reason you should avoid it by default.

In addition to the insurance company's structure and leadership, you should evaluate its ability to pay claims. If you deposit money in a bank, the Federal Deposit Insurance Corporation protects your checking or savings accounts. There is no equivalent for insurance companies. Instead, each state maintains a guarantee association to protect policyholders' benefits. Associations cap the level of coverage, and these caps vary by state. That said, insurance company failures are extremely rare. Struggling companies are more often bought and restructured, and policyholders may not even notice if the buyer continues to do business under the original company's name. Even so, it pays to do your research to try to avoid holding a policy with a company that proves an exception to the rule. You can ask your financial adviser (if you have one) to evaluate the carriers you are considering based on their financial strength.

You, your adviser or both will likely look at one or more of the assessments done by major ratings agencies. These evaluations provide information on various aspects of an insurer's financial position. The major ratings agencies are:

- **AM Best:** This agency focuses on the consistency of profits and growth. AM Best's ratings involve some qualitative measures but mainly rely on hard statistics.

- **Standard & Poor's (S&P)**: S&P is most concerned with a carrier's "claims paying ability." To this end, it looks at a company's liquidity, management strategy, earnings, investments, capitalization, business profile and financial flexibility.
- **Moody's** and **Fitch**: Both of these ratings agencies care mainly about an insurer's ability to generate consistent profits. They also consider the quality of the carrier's management team and its assets.
- **Weiss Ratings**: This agency differs from the four above in its methods. Unlike the others, Weiss bases its ratings only on publicly available data. It also does not take compensation from the companies that it rates. The other four agencies create their ratings primarily for financial professionals, while Weiss tailors its ratings to the general public.

Each of these agencies has its own rating scale. Generally, you should look for a carrier with a rating of at least A+ from AM Best (its second-highest rating); AA- from S&P (its fourth-highest rating); and Aa3 from Moody's (its fourth-highest rating).

Credit ratings are useful, but be aware of their limitations. Apart from Weiss, all the major ratings agencies are paid by insurance carriers, which creates an inherent conflict of interest. Ratings agencies also don't respond to changes in a carrier in real time, so it may take a while for carriers whose financial strength has deteriorated to get downgraded. Because of this, a financial professional can help you to better understand a carrier's ratings in context.

Beyond settling on a carrier that is unlikely to fail, you should also look for one that is likely to give you a good return on your premium dollars if you plan to buy a permanent policy. Ideally, a carrier will pay dividends beyond its guaranteed minimum rate of return. This is the difference between evaluating a company's financial strength and its financial performance. The best performing company is the one that generates the largest cash value and death benefits for a given level of premiums. You should also factor in the time value of money — the concept that money in hand today is worth more than the same amount available in the future. If a company's financial data suggests you can potentially earn a better return by buying a term policy and investing your money elsewhere, that is worth knowing before you sign a contract.

Four main factors affect an insurance carrier's financial performance. The first is mortality risk, or the rate at which it must pay claims. The second is investment risk, which is self-explanatory. The third is lapse risk, or the rate at which policyholders abandon their policies. And the fourth is expense risk, or the general costs of doing business. There are a variety of ways to measure all four of these factors, and a financial adviser will likely use several metrics to help you evaluate your prospective carrier. These may include:

- **Historical investment performance.** You may have heard the caveat that past performance does not guarantee future results. That's true. But looking at an insurer's performance trends can give you useful information about its current position and its future prospects, especially in combination with other data.

- **Ratio of nonperforming assets to asset valuation reserve (AVR).** An adviser will look at the actual composition of a carrier's investments. Specifically, the adviser will want to consider the ratio of "nonperforming" assets to "asset valuation reserve," or AVR. Nonperforming assets include bonds in or near default, real estate recovered through foreclosure, or mortgages in which the debtor has defaulted — essentially any form of debt that the borrower has stopped paying back. AVR is a pool of assets the carrier keeps on hand to protect against the risk of such nonperforming instruments.

- **Three-year lapse rate.** At first, it may seem that policyholders canceling their policies benefits insurance carriers, since policies that lapse will never pay out benefits. In reality, though, lapses hurt insurers in two ways. A policy may lapse before the insurer can recoup the initial costs of setting up the policy. Lapses can also fuel adverse selection — the concept that the people who expect their policies to pay out are unlikely to cancel, while those who are in good health may be tempted to let a policy go. This leaves insurers with a higher proportion of risk among the customers who keep their policies in place.
- **General expenses and commissions to total income.** Like any other company, an insurer must pay for administrative expenses like facilities, wages for staff and other forms of overhead. A carrier's cost-to-income ratio is a good way to measure its efficiency. However, sometimes a temporary factor can skew this measurement. For instance, a rapidly growing insurer may experience high commission costs in a particular year. The insurer will eventually make up these costs through the premiums the new policies generate, but it will take some time for the distortion to even out.
- **Return on equity (ROE)**. Return on equity is an overall measure of an insurer's financial performance. Like the expense ratio, it may be distorted by temporary factors, so a low or negative ROE is not an immediate deal breaker. However, it is a signal that you or your adviser should look for any underlying financial problems.

How To Pick A Policy

Once you have settled on what type of policy you want and you have identified a carrier you want to buy it from, it is time to get specific. You (and your financial adviser if you have one) should carefully go over a policy's details before you purchase it. The insurer will provide you with a "policy illustration," which will lay out the policy's particulars and demonstrate how it is designed to perform over time under various sets of assumptions. If done well, a policy illustration should answer any "what if" question you might have.

State laws and regulations govern what information a carrier must include on a policy illustration, so depending on where you live, the specifics will vary. One element an insurer should always include is a worst-case scenario, showing the minimum guaranteed results for a policy. Most illustrations also include a "current" scenario, which shows what will happen if key metrics remain essentially the same as today over time. If you like, you or your adviser can request additional illustrations to show results under various conditions, such as interest rates sharply rising or falling. Do not hesitate to ask; a reputable carrier will want to give you all the information you request before you commit to a policy.

How To Monitor Your Policy

Congratulations — the contract is signed and you are the proud new owner of a life insurance policy. You may be tempted to promptly put the policy out of your mind, but resist this urge. Whether you decided on a term policy or a permanent policy, treat your life insurance as part of your overall investment portfolio. Just like stocks and mutual funds, policies should not be left to their own devices indefinitely. It is important to regularly reassess how your policy is performing.

When you monitor your policy, evaluate the same factors you considered when shopping for it in the first place. If you notice signs of trouble in your insurer's financial position, look closer to try to identify the specific cause. Decreases in certain measurements can be signs of growth, not decline, but you should take the time to find out more before you decide which it is. A financial adviser can help you navigate performance information that is publicly available if necessary.

If you become dissatisfied with your policy's performance, you may eventually need to decide whether to let it go. Before you make the final call, answer three questions.

First, what is your health like compared to when you first bought the policy? If you have developed a serious or chronic health condition, or if you are just significantly older than when you bought the policy, a new policy may be much more expensive or offer much smaller benefits, if you can get one at all. It is always a good idea to obtain a new policy before you let your original one lapse, so you don't go without coverage if getting a new policy is harder than you anticipated.

Second, is switching worth the extra upfront costs? You already paid these costs on your original policy and won't recoup them, so you will need to weigh whether they're worth paying again.

Finally, if you have a permanent life insurance policy, you need to ask whether changing policies will be worth the potential income tax consequences. If your policy's cash surrender value is greater than the amount of premiums you have paid, the difference is treated as ordinary income, subject to federal income tax. You will also owe state income tax if you live in a state that levies one. (For more on federal and state income tax, see Chapter 15.) There is a technique, called a Section 1035 exchange, which lets you trade an existing permanent life insurance policy for a new permanent policy without incurring tax. For a Section 1035 exchange to work, the owner, the insured and beneficiary must be the same on the old and new contracts. It is best to involve a tax professional if you intend to pursue this technique.

Even if you decide to keep your current policy, you may want to adjust the way that you pay premiums. Universal life and variable universal life policies give policyholders the option of using dividend payments to cover future premiums, so a well-performing policy could become self-funding. When you evaluate whether you should set up your policy this way, consider not only the policy's performance, but also how much coverage your premiums can buy and the amount you could earn by investing money you would have paid in premiums elsewhere. This calculation can be complex. A financial adviser can illustrate a variety of scenarios based on different variables, both in and outside your control, which can help you make an informed decision.

CHANGING LIFE INSURANCE NEEDS

Your insurance needs will likely change over the course of your life. Certain major life events can mean it's time to revisit your life insurance coverage. These might include marriage, divorce, children, a decline in a parent's health, homeownership or career changes. It is also sensible to revisit your insurance coverage every so often, even in the absence of these major life changes. Your estate planning considerations may change, and it is likely any income you are protecting will grow as you progress in your career.

Beneficiaries

One aspect of your policy worth reviewing periodically is your beneficiary designations. When you first set up a policy, you will name a beneficiary. You can name one or more primary beneficiaries, as well as contingent beneficiaries who will receive the death benefit if the primary beneficiary dies before you do. Most married people name their spouse as their primary beneficiary. If you are mainly concerned about protecting business income, you can name the organization itself as beneficiary. For those planning to use life insurance as part of an estate plan, a charitable organization can also serve as a policy's primary or contingent beneficiary. If you name multiple primary beneficiaries, they will split the death benefit, either evenly or in proportions you choose. If you don't name a beneficiary at all, the insurer will pay the death benefit directly to your estate.

While your beneficiary is up to you, some states restrict whom you can name. You may need your spouse's consent to name someone else as beneficiary of a policy if you live in a community property state and the policy is purchased with community funds. (If you aren't familiar with community property laws, see Chapter 11 for an explanation.) Unmarried couples living together once faced the roadblock of proving an "insurable interest" — in other words, that the insured's death would financially impact the survivor. But these days such arrangements are more common and the rules have become less strict. However, you must still have an insurable interest to purchase life insurance. If you own a home together, co-signed for a lease, jointly own investments or have children together, proving an insurable interest will be fairly straightforward. Single parents should also note that naming a minor child as the beneficiary of your policy can create legal complications. Minors can't directly receive insurance benefits, which means that if they are named as the beneficiary, the courts will step in to manage distribution, potentially in ways you wouldn't choose. It often makes more sense to name the person who will serve as your child's guardian or another adult custodian as the beneficiary on behalf of your child, or to set up a trust on your child's behalf. Regardless of whom you name as a beneficiary, be sure to tell them, even if they are a contingent beneficiary. It's also wise to alert whoever is serving as your estate executor, so they know how to contact your policy's beneficiaries if necessary.

While your life insurance beneficiary is up to you, some states restrict whom you can name.

Generally, you designate a beneficiary as revocable or irrevocable at the outset. Revocable beneficiaries can later be removed from your policy, with or without notice. If you are single but think you may get married one day, you could name a parent or an adult sibling as your revocable beneficiary, with plans to switch it to your spouse in the future. Irrevocable beneficiaries cannot be removed from the policy without their consent. If you need to change a beneficiary, revocable beneficiaries are fairly straightforward but irrevocable beneficiaries are more involved by design, so think carefully about your designations. Also bear in mind that even if your beneficiaries' identities do not change, you will need to periodically make sure their contact information is still accurate. Some insurers allow you to update your beneficiaries online, while others require a physical form, so you will need to check your company's requirements. But in general the process isn't meant to be burdensome.

Adding More Coverage

If your financial position has changed and you need additional coverage, you could shop for an entirely new policy. As I previously mentioned, do not surrender your existing policy until you secure new coverage, and involve a professional if you intend to perform a Section 1035 exchange. But if you like your current policy, you may not need to start from scratch. Once you have a new amount of coverage in mind, your next step will depend on the type of policy you have. If you have a term policy, you cannot increase the coverage amount, so you may need to apply for an additional policy to expand coverage. Depending on your needs, you may look for a new policy with a shorter term than your original policy. Remember that your premiums will likely be higher, since you are older than when you first applied. If you have a permanent policy, you can check to see if your carrier offers a guaranteed insurability rider. This rider allows you to increase your coverage limit without going through the underwriting process a second time. Depending on the rider, you may be able to add coverage after a particular life event, such as the birth of a child, or after a certain number of years holding your original policy.

Canceling Or Surrendering A Policy

Because term life insurance is "pure" insurance, it has no cash surrender value. If you want to end the policy early, either because you have secured a different policy or because the need for your insurance went away sooner than expected, you can generally cancel it. You can either notify your insurer in writing or, in many cases, just stop paying premiums for long enough that your policy lapses. While you won't get any benefits, you won't pay any future premiums, either. In some cases, this can be a sensible approach.

Surrendering a permanent life insurance policy is more complicated. Each policy has its own forfeiture rules, so you will need to consult your policy documents to make sure you understand the particulars. In general, the first step will be to contact your insurer. Depending on how long you've held the policy, you may be able to cash it out. However, this transaction may be subject to significant fees within the contract's "surrender period," which may be as long as 10 or 20 years in some instances. During the first few years of the surrender period, there may be no cash value left to redeem after fees and penalties apply. Cash value from a policy is also subject to income tax if you receive a greater value than the premiums you paid in.

Some insurers offer a "reduced paid-up option" on permanent life insurance policies. This approach lets you stop paying premiums but maintain a reduced death benefit on your whole life policy. You won't have immediate cash in hand, but this can be a reasonable way to avoid income tax and insurer penalties if the option is available to you. Some insurers may also allow you to use the cash value of your plan to buy a smaller, less expensive policy. A financial adviser can help you to work through your options, depending on the reasons you are surrendering your original policy.

TAX PLANNING

If you plan to use your policy to transfer wealth or provide estate liquidity, it is important to make sure that you have structured your estate so that the policy doesn't create new liabilities for your heirs. Assets in life insurance policies accumulate income tax-free, and in most cases death benefits aren't subject to income tax either. But if you own your own policy, which is the case for most people, the policy's death benefit is included in your gross estate. If your estate is large enough to be subject to federal or state estate tax, this tax will reduce the total value of assets your heirs receive.

The best way to avoid this problem is to have someone else own your policy. This can be another person, such as a trusted relative. You can also place the policy in an Irrevocable Life Insurance Trust (ILIT). The trust becomes the policy's owner and its beneficiary. The trustee — who must be someone other than you — takes on the responsibility of managing the life insurance policy. If you don't want to designate an individual trustee, you can also designate a corporate fiduciary. A corporate fiduciary is an institution, such as a bank or a trust company, acting for the benefit of another (in this case, you and the named beneficiaries).

As the name suggests, an irrevocable trust involves permanently giving up control of your policy. You cannot make changes to the policy itself, or to the terms of the trust, once the ILIT is in place. This is why choosing a trustee is so important; depending on state law, the trustee may be able to make some changes to the policy, though even these are limited and may trigger tax consequences. Using an ILIT also means you give up the ability to borrow against your policy. In order for the trust to function as designed, you must give up any "incidents of ownership," including the ability to change beneficiaries or to surrender the policy.

Even though the trust is the policy's owner, the trustee you designate will usually not want to pay premiums out of pocket. Therefore, you will need to set up a way to fund the trust. Because any assets you add to the trust can be considered gifts to the beneficiary, you need to be mindful of gift taxes when setting up this funding. You can give a set annual amount — $18,000 per recipient in 2024 — completely gift tax-free. However, this gift must be of a "present interest" to the recipient; in other words, the recipient must be able to access the gift immediately.

Luckily, it is enough to give the recipients the option to withdraw the assets right away, even if they don't actually withdraw it. This technique is known as using "Crummey" powers. To qualify assets for the annual gift tax exclusion, the trustee must notify beneficiaries of their right to withdraw any money you give to the trust. Usually beneficiaries will have a set amount of time, such as 30 or 60 days, to make any withdrawals. After that, the assets are available to the trust for premium payments or other expenses. Beneficiaries usually understand this arrangement if you explain it to them. But the requirements of this setup mean you must time your gifts so that the money is available for the entire withdrawal window, even if you already know the beneficiaries will not exercise their rights to it.

If you decide an ILIT is right for you, it's usually best to create the trust first and then have the trust take out the insurance policy. You can move a preexisting policy into a trust. But for the first three years after the transfer, any death benefits will still be subject to estate tax if it applies, just as if the policy remained in your name. Similar timing considerations apply if you transfer an existing policy to another individual.

If you decide an Irrevocable Life Insurance Trust is right for you, it's usually best to create the trust first and then have the trust take out the insurance policy.

COLLECTING BENEFITS

By design, you will not be around when your beneficiaries collect the death benefit of your life insurance policy. But that does not mean you shouldn't do all you can to make it as easy as possible for them. Luckily, insurers try to make benefit collection easy. After the insured dies, the estate executor or the policy's beneficiaries should notify the insurance company. The carrier will usually provide a claims package with the necessary paperwork. The executor or beneficiaries should complete these forms and return them, along with a certified copy of the insured's death certificate. Once the insurer processes these documents and approves the claim, it will distribute the death benefit. Your part in all this is to keep your insurance records in good order and make sure that someone close to you knows where to find them. It is also a good idea to keep the beneficiaries' contact information with your insurance documents. If you have an estate planning binder or other master document, include your insurance arrangements and keep them up to date.

FINAL THOUGHTS

Many young professionals consider life insurance boring or unnecessary. In reality, it is an important part of your overall financial plan. You may want to protect your dependents or your business, or you may find life insurance a useful long-term wealth transfer and estate planning tool. Fully understanding what life insurance can do and how to secure the best policy for your needs can help you to make the most of it.

CHAPTER 11

MARRIAGE AND PRENUPS

David Walters, CPA, CFP®

Deciding to get married is a significant milestone, even for couples who have lived together for years before tying the knot. You and your partner are blending your lives into a single family unit legally, socially and, of course, financially.

In the busy time stretching between engagement and the wedding day, the last thing you may want to do is sit down with your soon-to-be-spouse to discuss the ways you will fit your financial lives together. But the time for these conversations is well before you say "I do." Not only will communicating now about finances set you up to reach your goals, but establishing a habit of talking about money can reduce stress throughout married life. According to research conducted by The Harris Poll on behalf of the American Institute of CPAs in 2021, 73% of married or cohabiting couples said that financial decisions had been a source of tension in the relationship at least once. Pushing through any discomfort and communicating honestly from the beginning can help you avoid this common source of relationship stress.

MARRIAGE: WHEN TWO (FINANCIAL LIVES) BECOME ONE

When you decide to marry your partner, one of the many implications is that you will blend your finances to some degree. This is why the first and most important step to approaching money as a married couple is to have open and honest conversations on the topic — before the wedding day. Many people find discussing money difficult, even with loved ones, but it really is essential to your future financial success.

Have a conversation, or several, in which you both set out a clear picture of your assets, debts and credit. One or both of you may be embarrassed, but it is better to get any potential issues out in the open as soon as possible. You will not improve the potential reaction by springing problems on your partner as a surprise in the future. If one (or both) of you carries major credit card debt, has a low credit score or has not resolved some outstanding tax issues, you should talk about how to approach these problems as a team. You should also know it is perfectly normal if you and your partner come to your union with different financial backgrounds. In particular, it is common for one to carry more debt into the marriage than the other, especially student loan debt. At this stage, the biggest red flag is not a past financial mistake or burden, but a partner who refuses to talk about money at all.

You and your partner should also discuss whether you prefer joint accounts, individual accounts or both. There is no right answer. The best approach depends on your circumstances and personalities. Both partners should communicate their needs and preferences, and listen to the needs and preferences of the other. Completely merging your accounts makes it easier to handle joint expenses and simplifies the work of keeping track of your accounts. However, it means a lot of checking in with one another day-to-day, with less privacy and independence for each of you. Separate accounts give you more autonomy but can make it more complicated to save for joint goals (like a house down payment) or to handle joint expenses on short notice. A blend of both joint and separate accounts can balance the downsides of an either-or approach. But this system requires you to determine what each of you will contribute to the joint account, and what expenses you will pay jointly and separately. Keep in mind that whatever choice you make needn't be permanent; if something isn't working, you can always try another approach.

Depending on where you live, state law may also affect your financial picture. Nine states — Arizona, California, Idaho, Louisiana, Nevada, New Mexico, Texas, Washington and Wisconsin — are "community property" states. In these, any property or debt that either spouse acquires during a marriage is considered the property or debt of both partners. If you live in one of these nine places, even if you decide to keep separate accounts, those accounts are considered property of the couple unless they predate the marriage (and, in some states, even then). Alaska, Florida, South Dakota and Tennessee have optional community property systems, in which couples can agree to hold some or all of their property in community under state law. If you may be subject to community property law, be sure to investigate the exact rules in your state, because the particulars can vary.

Your choice about whether to maintain separate accounts or to merge everything may depend on how compatible your saving and spending patterns are.

Realistically, even outside community property states, the choice to keep separate accounts does not mean your finances and your partner's will never affect one another. For example, in nearly all cases you are not on the hook for student loan debt your spouse incurred before you married. But every dollar your spouse spends to pay down that debt is a dollar that cannot go toward other joint financial goals. Similarly, your spouse's credit score does not directly affect yours. (See Chapter 3 for more information on the way credit scores work.) But if your spouse's credit is in bad shape, it could hinder your future plans to buy a house or jointly apply for any sort of loan. You may need to prioritize rebuilding your partner's credit score before you can pursue certain financial goals.

Your choice about whether to maintain separate accounts or to merge everything may, in part, depend on how compatible your saving and spending patterns are. If you have been together a few years, you likely have some sense of whether your partner tends to splurge or is scrupulously frugal, but you should have a frank discussion about your respective approaches to money. This should go beyond your shopping habits. What financial fears do each bring to the table? How do you feel about risk in long-term investing? Dig below the surface to really understand your partner's relationship with his or her finances.

In some cases, you may need to discuss different approaches to income. One of you may be used to a traditional job with a steady, biweekly paycheck. The other may freelance or be an independent consultant accustomed to sometimes unpredictable income. Or perhaps one is an entrepreneur who runs a business. In cases like these, you should discuss how each of you is used to handling income, and work on a plan for blending your approaches in a sensible way.

By the time you plan to marry, you have likely discussed some of your hopes and dreams. But it is worth taking the time to talk seriously about the financial component of these dreams, too. What career trajectory does each of you have in mind? Do you plan to have children? If so, does one of you plan to stay home, either part-time or full-time? For how long? If either has children from a previous relationship, you should discuss how you plan to provide for them.

All of this will naturally lead to a conversation in which you discuss your joint financial goals. Goals are key to both budgeting and investing, and it pays to align yours as a couple. You may want to prioritize paying off debt, repairing credit, pursuing homeownership or a variety of other potential goals. Perhaps one wants to travel abroad, while the other would prefer to save aggressively for early retirement. It may take time to talk through your goals and identify points of potential compromise, if necessary. Make sure you and your partner are on the same page about which goals you want to prioritize. Once you know this, you can start to consider how to achieve them.

You may already have individual budgets, but you will need to discuss how to merge them into a family budget that works for you both. Be willing to compromise. For instance, if you come up with very different numbers for what you'd prefer to spend on rent, listen to your partner's logic and priorities. You may settle on the lower number with the understanding that you'll revisit the situation in a year or two. Or maybe you settle on a higher rent, but split it 60-40 or 75-25, rather than 50-50. The most important thing is not the ultimate solution but a commitment to listen with an open mind and stay flexible. Good short-term budgeting goals are the wedding itself, a honeymoon or both. The two of you can talk through how much you each envision spending and how you are willing to rearrange your spending habits to save that amount. You and your partner may not naturally approach a budget the same way, but patience and communication are key to blending your approaches. (For more on ways to budget, see Chapter 3.)

Many couples divide financial responsibilities, while others leave most financial duties to one person. One spouse may have more of a talent or affinity than the other for paying bills, tracking expenses or managing investments. In that case, both partners may be happier if the split is not even. Or you may choose for one spouse to handle day-to-day budgeting and the other to handle investing. You should also discuss whether you want professional help, and if so, in what capacity. It is possible one partner already has a financial adviser, through parents or independently. You can discuss whether you prefer to keep that adviser or shop around as a couple. Including an adviser can also help couples resolve issues when partners differ in philosophy or approach.

For many couples, talking frankly about money is easier said than done. Even if you understand the importance of clear and honest communication, it can be emotionally difficult to start. It may be helpful to set up a monthly or quarterly family meeting to check in and make sure you are still on the same page. If financial discussions become a regular part of your lives, formally or informally, these conversations will become less daunting over time. Regular check-ins also make it less likely that major money conflicts will brew out of sight, threatening to crop up in a fight rather than in a calm discussion.

Taxes For Married Couples

Newlyweds face a major choice in their first tax season as a couple: how to file their income tax returns. The Internal Revenue Service offers two options for couples: joint or separate filing. In most cases, filing jointly means a lower overall tax bill. This is because joint filers are subject to higher income thresholds for certain taxes and deductions, so they can still access these tax breaks at a higher income level than each partner could separately. For example, married taxpayers who file jointly receive a standard deduction of $29,200 (as of tax year 2024). If you are filing separately, you get $14,600 each, with a catch: You must both claim the standard deduction or both itemize your deductions. (For more on the standard deduction and other tax topics, see Chapter 15.)

Couples who file separately are automatically disqualified from certain tax deductions and credits. For instance, if your modified adjusted gross income is low enough to allow you to deduct interest paid on your student loans, the only way to do so is to file jointly. Couples who file separately also may not be able to deduct contributions to employer-sponsored retirement plans if their incomes exceed a set threshold. Separate filers cannot claim the earned income credit, the American Opportunity Credit or the Lifetime Learning Credit. And if you have a child, generally only one spouse can claim the associated tax breaks if you file separately.

If you are not sure which tax filing status to use, calculate your tax liability both ways to see which option is more beneficial. Bear in mind that the best answer may change from year to year.

Despite these drawbacks, there are times when filing separately makes sense. A major example is when one spouse is enrolled in an income-based repayment plan for student loans. In most cases, if you file separately, your payment will be based on your income alone, not your joint income. Filing separately may be the best or only way to preserve the borrower's eligibility and keep monthly payments low if the other spouse has significant income. Another possible scenario in which separate filing makes sense is a year in which one spouse incurs high out-of-pocket medical expenses. The IRS allows taxpayers to deduct the amount of medical costs that exceed 7.5% of the taxpayer's adjusted gross income; this threshold may be easier to reach for couples who file separately, especially if the partners have very different incomes.

Beyond your filing status, marriage includes a variety of other tax changes, some of which are significant perks. For example, you can make tax-free gifts of any amount to one another (as long as the recipient spouse is a U.S. citizen), a benefit not available to unmarried partners. You can also make joint gifts to third parties, allowing you to give them a greater amount before triggering federal gift tax. (For more on gift and transfer taxes, see Chapter 16.)

Because marriage has such a major impact on your tax situation, you and your spouse may want to talk with a tax professional, especially before your first income tax season as a couple. Regardless, if you are not sure which filing status to use, the best plan is to calculate your tax liability both ways to see which option is more beneficial. As with other financial choices you make, bear in mind that the best answer may change from year to year.

Estate Planning For Newlyweds

If you don't already have an estate plan in place, marriage is a good trigger to sit down and get started. And if one or both of you already have one, take the time to thoroughly update it in light of your changed family circumstances.

First and foremost, you both need a will. While a will is important for everyone, it is critical if you already have children, either together or from previous relationships. If you die intestate — that is, without a will — the court will determine who gets custody of your children based on the laws in your jurisdiction. This can create messy custody battles, or it can mean that a family member is suddenly responsible for your children without having opted in previously. As part of estate planning, you and your partner should discuss potential guardians, and ensure the guardian or guardians you choose are up for the job. (Note that if one of you brings children to the marriage and shares custody with their other parent, you will need his or her consent for any guardianship decisions you make.) You may also want to set up a trust to safeguard any minor children's financial future. A will can provide instructions for the care of any pets, too, although you can't leave assets directly to an animal. Instead, you can name a new caregiver and leave assets designated for your pet's care to that person.

Apart from any dependents, you will need to discuss how you want to distribute any joint assets. As a married couple, you and your partner have new options when leaving assets to one another. All property you give to your spouse during life or leave to your spouse upon your death is free of federal gift and estate tax, if the surviving spouse is a U.S. citizen. Also, the "portability" rule means that married couples can treat their individual estate tax exemptions as one large, combined exemption. If the first spouse to die does not use all of his or her lifetime exemption, whatever is left can be transferred to the survivor. (For more details, see Chapter 16.) Marriage also gives you more options for using individual retirement accounts; if one spouse works and one does not, the working spouse may contribute to an IRA in the nonworking spouse's name, subject to certain requirements. You may also roll over a deceased spouse's IRA into the survivor's IRA without triggering immediate required minimum distributions. You may wish to update your will to name your spouse as your executor, though you always should name a backup executor as well. (For more on wills, see Chapter 12.)

You should take the opportunity to update the listed beneficiary on any retirement accounts or life insurance policies you already hold. Generally, beneficiary designations take precedence over a will, so it's important that your beneficiary designation reflects your wishes. Be sure to update any 401(k) plans, IRAs or brokerage accounts. Some other accounts may also offer the ability to directly designate a beneficiary through a "transfer on death" registration. If one of you has a pension, you can also elect survivor's benefits. Note that, in certain circumstances, if you don't want to designate your spouse as the beneficiary of a particular account, you may need to get your spouse's consent in writing. Be sure to pay attention to the requirements for various accounts and policies. If either of you brings property such as homes or cars to the marriage, you may also want to retitle the ownership documents if you plan to own the property jointly going forward.

It is also important to revisit your overall insurance situation together. For example, your life insurance needs may shift now that you are part of a family unit, and again if children enter the picture. In addition, you will likely want to consider your respective health insurance options. In most cases, it will be more economical to add a spouse to one of your existing plans than to maintain separate individual health insurance policies. Marriage qualifies as a special enrollment period, so be sure to time your adjustment accordingly. If both of you have cars, you may also save on premiums by merging your auto insurance policies.

You may wish to set up health care proxies for one another. While marriage gives your spouse more rights in making decisions about your care, naming your spouse as your proxy will give him or her greater leeway to proceed if you are incapacitated or unable to communicate. Of course, this means you should discuss your wishes regarding life-sustaining care and resuscitation in advance, too. You may also want to consider giving each other durable power of attorney. This legal document will allow your spouse to pay bills, manage bank accounts, file taxes and generally manage your financial life on your behalf if necessary.

Getting Married: A Financial Checklist

In summary, here are some major topics to cover before — and shortly after — you tie the knot.

Before The Wedding

- ✓ Discuss your existing assets, debts and credit scores.
- ✓ Identify separate and joint financial goals, long term and short term.
- ✓ Decide whether you want separate accounts, joint accounts or both.
- ✓ Determine whether you live in a community property state, as well as the particular laws in your jurisdiction.
- ✓ Create a blended household budget.
- ✓ Decide who will be responsible for various joint financial tasks.
- ✓ Determine whether you want a prenuptial agreement — and, if so, create and sign it well before the wedding.

Within The First Year

- ✓ Decide whether to file taxes jointly or separately.
- ✓ Create or update wills and other estate planning documents.
- ✓ Update beneficiary designations on existing retirement accounts and life insurance policies.
- ✓ Retitle any property such as cars and houses (if desired).
- ✓ Evaluate your joint insurance situation and make any necessary adjustments.
- ✓ Set up health care proxies and/or powers of attorney for one another.

PRENUPTIAL AGREEMENTS THAT WORK

Few engaged couples want to dwell on the possibility that their union may not last, so it is understandable that some people may resist the idea of a prenuptial agreement. Whether you feel you would be spending a lot of money and effort to create something you are confident you won't need, or you harbor a superstitious worry that you might "jinx" your upcoming marriage, it is easy to talk yourself out of a prenup. But for many couples, creating a prenuptial agreement is prudent and sensible. It no more demonstrates a lack of faith in the marriage than buying homeowners insurance demonstrates lack of faith in your home's construction.

Who Needs A Prenup?

A prenuptial or premarital agreement is a written contract two people enter into before marrying. At its most basic, it outlines how the couple will divide their assets and earnings in case of a divorce. Without such an agreement, the parties will have to decide how to divide assets during the divorce itself. Attempting to make reasonable decisions in the midst of a dissolving marriage is difficult at best and sometimes impossible. This can add costly attorney's fees for both parties, and if the parties can't agree on terms, the courts will use state law as a guide.

While any couple can benefit from a prenuptial agreement, in some cases they go from smart planning to a true necessity. Many people have the misconception that prenups are only for the very wealthy; this is not true. However, if the partners enter a marriage with vastly different levels of wealth, a prenuptial agreement is an especially good idea. Similarly, even if both partners have similar levels of assets at the time of the wedding, one may expect to earn much more in the future — say, after finishing an advanced degree. Or he or she may expect a substantial inheritance or be the beneficiary of a trust. One or both partners may also have children from a previous marriage to consider. Any of these circumstances mean the couple would benefit from negotiating a premarital agreement.

Another major indicator that a prenup is a good idea is that one of you owns a business. Amazon founder Jeff Bezos married a year before he launched his company; when he and his wife, MacKenzie Bezos (now MacKenzie Scott), divorced 25 years later, the split involved what had become the world's largest fortune. While this extreme case is obviously an outlier, entrepreneurs with ambitious plans should consider getting specific about control and ownership of business assets during the prenuptial-agreement process.

Finally, much like estate planning, prenuptial planning can benefit individuals concerned about their privacy. Without a premarital agreement, you may find yourself subject to your state's law or a judge's discretion concerning asset distribution in a divorce. Most states dictate equitable distribution of assets, though this may not mean equal distribution of assets. In states without community property laws, assets acquired during a marriage may not be split down the middle, but rather divided in view of the partners' relative potential earning power, the income each contributed during the marriage, and the value at stake if one partner stayed home with any children part- or full-time. The process of dividing marital assets without a premarital agreement puts the question of fairness in the court's hands, and opens your personal assets and earning power to public scrutiny.

Say you are convinced, or were already leaning in the direction of a prenuptial agreement, but you are worried about what your partner will think if you broach the topic. While there is no foolproof method to bring up a potentially sensitive subject, there are a few pitfalls to avoid. Bring up the potential of a prenup soon after the engagement, or even before you get engaged. Present it as something important to you, but avoid framing it as an ultimatum. Be honest about your own feelings, even if it is difficult. Do not produce a full agreement for your partner to take or leave; you and your partner should draft a prenuptial agreement together if you decide to make one. And if your partner has concerns, listen to them with an open mind. Like any other financial conversation, broaching a prenup is not always easy, but it needn't be the start of a fight if you approach it honestly and with an open mind.

How To Create A Solid Prenuptial Agreement

First and foremost, both partners need legal representation. While there are many times in your married life the same attorney can represent you both, this is not one of them. Many lawyers would not be comfortable representing parties on opposite sides of a negotiation. Even if you find an attorney who would agree to represent both of you, a court might not enforce such an agreement. For example, if the agreement appeared to tilt in favor of the party who paid the lawyer, the court might suspect the other partner had not been treated fairly. Both partners should secure legal advice from an experienced attorney who is not worried about split loyalty.

Once both of you have legal representation, the next step is to disclose all relevant information. This practice is not only fair but prudent to make sure your prenuptial agreement is binding. If it comes out that one partner hid assets or debts during the negotiation, it could invalidate the entire contract.

To start, create a list of all your current assets. For many people getting married, especially as young adults, the major asset may be each spouse's earning power. Then take stock of your projected income, future trust distributions, and any major gifts or inheritance you expect to receive. You may need to involve your parents or other relatives, and possibly consult with their financial advisers, to get a full picture of what you can expect. You should also inventory your educational loans or any other significant debt you carry. At this stage, you and your partner may want to agree to pull one another's credit report, too.

QUICK NOTES

Creating A Prenup — A Checklist

- ☑ Secure separate legal representation for both partners
- ☑ Disclose all relevant information, including assets and debts
- ☑ Make sure you understand the relevant state laws
- ☑ Complete the process well in advance of the wedding (no less than 30 days prior)

You should familiarize yourself with the laws of your state. Some states have adopted the Uniform Premarital and Marital Agreements Act (UPMAA), which provides a template for such agreements. Other states previously adopted the Uniform Premarital Agreement Act (UPAA), an older version of a similar template. Even with these templates, the details of state laws vary. Certain features are fairly consistent, however. Many states stipulate that a prenuptial agreement that is so unfair an informed party would never agree to it is unenforceable. For example, if an agreement's provisions would render one of the parties eligible for public assistance, it is unconscionable and a court is unlikely to uphold it. State law will also come into play as you and your partner consider the question of alimony. In certain states, spouses cannot legally waive the right to alimony in a prenuptial agreement. If you plan to include such a provision, make sure your state allows it first. Note, too, that some states automatically invalidate prenuptial agreements after a certain amount of time, or if the couple has a child. If you do not want to embrace such a sunset arrangement, you may need to explore other planning options, such as trusts.

Finally, give yourself plenty of time to complete the process. Aim to have everything done and signed well in advance of the wedding; a good rule of thumb is no less than 30 days prior to the big day. Not only does this mean you will not have to worry about your prenup while juggling the other stressors related to wedding planning, it will help your agreement stand up to legal scrutiny. Some courts have refused to enforce last-minute premarital agreements, on the grounds that at least one of the partners was under duress. Completing the process in advance allows both partners to approach the decisions involved thoughtfully and calmly.

Elements Of A Good Prenup

Each couple is different, so the details of each prenuptial agreement will reflect the unique assets and circumstances the partners bring to the marriage. Even so, all good prenups have a few factors in common.

First, you and your partner should approach the negotiation from a place of fairness. In a well-constructed prenup, there should be no losers. Your goal is not to extract every possible asset from your partner. Instead, you want to settle on an agreement that gives you both the assurance that you can exit the marriage with your finances — and self-esteem — intact. Presumably you love your partner. Even though you are on opposite sides of the negotiation, treat your partner with consideration and respect.

Second, a good prenup should be both clear and simple. Confine your prenup to the basic financial and legal issues you need to settle. Not only will this make negotiations smoother, but a court will be more likely to enforce your agreement as you intend.

The particular financial and legal issues will depend on your circumstances, but here are a few items to consider including.

A clear trigger. When will your prenuptial agreement take effect? A well-selected trigger is some event that is easy for a third party to observe or verify. Good choices may include a partner filing for divorce or the divorce taking legal effect. If one partner moving out is the trigger, be as specific as possible. What exactly does moving out entail? How long must he or she be gone before the agreement takes effect? Avoid vague terms such as "a separation." The more specific, the better. For example, you may define the triggering event as one spouse informing the other in writing of an intent to dissolve the marriage. Further specifying that such a notice should be sent via registered mail allows everyone to be precise about the trigger's date and eliminates potential ambiguity.

Vesting guidelines. Many prenuptial agreements include a mechanism by which one spouse's interest in the other's assets vests. If your main concern is a marriage falling apart quickly, you may not mind equitable division of marital assets by state guidelines after a longer union. In this case, you could decide that a spouse's interest in the other's assets vests over a certain term of years, or once you have a child together. Of course, you may also forgo vesting altogether, but bear in mind any sunset provisions built into your state's law.

Definitions of individual and joint property. One of the main purposes of a prenuptial agreement is to define separate and joint property. Do you plan to treat all assets and property you bring to the marriage as joint property once you say "I do"? What about retirement accounts, gifts from third parties to a particular spouse or future bequests? Discuss to what extent you plan to treat these assets as separate in case of divorce. Don't forget to do the same for any debts or liabilities one of you incurred before the marriage. If you do not live in a community property state, you should also discuss ownership of any property you acquire as a couple. The answers you arrive at are less important than the fact that you and your partner agree in advance on what constitutes individual property and joint property. This can lessen the chances of messy disputes in a possible future separation.

Advanced degrees and professional licenses. In some states, a professional license is considered an asset subject to division in the case of a divorce. Typically, this only applies to degrees a spouse earned during the marriage, though you should check your state's rules. If you earned your CPA license or became a medical doctor while married, the court may decide your spouse has a claim against a share of that credential's value. If your partner helped pay for your training or education, some compensation may be appropriate. But if you paid to obtain your license or degree yourself, you may wish to specify in your prenuptial agreement that your credentials aren't subject to division in case of a divorce.

Some other provisions will depend on the discussions every married couple should have. For example, if you decided to maintain separate bank accounts, it may be wise to specify that spouses are entitled to maintain separate accounts not subject to division in a divorce, but that assets in a joint account are joint property. Bear in mind that couples living in community property states may face additional complications, depending on their plans.

In addition to items to include, you should avoid some common pitfalls. A prenuptial agreement is not the place to decide how many children you want to have or how you plan to raise them. Don't include items such as where you will live or how you will celebrate major holidays, either. All of these topics are good to discuss before the wedding day, but that does not mean they should be in your premarital agreement. You should also avoid including frivolous items — for example, that you will always do the dishes while your spouse will always do the laundry. Such provisions are, at best, unenforceable. At worst, they may lead a judge to invalidate the entire contract.

Prenuptial agreements cannot determine custody or visitation for your future children with one another. They can, however, govern these matters for any children either spouse brings to the marriage. Prenups can also include details of potential future child support. But in general, it is better to specify that such arrangements will be determined by mutual agreement, or by the court, if they become an issue. Unless you have children from prior relationships, leave children out of your prenuptial agreement entirely.

You may have noticed that, throughout this chapter, I've returned over and over again to the importance of starting financial conversations and revisiting them over time. As in other areas of a marriage, successfully blending your financial lives is largely a matter of honesty and trust. Getting in the habit of frank communication, even when it makes you feel vulnerable, sets you and your partner up for financial success in all areas of your life. After all, while you will inevitably face highs and lows in your future, you are in it together.

CHAPTER 12

WHAT ESTATE PLANNING DOCUMENTS DO I NEED?

Shomari D. Hearn, CFP®, EA and Kasey Radney

Estate planning is not most younger adults' first priority. Many people have other priorities such as investing for long-term goals, establishing an emergency fund or preparing to purchase a home. Some may dread the topic of death. Whether out of distraction or discomfort, you may be tempted to put off estate planning until later in life or until you feel you have accumulated enough wealth.

You would not be alone if you gave in to this temptation. Many adults, especially those under age 40, wait too long to begin estate planning. A 2022 survey by financial services company D.A. Davidson found that 66% of Americans age 18 or older did not have an estate plan in place. In the same survey, 37% of respondents said they did not think they had enough money to need an estate plan, while 32% admitted to procrastinating. A full quarter of respondents said they did not have a plan because they did not know where to start.

Deciding what will happen to your possessions when you die may seem intimidating and not especially urgent, especially for young adults. However, although it is never too early to begin estate planning, it can be too late. While death or incapacity are less likely for younger adults, neither is impossible. If you have wishes about your own medical care, for example, making those wishes explicit can ensure your loved ones carry them out and can help to avoid unnecessary infighting. And while you may not feel you have accumulated enough assets to warrant a plan, if you have children, a will is absolutely critical. Your estate plan will determine where your children will go upon your death. Without a plan in place, the state will decide who will care for them. There is no guarantee the courts will choose the guardian you would have preferred.

If you are among those who simply do not know where to begin, we hope that you will find this chapter especially helpful. It is true that estate planning can be a complex and time-consuming process, depending on your personal and financial circumstances. In certain cases, it may be prudent to work with a professional adviser for additional guidance. But even a simple estate plan is much better than no plan at all.

ESSENTIAL ESTATE PLANNING DOCUMENTS

Wills

A last will and testament is a legally binding document that determines how your assets will be distributed upon your death. It may also appoint guardians for your children and other dependents (such as elderly relatives), or caregivers for pets. A will is one of the primary documents in an estate plan, and it is essential for providing information about your final wishes.

Generally, wills are presented to the local probate court, which is the section of the judiciary that oversees the handling of estates, guardianships and several related areas of law. A properly drafted will appoints an "executor," a person — or occasionally a group of people or an institution — who is responsible for carrying out the will's terms. (We will discuss executors in more detail later in this section.) After the probate court receives a valid will, the court will authorize the executor to distribute the assets according to the will's instructions. Executing the will and administering an estate may involve paying debts, distributing property, or dealing with outstanding tax obligations. When done well, a binding will ensures that your assets go to the people or organizations you choose, and that any dependents are placed with the intended guardians, who have agreed to serve in that capacity.

A well-written will can ensure the smooth transition of your assets and make sure your wishes are carried out. Your will should:

- Establish your identity
- Revoke any former wills
- Name an executor, and a successor executor if the primary executor is unable or unwilling to serve
- Name beneficiaries
- Name guardians for any minor children or other dependents
- State how any debts or taxes associated with the estate will be paid
- Provide for any pets*

Your will should not:

- Include instructions for the distribution of any business interests (which are better passed via trust)
- Include conditions for your gifts (for example, "My daughter will only receive inheritance if she divorces her husband")

- Include detailed instructions for your memorial service or funeral arrangements
- Express wishes regarding assets that pass outside the probate process (such as retirement accounts or life insurance policies)
- Arrange for the care of a beneficiary with special needs**

**You cannot leave assets or property directly to an animal, but you may name a new caregiver and name that person a beneficiary of the assets designated for the pet's care.*
***For a beneficiary with special needs, you may want to set up a special needs trust. (See later in this chapter for more about trusts.)*

Many people associate wills with attorneys, and if your situation is complex, it is likely wise to work with an estate planning lawyer to draft yours. That said, it is not always necessary to involve an attorney to create a legally valid will. States differ in the rules they use to determine a will's validity, so it is vital to prepare your will following your state's legal requirements to ensure the court recognizes it. Regardless of where you live, it is a good idea to type your will rather than writing it by hand. It must also be signed and dated when you complete it. Another crucial requirement is that two adult witnesses who are not beneficiaries of the document sign your will. These witnesses will watch you sign the will, and they will then sign the document themselves. While most states do not require wills to be notarized, notarizing the document offers another safeguard against challenges to your will in court. The notary, like the witnesses, serves to verify that you are of sound mind and not influenced by anyone when you create your will. Both factors are necessary to create a valid document.

You will likely cross many milestones between creating your first will and your death, especially if you create it as a young adult. Once you create a will, it is important to keep it up to date and accurate. You should update your will when you experience certain major life events, such as the purchase of a new home; a marriage or divorce; the death of a loved one; receiving an inheritance; the birth of a child; or any major changes in your financial situation. You may also simply change your mind about beneficiaries or guardianship choices over time.

Worse than dying with an out-of-date will is dying with no will at all. If you die without a will in place, you have died "intestate." In this case, your assets would be distributed according to your state's intestacy laws. These laws generally distribute your assets to your relatives. Even if you do not object to this in theory, the distribution may not happen in the order or in the amounts you would have liked. Each state has its own intestacy laws; however, many base their codes on the 1990 Uniform Probate Code. These laws determine the order the court distributes your estate based on the hierarchy of surviving family members as follows:

- A surviving spouse
- Children or direct descendents (such as grandchildren)
- Parents
- Descendents of parents (siblings, nieces or nephews)
- Grandparents
- Descendents of grandparents (aunts or uncles, first cousins)

If you do not have any of these surviving relatives, your assets will go to the state. Additionally, property you might have preferred to set aside for people who are not your relatives or for charity will not go to them, even if you expressed your intentions during your life. Without a valid will, the probate court will make all decisions about your estate.

The ramifications of intestacy go beyond losing control of how your assets are distributed. The probate process can be lengthy and expensive, potentially placing a significant time burden and great financial cost on your loved ones. Probate is also fully public. Consider the estate of the late pop icon Prince. The artist died intestate in 2016 with a large number of assets that were complicated to value, including his extensive music catalog. The complexity of his estate contributed to an especially lengthy probate process. Lawyers and consultants for the state's administrator and the court-appointed beneficiaries disputed several aspects of the estate administration, drawing out the process further. In the end, it took six years to resolve Prince's estate; two of his heirs died before the case could be resolved.

Intestacy can make a mess of your assets, but the stakes are even higher for guardianship of your minor children. In the absence of a will, the court will appoint the new legal guardian of any minor children who are left without a surviving custodial parent, either because they had only one or because they have lost both (for example in a car accident). The court will generally appoint the closest available relative, so as not to exacerbate the children's trauma. The court will also accept active petitions by family members who wish to become the child's guardian; however, the court will usually favor a living biological parent who did not previously have custody over other petitioners. For blended families, this can lead to the separation of siblings. An even more unfortunate situation is if more than one person, or no one, actively seeks custody of the children.

If there is no living biological parent, the court usually favors grandparents, aunts, uncles, or other relatives, regardless of whether these individuals are in the best financial position to care for your children. For example, children may have one grandparent who lives close to their existing home but who is not financially stable, and another grandparent who is well-off but lives out of state. In this case, the court may favor the grandparent who lives farther away, causing even more upheaval for the minor dependents. The court may sometimes take older children's wishes into account, but it is not bound by them. In some states, the court will not even consider nonrelatives, meaning if you wished to appoint a friend, a romantic partner to whom you are not married, or an unrelated godparent, the court will ignore these wishes outright. If there are no relatives or other suitable individuals who step forward, the child will become a ward of the state and enter the foster system.

In the case of intestacy, the court must also appoint a guardian for any property it distributes to a minor. A guardian of property is someone the court names to manage money and property for a person who cannot legally receive these assets outright. This is generally true of minors, but it can also be someone whom the court has found unable to effectively manage the assets, such as an adult with intellectual disabilities. In the case of minor children, the court's selected guardian often also fulfills this role, but not always.

The ramifications of intestacy go beyond losing control of how your assets are distributed. The probate process can be lengthy and expensive, potentially placing a significant time burden and great financial cost on your loved ones.

Both a guardian and guardian of property are fiduciaries, whether the court appoints them or you name them in your will. A fiduciary is a person — or organization — that acts on your behalf in good faith to carry out your wishes. Their legal and ethical duty is to put your interests before their own. An executor is also a fiduciary, though the scope of their role is different, as we will discuss in the next section.

Choosing An Executor

Choosing an executor for your estate is an important decision. Many people select their spouses, siblings, or an adult child. These may seem like default choices, so much so that some people worry about offending by not picking one of them. However, consider the responsibilities that the executor will take on in administering the estate. Some family members may find the role overwhelming in the wake of your death. Do not simply pick the person you feel closest to emotionally. Instead, you should select an executor who you know to be trustworthy, and who you believe can work with professionals such as your attorney or financial adviser to carry out your wishes.

Your executor will take on the following duties:

- Locating and proving the validity of your will
- Notifying financial institutions, insurers and the Social Security Administration of your death
- Selling any real estate and personal property if necessary
- Finding and contacting beneficiaries
- Filing all required documents with the probate court
- Obtaining date-of-death valuations for any assets in your estate
- Identifying any outstanding debts and overseeing payment
- Assessing your estate's tax liability for income and estate taxes, and filing all related returns (including making a portability election, if necessary)
- Arranging the payment of estate expenses until the estate is closed
- Managing the estate's assets until they can be distributed to beneficiaries
- Overseeing the distribution of the estate to beneficiaries once debts and tax obligations are satisfied

As we mentioned, executors are fiduciaries, meaning they must prioritize the interests of your estate (in the form of your expressed wishes) over their own. The same is true of a trustee for any trusts you created prior to or at your death. A fiduciary must be an adult by state law, usually at least 18 years old, but 21 in some states. Generally, you may choose a family member, a friend or an adviser to serve as an executor or trustee. However, some states do require a noninstitutional fiduciary to be a family member. Certain states also prohibit any non-U.S. citizens or individuals who have been convicted of a felony from serving as a fiduciary. Check your state laws before selecting an executor, as well as considering who is best suited to the complicated and potentially time-consuming task.

Estates can be intricate, and executors may not know how to handle every question or task that arises. You should therefore pick an executor who will be comfortable seeking advice from financial advisers and legal counsel (assuming you do not name an institution as your executor in the first place). You may also want to factor in geographical location. Over the course of the estate administration, some processes may require the executor to handle them in person, especially if they involve legal documents. Some states outright require that an executor be a state resident. If your state allows you to pick someone who lives farther away, keep in mind that your executor must be available to conduct estate business, sometimes over many months. Take into account the time and cost of traveling and working on the estate administration before you choose an executor who lives far away. If the person you named as your executor was once local and has moved out of the area, you may also want to consider whether to update your will.

You can select more than one executor if you like. The benefit of naming multiple executors is that the responsibility needn't overwhelm one person if the work is shared. Keep in mind, though, that if the executors disagree, the dispute may delay the distribution of your estate. In severe cases, executors disagreeing could lead to litigation, suspending your estate's administration until the legal action is resolved. If you name more than one executor, do your best to ensure they are people who can work together, and who both understand your wishes.

You may also name a successor executor; this person will only act as executor if the primary executor cannot or will not take on the role.

While you should never choose an executor out of obligation, you should also do your best to choose someone your family will accept in the role. In some cases, the surviving spouse or another relative can petition the court to remove an executor if they believe they have legal grounds. Such challenges invite more fighting and potential litigation, and can waste the estate's resources. For instance, if your spouse and your sibling do not like each other and you appoint your sibling as the executor, your spouse can challenge the appointment. Such a challenge would require your spouse to prove that your sibling legally cannot serve, which is a high bar to clear. But the dispute can still take up time and resources. This is one reason why it is essential that you talk about the contents of your will, including your choice of executor, with your loved ones while you are alive.

As we mentioned, in some states, you may select a professional such as a financial adviser, attorney, accountant or banking institution as your executor. These professionals are typically familiar with probate laws and have experience with estate administration. Choosing a professional provides the added benefit of an impartial executor with expertise and experience. On the other hand, professional executors may not be aware of delicate family dynamics. If you choose a professional or an institution, you should expect a strict and conservative reading of your will and other estate documents. This is because, compared to a family member, a professional such as a financial adviser or attorney assumes additional responsibilities and legal liability when serving as a fiduciary. Also bear in mind that asking a professional to serve as an executor typically incurs higher fees than paying for the professional to provide financial or legal advice to a family member serving as executor. If you select an institution like a bank to act as your executor, you should be prepared for a longer estate process, because the institution often will involve several employees in administering a particular estate. Weigh whether naming a professional or institutional executor is worth the additional cost and time, and the loss of flexibility, for your estate.

While your executor and the legal guardian of your minor children can be the same person if you choose, understand that administering your estate and taking on the care of your children at once could be overwhelming. Discuss your plans with potential executors and guardians well in advance, and listen honestly to any concerns they have. Asking separate people to serve as your executor and your children's guardian may be the more realistic route. If your estate involves trusts, many of the concerns we have touched on in this section will also apply to selecting trustees. (We will discuss trusts in more detail later in this chapter.)

Living Wills And Advance Health Care Directives

A living will records your wishes and instructions for life-sustaining medical treatment when you cannot make decisions. You may be incapacitated because of a physical injury, a condition that renders you unconscious, or a disease that affects your cognitive abilities. For instance if you are affected by dysarthria, a degenerative disease that causes patients to lose the ability to communicate, in the absence of written instructions, family members could disagree over the best course of action or hesitate in trying to guess what you would want. A living will serves as the specific instructions for what life-sustaining procedures you do or do not want, making it easier for your family members to carry out your wishes. You can also state your preferences regarding organ donation. Make sure to include your wishes for end-of-life pain management in your living will, as this is a common source of familial disagreement. Specific instructions can help reduce potential conflicts between your loved ones, especially if you discuss the contents of your living will with them when you create it.

One of the most common mistakes people make when drafting a living will is not being explicit enough.

A living will is one common form of advance health care directive. Advance directives are a set of written, legal instructions that express your wishes for medical care should you become unable to make your own decisions. These may include questions about life support, as in a living will, but may also include instructions about care if you should experience dementia, suffer a serious injury, or experience any other major health crisis in which you may not be able to express your own preferences. A common advance health care directive is a "do not resuscitate" order. A DNR order can be a stand-alone document or appear as part of a more comprehensive set of instructions.

No advance directive can cover every possible scenario. This is why you may want to designate someone as your proxy health care agent by granting them medical power of attorney. If you go this route, you should name someone worthy of your implicit trust. A good proxy should fulfill your wishes and do what is best for you regardless of their own emotions or agenda. Common choices include a spouse, sibling, or parent. Most states allow you to choose a friend or other competent adult if you prefer. Bear in mind that you are granting the proxy health care agent medical power of attorney only; thus, he or she will only be able to make decisions involving your medical care and not those regarding your financial or legal affairs. As with an executor or trustee, it is also wise to name a successor if your primary proxy health agent cannot take on the role.

A common pitfall when drafting a living will or other advance directive is not being explicit. Overly simple or cryptic language can make it hard for your loved ones to understand your wishes and can create additional stress at a strenuous time. Detailed language prevents burdening your family members with uncertainty in your last moments.

A PERSONAL EXAMPLE

My family was fortunate enough to experience peace during the last moments of my grandfather's life because of clear language in his living will. After he was diagnosed with lung cancer, my grandfather's health quickly deteriorated. He immediately revised his living will to clarify which life-saving procedures and end-of-life pain management options he wanted and did not want. He specified which measures he wanted to be taken to save his life but was emphatic that he did not want to live his last days in a hospital. He ultimately desired to have his pain managed and to pass peacefully, surrounded by family, even if he became incoherent (as most people do before death). Luckily, my family did not have to make any difficult decisions while carrying out his wishes. There were no arguments because he had a detailed living will in place when he became unable to express what he wanted. If the living will had been ambiguous, my family surely would have fought over deciding what procedures to allow for my grandfather, causing conflict at a tragic time.

— *Kasey Radney*

Power Of Attorney

As we mentioned in the previous section, a medical power of attorney only offers the legal power to make decisions about your medical care. For other aspects of your life, you may want to consider a general power of attorney, which will give the holder the right to handle your financial and legal affairs. The person who holds your POA, called an agent or an attorney-in-fact, may be given the authority to access your bank accounts to pay your bills, file your tax returns, manage your investments, and take care of a variety of other concerns if you are incapacitated.

As with an executor, you should trust the person you grant your power of attorney implicitly. While you may revoke a POA at any time, as long as you retain capacity, you are often granting significant power to your agent. Many people select a spouse, sibling or professional adviser. As with other roles we have discussed in this chapter, you should also consider arranging for a secondary agent in case your first choice is unavailable or incapable of taking on the duties involved. You may want to discuss the particulars of this arrangement with an attorney as well as the people you are designating. (For more details on durable powers of attorney, as well as medical powers of attorney and living wills, see Chapter 19.)

Memorial Instructions

Since many people avoid the topic of death, it isn't surprising that many people also avoid thinking about the details of their own funerals. That said, even if you have no strong preferences, leaving instructions for your funeral services removes some of the burden for your loved ones. No matter your age, it is important to think about these details sooner rather than later. Do not include your memorial instructions in your will, however. Settling your estate will take time, especially if it is complex or contested. Your loved ones may need to make decisions about a memorial within a few days. You should create a completely separate document and keep it with other estate planning materials. This will allow your family or friends to easily determine your wishes even if there are complicating factors with your will.

Consider several questions when thinking about your funeral:

- What type of gathering, service, or ceremony would you like?
- Where would you like the service to take place?
- Who should be invited?

- Would you like flowers, or would you prefer people make memorial gifts to a charity?
- How would you like your remains to be handled?
- If you opt for burial, where would you like to be buried? Do you already have a burial plot?
- Do you have a preferred funeral home?
- How would you like to pay for your funeral?*

** In some cases, if you arrange your funeral while you are still alive, you can opt for funeral insurance, which will guarantee current prices.*

If you have already arranged any of these details, be sure to keep that information with your other estate planning materials. As with all estate planning documents, be sure to discuss your wishes with your loved ones in advance, too.

Funeral costs can add up to an expensive memorial, especially if you die far away from a burial plot you have purchased in advance. According to a 2021 study by the National Funeral Directors Association, the median cost of a funeral that year was $7,850. This figure does not take into account cemetery, monument or marker costs or miscellaneous cash-advance charges, such as flowers or an obituary. Cremation is typically a less expensive option than burial, with a median cost of $6,970 in the 2021 survey. It is vital to set aside funds to cover the costs of your memorial services if you wish to avoid passing the bill to your family members. Generally, an individual's estate covers their funeral and burial costs, so plan ahead to ensure sufficient assets are available.

Personal Records

In addition to your will, advance health care directive, power(s) of attorney and memorial instructions, your executor and loved ones will need a variety of other documents to put your final affairs in order. It is a good idea to make a binder — either literal or the digital equivalent — to keep these documents organized. The type of documents will vary depending on the complexity of your personal and financial circumstances. It may be impractical to leave some of these documents in this central location. For these, sometimes a copy will serve equally well, but in some cases you will want to include up-to-date notes on where your executor or family members can find the originals.

Some documents to consider keeping in your estate planning binder include:

- Your birth certificate
- Your marriage license, along with any prenuptial or postnuptial agreements
- Your divorce decree and related documents
- Your Social Security card
- Death certificates for a predeceased spouse or any other relatives whose estate may affect yours
- Adoption papers for your children
- Your citizenship documents
- Your military records
- A copy of your driver's license or state-issued ID
- Your health insurance information
- Your life insurance information
- Your organ donor card (if separate from your state ID)
- Relevant business documents, including employment agreements, limited liability company or other corporate documents, leases or partnership agreements

- Your financial documents, including information about your bank and brokerage accounts, credit cards and retirement accounts
- Any original stock or bond certificates
- Real estate documents such as deeds, mortgage documents and title insurance policies
- Titles to your car and any other vehicles, along with the associated insurance policies
- Any outstanding student loan information
- Copies of your recent tax returns
- Inventories or valuations of your belongings

You may not have physical copies of all, or even most, of the documents we have listed. Your executor will need to have easy access to your digital files as well as any physical estate planning materials. Make sure to keep an accurate and complete record of all usernames and passwords for important websites such as your email, social media, and bank and investment accounts. This also includes private keys if you maintain digital wallets, for example to store cryptocurrency. Your executor may need to access your accounts promptly, and it can be time-consuming to gain access to a deceased user's account without the login credentials. As with other sensitive documents, be cautious with the list of your account information. If you use password management software, you may have the option to grant emergency access for a secondary user. We will also discuss secure storage more thoroughly later in this chapter.

Your estate planning documents can include your wishes for your social media and other public-facing online accounts upon your death. For example, you can state whether you would like for your Facebook account to be deactivated and deleted, or kept active as a way to honor your memory. Some sites allow you to express these wishes directly, but including them in your overall estate plan will ensure your loved ones don't have to hunt down each of these accounts individually.

Finally, you should keep a current and detailed list of contact information of family members, friends, colleagues, employers or employees, and professionals such as investment advisers and attorneys. The list should include the individuals' full names, addresses, relationships to you, phone numbers, email addresses, and any other contact information you can provide. This list will be essential for your executor, who may need to contact many of these people while administering your estate. It may also be helpful when your executor or another loved one sorts through who they need to alert that you have died.

DO I NEED A TRUST?

A trust is often thought of as a tool for those with vast wealth who want to pass it to their heirs. This is a common misconception. A trust can sometimes serve as an effective tool even for smaller estates. A properly structured trust allows you to control where your assets go and under what circumstances. Trusts also let you distribute your estate with more privacy, bypassing the probate process. You can pass assets to heirs such as your children or grandchildren through a variety of trust structures. However, trusts can be expensive to establish and administer, so they are not the right choice for everyone.

If your goal is simply to avoid probate, trusts are not the only way to do so. For example, joint tenancy with right of survivorship is a form of property ownership that allows the asset to pass directly from one tenant to another without being subject to probate. Married couples may also be able to own property as tenants by entirety, though this arrangement is not available in every state. Tenants by the entirety are able to own assets as a single legal unit. Some assets, such as retirement accounts, allow you to designate one or more beneficiaries. The assets held in these accounts will pass directly to the beneficiaries upon your death, again outside of probate. You should be sure to designate the beneficiaries for these accounts and periodically review and update them.

Revocable vs. Irrevocable Trusts

There are two primary types of trusts: revocable and irrevocable. Each type allows you to set aside assets for beneficiaries, but one offers more flexibility. A revocable trust allows you to avoid probate while also giving you flexibility and better control. As the creator — or grantor — of the revocable trust, you have the discretion to change beneficiary designations, add assets to the trust, and make changes to the trust's terms. You will typically serve as the trustee or co-trustee of your revocable trust. While revocable trusts are more flexible than irrevocable trusts, they can potentially be subject to estate tax, since the assets remain under your control during your lifetime. Upon your death, your revocable trust becomes irrevocable. (See Chapter 16 for more information on estate taxes, as well as more detailed information on types of trusts.)

In contrast, grantors of irrevocable trusts cannot change or end the trusts after creating them. In exchange for less flexibility, irrevocable trusts allow grantors to take advantage of tax-shelter benefits that revocable trusts do not offer. This type of trust can also protect assets from claims by potential creditors and can allow grantors to provide resources for one or more younger generations.

Irrevocable Life Insurance Trust (ILIT)

Once you have children and other loved ones who are dependent on you financially, you may want to consider taking out a life insurance policy. Depending on the size and complexity of your estate, personally owning your policy may create additional estate tax liabilities. This is because owning the life insurance policy yourself means the death benefit will be included in your taxable estate. If you think you may be subject to federal or state estate tax, having someone else own your policy can help you to avoid this outcome. One option is to set up an irrevocable life insurance trust (ILIT).

The most efficient approach is to set up an ILIT first, then have the trust purchase your life insurance policy from the insurer. If you have an existing policy in your name, you can still transfer the policy to the ILIT, but you will need to survive at least three years after the transfer to receive any estate tax benefit. Once the ILIT owns the policy, you will need to arrange for the trust to pay the policy premiums. Funding the trust can trigger additional federal gift tax consequences, so be careful in how your payments are structured. For further elaboration on this strategy, and on life insurance in general, see Chapter 10.

STORING ESTATE PLANNING DOCUMENTS

It is vital that you store all of your estate planning documents in a safe and secure location. For physical documents, you may want to invest in a fire- and water-resistant safe. Digital copies should be password-secured, though be sure your executor or another trusted person has the necessary credentials to access them. If you cannot keep all the documents in one place, it is a good idea to list the documents stored elsewhere, along with their locations, to keep with your will and other estate planning documents.

You may also wish to pass down specific heirlooms or other sentimental items to specific family members or friends. These items may be spread out in your home or elsewhere, so keep an updated list of where they can be found. Ensure that your executor knows how to access this list.

You may prefer to keep important documents or valuable items in a safe deposit box. In that case, you should ensure that both the box and the key are accessible to someone who is authorized to handle your estate, or your affairs if you become incapacitated. Many attorneys strongly advise against placing your original will in a safe deposit box. Some jurisdictions require that such boxes be sealed when the owner dies, to be opened only by a court-appointed executor. But the would-be executor will need access to the will in order to be appointed by the court.

Wherever you choose to store your documents, it is never a bad idea to keep a record of which documents exist and where you have stored them with your estate planning attorney. In addition, at least one member of your family should know where you are storing the documents and should know how to access them, whether that means having a key, knowing a safe combination, or having an up-to-date password. Remember that someone other than your executor may handle matters such as arranging your memorial or contacting your friends and extended family. You may want to give access to more than one trusted individual.

FINAL POINTS

Your estate plan should be holistic. Once you write your will and establish any trusts, it is important to revisit them regularly and make updates when necessary to ensure that your plan continues to address your objectives. Life can change quickly and, at times, unexpectedly.

When you experience events such as having a baby, purchasing a home, or receiving an inheritance, be sure to update your will and relevant estate documents. While you may believe that you are too young or that you have not accumulated enough assets to need estate planning, it is never too early to have your affairs in order. As you age, you may find that your estate grows more complex and will require more expertise to administer. Even if you draft your first will yourself, eventually you may want to seek guidance from an estate attorney to make sure your plans are documented as you intend.

Estate planning is a complex process. Though this chapter has discussed some of the basic steps of estate planning and the documents you will need, it cannot cover every intricacy. There are comprehensive internet resources devoted to estate planning, as well as entire books on the subject. For more immediate information, Chapter 16 of this book covers estate and gift taxes in detail. You may also want to consult our firm's book *Looking Ahead: Life, Family, Wealth and Business After 55.* While that book is designed for older adults, many of the concepts apply to younger readers too. If your specific situation is especially complex, you should move beyond DIY resources and consult professional advisers for the best results.

Few people enjoy the topic of death, especially their own. This can often cause us to procrastinate on preparing for a future beyond our own lifetime. Having a structured plan, however, can give you peace of mind that your family is prepared for your death, at least financially, and that they will have the resources they need. A good estate plan reflects your wishes for your assets, and taking care of your family's needs is often that plan's centerpiece.

CHAPTER 13

WHEN CHILDREN ARRIVE

Anthony D. Criscuolo, CFP®, EA

Here is all the advice you need about children and money: If you want to maximize your wealth, do not have kids. Just move on to the next chapter.

If you are still reading, then you, like me and many others, don't seek wealth maximization as your primary goal in life. Happiness maximization is a better goal, anyway. For some, a family with children is a big part of their personal happiness equation. Many view children as their ultimate legacy, well ahead of any wealth, business or other aspirations they may seek during their lifetime. But don't romanticize the idea of children too much. Children are a great deal of work emotionally, physically and financially. Having children is life-changing in a variety of ways, but in this chapter I'll mainly focus on one: the way having children alters your financial life.

I have three children myself. So first, you're welcome — that's three future taxpayers, three future workers, and three future consumers who will help drive our country and our economy forward. But having three kids is much more the exception than the norm these days. Like many countries, the United States has experienced fewer births overall in recent years. The Centers for Disease Control and Prevention reported that 3.66 million babies were born in 2022 (the most recent year with available data at this writing). While this represents a small bounce back after a low point in 2020, and a trivial increase over 2021, it is the third-fewest annual births since 1983. The fertility rate, at 56.0 births per 1,000 women between the ages of 15 and 44, remains well below the so-called replacement rate — the fertility rate that would keep the overall population more or less stable, apart from the effects of migration.

No one has a comprehensive answer for why the U.S. is experiencing a baby bust, but the economics of having and raising children are likely a significant factor. No matter where you live, kids are expensive. Yet just how expensive can vary widely depending on whether you live somewhere rural or urban, and in what region of the country you reside. The costs of pregnancy and delivery alone can range from thousands to tens of thousands of dollars. This is not to mention the additional costs for those who need fertility treatments, surrogacy or other assistance to have a child at all. Like most health care expenses, the exact figures can be hard to estimate because of the opacity of medical billing practices, as well as the fact that you cannot always know ahead of time whether a particular birth will be complicated or straightforward. For example, my twins were born early, at 33 weeks, which kept them in the neonatal intensive care unit (NICU) for 20 days and 30 days, respectively. This produced a six-figure hospital bill. I'm happy to say most of the cost was covered by insurance — and, most importantly, the care they received was necessary and wonderful, and my twins are happy and healthy today.

Of course, the financial responsibility of parenthood does not end with delivery. A 2022 estimate from the Brookings Institution — based on earlier figures from the U.S. Department of Agriculture — suggested that the average cost to raise a child from birth until age 17 is $18,271 per year, or $310,605 altogether. (The age cutoff means this figure does not include any costs for college.) Adjusted for inflation, this estimate is about $50,000 more per child than the average cost in 1960. The two main factors that drive the difference: the rising costs of education and health care. The rising cost of child care follows closely behind. In addition to rising costs potential parents face, many young adults start their lives with serious debt, especially student loans. This has pushed many people to delay parenthood or reconsider whether they can afford kids at all. Other parents, who might have otherwise wanted a large family, may choose to stop at one or two children.

No one else can tell you when you are ready for children, but from a financial perspective, there are a few signs to look for. Very few people save a full $18,271 before their first child arrives, much less the nearly $311,000 to cover an entire childhood. (This is not to mention the estimated 35.7% of U.S. pregnancies that are unplanned, according to the Centers for Disease Control and Prevention.) But it is still wise to consider your overall financial stability when facing the prospect of parenthood. How steady is your income and the income of your partner, if you have one? Do you live somewhere you can stay for the long haul or are you contemplating a big move in the next few years? How much debt do you carry? Have you built an emergency fund? (For more on emergency funds, see Chapter 2.)

Couples should talk seriously about all aspects of parenting before their first child arrives, including money questions. Many start with conversations about how much each partner wants children and spend a lot of time on aligning their wants. This is great — but don't stop there. Even assuming you are both enthusiastic about children in the near term, you have had different upbringings, with different parenting experiences you may want to mirror or avoid. You will also have to make changes to your monthly budget, and those changes could be dramatic depending on your circumstances. Parenting often involves financial trade-offs, as well as trade-offs in time and opportunities. Therefore it is critical that the two of you are on the same page from the beginning.

A CHILD'S IMPACT

Before Your Baby Arrives

If you have not already nailed down a baseline budget or a savings plan, the time to do both is before your child is born. (For more on budgets, see Chapter 3; for more on savings, see Chapter 2.) Assuming you have a budget that works, you will want to use it as a baseline. Start to look at adjustments you can make to be sure your new addition doesn't leave you financially unstable.

Adjusting Your Income

One of the biggest questions to decide in advance is how parenthood will affect your income. In a childless two-person household, it is likely (though not a given) that you have two incomes. Once you have kids, you face the choice of whether either of you will stay at home and, if so, which one. But this is not always a binary choice between working or not. Some parents may find it more practical for one of them to work part-time or pursue work that can be performed from home. Single parents may want to go back to their original careers or may consider changing course to secure greater flexibility. There are a variety of ways parenthood can shape your future career.

From a financial perspective, you should also consider whether child care would equal or exceed the income of the parent considering going back to work. In certain cases, the choice to preserve a second income may feel like less of a choice due to practical considerations. When thinking about staying home or returning to work, do not forget to consider the long-term effects, too. When you stay home, you are forgoing not only your present salary but also the Social Security and retirement benefits you would earn at work. This, in turn, means giving up the potential investment growth of those retirement assets over time.

You should also think about how long you plan to stay home if you won't return to work right away. Some parents go back once their kids are in school, while others may stay at home full- or part-time much longer. While it is often more challenging to return to the workforce after a long absence, it is not impossible. How difficult it is to secure a new job after a years-long gap will depend on your career and where you live, as well as the state of the economy at the time you wish to reenter the workforce. Note, too, that staying home can affect your lifetime earning potential. An analysis from the Institute for Women's Policy Research, quoted by the Center for American Progress, found that women who took one year of parental leave earned 40% less over the following 15 years than women who did not take time off.

Your particular circumstances, preferences and resources will inevitably shape your decisions about whether to return to work and in what capacity. Many parents have strong feelings about whether staying home or going back to work is the "right" choice. The real answer is that there is no single right choice — only the right choice for you and your family.

Adjusting Your Spending

Once you have thought through the potential changes in your family's income, you are ready to consider the necessary changes to your spending. The cost of raising a child varies significantly depending on where you live and the lifestyle you envision for your family. But those expenses will need a place somewhere in your existing budget.

As with any other major financial change, your first step is to sort your budget into mandatory and discretionary expenses. You can't stop paying rent or the mortgage — in fact, your housing expenses may go up if you need to find a place with an additional bedroom — and your grocery budget will increase with a new family member to think about. The most flexible items in your budget are discretionary expenditures such as vacations, entertainment and eating out. The line item for your biweekly date night is likely to turn into diapers and wipes. Depending on your circumstances, you may want to look at ways to reduce certain mandatory expenses too, even if you cannot eliminate them outright. For example, if your credit is good, you may want to consider refinancing student loans to reduce your monthly payments. (For more on refinancing education loans, see Chapter 4.)

If you can learn to live on less before your baby arrives, you can save up a cushion for "startup" costs and get used to your new budget before you are also getting used to a newborn.

If you can learn to live on less before your baby arrives, you can save up a cushion for "startup" costs and get used to your new budget before you are also getting used to a newborn. If you plan to live on one income after your child arrives, consider starting sooner if you can. Devote the second income to building savings while you test out your new, leaner budget. This test run will also let you make some adjustments, if necessary, while you still have greater room for error.

Remember that budgeting is not a one-time exercise. Prepare to regularly revisit your budget and revise it as necessary. Parenthood is inevitably full of surprises, the financial sort among the rest.

Adjusting Your Insurance

Insurers acknowledge that having a child is a major life event, which gives you an opportunity to make changes to your health insurance outside the annual enrollment period. Having a baby or adopting a child usually triggers a "special enrollment period" after the event, often lasting 60 days. If you and your partner both have access to health insurance through work, look at the terms and costs of each policy. Depending on the details, it may make sense to move to a family plan, though occasionally it may be better to split coverage and add a dependent to one parent's plan.

QUICK NOTES

Financial Checklist — Before Your Baby Arrives

- ☑ Determine how parenthood will affect your household income
- ☑ Adjust your budget to allow for new expenses
- ☑ Prepare to take advantage of the "special enrollment period" for health insurance
- ☑ Consider (or reconsider) life insurance coverage

If you are the parent who is pregnant, check with your employer to see if you are covered by short-term disability insurance as a work benefit. This form of insurance typically covers pregnancy and can replace a portion of your gross income after your child is born. In most cases, policies replace 60% to 70% of gross income for around six weeks after you give birth. (For more information on disability insurance, see Chapter 9.) If you are not covered by disability insurance, your employer may be required to grant you time off under the Family and Medical Leave Act. FMLA-mandated time off is unpaid, though some employers offer company-specific paid leave. Certain states, including California and New Jersey, also mandate some level of paid family leave. You, and your partner if you have one, should make sure you fully understand any applicable benefits and how to claim them.

A new baby also means it is time to consider, or reconsider, life insurance coverage. You may not have needed a mechanism to replace your income as a childless adult, but now you need to provide for your child if anything happens to you. New parents are prime candidates to consider term life insurance policies. For more on the details of life insurance, see Chapter 10. While you are thinking about the future, it is also wise to create or update your estate plan, including custody arrangements. For more on estate planning, see Chapter 12.

The Baby Years

Earlier, I mentioned "startup" costs. For a new baby, especially a first child, you will need to budget for one-time purchases that will not translate into items in your monthly budget. These expenses include gear such as a crib, car seat or stroller. You may also need to pay for childproofing items, such as drawer locks and gates for stairs. If you have more than one child, you can likely use these purchases again, but they represent a significant initial expense in addition to the costs of pregnancy and delivery. Since some of these items are only necessary for a short period of time, you may be able to save by looking for parents selling used gear. If you have family or friends who have recently moved past the baby stage, you may even be able to borrow or inherit some items. Be sure to do your research and look out for recalled products, however. Never purchase anything used that could pose a major safety issue, such as a car seat.

You will also need to factor in the monthly expenses specific to the beginning of your child's life. This category includes items like diapers, formula, clothes and baby food. Perhaps the most significant cost for many parents is child care. If you or your partner chooses to stay home, you may only need an occasional babysitter, and if you live near family and friends who are able to help, you might keep these costs low. But for most parents, day care or in-home employees (such as a nanny) represent a major cost. Day care is especially expensive for children under age 2, as infant care requires lower staff-to-child ratios than care for older kids. For reference, child care costs can easily run from $1,000 to $2,000 per month, or more. While numbers vary widely, I wanted to include a range, since this can be a real sticker shock to some new parents. If you are blessed with twins, like me, that cost is doubled. Remember, though, parenthood is all about happiness maximization.

If you hire a nanny, au pair or other in-home employee, be aware of potential tax considerations. If you pay a household employee more than a particular threshold — $2,700 annually as of 2024 — the Internal Revenue Service considers that worker to be a household employee, rather than an independent contractor. Therefore you, as the employer, must pay Social Security, Medicare, and federal and state unemployment taxes on the employee's wages. This rule is often colloquially known as the "nanny tax." If your parents watch your child, even if you pay them, you do not owe nanny tax; similarly, you are not responsible for taxes if your babysitter is under age 18 and is not primarily working as a caregiver. The complications of paying taxes to household employees is one significant reason that many parents hire nannies or au pairs through employment agencies. In these arrangements, the agency is responsible for the worker's taxes. Parents who take on the responsibility of employing household workers directly may want to work with a financial adviser, especially at first, to make sure they are meeting all the pertinent tax obligations.

While you are caring for a newborn, paying for your child's education may seem a distant concern. But starting educational savings early is a powerful tool to make the most of whatever you can set aside. Many discussions of educational costs focus on college. This is understandable, as the cost of postsecondary education continues to outpace inflation. However, don't forget to plan for K-12 educational expenses, too. If you plan to send your child to parochial or private school, you will also need to budget for tuition in the near term. And even kids who attend public school can expect to pay for textbook rentals, school lunch programs and other school-related costs. You can also consider private tutoring or after-school enrichment programs.

Section 529 savings plans are among the most popular ways to save for a child's education. A 529 is a specialty investment account that allows you to save and invest for these expenses in a tax-advantaged way. (There is a second type of 529 plan, called a prepaid plan. These operate differently. Both types are covered in more detail in Chapter 4.) All investment earnings in a 529 plan are tax-free as long as the assets are used to pay for qualified educational expenses. Since 2018, qualified expenses have included K-12 tuition up to $10,000 per year, per beneficiary. A long time horizon lets you make the most of compounding, so the sooner you can get a 529 started the better. This is true even if you have relatively small amounts to save; many states have very low minimum contribution requirements or no minimum at all. Friends or extended family members can also contribute — this is a great birthday or holiday gift for your child.

Tax Considerations For New Parents

The first step to filing taxes as a parent is to make sure your child has a Social Security number. You can — and should — request a Social Security card for your newborn at the same time you apply for a birth certificate. Securing one later is generally much more difficult. While your child won't need the number anytime soon, you will need it to claim him or her as a dependent on your tax return.

Married couples who were already filing jointly will likely continue to do so once a child arrives. If you are married but were filing separately, you may want to revisit your choice to see if it is still beneficial for your family's overall situation. Single filers who become parents may be able to file as a "head of household," which offers benefits including a larger standard deduction. To qualify, you must pay more than half of the annual cost of providing a home for your child. (For more on filing statuses, and income taxes more generally, see Chapter 15.)

Child Tax Credit

American taxpayers with qualifying dependents age 17 or younger as of the end of the tax year can claim the Child Tax Credit. Unlike a deduction, a tax credit reduces your tax liability dollar for dollar, making this a valuable tax break for parents. The Tax Cuts and Jobs Act, which passed in late 2017, raised the Child Tax Credit to $2,000 per child. The law also made $1,400 of the credit refundable. With inflation adjustments, the refundable portion had reached $1,700 by 2024.

Qualifying dependents must be U.S. citizens, U.S. nationals or U.S. residents. In addition, they must live with the adult who is claiming them for half the tax year or more, and that adult must be able to claim the children as dependents on the return. Adopted and foster children also qualify, as long as they meet these requirements. As for the taxpayer, the main qualification is related to income, as the credit phases out at higher income levels. At this writing, the credit is available to taxpayers whose modified adjusted gross income is below $200,000 ($400,000 for married couples filing jointly). These levels will revert back to previous, lower thresholds at the end of 2025 unless Congress acts to extend the current rules.

If you share custody with another adult who is not part of your household — for example, an ex-spouse — note that only one of you can claim the Child Tax Credit for a particular child. If custody isn't split evenly, the parent with primary custody usually receives the credit. But if you have joint custody, you will need to come to an arrangement about how to handle the credit. Some parents alternate claiming it each year, while others may make up the difference in some other way. The specifics are up to you, but the government will only issue the credit to one taxpayer per child, per year.

The Child And Dependent Care Tax Credit

Parents with children under age 13 may also qualify for the separate Child And Dependent Care Tax Credit. For up to $3,000 (or $6,000 for a couple) in care expenses, you can claim a credit between 20% and 35% of your costs, depending on your overall income. Unlike the Child Tax Credit, this credit is not refundable, which means it can reduce your tax liability to zero, but you won't get a refund if there is anything left over. The Child And Dependent Care Tax Credit does not disappear completely at higher income levels, though the percentage of allowable expenses decreases for high-income taxpayers.

In addition to the age requirement for your child, you must have earned income (for example, from wages). You must be paying for child care in order to work or to help with a job search. If you are married, you must file jointly to claim this credit. You will need to provide information about the care provider, too; note that you cannot claim payments for care provided by your spouse, the child's other parent or someone under age 18.

Some states offer their own versions of this credit. In many cases, they simply offer a percentage of the federal credit, but occasionally a state's law may offer expanded eligibility or include other incentives. Be sure to check the law in your state, assuming your state has an income tax.

Other Tax Considerations For Parents

When you add a child to your family, consider adjusting your withholding if you are an employee (rather than an independent contractor or a stay-at-home parent). Claiming a dependent generally decreases your overall tax liability for the year. You can file a new Form W-4 with your employer to claim an additional withholding "allowance," which will increase your monthly take-home pay.

Claiming your child as a dependent extends your eligibility for the Earned Income Tax Credit. These limits rise again for a second child, and again for parents with three or more children. Couples with three or more children can qualify for this credit if their adjusted gross income is anywhere below $66,819 (as of 2024).

Some employers offer "flex accounts," which provide a tax-friendly way to pay for child care. A flex plan lets you divert up to $5,000 of your pretax income into an account you can use to pay for child care expenses. This diverted income avoids federal and state taxes, as well as payroll taxes. Note that you can't double dip and claim the Child and Dependent Care Tax Credit on child care expenses you paid with flex account funds. But if you are married and filing jointly, you may claim up to $1,000 of additional child care expenses paid out of other funds before you hit the $6,000 threshold for the credit. In general, employees sign up for flex plan benefits during open enrollment but, as with health insurance, the birth of a child often triggers a special enrollment period.

If you are adopting a child, the federal government offers an Adoption Tax Credit. Assuming your expenses were not reimbursed by a state agency or your employer, you may claim the credit for expenses related to adoption such as court costs, home study expenses and money spent on travel related to the adoption. (You may be eligible to claim additional expenses if you are adopting a child with special needs.) This nonrefundable credit is worth up to $16,810 for tax year 2024, subject to a phase-out based on taxpayer income.

Certainly no one decides to have, or not have, a child based on tax laws. But you should understand the various rules and take advantage of any tax savings available to you. Tax rules also change, so be sure to keep up to date.

As They Grow

While infants mean a lot of upfront costs, they are notoriously easy to entertain. As your child grows, that will change. Costs for extracurricular activities and sports can add up quickly. You, and your partner if you have one, should take time to think seriously about your budget for these activities. You may need to comparison shop and weigh cost against convenience for a particular dance studio or sports league. Also talk to your kids about their priorities and try to determine which activities are most meaningful to them. If you're a single parent or both parents work, you will also need to figure out what to do with your kids during school vacations. This means budgeting for additional child care, whether in the form of babysitters, camps or other daytime activities.

As your children reach school age, you may want or need to consider moving due to the quality of public schools in a particular area. If you prefer private school, you will need to budget accordingly; note that private high schools are nearly always more expensive than private elementary schools. Revisit your education planning often, and remember that any funds invested in a 529 account should move toward increasingly safe investments as your child approaches college age.

PARENTING WITHOUT MARRIAGE

In 1968, only 7% of parents living with their children were unmarried. By 2017, that number reached 25%, according to data from the Pew Research Center. This shift reflects a variety of social changes, including a decline in marriage rates and an increase in the number of children born outside of marriage. This means many American children are growing up either in households where their parents are cohabiting but are not married, or in single-parent households. Parents in either of these situations face some extra financial planning concerns.

If you are not your child's blood relative, you will need to take legal steps to ensure your right to custody is protected.

Unmarried, Cohabiting Couples

If you and your partner choose not to marry, you will not have access to many of the legal protections and benefits that married couples receive. When you add children to the mix, it is essential to ensure that your child's future is secure, even if you and your partner break up, or if something happens to one or both of you.

If you and your partner are your child's biological parents, both of you have some inherent rights where your child is concerned. In some states, fathers who are not married to their child's mother must sign a voluntary declaration of paternity in order to put their name on the child's birth certificate. Under federal law, all states must offer unwed parents the opportunity to sign such a document, either at the hospital or subsequently. Even in states that do not require a paternity statement, you can prepare one to head off potential parentage disputes.

If one or both of you are not your child's blood relative, you will need to take legal steps to ensure your right to custody is protected. These concerns may apply to LGBTQ couples, couples who have pursued adoption or surrogacy, or couples co-parenting a child from a partner's previous relationship. Some states allow "second parent" adoption, in which an unrelated parent can adopt a child without the biological parent losing any rights. However, some states that allow this arrangement for heterosexual couples deny it to same-sex couples; similarly, some adoption agencies will not allow two same-sex parents to adopt a child. If second parent adoptions are not available to you in your state, you and your partner should create a formal co-parenting or custody agreement, ideally with an attorney's help. Such agreements outline how you will handle a breakup or the death of one partner. Couples in which a parent is not biologically related to the child should also take special care with wills and other estate planning documents to ensure that the nonrelated parent can retain custody if the biological parent dies unexpectedly.

Single Parents

Single parents face self-evident challenges, in that they lack the financial, emotional and practical help available to partnered parents. Even for couples where the other biological parent is still living, a parent with sole custody may or may not have much external support. The Pew Research Center found that only 22% of fathers who live separately from their kids see them once a week or more. According to the U.S. Census Bureau, the average amount of child support custodial parents receive is $460 per month.

Whether you started out single, or became single after divorce or the death of your spouse, you will need to go through the same budgeting exercises outlined earlier in this chapter, likely with less flexibility on your side. It is especially important for single parents to build a robust emergency fund. If you do not have disability insurance to replace your income in case you cannot work due to illness or injury, strongly consider getting it. Life insurance is also especially important for single parents, as is comprehensive estate planning. (See chapters 9, 10 and 12, respectively, for more on disability insurance, life insurance and estate planning.) Think carefully about who should get custody of your children if anything happens to you, and have detailed conversations with your candidates in advance to make sure they are ready to take on that responsibility.

BEYOND TRADITIONAL CHILDBIRTH

Not everyone is in a position to become a parent without help. Whether you choose fertility treatments, surrogacy or adoption, pursuing parenthood can sometimes involve major financial decisions long before your child arrives.

Fertility Treatments

Assisted reproductive technologies, often abbreviated ART, are an increasingly common part of parenthood for many Americans. The Centers for Disease Control and Prevention estimate that 2.3% of American babies are conceived with the help of ART. Yet many prospective parents are uncomfortable discussing the various medical procedures or technologies they consider. The truth is ART is not as rare as many people think. Individuals or couples considering these methods should plan for them, just as they would any other aspect of pregnancy and childbirth.

ART includes any fertility treatment in which medical professionals handle both eggs and embryos. (This excludes procedures such as artificial insemination or fertility treatments based on medication.) The method most people likely think of first is in vitro fertilization, or IVF, the most common option in the U.S. ART also includes procedures such as intracytoplasmic sperm injections, gamete intrafallopian transfers, zygote intrafallopian transfer and frozen embryo transfers. These options have been a boon for many parents, but the procedures involved can be costly. Because it often takes more than one cycle of treatment before the result is a viable pregnancy, patients can spend tens of thousands of dollars on the procedure overall.

Health insurers vary widely as to whether and to what extent they cover fertility treatments. It is important to dive into the details of your plan — and your partner's, if you have different coverage — to understand what you are likely to owe out-of-pocket. Fourteen states have passed IVF insurance mandates, requiring employers to offer at least one plan covering the procedure to employees. In seven additional states, plans must offer some form of fertility coverage, though not IVF specifically. The specific legal requirements vary from state to state, and small employers are often exempt from these requirements. According to FertilityIQ, a database for information about fertility benefits and treatments, approximately 64% of patients who underwent IVF paid for 50% of the procedure or more.

Because time can be a factor in the success of fertility treatments, many patients feel they cannot wait until they have saved all of the funds necessary. As always, if you take on debt, be mindful of the borrowing terms. Borrowing against your home or a retirement plan has risks and downsides, but is generally a better option than running up credit card debt, for example. You may have access to financing options through the fertility clinic itself, such as graduated repayment or even outcome-based pricing models. For instance, some clinics may issue refunds if you paid for multiple sessions upfront and ended up not needing them. Some clinics also offer lotteries for free or reduced-cost treatment cycles. You may be eligible to apply for grants from certain private foundations or to participate in clinical studies for new forms of fertility treatment. And certain employers offer fertility-related benefits separate from employee health insurance coverage. Be sure to explore all of your options.

Preserving your genetic material gives you the opportunity to delay parenthood or preserve your chance at biological children after an event that could affect fertility (for example, chemotherapy). This can be pricey, however. Many health insurance plans do not cover sperm banking or egg freezing, leaving patients to pay for these services out of pocket. In addition to the price of the procedure, many clinics charge an annual storage fee. Costs vary by location, and patients with cancer may sometimes be eligible for discounts. Some companies, especially tech startups, may defray some of these costs as an employee benefit, but this is still relatively uncommon.

It is important to dive into the details of your health insurance plan — and your partner's, if you have different coverage — to understand what you are likely to owe out-of-pocket on fertility treatments.

Surrogacy

If fertility treatments are not feasible, or you and your partner do not have the necessary biology to have a child on your own, you may consider surrogacy. There are two types. In "gestational surrogacy," one person (often you or your partner) donates an egg and the surrogate carries the child. In "traditional surrogacy," the surrogate also provides the egg, meaning the carrier will be biologically related to the resulting child. Gestational surrogacy is more common in the U.S. today, and some states prohibit traditional surrogacy outright. Either option may make sense, however, depending on the circumstances that led you to surrogacy in the first place.

Although legally you do not need to work with an agency in a surrogacy arrangement, most experts advise against going it alone. While an agency creates additional costs, the surrogacy process is often medically and legally complicated. At a minimum, you should expect to work with a reproductive endocrinologist, a lawyer, a psychologist and an insurance specialist throughout. As the size of this team suggests, surrogacy is an expensive option. The New York Times reported in 2019 that the average cost of surrogacy in the U.S. from start to finish was about $150,000.

As with fertility treatments, it is important to do research and make a budget before you begin the process. "Compassionate" or "altruistic" surrogacy involves a surrogate who does not ask for compensation; in many cases, this is likely to be a close friend or family member. If you connect with a surrogate whom you do not already know, expect to provide compensation for the time, effort and risk involved in pregnancy. You should also research your state laws to be sure your state allows commercial surrogacy. As for funding, many of the options available to fertility patients (such as grants and employer assistance) may also be available to families pursuing surrogacy. Be thorough and deliberate in exploring your options, and decide how you will fund your surrogacy journey before you begin.

Adoption

Some parents come to adoption due to health concerns or fertility struggles that make pregnancy impossible or impractical. Others know from the start that they want to adopt. Regardless of your path to adoption, it is important to consider the financial implications the same way you would any major long-term financial goal.

The costs of adoption vary widely depending on the circumstances. Adopting through your local community's foster system may cost very little upfront; some states even offer subsidies to encourage adoptions through the foster system. On the other hand, private or international adoptions can cost between $30,000 and $60,000, according to a 2022 report from the Children's Bureau and the Child Welfare Information Gateway (both federal agencies). These costs may include court fees, home evaluations, paperwork processing and post-placement supervision. In addition, international adoptions can involve multiple trips to your future child's country of origin, both before and after the birth. There are many types of adoption, and the full list of details a prospective adoptive parent should consider are beyond the scope of this chapter.

Whatever approach you take, do your research so you know what to expect when it comes to fees and requirements. Since adoption is inherently a legal process, you should expect to hire an attorney, regardless of whether your adoption will be domestic or international. As with other major financial decisions, such as buying a home, it is important to create a budget and stick to it.

You may have access to supplemental financial resources in pursuing adoption. Investigate your employer's benefit offerings; some workplaces offer specific adoption benefits. Certain religious and nonprofit organizations offer grants to prospective adoptive parents, which may also help offset some of your costs. And, as I mentioned earlier in this chapter, you may be able to claim a federal tax credit for some of your expenses. Since adoption may take multiple years, especially if you pursue private or international adoption, use that time wisely to build your savings for the process itself and the future care of your child.

FINANCES AND THE FAMILY

Grandparents

If you are lucky, your parents will be eager to help as you start your own journey with parenthood. While this help will look different depending on your family's resources, habits and geography, financial help can be especially useful — but also especially fraught.

The key, as with many places where family and money intersect, is clear, upfront communication. Ideally, your parents will initiate conversations with you about how and when they plan to help. But if not, you can and should take the first step. For example, if you plan to open a 529 savings account for your child, you can proactively let your parents know and alert them that they can contribute to that account directly if they wish.

You may also find it useful to be aware of some common financial planning techniques your parents may use to plan gifts to grandchildren. Many of these strategies allow givers to avoid triggering gift tax or generation-skipping transfer tax. (For more on these taxes, see Chapter 16.) For example, a grandparent may want to pay a grandchild's medical bills or tuition expenses directly, since such direct payments are not subject to transfer taxes. Talking to your parents can help you to coordinate this sort of gift.

Your parents may also want to set up trusts for the benefit of your children. There are many sorts of trusts, and the details are beyond the scope of this chapter. But if your parents mention naming your children as trust beneficiaries, don't be afraid to ask for the trust's details. Especially while your children are still young, it is important that you be aware of details such as the trustee's contact information or any restrictions on distributions. Similar considerations apply if grandparents want to set up a custodial account for your child's benefit. (See Chapter 4 for more on custodial accounts.)

If you need help and your parents are not in a position to offer outright gifts, you may want to discuss the potential of an intrafamily loan. For instance, your parents may be in a position to support you while they are working, but worry they may need funds after they retire or if their health deteriorates in the future. To avoid having the IRS treat forgone interest or even the principal itself as a gift rather than a loan, you must pay interest at a rate equal to or greater than the Applicable Federal Rate. (This rate will be lower than what you would owe to a bank if you took out a personal loan.) You and your parents should draw up a formal agreement, which includes the payment terms, the length of the loan, and any potential penalties for late payment or other violation of the loan's terms. Such an agreement is not only useful for tax purposes, but also to avoid future disagreements or misunderstandings between you and your parents.

Teaching Your Kids About Money

As a parent, one of your important duties will be to teach your children how to handle money. While this responsibility is not applicable to infants, you may want to start teaching your kids financial skills earlier than you think. If you are parenting with a partner, be sure you are on the same page when it comes to how you want to talk to your kids about money and what you plan to teach them. Will you give your kid an allowance? At what age, and how much? If and when your child has a phone, what limits will you put on spending in apps and other online payments? Will allowance be tied to chores? Will you let your children earn extra by going above and beyond expected contributions to the household?

The right answers will vary from family to family, but an allowance can be an excellent teaching tool if it is practical for you. If you plan to connect the allowance to the completion of chores or other tasks, make sure that connection is clear in advance and stick to it. When your child purchases something with allowance money, talk about the purchase later. This can be a useful way to illustrate the satisfaction of saving for something you really want — or to illustrate the dangers of buyer's remorse. You may also want to take a more direct hand in creating a system for your kids to manage their money, especially while they're young. Consider setting up three jars (or piggy banks): "save," "spend" and "give." This can help children get the hang of the basics of budgeting, and you can use the "give" jar to help them learn about how they can use their money to help others.

The most important thing, no matter how you approach finances with your kids, is to talk to them about money.

Once your child is old enough, encourage entrepreneurial inclinations. Help your child set up a lemonade stand, pursue Girl Scout cookie sales or pick up babysitting jobs. Such experiences are a useful introduction to the world of work and sales. If you think a teenager is ready, you may want to add your child as an authorized user to your credit card to teach him or her good credit card habits with a safety net. The best approach will vary depending on your child's temperament and your family situation, but giving kids room to try out managing their own finances, including earning money when practical, will set them up for future success.

The most important thing, no matter how you approach finances with your kids, is to talk to them about money. The more natural you make money conversations, the more comfortable your kids will feel coming to you when they are curious, or possibly in trouble. Many parents shy away from talking about money because they feel awkward, but this does your children a disservice. The FINRA Foundation reported that, in a 2021 survey, respondents averaged a score of 3.2 out of seven basic financial literacy questions. Only 23 states require students to take a course in financial management before graduating high school, which means that a lot of the responsibility for financial education remains with parents. Talking to your children about money is the first step in making sure they have the tools to manage their money well as adults.

You may also want to get an early start on thinking about your child's career. While this is ultimately a choice that children make for themselves, as a parent you will likely have opportunities to offer guidance. We all know the workplace is changing rapidly, driven by new technologies and increasing automation. Certain industries may be completely gone, or much different, by the time your children enter the workforce. Teaching your children to be adaptable, creative and resourceful will help lead them toward a successful career in whatever field of work may await them.

Boomerang Kids

It may seem too soon to think about your boundaries for adult children moving back in with you, but considering this possibility years in advance has many advantages. Multigenerational homes are on the rise in America; the Pew Research Center found that about four times as many American households encompassed multiple generations in 2021 than they did in the 1970s. This is another area where your background or your partner's may affect your thinking. If you moved back home and it gave you a useful leg up as a young adult, you may be more inclined to plan for this option. Conversely, if you had a bad experience as a "boomerang" kid, you may want to discourage your own children from returning home after college or an initial period of independence.

Like many parenting questions, there is no right answer to approaching the boomerang kid phenomenon. You (and your partner if you have one) should think through your potential ground rules for such an arrangement. You may want to attach conditions to your child's stay, such as actively hunting for a job, paying rent or helping with housework. Also realistically evaluate how much financial help you are willing and comfortably able to give your child after a certain age. If you plan to stay in your home, having your child return may not make a major difference in your plans. If you expect to downsize, you may have to reexamine your budget more seriously. As your child gets older, you can start conversations about the financial support you are and are not able to offer once your child is grown.

FINAL THOUGHTS

Children are not for everyone, and that's OK. But if you know you want kids, you should not let the financial considerations scare you away from parenthood. Yes, children are a major financial undertaking, but so are many of the most worthwhile experiences in life. My three children are certainly my greatest joy. Together, the staff at Palisades Hudson has 29 kids (at this writing) and growing, and I am confident my colleagues would also say the trade-offs are worthwhile. So remember that good financial planning is not about wealth maximization, but rather happiness maximization. You should plan your finances to help you reach your goals — including when your goals involve making and raising another human being or two (or three).

CHAPTER 14

EMPLOYMENT CONTRACTS

Benjamin C. Sullivan, CFP®, EA, CVA and Mamie Odom

As a young adult, your biggest asset is likely not your savings, your investment portfolio or even your home. It is almost certainly your future earning capacity.

As you will know if you have read Chapter 9, it is important to protect your future income through disability insurance. But you can also protect your earning capacity through your approach to your career. If your work is governed by a written contract, this means taking an educated approach to evaluating that contract before you sign. Even if your employment agreement is less formal, being proactive in carefully reviewing your offer letter or other written terms of employment before you agree to a start date can pay off.

Contract practices vary widely by industry, but most American employees receive offer letters rather than contracts. Contracts are more likely for high-level executives, government workers and commission-based sales positions. Like a contract, an offer letter sets down the terms of employment in writing. In rare cases, offer letters can create legally binding agreements. Most of the time, however, they merely summarize the terms that the employer and prospective employee have discussed previously. If you receive an offer letter, be sure that you know whether it is a legally binding agreement or simply a point of reference.

Occasionally, an employment agreement may be purely "implied" — based on verbal statements, along with employee handbooks, company policies or other general documents. If you receive an offer by phone or in person, it is smart to summarize your understanding of that offer in an email to the employer after whatever conversations you have about it. While such a communication is not legally binding, it can serve as a reference in case of future disagreement about a job's particulars or the outcome of a negotiation. Whenever possible, though, a formal offer letter or a contract is a better alternative.

While employee contracts are relatively rare in most fields, you may encounter them more often if you work for yourself. A 2022 survey from consulting firm McKinsey & Company found that 36% of U.S. workers surveyed reported identifying as "independent workers." This number included full-time freelancers, independent contractors, and traditional employees who engage in an additional "side hustle." Freelancers operate their own businesses and so, in many ways, are their own bosses. But in many fields, they often enter into contracts with clients to define the scope of work, payment terms and other details. Independent contractors may also take longer-term positions in which they work with a single client at a time. In these cases, the client may look more like an employer, though the contractor retains more independence than a traditional employee.

If your industry does not treat employee contracts as a given, you may still be able to arrange one. If this is something you want, raise the possibility after the employer has made the initial offer, during the phase in which you would negotiate salary and other terms of employment. Not every employer will be willing to commit to a legally binding document, but some will. As with other employment negotiations, senior employees or workers with in-demand skills have more leverage to ask for something the company normally would not offer.

This raises the question of why you would want a contract as an employee. The main reason is job security. Contracts create certainty by their nature. Years ago, a worker could spend an entire career working upward at the same company; today, such a trajectory is rare. According to the U.S. Bureau of Labor Statistics, at this writing the median tenure for an American worker is 4.1 years with an employer. The median for management is five years, and for public sector workers it is 6.8 years. Employers can attract candidates looking for security by guaranteeing they won't let go of the employee without cause for a certain number of years, or at all. A contract may also serve as a way to secure a more lucrative severance package if a position is eliminated or you are let go. However, not all contracts are created equal. Once a contract is signed, both parties must abide by its terms unless they agree to renegotiate. So it's important to make sure your contract includes enough flexibility to allow for unforeseen changes to your role or to the business.

Whether or not you have a contract, you should be aware of a few laws that govern U.S. hiring and firing practices. In the U.S., nearly all employment is "at will." Even contract employees sometimes work at will, if the contract affirms at-will employment rules. This means that either the employer or the employee can legally end the agreement at any time, for nearly any reason. The major exception is ending employment for a reason that could run afoul of legal protections against discrimination. Federal law prohibits employers from discriminating against applicants or employees for a set of protected categories, including race, religion, sex, age (for workers 40 and older), national origin or disability. The Equal Employment Opportunity Commission interprets "sex" to include sexual orientation and gender identity, a position that has been supported by the U.S. Supreme Court. Employers also cannot discriminate against applicants who are pregnant or workers who become pregnant. Finally, they cannot retaliate against an employee who complains about discrimination or participates in a discrimination lawsuit against the company. Some states have added other protected classes or have made presumed protections for certain classes more explicit. For instance, many states have added specific legislative protection for sexual orientation or gender identity.

If a contract specifies a company may not fire an employee at will, it will generally set out the various grounds that could result in termination. These may include misconduct, such as financial malfeasance; failure to hit specific goals, such as sales quotas; or outside events, such as the company's sale or a merger. At-will employment may also be restricted by state law. If you work in Montana, your employer is subject to state law that says employers may only discharge workers "for cause," unless it is during a probationary period. Montana is a U.S. outlier given its prohibition against at-will employment in most instances. A more common state restriction is a "right to work" law. At this writing, right to work laws exist in 26 states, mostly in the South, Midwest and interior West. In these states, employers cannot require employees at a particular workplace to join a union, even if those workers are protected by the union's collective bargaining agreement.

APPROACHING A CONTRACT AS AN EMPLOYEE

Getting a job offer is exciting, especially if you have dreamed of working for a certain company or if your job search has dragged on for many months. It can be tempting to accept right away. But whether a potential employer is submitting a contract or an offer letter, it is critical to take the time to fully read and understand it. While this section principally focuses on contracts, many of the same considerations apply to offer letters.

"Read the entire contract" may seem like basic advice, but it truly is important. Many of us are guilty of clicking "accept" on the terms and conditions of a website or app without worrying about the details. That is not ideal either, but when it comes to your career, the stakes are too high not to read and understand the entire document. As with any other contract, once you sign it, you have legally agreed to all the terms it contains. If there is anything that you find unclear or that deviates from your expectations, bring it up and ask for clarity.

When you read the contract, bear in mind which provisions are likely negotiable. Most people think of salary first, but other factors may matter as much or more. You may also want to negotiate when it comes to vacation time, schedule flexibility, the potential for remote work, or allowances for a car or smartphone. Don't hesitate to negotiate these terms, though you should prioritize what's important to you and remain realistic about how much you bring to the table. At worst, an employer will hold firm, but a reasonable company will not withdraw an offer simply because you asked for an adjusted salary or the option to work remotely on occasion. Approach negotiations in a thoughtful and reasonable way, and a good employer will respond in kind. Once you have signed the contract or offer letter, the opportunity for negotiation is finished.

Whether a potential employer is submitting a contract or an offer letter, it is critical to take the time to fully read and understand it.

The U.S. Labor Department sets minimum standards for terms of employment. It is worth making sure that your contract complies with legal guidelines for standard work weeks, overtime, mandated breaks, safety issues and minimum wage. State laws may also restrict what an employer can or cannot offer. The idea is not to accuse your potential employer of wrongdoing; that is needlessly adversarial. If you think they are knowingly breaking the law, it makes more sense to walk away. Instead, you should clarify if some provision of your contract seems legally murky or ambiguous. In certain cases, you may benefit from paying for an attorney to review your contract. If you find any language confusing or troubling, or if the contract includes strict limits such as confidentiality or noncompetition clauses, an expert can help you make sure you understand the terms you are agreeing to follow.

Specific Contract Provisions

Compensation

Most of us work, at least in part, to support ourselves and any dependents we may have. So it is understandable that one of the first contract provisions many employees want to review is compensation. Your contract should clearly outline your salary level — which should match your expectations based on the interview process or previous negotiations — but it should also go further. For instance, it should specify whether you are entitled to overtime pay and how such pay will be calculated. In some cases, the contract may lay out guaranteed changes to the base salary to reflect cost of living increases. It should note when such changes happen and how they are calculated. Some companies also include a right to reduce base salary by a certain percentage if other employees' salaries are similarly reduced, which gives the employer some room to cope with unforeseen financial challenges. If this provision is present, make sure you understand when and how such a change could happen.

Your compensation may be entirely fixed or it may include variable compensation. Variable compensation is any compensation that is not guaranteed, and it often takes the form of discretionary bonuses. Your contract should clearly explain how the company pays bonuses, if it does. Are they available quarterly or annually? Are they guaranteed or discretionary? If they aren't guaranteed, are they based on your personal performance or the company's overall growth? In some companies, bonuses will reflect particular achievements or milestones, while other companies issue bonuses wholly at the discretion of company leadership. For performance-based bonuses, the contract should be specific about how the company will measure that performance. If you were offered a signing bonus, that should appear in your contract too.

If part of your compensation is deferred, such as employer contributions to a retirement plan, the contract should outline any vesting schedule that might apply. (For more on retirement plans, see Chapter 18.) Your contract should also lay out any details of equity that you receive as part of your compensation, most often in the form of company stock or stock options. Equity grants are often subject to vesting schedules, and your agreement should clearly lay out these requirements. If you will receive stock options, the price to exercise them should be clear, as should the rules about exercising them if you are terminated or resign.

Some extra care is necessary if you are receiving equity from a private company. Be sure you understand what percentage of the company your equity represents and how that will change as the company issues more shares. In most cases, though not all, issuing more shares will dilute your position. Valuing shares in a private company is also less straightforward than equity in a public company, so ask how your interest will be valued, as well as if you are subject to restrictions on selling it. What will happen to your equity if you leave the company should be clearly documented, and you should inquire about any other agreements that might affect the outcome. For example, a buy-sell agreement might dictate a requirement to sell your interest back to the company or other shareholders when you go.

The contract should also make clear what will happen to your equity in case of a sale or public offering. As all of this suggests, equity in a private company can be complex, so you may want to consult a third party such as your financial adviser or attorney.

EQUITY COMPENSATION

Being offered any form of ownership in a company you work for can be exciting and potentially lucrative. Equity compensation might come in the form of stock options, restricted stock, restricted stock units (RSUs) or outright shares of a company.

Just as when you receive cash as compensation for your work, you should generally expect that any stock you receive from your company will be taxable as ordinary income. You will owe that tax when you no longer risk forfeiting the compensation, unless special rules apply to the specific form of equity.

At their most basic, stock options are an agreement in which a company grants an employee the right to buy shares of stock at a set price, known as the strike price or exercise price. When the company trades below that set price, your options are worthless. As the stock price increases beyond the strike price, your options will become more valuable.

Companies may offer nonqualified stock options or incentive stock options. Nonqualified stock options are more common; incentive stock options offer some tax benefits but can potentially trigger the complexities of the alternative minimum tax. (For more on the AMT, see Chapter 15.) In some cases, the company may offer you a choice between nonqualified and incentive options. In others, the company will only offer stock options of one of these types. Companies can offer incentive stock options only to employees, but can offer nonqualified stock options to contractors and consultants as well.

When you exercise a nonqualified stock option, you will owe tax at ordinary income rates on the difference between the exercise price and the stock's market price at the time. If you have access to incentive stock options, you will incur long-term capital gains tax on all appreciation over the exercise price, as long as you hold the acquired shares for at least two years from the date of option grant and one year from the date of exercise. This can represent a significant tax savings. The rules about vesting and exercise of your options can vary substantially between companies, so it is important to carefully read the terms governing your options and make sure you understand them.

Restricted stock refers to shares subject to certain stipulations. Most commonly, a company will stipulate that restricted shares will vest after you maintain employment with the company for a set period. So long as you haven't met the milestones in question, you risk receiving no value for your restricted stock. Therefore, you typically would not include the value of restricted stock received in your income before it vests. However, if you expect to stay with the company and have high expectations for the stock's performance, you could benefit from making a special election to include the equity compensation in your income when it is granted, rather than when it vests.

Named for the relevant section of the Internal Revenue Code, an 83(b) election allows you to do just that — to recognize, at the time of the award, the fair market value of the stock as ordinary compensation income. This accelerates the taxability of the stock award to its grant date, rather than the later vesting date, when the stock may have appreciated in value. Assuming the stock appreciates between the grant date and the vesting date, the election saves you from additional ordinary income taxes. Whether or not you make an 83(b) election, you still will have to pay capital gains tax on any appreciation that occurs between the point at which you include the restricted stock as ordinary income and the future date when you sell the shares. While you recognize the same amount of total income either way, the 83(b) election allows you to characterize more of that income as favorable capital gains rather than as ordinary income, assuming the price of the stock increases.

This strategy comes with risks. If you lose your right to the property before it vests, you needlessly paid tax on income you never received. Similarly, if the value of the restricted stock decreases between the date of grant and date of vesting, you will recognize more ordinary income by making an 83(b) election than without it. Because you must notify the IRS that you are making an 83(b) election using specific procedures and within tight deadlines, it is a good idea to consult a tax professional as soon as you receive a restricted stock award to be sure you make the election correctly.

Understanding equity compensation can help you accurately evaluate how lucrative a job may be. Proper planning for it can help you minimize the associated tax burden and make the most of your benefits.

Your compensation includes any benefits offered or negotiated during the interview process. These may be one-time perks, such as relocation assistance, or ongoing benefits such as health, disability or malpractice insurance. The document should lay out any eligibility requirements for benefits, too. For instance, some employers do not extend certain benefits until the employee has been with the company for 90 days, or until the worker has completed a particular orientation procedure. The contract should also lay out whether your rights to any of your benefits lapse under certain circumstances, or whether you are entitled to accrue them for future use.

One area in which accrual, or the lack thereof, matters a great deal is vacation time and sick leave. In some workplaces, workers can bank vacation time from year to year, while other workplaces have a "use it or lose it" approach. Sick leave, holiday pay and vacation may be separate banks or one combined pool; banked time may or may not be payable when your job ends. Be sure that the contract covers any potential vacation blackout periods as well. If you work in a business that involves retail sales, for instance, you may not be able to take much or any time off during the holiday season, whereas a tax-preparation firm is unlikely to offer vacation in the weeks leading up to major tax deadlines. You should also be sure you have detailed information on the company's parental leave policy if you think you may take advantage of it in either the short or the long term.

It isn't necessary for a contract to cover every single benefit an employer offers. Smaller matters such as when you can take your lunch break, whether the office provides free coffee or how gas mileage is reimbursed are more likely to appear in an employee handbook. But anything that contributes to your compensation in a significant way, and especially anything you specifically negotiated, should appear in writing. In general, if you discussed anything in the interview or negotiation process related to pay or compensation, expect to see it in the contract and ask if it isn't there.

Terms Of Employment

Your contract should make clear whether you are a full-time or a part-time employee, or whether you are an independent contractor. Note that whether you are an employee or a contractor is not up to your employer. The difference between the two is determined by statute, so you can ensure that the classification aligns with the factors that determine it. (See the section on concerns for contractors later in this chapter for more information.)

Assuming you are an employee, your contract should make clear what hours you are expected to work. If the employer allows flextime, the contract should explain how that benefit is structured. It should also specify whether you will be paid as a salaried or hourly worker. Most U.S. jobs are covered by the federal Fair Labor Standards Act, or FLSA. Major exceptions include elected officials, as well as their staff or appointees. If the FLSA applies, your position should be classified as "exempt" or "nonexempt." Like the distinction between employee and contractor, these classifications are governed by legal rules rather than employer preferences. Exempt employees must generally be salaried workers who receive an annual income over a certain threshold: $684 per week or $35,568 per year for a full-time worker as of 2024. In addition, FLSA-exempt workers must perform relatively high-level job duties such as management, engineering, teaching or administrative work. Nonexempt workers are entitled to overtime pay, while exempt employees generally are not. If your contract specifies that you are exempt, or that you will not receive overtime, make sure your position fits the FLSA's definition.

Your contract will likely touch on the job's duration, even if the position is open-ended. In addition to your start date, the contract may outline a probationary period, or a specific end date for a position designed to last only a year or two. For jobs meant to last indefinitely, the contract will likely build in an end point, after which you and the employer can renew or renegotiate your agreement. Many employment contracts include an "evergreen" provision, which states that the contract will renew automatically unless either party chooses to terminate it. If your contract automatically renews, you should begin a discussion about any possible renegotiation well before the original term expires.

Like the distinction between employee and contractor, the classification of a position as "exempt" or "nonexempt" under the Fair Labor Standards Act is set by legal rules rather than employer preferences.

Your contract will likely not spell out future growth opportunities explicitly, but it is worth considering your potential path when you are evaluating a job offer. Ideally, you have already asked about the potential for career advancement by the time you have an offer in hand, but if not, you should raise the subject with the hiring manager. You may also want to look for provisions in the contract that could support your professional growth. For example, the employer may offer to reimburse you for membership in a professional organization or for continuing-education courses. If you want to obtain a certification or credential, note whether the company will reimburse you for testing fees or allow you to study for a related exam as part of your job duties. Your contract may also specify whether the employer offers any education funding and, if so, what the requirements are to secure it.

Your contract will generally state where you will work. It should also cover whether, and to what extent, remote work is permitted. If flexibility about location was a point of negotiation, be especially sure that the contract reflects the terms you and the employer settled on. In cases where you agreed to be on site full time at first, look for a specific timeline for when you can begin working remotely some or all of the time. If the employer does business in multiple locations, or even if the company is just likely to expand in the future, a contract may also cover whether an employer can require you to move to another location without your consent and how much notice such a move requires.

Some employers ask applicants to pass a drug test before starting work. Most states allow such testing or allow it under certain circumstances. It is rarer for a workplace to require current employees to undergo random or periodic testing. Some states prohibit blanket testing outright due to privacy concerns. If your state does not, note whether your employer tests employees and under what circumstances. Employees may always refuse testing, but in most cases, they can be fired over that refusal (and, in some states, they may be denied unemployment benefits).

In addition to these clauses, a contract should include your job title and an overview of the basic duties of the position. The details will depend on the job and the industry. Occasionally, you will want very specific and detailed descriptions of what your job will — and will not — entail. But in many other positions, such specificity would be needlessly restrictive. If you are not already familiar with what is typical in your field, ask a trusted colleague or mentor. Regardless of the detail, be sure that the title and description provided match what you expected after the interview process. Speak up about any discrepancy you notice.

Restrictions

One of the principal reasons a company might offer a contract rather than a nonbinding offer letter is to include position- or industry-specific restrictions. For example, businesses with relationship-based revenue are much more likely to insist on formal noncompete agreements. While these agreements are in force, employees agree not to work for direct competitors and not to set up a business in direct competition with their former employer. These provisions are common for sales positions, but also in medical practices, research positions and technology companies (among others). Most noncompete agreements have a set term for how long they extend after you leave, and many are also restricted by geographic area. In general, noncompete provisions cannot be broader than necessary to protect the employer's business. State law varies on how restrictive a noncompete may be while remaining legally binding; in California, most noncompete clauses are automatically void. Educate yourself on your state's requirements to be sure the proposed noncompete complies with these rules. An overly restrictive noncompete can make it hard to get a new position in your industry. Be wary if the terms seem too broad, even if they are legal in your state.

Certain contracts may also include nonsolicitation clauses. These restrict employees from soliciting work from the business's customers. For a full-time employee, a nonsolicitation clause is generally designed to protect the business after the employee's departure. It may also apply to independent contractors whose business offerings overlap with the client's. Like noncompetes, nonsolicitation clauses should not be open-ended. Make sure that such clauses are not so far-reaching that they would make it difficult or impossible to work after you leave. Nondealing clauses similarly prohibit you from dealing with an ex-employer's customers, but differ in that they forbid you from accepting work from customers who approach you, even if you don't actively seek them out. Nonpoaching clauses prohibit you from taking colleagues and other staff with you when you leave your employer.

In some positions, you may be required to sign a confidentiality or nondisclosure agreement. This generally means agreeing not to share any proprietary data, processes, plans or other sensitive information. Unlike noncompete and nonsolicitation agreements, most nondisclosure agreements last indefinitely. If you sign a confidentiality agreement, be sure that the agreement spells out clearly what information the employer considers confidential. The less uncertainty in this area, the better.

If you are an employee who wants to hold down a second position, whether a part-time job elsewhere or the occasional freelance gig, it is important to make sure your contract allows moonlighting. In most cases, this is easier to negotiate if your other work is unrelated to your employer's industry. Most employers want to ensure that your other work will not run afoul of noncompete rules or create conflicts of interest. This is the same reason a contract may prohibit employees from becoming a shareholder or director in another business within the industry. Similarly, if you want to serve on a nonprofit board or take on other significant community work, it is worth ensuring that this won't conflict with any of your new employer's policies. (For more on serving on a nonprofit board, see

Chapter 20.) If you already have a side business or plan to start one in the future, it is better to discuss the situation upfront, before you accept an offer, than to face a potential legal headache once you've started your primary job.

You may generate intellectual property in the course of your work, including written compositions, graphics or audiovisual materials. Intellectual property concerns also apply to all sorts of research and development positions, including software developers, pharmaceutical researchers and many others. In most cases, employees creating work as part of their normal job duties do not have the right to copyright or patent that work. Work within the employee's "scope of employment" automatically belongs to the employer in nearly all circumstances.

The issue becomes murkier when employees make a discovery, invent something new or generate creative work on their own time that somehow relates to the employer's business. Some companies ask employees who focus on invention or product development to sign "assignment agreements," which are broad in scope and don't always end when an employee departs. These clauses cover work created using company resources and often rely on the fact that it can be difficult to definitively prove when you have had an idea. Some states limit the scope of such agreements by statute. Make sure that your employer's definition of the scope of your employment is not overly broad, especially if your work is creative or you produce even tangentially related work on your own time.

QUICK NOTES

Potential Restrictions In A Contract Or Offer Letter

Type	What Employees Agree To
Noncompete Clause	► Not to work for direct competitors and not to set up a business in direct competition with a former employer
Nonsolicitation Clause	► Not to actively pursue work from the business's customers
Nondealing Clause	► Not to accept work from the business's customers for a certain period, even if they seek the employee out themselves
Nonpoaching Clause	► Not to take colleagues or other business staff along when leaving
Confidentiality/ Nondisclosure Agreement	► Not to share any proprietary data, processes, plans or other sensitive information
Prohibition on Moonlighting	► Not to engage in a second job (either in the same industry or of any kind, depending on the provisions)
Assignment Agreements	► That the business has a legal stake in creative work made using company resources, even outside the employee's regular scope of employment

Disputes

Most contracts include some provision for how the company resolves disputes with employees. At a minimum, they will generally specify "choice of law" or "governing law" — in other words, which state's law will govern the employment relationship as laid out in the contract. This matters less if you and your employer operate only in one state; for example, if you are a chef at an independently owned restaurant with only one location in Illinois, your employment will be subject to Illinois law. But for companies with locations in multiple states, or which do business online, governing law is less of a foregone conclusion.

Some contracts also include arbitration clauses, in which the parties agree that they will submit any serious disagreement to arbitration rather than seek resolution in the courts. This provision may specify whether the arbitration is binding or how the parties will find an arbitrator if they need one. It will also generally specify whether arbitration is confidential, and where such disputes must be arbitrated. If you and the employer enter into arbitration — or a legal dispute — the contract may specify that the prevailing party is entitled to recoup any related fees.

Unions are rarer than they used to be, especially in the private sector. But if workers at your new employer are unionized, it is likely that your contract will be shaped by collective bargaining. Depending on the type of "shop" that exists at your workplace, you may be required to join the union to take a position there. In states with right to work laws, such a requirement is not permitted. A collective-bargaining agreement may also include provisions about arbitration and dispute resolution between the company and employees. Therefore it is important to fully understand any agreement governing your particular workplace. Note, too, that in most cases the National Labor Relations Act prohibits employers from interfering with their workers' right to organize, so if a union does not already exist, your contract should not include provisions that would make your position contingent on refusing to support unionization.

Consider both the near-term and long-term implications of dispute-resolution clauses in your contract. Employees typically do not enter into contracts with employers because they expect the company to act in bad faith. At the same time, you should feel confident that your contract protects your interests if something goes wrong. Ideally, a contract should work for you whether things go as planned or not.

Departure

Few people have termination on their minds when accepting a new job. Yet it is smart to carefully review the contract's rules about voluntary and involuntary departure. Some employers are willing to lock in a desirable employee for a certain term, during which the employee can only be terminated for cause. If this applies to you, the grounds for potential termination should be clearly defined in your contract. For example, potential circumstances under which you might be fired for cause include breaching the terms of the employment contract or theft from the employer.

Even if your contract defines your employment as "at will," it may spell out other important terms of your departure. If your employer terminates you without cause, you may be entitled to severance pay; if so, the contract should state how much, and whether it is payable as a lump sum or over time. The employer may specify that if you accept a severance payment, you must sign a release of liability. The contract can also specify how much notice either party must give before ending the arrangement. Under an at-will arrangement, neither you nor your employer must give advance notice, but a contract may specify that your employer must provide you with a notice of termination.

While most workers hope they will not leave a job due to severe disability or death, this sometimes happens. Your employer should make clear whether you or your family members will continue to receive benefits for some amount of time after the position ends in these circumstances.

FREELANCERS AND INDEPENDENT CONTRACTORS

Most of the advice in the preceding section also applies to freelancers and contractors. But these workers may have additional concerns when reviewing a contract. It is possible that you may be responsible for offering the contract yourself, if your client is not prepared to do so.

As we mentioned earlier in this chapter, whether a worker is an independent contractor or an employee is not up to the employer. Rather, the two terms describe distinct ways of doing work on an employer (or client's) behalf. Since 1978, the Internal Revenue Service has issued guidance to help employers make sure they are classifying workers correctly. This means that if you are working as a contractor, your contract should align with these legal requirements. The overarching principle is that an employer has a right to control when and how employees do their work; contractors have the right to control their own working conditions. For instance, in most cases, if you are required to be at a company's office between 8 a.m. and 5 p.m. every day, you are an employee. Contractors generally agree to produce a certain result by a certain deadline, but can determine when and where they work.

Based on IRS guidance, contractors retain behavioral control and financial control of their work. Clients can pay contractors per task or by the hour. As a contractor, you may have some control over whether you prefer to charge by the hour or by the project. Companies also typically cannot require contractors to sign noncompete agreements or forbid them from working for other companies without running afoul of IRS rules. In turn, contractors seldom have access to benefits such as company-paid health insurance or retirement plans. As self-employed workers, they must also handle their own taxes. (For more on self-employment and quarterly estimated taxes, see Chapter 15.)

Employers offer contracts to freelancers more frequently when they will be doing a significant amount of work or potentially entering into a long-term arrangement. But even if you are agreeing to work on a one-off project, it is smart to get the agreement in writing. This may be a "letter of agreement" (more often an email of agreement in practice), which is an informal written summary of the terms you and your client have discussed. Many freelancers use a "statement of work" or "scope of work" arrangement, which is more detailed than a letter of agreement but less formal than a full contract. Some freelancers prefer to hire an attorney to help them create a more formal contract template, which they can customize for various clients. Unlike an employee contract, a freelance contract will not include items such as working hours or benefit details. But it should outline any agreed-upon deadlines for the work, a description of the work you have agreed to produce, and when and how the client will compensate you for that work. If you and your client have negotiated an upfront fee, include that too.

Some businesses may want you to sign a nondisclosure agreement as a freelancer or contractor. This request is not unreasonable on its face, provided it is structured so that it does not represent an overreach. Be sure to review any nondisclosure agreements carefully and bring up any questions or concerns before you sign it.

Your agreement or contract should also lay out how you will deal with any proposed extra work that might arise. You will want to make the original scope of the project clear and address how any work beyond that scope will be addressed. Are you open to adding additional work for a fee? Is there certain additional work you will not do? For example, if a company hires a writer to produce a manuscript, she may want to make clear that the project includes no subsequent edits under any circumstances. Or she may offer two rounds of editing in the project's original scope, with any more requiring an additional fee. However you want to approach "scope creep," your contract should outline what work is and is not included in your agreement. This is much more important for a contractor than for an employee, whose job is likely to grow and change over time.

QUICK NOTES

Employee vs. Independent Contractor

Employee

- Employer can control when and where employee works
- Can be subject to noncompete clauses in most cases
- Often has access to benefits such as employer-paid health insurance
- Employer handles employment taxes and can withhold income tax
- Most creative work within scope of employment is automatically the employer's property

Independent Contractor

- Contractor controls own hours and work environment
- Usually can't be required to sign a noncompete agreement
- Seldom has access to benefits through clients
- Contractor is responsible for employment taxes and paying quarterly estimated tax
- Contractors can negotiate with clients how they will handle rights to creative work

Many freelancers are creative workers, such as writers or graphic designers. This means intellectual property rights are likely to be an important part of any contract or agreement. Depending on what you are hired to do, your contract may include a "work made for hire" provision, which specifies that the work you are agreeing to perform will belong to the client. In many cases, this is normal and will be reflected in your compensation. In other situations, you may want to preserve certain rights or have rights revert to you after some time. You may want to retain the rights to display your work as part of a portfolio without having to consult or compensate your client, for example. If you plan to license your work and the client seems open to the arrangement, you will likely want to involve an attorney who has experience with intellectual property to help create or review your contract, as the law can be complex. Many freelancers specify that they retain intellectual property rights to their work until the client pays them, as a way to ensure an unethical client does not start using their work without compensating its creator. The crucial point is that you and your client should be on the same page about who will own the creative work before you get started. A contract should confirm your understanding.

You and your client may agree to part ways before your contract ends for a variety of reasons. Therefore, it's worth touching on termination, even in a relatively short-term contract. Like an employment contract, a freelance contract may dictate that each party must give a certain amount of notice before ending the arrangement. You may also want to include a provision for "inactivity," in case you cannot reach your contact at a company for an extended period. You should agree on a fair payment system for time spent or the amount of work completed if a project is cut short; you can outline how you plan to invoice on a pro rata basis, for instance.

ENFORCEMENT AND PENALTIES

The trade-off for the security and clarity a contract offers is that both parties agree to be bound by its terms. If either you or your employer violates those terms, the consequences can be serious.

The precise consequences will likely be stipulated within the contract itself. At a minimum, if you violate the terms, your employer can terminate you. A breach of contract also opens you to legal liability. Legal action is a last resort for most companies, as direct conflict resolution or even out-of-court mediation is less costly and less time-consuming. For a company, a lawsuit can also entail negative publicity. However, if either party violates the contract's terms, legal action is possible. For instance, if you signed a contract with a noncompete clause and your ex-employer thinks that your new job violates that agreement, the company can sue you and seek injunctive relief — that is, making you leave your new employer — or seek financial damages. For a situation in which you are on the other side of a breached contract, if you decide to pursue legal action you should involve an experienced attorney who is familiar with the applicable state law. In general, you can seek damages to compensate you for the particular financial harm the breached contract caused. Breach of an employment contract seldom leads to compensation for emotional distress or other less concrete damages.

You may go your whole career without encountering a formal employment contract, or you may deal with them frequently. Whether you fall at either extreme, or anywhere in between, it is important to approach a new professional position thoughtfully and methodically. A good employer puts significant time and effort into creating the employment offer in front of you. You should do the same before signing on the dotted line.

CHAPTER 15

INCOME TAXES

Melinda Kibler, CFP®, EA

Most Americans think of "tax season" as between March 1 and April 15, perhaps because this is when we are inundated with commercials and news reports reminding us to file. The average American only thinks about income taxes for this short period of time, then puts all tax-related matters on the back burner.

Yet you can — and should — plan for taxes year-round. It will minimize your overall stress, especially if you tend to procrastinate. By planning ahead, you can also avoid rushing to make last-minute decisions, with potential negative consequences. Making tax planning a routine part of your financial maintenance can benefit anyone, but it is especially useful for people with complex situations or in changing stages of life.

Many people who approach professional tax preparers want to find ways to cut their overall tax liability. A reputable tax expert can help you analyze your situation and identify how you may be overpaying. In this sense, minimizing your taxes is perfectly legal. The courts have repeatedly confirmed that arranging your affairs to minimize taxes while following the law is in no way sinister. On the other hand, paying less than you legally should is tax evasion. Whether it means fudging numbers or breaking the rules outright, tax evasion is illegal. Fraud — the act of intentionally paying the government less than you should — can result in hefty fines and jail time.

In general, the primary rule of financial planning is not to let the tax tail wag the dog. Never jeopardize your long-term financial stability in pursuit of a lower tax bill. For example, you may be tempted to stash every spare dollar into a tax-advantaged account, but that impulse can be costly if you find yourself needing cash and facing potential early-withdrawal penalties. Like all other aspects of financial planning, you should consider your tax situation as part of a bigger picture.

GETTING STARTED

When you prepare to file income taxes, start with your federal return. If you live in a state with an income tax, you can prepare your state tax return after the federal return. (For more on state income taxes, see the section later in this chapter.)

What Documents Do You Need?

While everyone's tax situation is unique, there are a few key documents you are likely to need to file your taxes.

- **Form W-2, Wage and Tax Statement.** If you are an employee, you should receive one of these forms every year. Companies use Form W-2 to report wages they paid to employees, as well as any taxes they withheld from those wages. Withholdings routinely include federal and state income tax, Social Security tax and Medicare tax.

- **Form 1099-NEC, Nonemployee Compensation.** Freelancers and independent contractors are likely to have at least one, or more commonly several, of these forms, unless they have organized their business as a corporation. Form 1099-NEC reflects income from any source that paid you $600 or more over the course of the year. Payers who issue 1099s are not required to withhold Social Security and Medicare tax, which means you are responsible for paying these taxes. (See the section on estimated taxes later in this chapter for more details.) If you requested it, the issuer may have withheld federal or state income tax, but this is rare.

- **Form 1099-MISC, Miscellaneous Income.** If you received at least $10 in royalties or at least $600 in rents, prizes or awards, you may be issued this form to report the income. As with Form 1099-NEC, issuers are not required to withhold income tax on the funds. For example, if you won a travel package or concert tickets worth $600 or more through a contest, the value of the prize is taxable and will be reported on the Form 1099-MISC.

- **Form 1099-DIV, Form 1099-INT or Form 1099 Composite.** If you have bank or investment accounts, generally you will receive one of these documents. Institutions use them to report any income in excess of $10 you gained from interest or dividends, as well as any capital gains or losses on your investments.

- **Schedule K-1.** If you are a partner in an investment or a business, this form will report your share of the partnership's earnings, losses, deductions and credits. Certain other organizations, including S corporations, also issue K-1s to owners or beneficiaries.

You may routinely receive a variety of other tax forms depending on your situation. These can include forms documenting student loan interest you paid, contributions you made to a health savings account, or contributions you made to a traditional individual retirement account. When you receive forms from a financial institution, it is a good idea to save them in a single location, so they will all be ready to go when you prepare to file your tax return.

If you may benefit from itemizing your deductions, you will also need miscellaneous data to support those deductions. These may include Form 1098, which documents mortgage interest; property tax records; receipts for medical expenses; and receipts for qualifying charitable donations. Note, though, that because the Tax Cuts and Jobs Act of 2017 significantly raised the standard deduction, you may not find it worthwhile to itemize unless your deductions are significant. However, this higher standard deduction may end if Congress does not extend the act's provisions, at which point more taxpayers may return to itemizing their deductions.

U.S. citizens need to report and pay tax on all income, domestic and international. This means you should document it all, including income you received without an associated tax form. However, there are a few ways you can receive assets that are legally excluded from what is called your "gross" income for personal income tax purposes. These items include gifts, inheritances, and most workers' compensation and life insurance proceeds, among a few other categories. You do not need to include income from these sources on your return.

Which Forms To File

Form 1040 is the form that all U.S. citizens, permanent residents and nonresidents married to U.S. citizens must file annually to report income, along with any claimed deductions or credits. It is usually due on April 15 of the following year. If you cannot meet the deadline for any reason, you can file Form 4868 to request a six-month extension. It is important to know this is an extension to file, not an extension to pay. Even if you extend your filing deadline, you must estimate any taxes you owe and pay the estimate by April 15 to avoid penalties.

Form 1040 is also important for business owners if they own a pass-through business. In these organizations, business income "passes through" to be taxed on the owner's (or owners') personal income tax return. If you are the owner of a single-member limited liability company, report all of your business income on Schedule C of Form 1040. Partnerships must file Form 1065 and then issue a Schedule K-1 to each partner. An S corporation must file Form 1120-S and then similarly issue a Schedule K-1 to each shareholder. Owners report the Schedule K-1 information on their individual Form 1040.

Taxpayers in particular situations may need to file additional schedules or forms. While this chapter will not cover every potential situation, I will mention a few of the more common forms and schedules when discussing the relevant circumstances.

TAX RATES

Tax rates, as well as income and deduction thresholds, are not static — far from it. They can change annually, if they are indexed to inflation or some other measure. In years when Congress passes major legislation, the rates may change even more significantly. A "permanent" tax rate typically lasts only a few years, according to historical data compiled by the Tax Foundation. The Tax Cuts and Jobs Act made major changes to the tax brackets and the standard deduction in 2017. It also changed which expenses were deductible and added new categories such as qualified business income, which I will discuss later in this chapter.

If you can't meet the income tax deadline for any reason, you can file to request a six-month extension. But even if you extend your filing deadline, you must estimate any taxes you owe and pay the estimate by April 15 to avoid penalties.

Many people do not have a clear idea of how federal tax rates work. Federal income tax rates are progressive and graduated. This means that for most people, not all income is taxed at the same rate. When your income passes a new tax bracket threshold, only the income exceeding that amount is taxed at the higher rate. For example, a single taxpayer earning $650,000 would be subject to the highest tax bracket for ordinary income — 37% as of this writing. However, the taxpayer does not owe 37% of the entire amount. Instead, he owes 10% on the first chunk of income, 12% on the next piece, and so on. Only the amount above the highest threshold ($609,350 for a single taxpayer at this writing) is subject to the highest rate.

You can determine your effective tax rate by dividing your total tax liability by your taxable income. Unless your income is such that all of it is subject to the lowest bracket, your effective tax rate will generally be lower than the rate you pay on the last dollar of your total income, which is described as your "marginal" tax rate.

In addition to your income, your filing status will also affect the rate you pay. This is because tax bracket thresholds vary based on filing status. Your status depends largely on your family structure. If you are single, you will generally file as "single." In some cases, you may instead qualify to file as "head of household" if you have dependents, or as a "qualified widow or widower" for the two years after the year your spouse died. In any of these cases, there is no real choice to make. You will select whichever status accurately describes your situation.

Married couples, on the other hand, may choose between two statuses: "married filing jointly" or "married filing separately." Most couples elect to file jointly. In this case, the spouses pool their income and the government taxes the couple as a single economic unit. Generally, couples who file jointly pay less than couples who file separately. There are, however, circumstances in which filing separately makes more sense. For example, if one spouse is on an income-based student loan repayment plan, filing separately could keep the monthly loan payment lower than it would be if both spouses filed together.

Tax Rate	Single	Married Filing Jointly/ Qualified Widow(er)	Married Filing Separately	Head Of Household
10%	Up to $11,600	Up to $23,200	Up to $11,600	Up to $16,550
12%	$11,601 to $47,150	$23,201 to $94,300	$11,601 to $47,150	$16,551 to $63,100
22%	$47,151 to $100,525	$94,301 to $201,050	$47,151 to $100,525	$63,101 to $100,500
24%	$100,526 to $191,950	$201,051 to $383,900	$100,526 to $191,950	$100,501 to $191,950
32%	$191,951 to $243,725	$383,901 to $487,450	$191,951 to $243,725	$191,951 to $243,700
35%	$243,726 to $609,350	$487,451 to $731,200	$243,726 to $365,600	$243,701 to $609,350
37%	$609,351 or more	$731,201 or more	$365,601 or more	$609,351 or more

Figure 6: Tax Rate Table

(Source: Internal Revenue Service for tax year 2024)

CAPITAL GAINS TAX

If you sold any assets during the year, either for a profit or at a loss, then you must report that gain or loss on your tax return using Schedule D. For most people, this situation arises because they sell assets within an investment portfolio. Gains or losses can be either short-term or long-term, depending on how long you held the asset before you sold it. If you held the asset for one year or less, you recognized a short-term gain or loss; anything longer than one year, and it's a long-term gain or loss.

Short-term capital gains are taxed at ordinary income tax rates. Long-term gains, however, are taxed at preferential rates. The precise long-term capital gains rate will depend on your total taxable income and your filing status.

	Single	Married Filing Jointly	Married Filing Separately	Head Of Household
0%	Up to $47,025	Up to $94,050	Up to $47,025	Up to $63,000
15%	$47,026 to $518,900	$94,051 to $583,750	$47,026 to $291,850	$63,001 to $551,350
20%	$518,901 or more	$583,751 or more	$291,851 or more	$551,351 or more

Figure 7: Long-Term Capital Gains Tax Rate Table
(Source: Internal Revenue Service for tax year 2024)

These brackets are indexed for inflation.

You may not end up paying tax on all of your capital gains. You can use capital losses to offset capital gains for tax purposes. If you sell an investment for less than its original cost, you can effectively cancel out some or all of a capital gain. If you have more capital losses than gains for the year overall, you can also reduce your ordinary income by up to $3,000 (or $1,500 for married taxpayers filing separately). If you offset your capital gains and $3,000 of ordinary income and still have additional capital losses, you can carry them forward to offset future capital gains. You should report individual gains and losses on Form 8949, and the total summary on Schedule D.

One exception to the general capital gain rule is personal property. The Internal Revenue Service taxes gains on personal-use property, which is property individuals own for their own enjoyment rather than for investment or business. However, a taxpayer cannot deduct the loss on a sale of personal property.

If you plan to contribute to a tax-exempt charitable organization, you may want to consider a gift of an appreciated asset. Like cash gifts, gifts of appreciated assets are tax deductible if you itemize deductions. But as an additional feature, giving appreciated securities allows you to permanently avoid capital gains tax on the appreciation. This can make your generosity go further, since the charitable institution also will not realize any taxable gain when it sells the asset.

SELF-EMPLOYMENT TAXES

As I mentioned earlier in the chapter, self-employed taxpayers such as freelancers or sole proprietors of businesses generally should not expect clients or companies for whom they work to withhold Social Security and Medicare taxes. They do, however, still owe these taxes.

The self-employment tax rate is 15.3%, which breaks down into 12.4% for Social Security and 2.9% for Medicare. If you are a sole proprietor or independent contractor, you will use Schedule C of Form 1040 to determine your net self-employment earnings and Schedule SE to calculate your self-employment tax liability. Self-employed workers can also deduct a portion of their self-employment tax —

the equivalent to the portion that an employer would contribute for a wage earner — from their gross income.

MEDICARE SURTAX

In addition to the standard Social Security tax and Medicare taxes that workers owe on wage income, wages or self-employment income above a certain threshold are subject to an additional 0.9% Medicare surtax. The taxpayer is generally responsible for this surtax. However, employers are required to withhold this tax on wages in excess of $200,000 paid to an employee.

The wage threshold for triggering Medicare surtax on your return varies depending on your filing status. If you are married and filing jointly, you must combine wages with self-employment income to determine if you have surpassed the threshold. For married couples filing jointly, that threshold is $250,000. For married taxpayers filing separately, it is $125,000, and for single filers or heads of household, it is $200,000.

Since the employer-withholding threshold differs from the filing-status threshold, there may be situations where an employee may exceed the total income threshold, triggering Medicare surtax, but be underpaid because the employer was not required to withhold the surtax. Alternatively, an employee may have Medicare surtax withheld, then receive a refund. For example, consider an employee with a salary of $225,000 who is married to a spouse who does not work. They are above the $200,000 wage threshold, causing the employer to automatically withhold an additional 0.9% Medicare surtax. However, when the couple files their personal tax return, they will receive a refund, because the $225,000 of income is below the married filing jointly threshold of $250,000. To request a refund, the taxpayer must complete Form 8959, Additional Medicare Tax.

NET INVESTMENT INCOME TAX

Taxpayers who earn investment income may face the 3.8% surtax on net investment income. To understand whether you need to worry about this tax, you must determine two things: whether your modified adjusted gross income (MAGI) surpasses a certain threshold, and what "investment income" means in this context.

Modified adjusted gross income is your adjusted gross income with certain deductions added back. (I will discuss adjusted gross income in more detail later in this chapter, but as the name suggests, it reflects your gross income less certain adjustments.) MAGI serves as the basis for determining whether a taxpayer qualifies for certain deductions or, in this case, must pay certain taxes. For the net investment income tax, your MAGI must exceed $200,000 for single taxpayers or taxpayers filing as the head of a household. For married couples, the thresholds are $250,000 for a couple filing jointly or $125,000 for spouses filing separately. Estates and trusts may also owe net investment income tax, depending on their income.

Once you determine whether your MAGI exceeds the applicable thresholds, you will need to know what sources of income are subject to this tax. Investment income mainly includes interest, dividends, certain annuities, royalties and rents (unless those rents are income from a trade or business to which the net investment income tax specifically doesn't apply). It may include income earned in a business or trade that the IRS defines as "passive." Net gains from the disposition of property can also be subject to this tax, unless the property was held by a trade or business exempt from the net investment income tax. As this incomplete list suggests, those who may be subject to this tax will likely want to speak to a tax expert about their situation. The IRS rules regarding passive activities are especially complex and best parsed by a professional.

Net investment income tax is charged on the lesser of your total net investment income or the amount by which your MAGI exceeds the threshold. A couple of examples may help make this clearer. Consider a single taxpayer with $170,000 of wage income and an additional $80,000 of investment income. This makes her MAGI $250,000. The threshold for a single taxpayer is $200,000. Therefore, the 3.8% surtax is charged on the amount the MAGI exceeds the threshold — $50,000 — instead of the full $80,000 of net investment income.

In contrast, consider a single taxpayer with $220,000 of wage income and $40,000 more of investment income. His total MAGI is $260,000. The 3.8% surtax will be charged on the full $40,000 of net investment income, since it is lower than the amount by which the MAGI exceeds the $200,000 threshold ($60,000).

ALTERNATIVE MINIMUM TAX (AMT)

Congress created the Alternative Minimum Tax, usually abbreviated AMT, to ensure that all taxpayers pay a minimum level of tax, regardless of deductions or other exclusions. While it applies to relatively few taxpayers, it is important to confirm whether it applies to you.

The AMT involves an entirely separate tax calculation, which eliminates or reduces many exclusions or deductions. Each time you file an income tax return, you (or your tax preparer) must calculate AMT. Taxpayers are required to pay the higher of regular tax or AMT.

The Tax Cuts and Jobs Act significantly reduced the number of taxpayers subject to AMT. Earlier versions of AMT calculations included adjustments for large state and local tax (SALT) deductions, as well as for "miscellaneous itemized deductions" (a category that included deductions for legal fees, investment advisory fees and other items). The Tax Cuts and Jobs Act eliminated miscellaneous itemized deductions entirely and capped SALT deductions at $10,000 per year, or just $5,000 for married individuals filing separately. Without these common triggers, fewer people now owe AMT. The remaining adjustments that can trigger AMT are much less prevalent. These include adjustments related to substantial income from municipal bonds classified as private activity bonds, investment interest, and depletion from oil, gas, timber, mining or similar activities. Note that, as with many provisions of the Tax Cuts and Jobs Act, the provisions affecting AMT are set to expire after 2025 unless Congress chooses to extend them.

For ordinary income, AMT rates are set percentages. Taxpayers calculate their taxable income, making adjustments for AMT rules that eliminate certain tax deductions or exclusions as I described in the previous paragraph. Then income is reduced by an AMT exemption unless the taxpayer's income exceeds $609,350 for single filers or $1,218,700 for married taxpayers filing jointly. (These are 2024 thresholds, subject to annual inflation adjustments.) For single taxpayers in 2024, the exemption is $85,700; for married filing jointly, the exemption is $133,300. The remaining income amount after exemption is subject to AMT tax rates. The first $232,600 of income is taxed at 26%, and the remaining income is taxed at 28% for all filers except married filing separately. Since taxpayers pay the higher of the two calculations, it is important to always calculate both ordinary income tax and AMT.

DEDUCTIONS

Tax deductions reduce the amount of your income that is subject to tax. Taxable income is the difference between a taxpayer's adjusted gross income (AGI) and either the standard deduction or allowable itemized deductions, as well as a deduction for qualified business income. The standard deduction is available to all taxpayers. The amount of this deduction varies based on filing status and is indexed to inflation, and so changes from year to year.

Filing Status	Deduction
Single or Married Filing Separately	$14,600
Head Of Household	$21,900
Married Filing Jointly or Qualifying Widow(er)	$29,200

Figure 8: Filing Status Standard Deduction Chart
(Source: Internal Revenue Service for tax year 2024)

Taking the standard deduction is much easier than the alternative, and it is also the most beneficial option for most Americans after the passage of the Tax Cuts and Jobs Act. In general, taxpayers should only itemize deductions if they are greater than the applicable standard deduction. Itemizing involves preparing Schedule A, attached to Form 1040, and reporting the particular dollar amounts spent on deductible expenses.

Some deductions affect AGI directly, before the calculation of taxable income. These are available to all taxpayers, regardless of whether they choose to itemize. Any deductions that affect AGI are known as "above-the-line" deductions. For example, a contribution to a traditional IRA is a deduction of this type. "Below-the-line" deductions make up the difference between a taxpayer's AGI and total taxable income. The standard deduction is a below-the-line deduction, as are charitable contributions and other itemized deductions.

Above-the-line deductions are more valuable, because lowering AGI can increase your available tax benefits or open new ones. For example, you can deduct medical expenses to the extent that they exceed 7.5% of your AGI, within certain limits. A lower AGI means a lower dollar threshold before such expenses become deductible.

Below-the-line deductions, however, can still make a significant difference in how much tax you owe. While most taxpayers are likely to take the standard deduction — at least through 2025, when many of the current law's provisions will end unless Congress extends them — taxpayers in certain situations can continue to benefit from specific deductions. For example, if you live in a state that imposes a high tax burden, you may benefit from itemizing, since state and local income taxes are deductible. However, as I mentioned in the previous section, each taxpayer may only deduct $10,000 of state and local tax (SALT) per year.

Homeowners also may benefit from itemizing. Mortgage interest is deductible on loans up to $750,000, or up to $1 million if you purchased your home on or before Dec. 15, 2017. Bear in mind that if you use your mortgage debt for purposes other than acquiring or improving your home, it is actually home equity debt, and the interest no longer qualifies as an itemized deduction under the 2017 tax law. This doesn't mean a home equity loan is never deductible. It is how you use the funds, not the nature of the loan, which determines whether you can deduct your interest. A home equity loan whose proceeds are used to fund a business can generate interest that is deductible as a business expense, for example. Homeowners may also deduct real estate or other property taxes. However, personal real estate taxes are subject to the $10,000 annual SALT limit.

Qualified Business Income

The Tax Cuts and Jobs Act created a new concern for owners of pass-through businesses. In an effort to make business taxation fairer for enterprises that are not corporations, lawmakers created a new deduction for "qualified business income," often shortened QBI. A taxpayer may deduct 20% of qualified business income that comes from a domestic business operated as a sole proprietorship, or from his or her interest in a partnership, limited liability company or S corporation. Trusts and estates may also be eligible to take the QBI deduction.

Qualified business income is the net qualified income, gain, deduction or loss from any qualified trade or business. This income must be effectively connected with a U.S. trade or business. There are several categories that are specifically not QBI, including capital gains or losses, certain dividends, interest, W-2 income and guaranteed payments from a partnership.

QBI is also subject to a variety of limitations. Factors including the taxpayer's overall income, the nature of the trade or business, the amount of W-2 wages the qualified trade or business paid, and the unadjusted basis immediately after acquisition of qualified property the trade or business held can all reduce or eliminate this deduction.

If your annual taxable income is below $191,950, or $383,900 for married taxpayers filing jointly (these are 2024 amounts that will be inflation-adjusted in later years), you can take the qualified business income deduction freely. For taxpayers with higher taxable incomes, the nature of the business becomes relevant. Above the threshold, income from "specified service businesses" are not fully eligible for the deduction. The IRS designates a list of specified service trades or businesses, including services in the fields of health, law, accounting, actuarial science, performing arts, consulting, athletics, financial services, investing and trading. The list also includes a catch-all description for businesses where the principal asset is the skill of the owners or employees. Taxpayers who receive income from these enterprises can only partially deduct QBI. This deduction phases out as taxable income increases. Once a taxpayer's income reaches $241,950 (or $483,900 for couples filing jointly), the deduction vanishes entirely for those with QBI income from a specified service business. These income ceilings also are 2024 amounts subject to future inflation adjustments.

The QBI deduction is still relatively new, and there is not yet extensive case law to guide taxpayers or professionals as to how tax courts will judge various applications of these rules. If you expect to receive QBI, especially if your income exceeds the base thresholds, proceed with care. But these rules can also offer planning opportunities.

CREDITS

Like deductions, tax credits reduce your overall tax bill. But they work slightly differently. While deductions reduce your taxable income, a tax credit directly reduces the tax you owe dollar for dollar. In other words, a tax credit valued at $1,000 lowers your tax bill by $1,000, whereas how much you save due to a $1,000 deduction would vary depending on your tax bracket. This means that, on balance, tax credits are generally more valuable than deductions of a similar dollar amount.

Common Federal Income Tax Credits

The IRS offers the foreign tax credit to alleviate the potential burden of double taxation for Americans who owe taxes in a foreign country. The most common reason American taxpayers can claim this credit is due to holding investments in international enterprises, often through mutual funds. If a mutual fund invests in a company outside the U.S., it will typically pay foreign income tax. The fund then reports the pro rata share of tax to investors on Form 1099. You may also be eligible for this credit if you are living and working abroad; for more details on this scenario, see Chapter 17. Taxpayers who are eligible for this credit will prepare Form 1116.

On balance, tax credits are generally more valuable than deductions of a similar dollar amount.

The child tax credit is also common. The credit is worth up to $2,000 per child under the age of 17. The credit can be limited, depending on income level. In certain circumstances, caretakers may also be eligible for a $500 credit for adult dependents who are physically or mentally unable to care for themselves. Separately, there is a Child and Dependent Care Credit for expenses incurred while taxpayers are working or looking for work. The credit applies to expenses related to qualifying children under the age of 13 and dependents who are incapable of self-care physically or mentally. The credit is for 20% to 35% of qualified expenses, with a maximum $3,000 for one qualifying person, and $6,000 for two or more qualifying persons. To calculate this credit, taxpayers should use Form 2441. You can read more about these credits in Chapter 13.

Qualified higher education expenses can also result in credits. The American Opportunity Tax Credit, up to $2,500 annually, and the Lifetime Learning Credit, up to $2,000 annually, both allow taxpayers to benefit from qualified educational expenses, such as tuition and fees for an eligible postsecondary institution. Taxpayers may claim both credits in the same year but not related to the same person. Claiming either (or both) requires filing IRS Form 8863.

Homeowners who install certain renewable-energy generation devices may be eligible for credits through the Residential Clean Energy credit. Solar electrical panels, residential wind turbines and geothermal heat pumps may all apply under certain circumstances. Eligible taxpayers can use Form 5695 to calculate this credit, which can be up to 30% of the cost of the property installed. Similarly, the Energy Efficient Home Improvement Credit offers tax credits up to 30% of the cost of qualified expenses with a maximum credit of $1,200 for energy property costs, such as exterior windows and doors. The maximum credit extends to $2,000 per year for qualified heat pumps, biomass stoves or boilers.

Taxpayers who own plug-in electric passenger cars or light trucks may be eligible for a credit of up to $7,500, depending on the vehicle's battery capacity, critical minerals and battery components. The manufacturer's suggested retail price (MSRP) cannot exceed $80,000 for vans, pick-up trucks and SUVs and $55,000 for other vehicles as of late 2023.

TAX PLANNING STRATEGIES

As this chapter has likely illustrated, the tax code is complex. Effective tax planning will vary depending on your particular situation. That said, there are some tactics that will help many people take full advantage of existing deductions and credits, or potentially streamline their tax compliance.

Tax-Advantaged Saving

Contributing to a traditional (as opposed to a Roth) IRA offers immediate tax benefits if you and your spouse do not have access to a retirement plan at work. You can deduct the full amount of your contribution, up to $7,000 in 2024, if you are under age 50. If you or your spouse has access to a retirement plan at work, your MAGI will determine how much you can deduct, if anything. IRAs are especially useful for tax planning because you can contribute up until April 15 of the year you file your return. For example, you can make a 2024 IRA contribution, deductible on your 2024 income tax return, until April 15, 2025.

If your employer offers a 401(k) plan, contributing to it also offers tax advantages. You can contribute pretax dollars, bringing down your annual taxable earned income. 401(k) earnings, like IRA earnings, accumulate on a tax-deferred basis, which means you will not owe tax on capital gains or dividends within your plan. This ability to compound income tax-free is a major benefit. In retirement, when you begin drawing on the plan, withdrawals will be taxed as ordinary income. Contributing to a nonqualified retirement plan or participating in a commuter allowance plan, if your employer offers either, can also reduce your earned income, and thus tax owed. (For more on qualified versus nonqualified retirement plans, see Chapter 18.) As a reminder, Roth 401(k) plans, which have grown increasingly popular in recent years, do not reduce your earned income like traditional 401(k) plans do, but they do offer long-term tax-free growth and are not taxable at the time of distribution.

Paying with pretax dollars also comes in handy if you have access to a flexible spending account (FSA) or a health savings account (HSA). Both are designed to fund medical expenses. An HSA is only available to individuals with high-deductible health plans. It is a portable account that you can keep if you change jobs, or even if you are self-employed. (For more information about HSAs, see Chapter 9.) An FSA is available to all employees, regardless of their health insurance plan. It is controlled by the employer, and funds do not roll over from year to year. In either case, participating employees can make pretax contributions, lowering their taxable income. In an HSA, any interest earned is also tax-free. If you have an HSA and your employer does not offer a program to let you make pretax contributions, you can take a deduction on post-tax contributions. Note, however, that the IRS limits annual HSA contributions, including employer contributions.

Strategies For The Self-Employed

Whenever you can, you should accelerate deductions and push income into the next tax year. Unlike many regular employees, taxpayers who work for themselves may have various opportunities to time deductions and income in ways that can limit tax liability. If you work for a business, asking to receive a bonus in January instead of December may or may not go over well. But when you run your own enterprise, such decisions are in your hands. For example, you may delay client billing at the end of the year so that you receive payments in January. Conversely, you can purchase new equipment and supplies in December to ensure they are deductible in the current year — though such equipment must be "placed in service" before the end of the year for this strategy to work.

Self-employed taxpayers should also be sure that they fully understand the idea of "constructive receipt." If you receive a check in a certain year, you must report it as income for that year, even if you do not deposit it into your account until the next year. Constructive receipt means that you could have deposited those funds, even though you chose not to do so. This concept is not always intuitive, but it is important when you report your business income. Constructive receipt also applies to employees, though with the prevalence of direct deposit, fewer wage earners need to bear it in mind.

Saving for retirement can also offer tax benefits for self-employed workers. Simplified Employee Pensions, most often called SEP IRAs, are a common choice. SEP IRAs allow self-employed individuals to fund a tax-deferred retirement account on a much larger scale than a traditional IRA, but the mechanism is largely the same. Like a traditional IRA, a SEP IRA offers an above-the-line deduction for contributions, though the maximum amount you can contribute varies depending on your net self-employment income. At most, a taxpayer can contribute $69,000 (as of 2024). The deadline for contributing to a SEP IRA is the due date of the federal tax return, including extensions. In 2023, the Secure Act 2.0 created the new option of SEP Roth IRAs. The funds contributed to these accounts are included in income, so the taxpayer doesn't receive a tax break at the time of contribution. However, the funds can grow tax-free, and withdrawals from a SEP Roth IRA are not taxable income after age 59 1/2.

Self-employed taxpayers may also offset their income with business expenses, an option no longer open to most traditional employees, with the exception of educators, performing artists, military reservists and some government officials. As I mentioned in the self-employment tax section earlier in this chapter, self-employed workers can also take an above-the-line deduction for half of their self-employment tax liability.

Minimizing Taxable Income In Your Portfolio

When managing your investment portfolio, there are a variety of ways to minimize taxable investment income. Funding pretax retirement accounts first is a useful way to reduce your current income, as well as to avoid taxable investment income on the account growth, since these accounts do not pay tax on investment income annually. Similarly, Roth IRAs and Roth 401(k)s allow you to compound growth without paying tax on capital gains, dividends or interest. While contributing to a Roth IRA or Roth 401(k) will not reduce your AGI, these accounts provide tax benefits in the future, since you can withdraw appreciated funds tax-free.

Consider favoring tax-efficient mutual funds or exchange-traded funds in taxable investment accounts. Funds that avoid frequent trades and focus on long-term results are more tax efficient overall. Index funds are among the most tax-efficient options available to investors and are therefore often a wise choice for exposure to certain areas, such as U.S. large-company stocks. You should, of course, focus primarily on the quality of the investment when selecting a fund, as well as asking what part the investment plays in your overall strategy. However, tax consequences are always worth considering.

If you are using a long-term investment strategy, which we recommend at Palisades Hudson, you should be rebalancing your portfolio regularly. (For more information about what rebalancing is and when to do it, see Chapter 5.) When you or your investment adviser rebalances, you can and should consider a trade's tax consequences. Consider adding money to the portfolio by purchasing underweighted investments, rather than selling overweight investments and triggering capital gains. Minimize sales of appreciated assets as best you can. If you must trigger gains, remember that — all else being equal — it is better to trigger long-term capital gains, because of the advantageous tax rate.

Traditional IRAs and 401(k)s are a great place for relatively tax-inefficient assets, such as actively managed mutual funds.

You should also look at your portfolio as a whole and consider which account is the best place for particular assets. For example, traditional IRAs and 401(k)s are a great place for relatively tax-inefficient assets, such as actively managed mutual funds with high turnover of their securities. Also, interest income from bond funds is taxed less favorably than qualified dividends and long-term capital gains from equities, which can affect asset location choices. Taxable, tax-deferred and tax-free accounts all have a useful place in your overall portfolio. By holding assets in accounts with different tax treatments, you can balance current and future tax benefits.

ESTIMATED TAX

While no one should ignore their tax situation for 11 months out of the year, taxpayers in certain situations have a more pressing motivation to keep their taxes top-of-mind. People who are self-employed and those who have significant unpredictable income, such as from a partnership or an investment portfolio, may need to complete quarterly tax projections. This is because the United States has a "pay as you go" tax system, in which you are expected to pay most tax over the course of the year, with the balance due on Tax Day.

For those who receive the bulk of their income from wages, which is most workers, paycheck withholdings should cover the estimated tax. But for freelancers, sole proprietors or anyone else with significant income not subject to withholding, pay as you go generally means running projections on year-to-date income and expenses to estimate the corresponding tax liability. To avoid penalties, people who pay estimated tax remit vouchers — Form 1040-ES — and payment each quarter. A taxpayer can pay either 90% of their current year's anticipated income or 100% of the previous year's liability. (That figure goes up to 110% of the previous year's liability for taxpayers with AGI above $150,000 for the year, or $75,000 for married taxpayers filing separately.)

If you elect to pay 100% of the previous year's liability, you can avoid running quarterly tax projections. However, this may lead to more unpredictability on your outstanding liability or refund when you file the next April. If your liability the previous year was significantly higher than your anticipated tax in the current year, you will essentially be providing the government an interest-free loan by submitting far more tax than required.

Taxpayers who are W-2 employees with significant additional income have the option to either increase their wage withholding to cover a larger anticipated tax bill or pay quarterly estimated tax vouchers in addition to paycheck withholding. Some workers may also need to pay estimated tax to a state, especially if the state where they live and the state where they work are not the same. More on this in the next section.

STATE INCOME TAXES

For many Americans, finishing up a federal income tax return is not the end of their income tax obligations. The majority of states impose their own income taxes, and these systems can vary significantly. Seven states — Alaska, Florida, Nevada, South Dakota, Tennessee, Texas and Wyoming — charge no personal income tax at all. As of this writing, New Hampshire does not charge income tax on capital gains, wages and self-employment earnings, but levies a flat tax on income from dividends and interest. Washington levies a capital gains tax on long-term capital gains of tangible personal property located in Washington (or, in some cases where the property is located elsewhere, for residents of the state), and on intangible property (for example, stocks) for taxpayers domiciled in the state. Washington specifically excludes taxing capital gains from the sale of real estate. Many cities and municipalities also impose additional taxes on residents. This chapter cannot cover all the potential tax rules a U.S. resident may have to navigate, but there are some major considerations every taxpayer should bear in mind.

Where To File

Most people live and work in a single state, which makes state income tax relatively simple. If this describes your situation, congratulations. With a few exceptions, it is likely you simply need to file in your state, assuming it levies an income tax at all.

Some people, however, face a more complex tax scenario. Some workers commute to work across state lines; for example, many who work in New York City live in New Jersey or Connecticut. Still others may own investments or rental real estate in a state where they do not spend most of their time. No matter where you live, income should be sourced to the state where you earned it. So a Connecticut resident who works in New York City should file a New York state return to cover wages earned in New York. That individual will also need to file a Connecticut return, which will reflect all of the taxpayer's income, including what was earned in New York.

If you are invested in a partnership, your Schedule K-1 will indicate where the income is sourced and may sometimes indicate that it is sourced to multiple states. In the latter case, you should file in any state where your income exceeds that state's filing threshold. In cases where the income is below the state's filing threshold, you may still want to file if tax was withheld, since you could receive a refund. Some partnerships will file composite returns for investors. Composite returns are group returns that report the income and pay the associated tax on the investors' behalf. This can alleviate the individual investor's filing responsibilities.

You probably spotted the immediate downside of living in one state and having income sourced elsewhere. Not only do you need to file two or more state returns, but you will pay tax to multiple states for the same dollar of income. Luckily, the law softens this blow. You can generally receive a credit for the tax you pay to the nonresident state to offset your home state's taxes. This lets you avoid double taxation. However, if the state where you live imposes a higher level of tax than the state where you earned the income, it is likely that the credit will not completely offset your tax obligations to your home state.

Some states have reciprocal arrangements, which can simplify this situation. These states, usually geographic neighbors, will exempt the earned income of residents in neighboring states from income taxes. If you live in State A and work in State B, you can file an exemption form with your State B employer requesting that they withhold State A taxes from your wages. In some reciprocal arrangements, workers may have to pay estimated tax instead. Either way, at the end of the year, the worker will only need to file a State A tax return. This saves taxpayers the extra work and expense of filing an additional return.

Some taxpayers travel a great deal and may earn income in various places as a result. These people should keep a calendar to track the number of days they work in various states, in order to source income properly. States' requirements as to who needs to file a nonresident return can vary tremendously, which can create major headaches for professionals who travel often for work.

If you move across state lines, take steps to document your move and establish your new domicile. Some states — especially those that impose high income taxes — are reluctant to let former residents go.

The rise of telecommuting, particularly in a post-COVID world, has complicated income sourcing rules. They vary from state to state, so it is important to understand those that may particularly apply if you work from home but your employer is in another state. Generally, however, one major question comes into play: convenience. Are you working at home for your own convenience or for your employer's? The answer will often affect how the income is treated.

For example, in 2019 Connecticut changed their rules on telecommuting. Employees who work remotely for a Connecticut employer must treat their wages as Connecticut-source income if the remote work is for their own convenience and their home state has similar rules. So, for instance, a New Yorker who works for a Connecticut-based firm but who negotiated working from home as a benefit will still owe nonresident tax for those wages, even if she is rarely within Connecticut's borders.

Domicile

In the previous section, I mentioned residency several times. Residency has a particular meaning when it comes to tax planning. States that levy income tax permit individuals to file either resident or nonresident returns, depending on their status. In general, nonresidents pay tax only on income sourced to the state; residents pay tax on all of their income. You are typically a resident of a state if you physically live there or maintain a permanent home within its borders. A nonresident is someone who earned income sourced to the state but did not live there during the tax year in question.

A related but separate tax concept is that of domicile. You may reside in multiple states, but for tax purposes, you have only one domicile. Your domicile is your primary home, where you intend to live permanently. You are automatically a resident of the state where you are domiciled. For many people, domicile is clear-cut, because they have a single residence and only travel a few times a year. Their domicile is the place they return after traveling, where they spend the bulk of their time. In these cases, domicile and residence are the same, and the distinction is essentially irrelevant.

If you move across state lines, however, you should take steps to document your move and establish your new domicile. This is because some states — especially those that impose high income taxes — are reluctant to let former residents go. States like California and New York often aggressively assert that former residents are still domiciled there, even after they move away. This is because if you remain a resident, the state can continue to tax all of your income. If your former resident state audits you, it can pay to have a lot of concrete proof that your domicile really has changed, as well as ways to pinpoint when the change happened. Also note that, if you move mid-year, you will need to file a part-year resident return in both your old state and your new one for the year that you relocated.

Unfortunately, there is no single way to definitively prove a change in domicile. The burden of proof typically rests with the taxpayer. A strong case for a new domicile involves cutting old ties and establishing new ones. Assuming you are not maintaining your former residence, you should document the move itself well. Save dated moving receipts, copies of your lease or closing documents, and other supporting evidence that will illustrate the timeline of your relocation.

In your new state, you should take steps to make your intent clear. Creating a paper trail can benefit you in case of an audit. Some steps to include:

- Transfer your driver's license and vehicle registration to your new state.
- Register to vote in your new state and vote when you have the chance.
- File for a homestead exemption in your new state if you qualify (and be sure to renounce any homestead exemption in your former state).
- Change the address on your bank and investment accounts.
- If you have professional licenses, make sure you have transferred or obtained them in your new home.
- Establish relationships with professional service providers, such as doctors, lawyers or accountants, in your new state.

While no single step will definitively prove or disprove domicile, the more evidence you can offer that your new state is your permanent home, the stronger your case.

Taxpayers who often travel between states for personal or professional reasons may find establishing domicile even more of a challenge. You may still have family or business in your old state that takes you back, or you may split your time between two states fairly equally. In these cases, you will need to be deliberate about establishing domicile. Extra steps may include moving family heirlooms or other sentimental items to the home you intend to be your permanent residence. Consider, too, where your pets live and where your children attend school. States typically levy income tax on the worldwide income of someone domiciled there even if that person spends only a short time in the state in a given year. Most states have safe harbor rules that treat people domiciled there as nonresidents if they are out of the state for a specific number of days, but you will need to investigate your own state's particular rules.

You may also need to take steps to make sure you do not accidentally trigger residency rules that could mean more than one state will tax your entire income. Unlike domicile, residency can often be determined by clear-cut measures. In some states, residency is determined by statute. The most common measure is time spent in the state. Often, if you spend more than 183 days in a state per year and maintain a dwelling there, the state will consider you a resident, regardless of other factors. It pays to be careful to avoid triggering statutory residency in states you visit often but don't live in. Many frequent travelers find it helpful to keep a calendar or a log, both for their own use and to document their whereabouts in case of an audit.

CONCLUSION

As this chapter has likely made clear, every individual faces a unique tax situation, and thus has access to different opportunities to legally minimize tax obligations. Planning steps such as staying mindful of timing income and expenses, pursuing appropriate deductions, taking advantage of pretax employee benefit programs, and managing your investments in a tax-efficient way can all have a major impact on your overall wealth.

Tax rules are complex and dynamic. While not every taxpayer needs professional help every year, a good tax preparer can guide you in years of significant change, particularly years that include high income, a move, a change in family status or a change in tax law. A professional can also give you peace of mind, ensuring that you are complying with the law without needlessly overpaying. Whether you handle your taxes yourself or with help, keeping tax consequences in mind all year long can yield concrete benefits.

CHAPTER 16

ESTATE AND GIFT TAXES

David Walters, CPA, CFP®

If you have read Chapter 12 of this book, or just given substantial thought to your overall approach to financial planning, you have likely come to the conclusion that you need to do some basic estate planning. Even if you have only taken the time to create a will, you are still ahead of many other American adults; a 2021 survey from Gallup found that 54% of adults had not created one. This problem has not spared those with the largest estates, either. A survey from Charles Schwab in 2023 found that one in five Americans with investable assets exceeding $1 million lack a will.

While everyone needs a will, only a small percentage of people actually owe estate and gift taxes. Yet for those who will owe these taxes — or even those who might — understanding how they work is essential to effective estate planning. The federal transfer tax tops out at a hefty 40% as of this writing. The good news is that, with thoughtful planning, you can make sure that more of your assets flow to beneficiaries, such as family members and charitable organizations, than to Uncle Sam.

This chapter is designed not only for taxpayers who face gift or estate taxes in the short term, but for those who could face these taxes in the future. For instance, you may accumulate sufficient wealth in your lifetime to make transfer taxes relevant. After all, Jeff Bezos once ran Amazon out of the family garage; your present and your future may look very different. On a less optimistic note, Congress could one day redesign the tax law so that a wider cross section of taxpayers are subject to federal gift and estate taxes.

Even if your own finances do not suggest you will likely need to worry about transfer taxes, your parents' finances may involve these issues. Depending on your relationship to your parents, they may involve you in their financial affairs as they age. Or you may need to step in to help due to health or capacity concerns. Having a basic grasp of transfer taxes in advance may make it easier to understand your parents' planning choices.

Your parents (or someone else close to you) may even ask you to serve as the executor of their estate. This responsibility goes well beyond taxes, but taxes can make up a major portion of an executor's concerns. While much of this chapter focuses on how to plan for your own estate and gift taxes, it will also touch on some major points executors should bear in mind. A note on terminology: If all the assets of the person who died — the decedent — are held in trust, a trustee will fill many of the same functions as an executor. In the event the decedent left no will, the probate court will appoint an administrator. While this chapter mainly refers to executors to keep things simple, know that a trustee or an administrator may fill the same roles when it comes to estate tax.

HOW DO TRANSFER TAXES WORK?

For federal tax purposes, the estate tax and the gift tax are two sides of the same coin. This is why financial planners often discuss the two together. The gift tax mainly exists so that taxpayers who would be subject to the federal estate tax cannot avoid it by simply giving away the bulk of their assets during their lifetime. Therefore, at least at the federal level, it is useful to understand both taxes individually and in conjunction with one another.

The Federal Estate Tax

For tax purposes, your estate includes everything you own, or have certain interests in, on the day you die. Its value is calculated as of the date of your death, or six months later if your executor makes an alternate valuation date election. Depending on your assets, the particular date may not matter much, or it may matter a great deal. This is because your estate's value comes from your assets' fair market value on the date in question; what you paid for those assets is not important in calculating estate tax. ("Fair market value" is the price at which an asset would sell between a willing and knowledgeable seller and an equally willing and knowledgeable buyer — in other words, two people who are not operating under duress or without full information.) In some cases, such as publicly traded stock, fair market value is very simple to determine. In others, such as a piece of fine art, determining value is more complex.

The Internal Revenue Service considers your "gross estate" the fair market value of everything you own or have certain interests in when you die. Note that, while life insurance proceeds are generally income tax-free, they do count toward a decedent's gross estate. Your estate's value typically includes both probate and nonprobate assets. For more on probate, see Chapter 12.

As of this writing, very few Americans will need to pay the estate tax prior to 2025, and possibly for some time after. This is because Congress has set the personal exemption — also known as the "unified credit amount" — quite high. In 2024, the exemption was $13.61 million per individual, or $27.22 million for a married couple. This amount will be indexed to inflation until at least 2025, and possibly longer if Congress acts to extend current rules. If your gross estate is less than the personal exemption, generally no tax will be due at your death. However, if you make taxable gifts during your lifetime, you will have used up some portion of your personal exemption in advance (thus the "unified" credit).

If your gross estate is large enough to be subject to tax, that does not automatically mean you will need to pay. You may be able to lower your taxable estate through various allowed deductions. In addition, married individuals have a mechanism called "portability" at their disposal. Portability essentially allows couples to treat their two personal exemptions as one larger combined exemption. If the first spouse's estate does not use up all of that individual's exemption, the remainder can essentially roll over to the surviving partner. While the unused exemption is no longer increased for inflation after the first spouse's death, it adds to the surviving spouse's overall exemption amount. Portability is incredibly useful, but it is not automatic. Executors must timely file an estate tax return (Form 706) in order to make a "portability election," even if no tax is due. If you serve as an executor, you should bear in mind that you may need to file to ensure a surviving spouse receives this benefit.

As an executor, you may encounter transfer tax requirements in other ways too. If the deceased's estate is greater than the personal exemption, an executor must file an estate tax return, even if no tax is ultimately due after deductions and other considerations. An executor must file the return within nine months of the individual's death, although a six-month extension is allowed as long as the initial deadline hasn't passed. This sixth-month extension is also available to estates filing solely to make a portability election. In the case of an extension, bear in mind that any estimated tax is still due by the nine-month cutoff. An estate may also need to file an income tax return in certain circumstances. This is a separate return from the decedent's final income tax return, which an executor will need to file regardless of the estate's size (unless a surviving spouse plans to file a joint return). Given these complexities, if you serve as an executor, it is a good idea to consult an attorney or a tax professional, such as an accountant or an IRS Enrolled Agent.

Federal Gift Tax

Both outright gifts and transfers for less than fair market value are considered gifts for gift tax purposes. Because it can be hard to determine the fair market value of gifts that are not cash or publicly traded securities (like stocks), you may want to hire an independent valuation expert or appraiser for large gifts. While the IRS may not agree with the assessment, the ability to support a particular valuation with evidence can help in any subsequent dispute.

Portability allows couples to treat their two personal lifetime exemptions as one larger combined exemption.

Note that the IRS is not only concerned with gifts where the giver gets nothing in return. Any irrevocable transfer at less than fair market value can trigger tax, regardless of the giver's intentions. A common example is an interest-free loan between family members. Even if the borrower pays the loan back in full, if the interest does not meet the minimum rates set by the IRS, any forgone interest counts as a gift. The same rules apply if you sell something at less than its full value.

Gift tax is only assessed on the person giving the gift, not the recipient. Certain gifts are not subject to gift tax at all. Every taxpayer can make a certain amount of tax-free gifts each year. If you give less than the "annual exclusion amount"— $18,000 in 2024 — you are not subject to tax. This amount applies per recipient. So, for example, if you have four grandchildren, you could give each of them $18,000 ($72,000 total) in 2024 without being subject to gift tax. The annual exclusion applies per taxpayer, so a married couple can each give $18,000 to the same person, or $36,000 total.

In addition to gifts below the annual exclusion amount, certain gifts are always tax-free. If you are married, you can give any amount to your spouse without triggering gift tax, as long as your spouse is a U.S. citizen. You can also pay someone else's tuition or medical bills, in any amount, as long as you do so directly. Any gifts to political organizations, within campaign finance rules, or to certain qualifying charities are also tax-free, regardless of their size.

If you give a gift that is subject to tax, you must file a gift tax return. This return is due at the same time as your federal income tax return, in most cases April 15 of the following year. However, while you must file, you will not actually owe any tax to the IRS until your lifetime personal exemption is used up. Any personal exemption you have not used on lifetime gifts will shelter assets in your estate at your death.

In some rare cases, a gift recipient may arrange to pay the tax on a lifetime gift. In these situations, both the giver and receiver should consult a tax professional.

Generation-Skipping Transfer Tax

Generation-skipping transfer tax, as its name suggests, applies when someone makes a gift when "skipping" a generation. In other words, if someone makes a gift to a "skip person" two or more generations down — typically a grandchild or great-grandchild — the giver may owe this tax. Lifetime gifts and bequests at death can both trigger the GST tax. Like other transfer taxes, the giver (or the giver's estate) is usually responsible for paying it.

Like the gift and estate tax, the GST tax only applies after a taxpayer exhausts a lifetime exclusion amount. Congress has linked the GST exemption to the personal exemption, so as one changes, the other does too. As of this writing, the GST tax exemption is the same as the regular estate tax exemption, $13.61 million. As with the personal exemptions, the exemption is linked to the giver, not the recipient. Likewise, each taxpayer has an annual exclusion amount for GST tax purposes equal to the regular annual exclusion, currently $18,000 per year.

A GST transfer may be direct or indirect. As the name suggests, a direct transfer is a gift or bequest directly to the skip person. It may also be a transfer to a trust for the skip person's benefit. An indirect skip gift usually consists of a gift to a trust that could benefit both skip and nonskip beneficiaries. In the case of a direct skip, the transferor is responsible for any GST tax beyond his or her lifetime exemption. Indirect skips are a bit more complex. These come in two varieties: taxable terminations and taxable distributions. A taxable termination is the moment when the interest of the last nonskip beneficiary ends. Taxable distributions occur when a trust distributes assets to a skip person.

Say your parents created a trust for you and your son. The trust is structured so that if you die, any property remaining will stay in the trust for your son's benefit. In this scenario, your death would be a taxable termination, since you are the only nonskip beneficiary. If the trust distributes any assets directly to your son while you are still alive, on the other hand, it would be a taxable distribution. In either event, the trust would be subject to GST tax (or would use up part of your parents' exemption).

Because the personal exemption for gift and estate taxes is unified, the timing of a lifetime gift or a bequest may only have minor effects on an individual's overall tax bill. GST tax is a different matter. Timing can have a major impact on skip generation gifts. For instance, if you make a large gift to a trust designed to benefit your descendants and apply your GST exemption, any future appreciation in the trust can go to your grandchildren or great-grandchildren without additional GST tax, no matter how much those assets grow. On the other hand, if the trust ends up distributing all its assets to your children, you will have wasted that portion of your GST exemption. This means you should plan carefully about when and how to claim your exemption, especially for indirect skip transfers.

State Tax Concerns

Depending on where you live, you may also need to plan for state-level estate taxes. As of this writing, 12 states and the District of Columbia levy estate taxes. If you live in Connecticut, Hawaii, Illinois, Maine, Maryland, Massachusetts, Minnesota, New York, Oregon, Rhode Island, Vermont or Washington, or if you serve as an executor for someone who does, you should consult a tax expert familiar with the state in question. In general, states tax residents' estates at a lower rate than the federal government does, but the tax often applies at a much lower threshold.

A few states impose an inheritance tax. These taxes affect beneficiaries, not estates. An inheritance tax never applies to a spouse and seldom applies to close relatives like children. Bequests to charities are also sometimes exempt. Unlike estate taxes, an estate's size is generally irrelevant in determining inheritance tax. Instead, it is the size of the bequest that generally triggers the tax. At this writing, Iowa, Kentucky, Maryland, Nebraska, New Jersey and Pennsylvania impose an inheritance tax. (As you may have noticed, Maryland charges both an estate tax and an inheritance tax.) Note that for an inheritance tax, it is the recipient's residency that matters, not that of the decedent. However, the estate's executor is responsible for the filing, regardless of how many beneficiaries are involved and where they live.

As of this writing, no states other than Connecticut impose a gift tax.

In general, people who are subject to state-level gift, estate or inheritance taxes can use the same techniques to reduce their potential tax burden as they would to reduce federal transfer taxes, some of which the following section will cover. Some individuals may also consider moving to reduce potential state transfer taxes, but this can be a complicated proposition if you still spend a lot of your time in more than one state. See Chapter 15 for more details on domicile and other state tax concerns.

MINIMIZING AND MANAGING TRANSFER TAXES

As with any tax obligations, it is important to pay the government what you owe. But that does not mean you cannot structure your own affairs to minimize your tax liability. If you expect to encounter estate and gift taxes on your own assets or as a beneficiary, you can take steps to ensure that you don't pay more than your fair share.

Personal Exemptions And Annual Exclusions

Many Americans never owe transfer taxes at all. In part, this is because the threshold for owing such taxes is relatively high. As I mentioned earlier, every individual can also make gifts up to the annual exclusion amount with no gift tax consequences. If you are married, you and your spouse can double up by giving away jointly owned property, since you are both allowed to use your full annual exclusion on the gift. "Gift splitting" also allows married couples to count a particular gift as coming half from each spouse, regardless of which of you actually makes the gift. (Note that, in the case of gift splitting, you and your spouse must file gift tax returns to document your intentions, even if you owe no tax.)

For gifts and bequests that exceed the annual exclusion, transfer taxes still do not kick in until each taxpayer has used his or her lifetime personal exemption. The personal exemption, or unified credit, applies to both gift and estate tax. Any estate valued at less than the exemption amount, after subtracting the value of any taxable lifetime gifts, does not owe federal estate tax.

Every individual can make gifts up to the annual exclusion amount with no gift tax consequences. If you are married, you and your spouse can also double up by giving away jointly owned property.

Say that Adam made three taxable gifts in his lifetime at the following values: $300,000, $400,000 and $1 million. At the time of his death, Adam's gross estate was $7 million. If the personal exemption is $13.61 million, Adam's executor will not have to pay estate tax since the gifts and estate together only took up $8.7 million of Adam's personal exemption. (Remember, any annual gifts of less than $18,000 did not count toward this total.)

If a person's gifts and gross estate together meet or exceed the personal exemption, the estate may or may not owe federal tax, depending on other potential credits or deductions that can affect the taxable estate amount. However, whether or not the estate owes tax, the executor will need to file an estate tax return if the gross estate exceeds the threshold.

The estate and gift tax system has long been a site of tension for lawmakers and uncertainty for taxpayers. The current personal exemption levels were bolstered by the Tax Cuts and Jobs Act of 2017, but unless Congress takes action, this change will expire at the end of 2025. Based on recent decades, it is fair to expect the federal transfer tax system to undergo more legislative shifts in the future, which means it is important to pay attention to rule changes and to keep estate plans flexible.

Other Tax-Free Gifts

Congress permits tax-free transfers in a few specific situations beyond the general exclusions and exemptions I discussed in the previous section. For example, as I mentioned earlier in this chapter, you can pay someone else's tuition or medical expenses in any amount without triggering gift tax liability as long as you pay the school or medical facility directly. You can also give any amount of property to your spouse during your life or bequeath any amount of it at your death without owing tax, as long as your spouse is a U.S. citizen. Spouses who aren't citizens can still receive a certain amount tax-free in lifetime gifts above the general annual exclusion amount ($185,000 per year as of 2024). And you can give or bequeath unlimited amounts to qualifying charities without triggering federal transfer tax. Making such gifts during your lifetime can reduce your estate without using up your personal exemption.

Deductions Against The Estate Tax

Just as deductions can reduce your annual income tax, a variety of deductions can reduce your estate's value for tax purposes. Bequests to your surviving spouse are generally deductible from your taxable estate. Your estate may also be able to deduct mortgages and other debts; funeral and estate administration expenses; any casualty losses (such as flood damage, for example) that estate property incurs during the time your executor is administering the estate itself; or state death taxes related to any estate or inheritance taxes your estate owed at the state level. If the decedent faced significant medical expenses in the final year of his or her life, the executor may also choose to deduct these expenses on the estate tax return rather than the individual's final personal income tax return.

Portability, which I discussed earlier in the chapter, may reduce or wipe out the liability of an estate that would otherwise be subject to tax. Remember that an estate's executor must file an estate tax return to make use of a portability election, even if no tax is due. If you are serving as the executor for someone with a surviving spouse, be sure you take advantage of this benefit.

Trusts And Transfer Taxes

Many people use trusts to transfer wealth to their heirs without losing a major portion to estate or gift taxes. Even after the annual exclusion, personal exemptions and potential deductions, some estates may still owe significant tax. Careful estate planning can minimize or eliminate such taxes.

At the most basic level, a trust is a legal vehicle that allows a trustee to hold assets on behalf of one or more beneficiaries. If structured correctly, a trust can effectively mean giving up assets while still maintaining some control over how they pass to your intended recipients, which is why they are so useful for estate planning purposes. Trusts do come with expenses and administrative work, which means they are not for everyone. But working with an experienced attorney can allow you to build a trust tailored to your particular goals.

Estate planners use a variety of trusts depending on an individual's situation and goals. Trusts come in a variety of forms, to meet the needs of families in different situations. Note that your gross estate may include nonprobate assets, so simply keeping property out of probate — in a living trust, for example — is not sufficient to remove it from your taxable estate. (For more about the difference between probate and nonprobate assets, see Chapter 12.) While a comprehensive discussion of trusts would exceed the scope of this chapter, here are a few common types of trusts you may encounter in your own planning or in discussing your loved ones' plans.

Irrevocable Trusts

Irrevocable trusts are the primary tool planners use to remove assets from an estate that may be subject to tax. As the name suggests, any assets the grantor places in an irrevocable trust are fully out of the grantor's control. Once you have created an irrevocable trust, you generally cannot alter it. In addition to reducing the grantor's estate, an irrevocable trust can protect assets from creditors. And if the beneficiary leaves the assets in the trust, they can eventually pass to the heirs outside that person's estate too, subject to certain rules.

You may owe gift tax on transfers to an irrevocable trust. A major factor is whether the beneficiary has a "present interest" in the assets — essentially, whether he or she has some access to the gift right away. If the trust is structured so that beneficiaries have the right to withdraw the funds for a certain amount of time after the gift, called a "Crummey" power, then the annual exclusion can apply. If the trust has multiple beneficiaries, the annual exclusion applies to each of them. All other transfers to the trust use part of your lifetime exemption. However, if assets grow within the trust, that growth remains entirely outside the grantor's estate.

Credit Shelter Trusts

Before the portability election existed, credit shelter trusts allowed spouses to take full advantage of both partners' personal exemptions. These trusts, which are also sometimes called "bypass trusts," were typically designed for partners who planned to leave all or most of their assets to each other. Before portability, the first partner to die would often leave much of his or her personal exemption unused, since assets pass to a spouse tax-free. This meant the survivor had a larger estate, but could only apply a single personal exemption.

Credit shelter trusts allowed couples to work around this result by dividing an estate into two pieces. The "marital share" can pass to a surviving spouse outright or remain in trust; either way, it's meant to provide the survivor with financial support for life. The "family share," on the other hand, remains entirely in trust, though most credit shelter trusts are structured to allow the surviving spouse to access the family share if the marital share runs out.

Because of portability, fewer families choose to set up new credit shelter trusts today, but they are not entirely obsolete. For instance, younger couples may choose a credit shelter trust because they expect a surviving spouse to live for a long time after their partner's death. Portability locks in the remaining exemption level at the time of the first spouse's death, while a trust lets assets appreciate outside the estate, which is a more attractive prospect with a longer time horizon. Credit shelter trusts also allow estate planners to avoid some of the potential complications that can arise if a surviving spouse remarries. Alternatively, they can be useful in cases where GST tax is a significant concern. These trusts can also offer effective protection against creditors.

AB Trusts

An AB trust was another common solution to the problem of securing both spouses' personal exemptions before portability. Rather than bequeathing property directly to one another, in this strategy both spouses can leave their property to an irrevocable trust. When one spouse dies, the trust begins to pay income to the survivor. Under some circumstances, the survivor may also have access to the principal. After the second spouse dies, any remaining property passes to beneficiaries (often the couple's children).

Like credit shelter trusts, AB trusts are less popular since portability solved the problem of "wasted" personal exemptions. But they still have uses. For example, individuals who feel strongly that they want their children to inherit certain property even if their partners remarry can set up an AB trust to ensure this outcome. A couple may also set up an AB disclaimer trust. In this structure, the surviving partner can "disclaim," or decline to inherit, assets bequeathed by the deceased partner. Disclaimed assets pass directly into the trust. If structured properly, a disclaimer trust gives the survivor the option not to create the trust at all, preserving flexibility if changes in personal circumstances or tax law mean it is no longer the best option. However, the survivor must remember to disclaim any assets promptly if that is the plan.

Qualified Terminable Interest Property (QTIP) Trusts

You will usually hear a Qualified Terminable Interest Property trust designated in its short form: a QTIP trust. A QTIP trust does not eliminate estate tax. It does, however, postpone the tax until the surviving spouse's death, as long as the surviving spouse is a U.S. citizen. A funded QTIP trust can provide the surviving spouse with a life estate and any income that the trust assets earn. The survivor may also use any real estate included in the trust, though he or she cannot sell or give away such property. Because the QTIP is exclusively for the spouse's benefit for life, the bequest falls under the marital deduction and is thus exempt from estate tax. After the survivor's death, any trust assets go to a "remainder beneficiary" — again often, though not always, the couple's children.

QTIP trusts are common when parents or other grantors want to put conditions on gifts or bequests. These trusts can also allow the executor some leeway in deciding how much, if any, of the property earmarked for the trust should actually go into it. This makes them a relatively flexible trust option. Because a QTIP trust allows you to be so specific, it can be helpful when creating an inheritance structure for a blended family or other complex situation. For example, you can provide for your current spouse during the person's lifetime and opt for the remaining assets to go to your children from an earlier marriage after your spouse dies.

Executors must take care to make the QTIP election on the estate tax return of the first spouse when he or she dies. This means that the executor must file a return, even if the estate owes no tax. This is the point at which the executor can specify how much of the assets set aside should actually go into the trust. (If the executor chooses only some of the earmarked assets, it is known as a partial QTIP election.)

Irrevocable Life Insurance Trusts (ILITs)

Irrevocable Life Insurance Trusts (ILITs) are, as you would expect, trusts designed to hold life insurance policies. Transferring a substantial policy to an irrevocable trust can offer additional protection and control to your plans to provide for your beneficiaries. Any policy you own at the time of your death will be a taxable asset for estate tax purposes. On the other hand, policies held in an ILIT are generally excluded, so long as you are not a trustee and the policy was transferred to the trust at least three years prior to your death.

If you have an Irrevocable Life Insurance Trust in mind from the start, choosing a single-premium policy means the trust does not have to manage recurring premium payments.

If you have an ILIT in mind from the start, you can choose a single-premium policy, so the trust does not have to manage recurring premium payments. If this is not practical, or if you already have a life insurance policy in place, you can pay premiums by making additional gifts to the trust for that purpose. (For more about life insurance, see Chapter 10.) It is important to remember to structure an ILIT with donor powers, beneficiary powers or trustee powers that will provide sufficient flexibility in case your family situation or the estate tax landscape changes in the future.

Qualified Personal Residence Trusts (QPRTs)

A Qualified Personal Residence Trust is designed to facilitate transfers of real estate, specifically a primary or secondary residence. A properly designed QPRT will allow you to continue to live in a home for a predetermined amount of time (the "retained income period"). The residence then passes to your beneficiaries. If you continue to live there after the retained income period, you must pay fair market rent.

While a transfer via QPRT counts as a gift for federal transfer tax purposes, that gift is valued below full market value, since the beneficiaries do not have full immediate use. At the same time, this strategy removes the value of the property from your estate without requiring you to move or find new accommodations. Any rent you pay after the retained income periods does not count as a gift, allowing an additional transfer of assets to your beneficiary.

A QPRT comes with a major caveat: You must outlive the trust term in order for the trust assets to pass out of your estate. If you die before the term ends, it essentially undoes the advantages of the planning strategy.

Beneficiary Rights

While it is never too early to start thinking about planning your own estate, in many cases your first encounter with estate planning will be as a beneficiary. Your particular rights as a beneficiary will depend, in part, on the terms of the trust. You should also bear in mind that interpreting trusts is generally a matter of state law, which means the particulars of your situation may vary based on the jurisdictions involved. In some instances, beneficiaries may have the right to request information regarding the trust or annual trust accountings. Depending on the trust terms, beneficiaries may also have the right to remove or replace trustees. Such rights are often subject to the specific terms of the particular trust, coupled with state law.

If you are both the beneficiary and the trustee, you may have the discretion to make distributions to yourself. This gives you access to the assets immediately, and it also allows the grantor to take advantage of the annual exclusion amount when funding the trust. However, this generally means the assets are vulnerable to your creditors or to an ex-spouse in divorce proceedings (absent a prenuptial agreement stating otherwise). On the other hand, if a third party serves as trustee or co-trustee, the assets may or may not be vulnerable. It will often depend on the court's evaluation of the relationship between the trustee and beneficiary.

The trust's structure will determine how much discretion the trustee has regarding distributions. In some trusts, a mandatory provision directs the trustee to pay income or principal to the beneficiary at certain intervals or in response to certain events. These may include marriage, educational achievements or a variety of other milestones. Still other trusts leave distributions more fully to the trustee's discretion. If you are the beneficiary of a trust, it is important to make the effort to understand the specific terms, so you can stay abreast of your rights and responsibilities.

BASIS STEP-UP

In many cases, families must consider the interplay between estate tax planning and planning for capital gains taxes. Capital gains taxes are assessed when you sell an asset, such as investments or real estate, that has appreciated in value from the time you purchased it. (For more information on capital gains taxes, consult Chapter 15.)

The law gives beneficiaries who inherit capital assets an advantage in the form of basis step-up. If an individual bequeaths an asset and the beneficiary chooses to sell it, that asset's sale price will be compared to its value at the date of the giver's death (or, in some cases, six months after), not the date the giver originally acquired the asset. The basis — that is, the original price of the asset as far as calculating capital gains is concerned — is "stepped up" as of the bequest. This means that if the beneficiary sells the asset soon after the original owner's death, he or she is unlikely to realize any significant capital gains.

In this sense, bequests have a major advantage over lifetime gifts, at least when it comes to assets that appreciate. Lifetime gifts do not receive a step-up in basis, which means the giver passes along the untaxed appreciation to the recipient along with the asset itself. The basis step-up mechanism for bequests allows individuals to transfer greater value to their heirs by resetting the clock on capital gains.

In a down market, estate and gift planning may involve purposely transferring investments that have lost value. In a low interest rate environment, you can take advantage of more sophisticated transfer strategies. For example, an individual may set up a grantor retained annuity trust (or GRAT), which allows the grantor to transfer most of the future appreciation without incurring gift tax, while also reducing the eventual value of the person's estate. Putting assets in trust in exchange for an interest-bearing promissory note can secure similar results.

OPPORTUNITIES FOR CHARITABLE PLANNING

For many people, philanthropy is a major component of estate planning. (For more information about charitable giving, see Chapter 20.) Lifetime gifts to IRS-approved charities are not subject to gift tax, which makes them a useful way to reduce your eventual estate without using up your personal exemption. Leaving a charitable bequest, however, creates a few additional unique planning opportunities.

In some cases, a person is owed income after his or her death. This income can come from a variety of sources, commonly including individual retirement accounts, 401(k) plans or other qualified retirement plans. Income in respect of a decedent, often abbreviated IRD, counts toward the decedent's taxable estate and is also subject to income tax in most cases. While the beneficiary will owe the income tax in this case, the tax will reflect what the decedent would have paid were he or she living. In other words, there is no basis step-up for IRD.

One way to avoid the double tax hit of IRD is to use such income when designing the philanthropic portion of an estate plan. If the recipient is a tax-exempt organization, it will not pay income tax on the gift, making the asset more valuable than it would be to most other beneficiaries. IRA assets or other forms of IRD can serve as a tax-efficient source of charitable funds. As long as the bequest is structured correctly, both the individual and the chosen philanthropic organization can benefit.

The simplest way to leave IRD to a charitable organization is to designate the charity directly as the beneficiary of the full value of your IRA or other qualified retirement plan at your death. Or you can split the account's value among multiple tax-exempt entities, if you like. As long as all the necessary paperwork is in order, this is a simple and straightforward technique. You can also divide an account between a charity and noncharitable beneficiaries, but this process is more complex (unless the only noncharitable beneficiary is your spouse).

If you prefer not to name the charitable institution as a direct beneficiary of a retirement account, you can leave the benefits to a trust and instruct the trustee to distribute the assets to one or more organizations. Or you can leave the benefits to a donor-advised fund instead. Using a trust for this purpose likely means involving a professional to serve as the trustee, as the rules around minimum required distributions and fiduciary income taxes can become complex.

Yet a trust will offer more control than a donor-advised fund. As with many estate planning choices, the right answer will vary depending on your particular situation.

You may encounter an opportunity to redirect retirement funds to a charity as a beneficiary, too. For example, the decedent could have set up a disclaimer-activated gift, naming you as the primary beneficiary and a tax-exempt charitable institution as a contingent beneficiary. This means that you can choose to disclaim all or part of the bequest. If you do, the charity will receive whatever assets you disclaim without you having to pay income tax on them first.

MISTAKES TO AVOID

When it comes to planning your own estate or gift-giving strategies, there are some common pitfalls you should avoid.

If you are married, a common trap is a "sweetheart" will, in which you simply leave all of your assets to your spouse. Frequently, both spouses will create such documents, compounding the problem. There is nothing inherently wrong with wanting to leave your assets to your partner. But depending on the complexities of your personal situation, there may be better ways to go about it. A sweetheart will offers no protection from creditors or liability. Or say that your spouse remarries. If there is no prenuptial agreement in that marriage, nothing will protect the assets you left your spouse if a divorce occurs. If you and your spouse have children, a sweetheart will can also potentially shut them out, especially if your spouse does remarry.

In addition, a sweetheart will has no built-in flexibility to address future changes in tax law. The personal exemption could shrink or grow significantly by the time of your death. Congress could revoke portability. Some entirely new legal consideration could arrive. Like any will, a sweetheart will is better than not having a will at all. But if you think you may be subject to the federal estate tax, it is wise to consider more sophisticated planning options.

QUICK NOTES

Pitfalls To Avoid

- ☑ Leaving all assets to your spouse ("sweetheart wills")
- ☑ Not making irrevocable gifts only out of worry about cash flow
- ☑ Failing to request a "closing letter" as an estate's executor
- ☑ Avoiding estate planning altogether

As you likely noticed throughout this chapter, many estate planning options involve irrevocable gifts. These strategies understandably make some people nervous. What about cash flow in the future? But given the variety of trusts and other techniques available, you can generally arrange to control how and when gifts are made. Some trusts are even designed to provide an income stream back to the grantor, even though the gift itself is irrevocable. You should talk to your financial planner about any concerns you have about balancing estate planning with maintaining a comfortable future lifestyle.

Executors, too, should be careful. The IRS has laid at least one additional tripwire specifically for them. Since 2015, it has required that executors actively request a "closing letter," a document that states the estate has satisfied its outstanding liabilities. Such a request must be made online at pay.gov, no sooner than nine months after filing the estate's return. While remembering to make the request is one more item on an already long executor to-do list, executors shouldn't neglect it. In many cases, beneficiaries cannot sell a decedent's real estate without a closing letter in hand, and courts may not distribute remaining assets to heirs until the letter arrives. While sometimes an account transcript will serve in place of a closing letter, executors should take care to understand which they need and make a request if necessary.

Many young adults, or even adults in middle age, avoid estate planning in part because it is uncomfortable to think about their own mortality. It may seem that there is plenty of time for estate planning down the road. With luck, there will be — but life is ultimately unpredictable. Even if your plan does not go into action for many years, getting a head start means you can avoid the prospect of estate planning paralysis when emotions may be running higher. Planning for taxes is one component of that process. A good estate plan is inherently flexible, and if you get into the habit of revisiting it on a regular basis, it will become a more comfortable topic over time.

CHAPTER 17

LIVING AND WORKING ABROAD

Shomari D. Hearn, CFP®, EA and ReKeithen Miller, CFP®, EA

So you've decided that vacations abroad are no longer cutting it, or you receive a career opportunity you cannot resist. Making a long-term or permanent move overseas to live, work and possibly raise a family may be an exciting prospect, but it is not a simple one. Where do you begin? The best way forward is to prepare in advance for the financial, tax and personal matters in play. The more you know before you move, the better your chances of making a successful transition.

BANKING AND INVESTING

In the United States, opening and maintaining a bank or investment account is typically quick and easy. Many banks and investment firms in North America offer accounts with either low or no minimum balance requirements. The same may or may not be true for the place you are moving. In certain countries, opening a new account may entail weeks of hassle and paperwork, including identification documents, letters of credit and references from your U.S. bank.

Initial deposit or salary requirements can make it difficult to open accounts with certain banks at all. For example, HSBC Bank offers an expat bank account for U.S. citizens moving abroad. However, to be eligible, you must have a valid reason for opening an account overseas as determined by HSBC; depending on your destination, you may need to meet other requirements to open an account. (These specific terms were accurate as of late 2023, though they may subsequently change.) You should investigate your banking options in advance and establish an account with a bank quickly upon arriving in your new country. An international bank may facilitate opening your account before you leave home, which is often ideal.

Part of the problem American expatriates face is due to the Foreign Account Tax Compliance Act, often abbreviated FATCA. The law essentially requires all foreign banks with U.S. accountholders to report annually to the Internal Revenue Service about their American customers' activities. This major administrative headache has made many non-American financial institutions reluctant to allow Americans to open accounts. Some U.S. banks and brokerage firms have also restricted or closed the accounts of Americans living abroad due to regulatory compliance burdens. FATCA was designed to prevent Americans living in the U.S. from evading taxes using foreign accounts, but it has created major hurdles for expatriates. Your best option is to research thoroughly ahead of your move.

You will need an account with a local bank one way or another, since you likely will be paid in local currency, and you certainly will need to pay your living expenses in local currency. But assuming you don't plan to renounce your American citizenship, most financial advisers suggest you keep the bulk of your assets in U.S. accounts and transfer funds to your local foreign bank as needed. Staggering the transfers removes some of the risk of currency fluctuations over time. Keeping most assets or savings in U.S. accounts protects you if your new country has an economy less stable than that of the United States. It also makes returning to the States simpler.

If you will be working for a U.S. employer in a foreign country, you should ask the human resources department whether you can participate in your company's qualified retirement plan while you are abroad. (For an explanation of qualified and nonqualified retirement plans, see Chapter 18.) Participating in a plan such as a traditional 401(k) will allow you to benefit from tax-deferred growth of your investments and defer some compensation, thus reducing your taxable income for U.S. income tax purposes. However, participating may result in double taxation if your country of residence taxes your contributions while the U.S. does not. In this case, you may be better off opting for a Roth 401(k) plan if your employer offers one. In a Roth 401(k), contributions are made with after-tax earnings. This lets you avoid the potential double-taxation issue while benefiting from tax-free growth, so your withdrawals will not be subject to U.S. income tax in retirement (when you may be in a higher tax bracket than you will be while living abroad). In either type of plan, you may also receive employer-match contributions, and you never want to pass up free money. Further, the investment options available within your company retirement plan will likely be low cost and provide diversification that may be otherwise difficult to access as an expat. You should consult your tax adviser before participating in a foreign retirement plan, however. While certain retirement plans might qualify for preferential tax treatment in a foreign country, that does not mean the U.S. will view the plans as favorably. The IRS may require additional reporting and disclosures related to the plans. In addition, contributions to foreign retirement plans and any earnings in these plans might be treated as currently taxable income. Some tax treaties have special provisions for various foreign retirement plans, but each treaty is unique, so relying on generalizations won't suffice.

If you have an existing 401(k) account with a former U.S. employer, you should either leave the assets in the plan or consider rolling them over to an individual retirement account before you move abroad. You will not be able to take the funds abroad without triggering U.S. income taxes and an early withdrawal penalty of 10% for withdrawing funds before age 59 1/2. You would also be forsaking the benefit of continued tax-deferred growth.

If you don't have a traditional or Roth individual retirement account, consider establishing one before you leave the country. However, be aware that living abroad may affect the contribution rules. For example, Americans working abroad can often exclude part of their earned income from taxation, which we will discuss in the next section of this chapter. But to make IRA contributions, you must have earned income above and beyond the income you exclude. Self-employed workers living abroad may also establish and contribute to retirement plan options such as a SEP IRA or Solo 401(k). (For more on the general rules governing IRAs and the characteristics of retirement plan options for self-employed workers, see Chapter 18.) If you plan to make contributions while abroad, it is best to consult a tax professional with experience handling expatriate clients.

Assuming you don't plan to renounce your American citizenship, most financial advisers suggest you keep the bulk of your assets in U.S. accounts and transfer funds to your local foreign bank as needed.

Maintaining your existing nonretirement investment accounts, or establishing new ones in the U.S., may be more difficult when you move abroad. U.S. investment firms may require you to convert your existing account to an international brokerage account. In some cases, the brokerage company may even prohibit you from maintaining existing accounts on their platforms if you move to certain jurisdictions. Most brokerage companies have a list of foreign jurisdictions on their websites outlining the various restrictions residents of those jurisdictions face. If you cannot find a list online, it is always a good idea to contact the brokerage company directly to get more details about any hurdles you could face once you move. If you can maintain your account after your move abroad, you can continue to trade stocks, bonds and exchange-traded funds in these accounts, but you generally cannot purchase mutual funds unless they are organized, or domiciled, abroad. (These funds are known as "offshore mutual funds.") Further, the Securities and Exchange Commission and the Financial Industry Regulatory Authority, or FINRA, have established rules for investment managers that restrict their trading on behalf of clients living outside the United States. If you plan to move abroad and want to keep working with your investment adviser, you will need to confirm the adviser's ability to handle your accounts while you live outside the country. If your adviser has the ability and inclination to continue working with you and you are otherwise pleased with the service, we recommend you keep him or her, as well as your existing accounts.

Whether or not you work with a U.S.-based adviser, if you have to invest through an offshore account, you will likely encounter higher fees and fewer investment options. You should also exercise extreme caution in opening a foreign investment account. Extensive regulations govern those accounts held by U.S. citizens. (We will touch on some of them later.) One possible strategy that works within these regulations is to establish a revocable trust for yourself, and name a trusted relative or friend who lives in the U.S. as a co-trustee. You can then open a U.S. brokerage account using the co-trustee's U.S. address. However, you will want to tread carefully, since choosing the wrong person could put your assets at risk.

TAXATION

As a U.S. citizen, you are still required to file U.S. income tax returns and pay federal (and possibly state) income tax even if you live and work abroad. This is because the United States is the only major country that taxes its citizens and resident noncitizens on their worldwide income. The U.S. does cut you some breaks if you live outside the country, however.

As a U.S. citizen or resident living and working abroad, or as part of the U.S. military stationed outside the country, you receive an automatic two-month extension to file your federal income tax return and pay your federal income tax liability. However, you will pay interest on any tax that you have not paid by the regular filing deadline of April 15. If you need more time beyond the two-month extension, you can file IRS Form 4868, "Application for Automatic Extension of Time To File U.S. Individual Income Tax Return," to receive an additional four-month extension. Form 4868 gives you more time to file your tax return, but not more time to pay any taxes due. You will need to estimate your tax liability using the information available to you and submit a payment with the extension form.

If you are moving abroad because your U.S. employer is sending you there, your employer will likely engage in "tax equalization." In this process, the employer takes steps to make sure that you are no better or worse off for tax purposes as an expat employee than if you were working in the U.S., despite the potential for double taxation. Typically, the employer will calculate the hypothetical (or "hypo") tax that an expat worker would pay in the U.S., including federal taxes, state taxes, and Medicare and Social Security taxes. Your employer then withholds this amount from your compensation. In some cases, employers may also pay their workers' foreign tax liabilities to the foreign tax authorities directly. Companies conduct tax equalization calculations annually, once the final income and deduction amounts are known. The results are then compared with the hypo tax deductions withheld by your employer. If the actual tax liability is higher than the hypo tax withheld, your employer will pay the difference. If the actual tax due is lower than the hypo tax, your employer keeps the difference. Before you move, talk with your employer and make sure you understand what steps the company will take to ensure tax equalization while you work overseas.

It may seem counterintuitive to talk about noncitizen "permanent residents" of the U.S. who live in a non-U.S. country, but the situation can arise. Permanent residents are foreign nationals who may be subject to U.S. taxation because of the "substantial presence test." Say you are a Brazilian citizen who lives principally in London but who often travels to New York City for work. If you are physically present in the U.S. at least 31 days during the current calendar year, and a total of 183 days split between the current year and the two previous years, you may be subject to U.S. federal tax law. In this way, even noncitizens who live abroad may find themselves within the IRS' reach.

Foreign Earned Income And Foreign Housing Expenses

As long as you meet certain requirements, you are allowed to claim a foreign earned income exclusion that may shield some or all of the income you earn abroad from U.S. income taxes. "Earned income" consists of salary, wages, commissions, bonuses, professional fees and gratuities. It does not include certain categories of income such as interest, dividends, capital gains or alimony.

For 2024, the exclusion amount is $126,500; this is adjusted for inflation annually. To qualify, your tax home — your main place of business or employment — must be outside the United States. As you would expect, you must also have foreign earned income. Finally, you must be a U.S. citizen who is a bona fide resident of one or more foreign countries for an uninterrupted period that includes an entire tax year; a U.S. resident who is a citizen or national of a country that has an income tax treaty with the United States and a bona fide resident of one or more foreign countries for an uninterrupted period that includes an entire tax year; or a U.S. citizen or resident physically present in a foreign country or countries for a minimum of 330 full days during any period of 12 consecutive months. If you don't expect to meet the bona fide resident or physical presence tests by the due date of your tax return, the IRS allows taxpayers to request a special extension of time to meet the requirement by filing Form 2350. The extension to file your return provided by Form 2350 will generally be 30 days after the date on which you expect to meet either the bona fide residence test or the physical presence test. This request only extends the time to file your return and does not extend the time to pay any taxes that are due.

If you qualify for the foreign earned income exclusion, you may also claim either an exclusion or a deduction for your "foreign housing amount." This includes such expenses as rent or the fair market value of any housing benefit your employer provides; utilities (other than telephone expenses); furniture rental fees; and nonrefundable occupancy taxes. However, you cannot claim mortgage principal or interest, real estate taxes, home improvements that increase the value of the property, furniture you purchase for the home, domestic labor costs, paid television subscriptions or any expenses the IRS may consider "lavish." You cannot exclude or deduct more than the amount of your foreign earned income for the year.

The housing exclusion is available to those who use employer-provided funds to pay for housing costs. You may only claim the housing deduction when you pay these costs with earnings from self-employment. However, in either case there are limits to how much you may claim. You must subtract the base housing amount, which is 16% of the maximum foreign earned income exclusion, from your total housing expenses to determine your housing amount. For 2024, the base housing amount was $20,240. Dividing this amount by 366 (because 2024 is a leap year) determines the daily rate ($55.30). You would then multiply the daily rate by the number of qualifying days in the tax year that you were in the foreign country. The IRS also sets a ceiling on the amount of qualified housing expenses you can claim.

Generally, the maximum is capped at 30% of the maximum foreign earned income exclusion ($37,950 for 2024). This is also converted to a daily rate of $103.69 and multiplied by your number of qualifying days in the tax year. If you live in what the IRS considers a high-cost city, you can claim housing expenses that exceed the standard limit. For example, the IRS considers São Paulo, Brazil, a high-cost city. For 2023 (the most recent information available as of this writing), it set the housing expense limit there at $56,600, or $155.07 daily. If São Paulo was your tax home for all of 2023 and you incurred $55,000 of housing expenses that you paid for with funds provided by your employer which were included in your foreign earned income, you could have used the amount above the base housing amount ($55,000-$19,200=$35,800, which were the applicable figures for 2023) to determine your housing exclusion.

To claim the foreign earned income exclusion, as well as the housing exclusion or deduction, you must complete IRS Form 2555, "Foreign Earned Income," and attach it to Form 1040 when you file your U.S. income tax return. You may be able to file the simpler Form 2555-EZ, "Foreign Earned Income Exclusion," if you earned foreign wages or salary but no self-employment income; if your foreign earnings were less than the maximum foreign earned income exclusion; and if you are not claiming a housing exclusion or deduction. If you are married and your spouse also qualifies for the earned income exclusion, you may both claim it, excluding as much as $253,000 of your 2024 joint income from U.S. taxation.

The U.S. has negotiated income tax treaties with a number of countries to help citizens avoid double taxation. Each bilateral tax agreement is unique, so investigate whether a treaty exists between the country where you will live and the U.S.

Tax Treaties

You will likely be subject to income tax in your country of residence, as well as to U.S. income tax. It seems unfair to have to pay tax on the same income to both the country you're living in and to the United States. Because of this, the U.S. has negotiated income tax treaties with a number of countries (67 as of this writing) to help citizens avoid double taxation on certain categories of income, such as business profits, wages, investment income and royalties. Each bilateral tax agreement is unique, so investigate whether a treaty exists between the country where you will live and the U.S. and, if so, what that treaty covers. If you are unable to resolve a double taxation matter with the tax authorities in your country of residence, you can seek assistance from the IRS.

Foreign Tax Credit Or Deduction

If no tax treaty exists, or if the treaty does not address double taxation of earned income, you can claim a foreign tax credit or a deduction on your U.S. tax return for the income taxes you pay to a foreign country. However, you can only claim a credit or deduction for the taxes you paid on foreign-source income in excess of the foreign earned income exclusion amount. The IRS does not allow double-dipping; you cannot claim a credit for foreign income taxes you pay on earned income excluded from U.S. taxation.

Most taxpayers will receive a greater benefit from claiming a credit for qualified foreign taxes. A credit lowers your U.S. income tax bill on a dollar for dollar basis, compared with a deduction that only reduces your income subject to tax. (For more on the difference between tax credits and tax deductions, see Chapter 15.) Further, you can claim the foreign tax credit even if you do not itemize deductions on your U.S. return; if you plan to claim the deduction, you must itemize. Due to the Tax Cuts and Jobs Act, which Congress passed in late 2017, fewer taxpayers find it worthwhile to itemize deductions in light of the increased standard deduction the law created. However, despite the credit's advantages in general, some taxpayers may find a foreign tax deduction more beneficial than the corresponding credit. You should still consider both options to see which one will lead to the most tax savings each year.

You can claim the credit in either the year you accrue the qualified foreign tax liability or the year in which you pay it. This will depend on which accounting method you use: accrual or cash. If you use the accrual method, you will report your income when you earn it, rather than when you receive it, and deduct your expenses when you incur them rather than when you pay them. If you are an accrual basis taxpayer, you can only claim the tax credit in the year in which you accrue the foreign tax. Typically, you will accrue foreign taxes when all the events that fix the amount of the tax and your liability happen — usually the last day of the foreign tax year. However, most individual taxpayers use the cash method of accounting. You report income in the year you actually or constructively receive it and deduct expenses only when you pay them. With the cash method, you have the choice to claim the foreign tax credit in either the year you pay the tax or the year you accrue it.

A common expression holds that timing is everything. It may not be everything, but smart timing can certainly reduce your tax obligations. In most cases, U.S. citizens will want to claim the tax credit for foreign earned income in the year the tax is accrued. Doing so helps to avoid a timing issue that could limit the credit and result in double taxation. If, for example, you claimed the foreign tax credit on a cash basis, you would claim the credit for the foreign taxes paid in year 2 for income earned in year 1. If you earned significant foreign income in year 1 but expect that your foreign income will be lower the next year, the credit in year 2 will be limited due to the lower foreign income. This will result in an overall higher tax bill for year 1.

Social Security And Medicare Taxes

Your earned income may also be subject to Social Security and Medicare taxes in the United States, and to similar social security taxes in the foreign country where you work. The U.S. has entered into totalization agreements with 30 countries to eliminate dual social security taxation for U.S. citizens and residents working abroad. These bilateral agreements ensure that the worker only pays social security taxes to one country. Totalization agreements generally state that a U.S. citizen or resident will pay Social Security taxes to the U.S. if sent to a foreign country to work for a single American-based employer for five years or less. If the workers are sent to work abroad for more than five years, they will pay social security taxes to the foreign country. The agreements also typically govern whether workers will pay social security taxes to the foreign country if they are employed by a foreign company or are hired by a U.S.-based employer while living abroad. Either the worker or the employer must request a Certificate of Coverage from the country in which the worker is employed or from the country of residence to substantiate a claim of exemption under a totalization agreement. You should investigate whether the U.S. has a totalization agreement with the country in which you reside. If so, you should coordinate the request for a Certificate of Coverage with your employer. If no totalization agreement exists, you will be responsible for paying social security taxes to both countries.

In the case of self-employed individuals, U.S. Social Security benefits typically extend to U.S. citizens whether the citizens performed work in the U.S. or abroad. That means they can be subject to dual coverage on their self-employment income when working abroad, since the resident country will typically cover them too. However, many of the totalization agreements eliminate this dual coverage by assigning coverage to the country of residence. In some cases, dual citizens — depending on where they reside — have the option to elect which country will cover them by filing a Certificate of Coverage.

Property Taxes And Mortgage Interest

Under the Tax Cuts and Jobs Act, you can no longer deduct foreign real estate taxes on your U.S. income tax return. You may only claim a deduction for property taxes you pay on a home or land you own within the United States. The law also caps the deduction of state and local taxes, including U.S. property taxes, at $10,000 total per year. If you hold on to U.S. real estate while you live abroad, you may deduct U.S. property taxes up to this limit as long as they are based on the property's assessed value and are charged uniformly against all property in the taxing authority's jurisdiction. However, taxes charged for local benefits and improvements that increase the property's value are generally not deductible. Neither are itemized charges for services like trash collection that are assessed against specific property or certain people, even if the state or local tax authority is assessing them.

You may deduct mortgage interest on a foreign residence, just as you would a U.S. property. You are allowed to deduct mortgage interest for a primary and a secondary home you own. The IRS generally defines a taxpayer's principal residence as the home in which the person lives most of the time. For any mortgages taken out from Dec. 16, 2017, through the end of 2025, you may only deduct mortgage interest on a maximum of $750,000 in mortgage debt to acquire or improve a home. This amount applies in aggregate across your primary residence and second home, if you have one. For mortgages obtained on or before Dec. 15, 2017, you may deduct interest on up to $1 million of debt.

State Income Taxes While Living Abroad

Whether you have to pay state income taxes while living abroad depends largely on the rules about domicile and residency in the state where you lived before leaving the country. If you take steps to terminate tax residency and domicile ahead of your move, you can often eliminate your state tax burden while living outside the United States. (For definitions of tax residency and domicile, see Chapter 15.) Some states make it easy to terminate domicile, while others require much more proof that you have left the state behind. You will need to research the particulars of your state, but in most cases — assuming the state levies income tax at all — you will need to file a part-year state return for the year that you move to signal the end of your residency. Be prepared to substantiate your change in residency status in case of an audit.

In some cases, you may be unable or unwilling to terminate your domicile. For example, you may want to maintain your U.S. residence, which a state can cite as proof that you intend to return. This logic may also apply to a houseboat or a mobile home you leave behind but continue to own. Some states will only allow you to move your domicile to another state within the U.S., which could leave you subject to tax on your worldwide income. In these cases, it may make sense to move in stages if you are able. Moving to a state without state income tax before you move abroad can save you both money and aggravation. But be aware that many high-tax states have a reputation for aggressively auditing former residents' moves to lower tax states. Be sure to demonstrate that your intent to move is genuine and establish as many new ties as you can.

If you take steps to terminate tax residency and domicile ahead of your move, you can often eliminate your state tax burden while living outside the United States.

As you have likely gathered, tax compliance for a U.S. citizen living and working overseas can be complex. We recommend seeking the services of qualified tax professionals, in both the U.S. and your host country, who have experience working with expats. Ensure that these professionals coordinate their efforts to see that you pay the minimum amount of tax in both countries.

Foreign Bank And Financial Accounts Reporting

As we mentioned earlier, holding foreign financial accounts as a U.S. citizen or permanent resident can subject you to strict requirements. Among the most important are reporting requirements for bank and financial accounts outside the United States. Taxpayers who qualify must file an annual "Report of Foreign Bank and Financial Accounts," FinCEN Form 114. Financial professionals often refer to this form as an "FBAR." You will need to file an FBAR if you meet the following criteria:

- You are a person (or entity) with a financial interest in, or signature authority over, at least one financial account outside the U.S., and
- The aggregate value of your foreign financial accounts exceeds the equivalent of $10,000 (U.S.) at any point during the calendar year.

When calculating your accounts, remember to include bank accounts, investment accounts, trusts or any other accounts based outside of the United States. You may need to file even if your foreign accounts produce no taxable income over the course of the year. You will need to answer certain questions about your accounts on IRS Form 1040, as well as filling out the FBAR, if you meet the conditions above, with few exceptions. For married couples with joint foreign accounts, if one spouse reports these accounts on an FBAR, the other spouse may not need to file a separate FBAR under certain conditions. Unlike income tax returns, FBARs offer no joint filing option. IRAs and tax-qualified retirement plans that hold an interest in a foreign financial account are generally excluded. Trust beneficiaries may also not need to file if another person reports the account on an FBAR filed on the trust's behalf.

Like a federal income tax return, the FBAR is due on or before April 15 of the next year. However, you are automatically granted a six-month extension to file by Oct. 15. Failing to file can result in steep civil penalties, up to $24,793. Purposely hiding foreign accounts can trigger both major civil penalties — the greater of $156,107 or 50% of the account balance at the time of the violation — and potential criminal charges, which carry even higher penalties and possible jail time.

In addition to the FBAR, you may need to file IRS Form 8938, "Statement of Specified Foreign Financial Assets." This form is filed along with your federal income tax return and does not replace the FBAR; some taxpayers may need to file both.

As this section suggests, reporting foreign accounts is complex. You should enlist the help of a tax professional with experience in this area if you know you have accounts subject to reporting or think you may be close to the relevant thresholds.

	IRS Form 8938	FinCEN Form 114 (FBAR)
Who must file?	Specified individuals and specified domestic entities that have an interest in specified foreign financial assets and meet the reporting threshold Specified individuals include U.S citizens, residents and certain nonresidents Specified domestic entities include certain domestic corporations, partnerships and trusts	U.S. persons, which include U.S. citizens, residents, trusts, estates and domestic entities that have an interest in foreign financial accounts and meet the reporting threshold
Reporting threshold (total value of assets) for individuals living outside the U.S.	Specified individuals living in the US: • Unmarried individual (or married filing separately): Total value of assets was more than $50,000 on the last day of the tax year, or more than $75,000 at any time during the year. • Married individual filing jointly: Total value of assets was more than $100,000 on the last day of the tax year, or more than $150,000 at any time during the year. Specified individuals living outside the US: • Unmarried individual (or married filing separately): Total value of assets was more than $200,000 on the last day of the tax year, or more than $300,000 at any time during the year. • Married individual filing jointly: Total value of assets was more than $400,000 on the last day of the tax year, or more than $600,000 at any time during the year. Specified domestic entities: • Total value of assets was more than $50,000 on the last day of the tax year, or more than $75,000 at any time during the tax year.	Aggregate value of financial accounts exceeds $10,000 at any time during the calendar year. This is a cumulative balance, meaning if you have two accounts with a combined account balance greater than $10,000 at any one time, both accounts would have to be reported.

	IRS Form 8938	FinCEN Form 114 (FBAR)
What must you report?	Maximum value of specified foreign financial assets, which include financial accounts with foreign financial institutions and certain other foreign nonaccount investment assets	Maximum value of financial accounts maintained by a financial institution physically located in a foreign country
When is it due?	Form is attached to your annual return and due on the date of that return, including any applicable extensions	Received by April 15 (six-month automatic extension to Oct. 15)
What are the penalties for failing to file?	Up to $10,000 for failure to disclose and an additional $10,000 for each 30 days of nonfiling after IRS notice of a failure to disclose, for a potential maximum penalty of $60,000; criminal penalties may also apply	Civil monetary penalties are adjusted annually for inflation. For civil penalty assessment prior to Aug. 1, 2016, if nonwillful, up to $10,000; if willful, up to the greater of $100,000 or 50% of account balances; criminal penalties may also apply

Figure 9: IRS Form 8938 vs. FBAR Table
(Source: Internal Revenue Service. Data retrieved Sept. 5, 2023.)

Fixing Mistakes

While working with a professional from the start is the best way to avoid problems, you may still discover a filing or reporting requirement too late. If you discover you should have submitted a form or document in the past, it is critical to be proactive rather than passively hoping tax authorities or regulators don't notice your mistake. As we mentioned in the preceding section, both civil and criminal penalties can be severe for errors involving international accounts. Coming forward voluntarily does not mean your mistake will be consequence-free, but it increases the odds of a good outcome significantly.

For unintentional errors in dealing with the IRS, the Service provides "streamlined compliance procedures." These procedures offer the chance to come back into compliance after a nonwillful failure to file. Depending on the circumstances, you may owe lower penalties, or no penalty at all (though you will still owe any unpaid tax that is due). Note that part of using these procedures is an understanding that you will comply in future years, and that you may be more likely to become the target of a future exam after completing them. There are separate sets of procedures for taxpayers who reside abroad and those who are based in the U.S. Even more so than with upfront reporting and tax compliance, taxpayers who plan to use the streamlined compliance procedures would be best served by consulting an experienced tax professional.

If you failed to submit an FBAR that you should have filed, the Treasury Department offers a mechanism to file a delinquent form. Proactively filing a delinquent FBAR can keep penalties to a minimum, and if the Treasury finds that you had "reasonable cause" for your failure to file, you may not face any penalties from the department at all. The IRS will not impose any additional failure to file penalties as long as you properly reported the income from the unreported foreign accounts and paid the associated tax, and the IRS has not previously contacted you about delinquent returns for the years in question.

Taking the time to proactively handle any problems with your international account filings offers the potential to save you considerable pain from harsh financial and legal penalties. It is also the right thing to do.

CITIZENSHIP

Renouncing Citizenship

Given the long reach of the U.S. tax authorities, you may wonder whether you would be better off renouncing your citizenship. The decision is a serious one and should not be made lightly. This is certainly the case for any American, but even more so for working-age adults. You should carefully weigh a variety of factors. Will future career advancement or business opportunities require you to move back to the U.S.? What would happen if you lost your current job? When you start a family, will you and your partner want to raise your children in the U.S.? If political or economic instability develops in your new country, would you want to return to the U.S. for safety and stability? If you should become ill, what is the level and cost of medical care that would be available to you in your new country? Will you want or need to move back to the U.S. in the future to be closer to family or to take care of aging parents? Although getting citizenship back once renounced is not impossible, it is not easy.

If you choose to renounce your U.S. citizenship, the first step should be pursuing citizenship in your new country. Going through the naturalization process can be very difficult or relatively easy, depending on the country; either way, it will likely take some time. It is imperative you be naturalized before you renounce your U.S. citizenship. Otherwise, you risk becoming stateless. Consult with the government of your new country, so you are sure you understand the process for naturalization there and meet the necessary requirements.

Once you have secured citizenship abroad, there are several ways to end your American citizenship. The most common method is formally renouncing American citizenship. This involves signing an oath of renunciation, which must be done in the presence of a diplomatic officer (generally at an embassy or a consulate). Expatriates must also file IRS Form 8854, "Initial and Annual Expatriate Statement." Revocation is final when the State Department issues a Certificate of Loss of Nationality.

In some cases, you may owe an "exit tax" upon renouncing your citizenship. This tax was established by the Heroes Earnings Assistance and Relief Tax Act of 2008 (the HEART Act). It applies to "covered" expatriates, who (with limited exceptions) are defined as any of the following:

- Those whose average annual net income tax for the five years prior to the date of expatriation is more than a specified amount. (This amount, adjusted for inflation, is $201,000 in 2024.)
- Those with a net worth of $2 million or more as of their expatriation.
- Those who fail to certify on Form 8854 that they have complied with all U.S. federal tax obligations for the five years prior to expatriation.

Covered individuals owe exit tax on the unrealized gains on their property. The expatriate is deemed to have sold his or her worldwide assets for their fair market value as of the day before expatriation. Those hypothetical sales are subject to U.S. short- or long-term capital gains taxes. A portion of the gains, the amount of which is adjusted for inflation, can be excluded. (In 2024, the exclusion amount was $866,000.) Similarly, tax-deferred accounts such as IRAs and Section 529 plans are treated as though the account owner received a full distribution as of the day before expatriation. There is some leniency with the standard rules of those distributions. For example, if covered expatriates are under age 59 1/2 at the time of distribution, they are not charged the 10% early withdrawal penalty tax that would normally apply. The total exit tax is due with the federal income return for the year in which U.S. citizenship was renounced.

If you fail to file IRS Form 8854 upon expatriation, you could face a $10,000 penalty, whether or not you are a covered individual. Form 8854 and the exit tax were designed largely to keep Americans from renouncing their citizenship merely to avoid tax obligations.

The HEART Act also affects transfer taxes on gifts or bequests from a former citizen to a current U.S. citizen. American citizens or residents who receive gifts or bequests from former citizens over the annual gift tax exclusion ($18,000 in 2024) incur liability for the transfer tax at the highest applicable rate, unless the former citizen reports the transfers on a U.S. gift or estate tax return. (For more information about transfer taxes, see Chapter 16.) Otherwise, the American citizen or resident recipient must file Form 708, "U.S. Return of Gifts or Bequests from Covered Expatriates." (Note that this form is not yet available as of this writing.) If the former citizen gives assets to a U.S. trust, the trust must pay the transfer tax. If the former citizen gives to a foreign trust, however, no tax is due unless there is a distribution to a U.S. citizen or resident.

Renouncing your citizenship also makes deferred compensation more complicated. Regulations make a distinction between eligible and ineligible deferred compensation plans. Eligible plans are those in which the payer is a U.S. person (or a non-U.S. person electing to be treated as a U.S. person), and the payee has notified the payer of his or her status as a former citizen and has irrevocably waived any right to claim a withholding reduction on taxable distributions. For eligible plans, the payer must deduct and withhold a tax of 30% on any taxable payment. Any deferred compensation plans that do not qualify under the rules stated above are deemed ineligible. Ineligible deferred compensation items are taxed as though the payee received the current value of all accrued benefits on the day before expatriation. Additionally, the covered expatriate must file Form W-8CE, "Notice of Expatriation and Waiver of Treaty Benefits," with the ineligible plan payer. The plan payer then responds with a written statement that includes the current value of accrued benefits for documentation purposes.

Even if you renounce your citizenship, you may still be subject to tax on FDAP (Fixed, Determinable, Annual or Periodical) income. FDAP income is any type of U.S.-sourced income, with the exception of: income effectively connected with a U.S. trade or business; gains derived from the sale of personal or real property; and income typically excluded from gross income. A tax of 30% applies to any FDAP income, except in cases where a tax treaty reduces this amount. You may not take any deductions against the FDAP income. Even Social Security income is subject to the FDAP rules, and up to 85% of Social Security income may be taxed at the 30% rate. For a nonresident present in the U.S. for 183 days or more during the year, capital gains also will be taxed at the 30% rate (again, unless a treaty applies). When considering whether or not to renounce your citizenship, keep in mind that former citizens may still find it difficult to avoid the U.S. income tax system entirely.

Dual Citizenship

Even if you do not plan to give up American citizenship, you may want to secure citizenship in your new country if you can. In some places, you must be a citizen to qualify for certain government benefits or to purchase real estate. Some countries may limit certain jobs and investment opportunities to citizens. If you plan to stay in your new country permanently or long enough that you anticipate traveling back and forth, dual citizenship can also give you peace of mind about the permanence of your new home. You will generally be able to remain in the country and seek employment without a visa or permit, and you will be allowed to vote in local elections. If you think your children are likely to attend university in your country of residence, citizenship may allow for reduced tuition or eligibility for certain forms of financial aid.

As with most of the topics in this chapter, dual citizenship's advantages and disadvantages will depend in part on the country in question. Some countries prohibit dual nationality outright. Be sure to investigate both the details of naturalization and whether the local law permits you to maintain your existing citizenship if you become a citizen of your new country. Be aware of potential drawbacks of dual citizenship, too. You may face additional obligations, including the potential double taxation if no tax treaty is in place. The process of becoming a citizen can also be quite expensive, depending on the country.

HIRING DOMESTIC HELP

Depending on where you move, you may consider hiring domestic help even if you never managed household employees in the United States. This could be because of a lower cost of living, cultural differences or your family's changing needs. Whatever the reason, take the time to approach the process methodically. That way you will be sure you are meeting your responsibilities and that you can set yourself up for the best possible fit with your staff.

Before hiring anyone, be clear on precisely why you need help. If you have a partner, be sure both of you are on the same page regarding "must haves" and "nice to haves" when it comes to domestic workers. Do you need help mainly with cleaning or yard work? Help with your children? Do you want live-in help or part-time help? Would you prefer fewer employees who can perform various tasks or someone who specializes in what you need?

Once you know what you are looking for, research the norms of the community where you will live. If practical, you may want to consider hiring through a local agency. Look for established businesses with at least three years of experience, and make sure the agency staff speaks your language and the employees' language, if those are not the same. As with any professional service, look for a provider that is organized, efficient and pleasant to deal with. A good agency can offer a variety of advantages, including:

- Vetting and background information on employees
- Documentation for professional arrangements
- Worker training
- Ongoing support to ensure the employees' welfare and client satisfaction
- A source for replacing a worker who does not work out or who chooses to leave

If you do not go through an agency, either because one is not available or because you prefer to make a direct arrangement with your employee, bear in mind that you will need to do many of the agency's functions yourself. Be sure to gather full contact information, as well as letters of recommendation or references, before the employee begins work. Also be prepared to meet any employer obligations, including any wage and tax requirements that apply.

Whether you hire staff directly or go through an agency, be mindful of the cultural and social norms of your new country, which may differ from what you are used to in ways big or small. Rules for tipping, dietary restrictions, holiday observances and other practices may take you by surprise. Do your research upfront to the extent possible, and stay open and honest about what you don't know. Make sure your own expectations are clear from the start and, just as you would in the U.S., treat your employees with fairness and integrity.

LONG-TERM CONCERNS

Family Planning

Most Americans know that the child of a U.S. citizen is a U.S. citizen, even when that child is born abroad. But there are some serious restrictions in play that prospective parents should know about in advance. Certain residency requirements apply, and there are extra requirements for unmarried couples if the child's father is a citizen but the mother is not. Matters get truly complicated if a couple turns to assisted reproduction or surrogacy. (For a more general discussion of these topics, see Chapter 13.) That is because the U.S. State Department requires at least one of the child's biological parents to be a citizen for the child to secure U.S. citizenship, even if a citizen parent without biological ties is listed on the birth certificate. This rule has caused major legal headaches for expatriate American families, especially same-sex couples in which one spouse is a citizen and the other is not. While these rules may evolve, for now couples may have to make some difficult choices if they want to be certain of securing U.S. citizenship for their children.

A child born abroad may automatically obtain dual citizenship, depending on the circumstances. In addition to paying attention to your child's U.S. status, be sure to investigate the rules in the country where you live. As with your own citizenship, take special care to ensure your child does not inadvertently end up stateless.

Education

If you have school-age children or intend to remain abroad long enough for your children to reach that age, you will need to think about your education preferences. Planning for educational costs can be complex even at home (see Chapter 4), but adding a second country to the equation means an extra set of questions to answer. Do you want your children educated in local schools, an international school if there is one nearby, or somewhere far enough away that they will need living accommodations? What language do you want your child principally instructed in? What level of tuition can you afford if you opt for private schooling? Like any long-term financial goal, paying for your child's education will be easier the sooner you get started on budgeting and saving for it. But outlining a plan and estimating the likely costs will help you tailor your savings to make sure your goals and resources align.

Estate Planning

If you plan to live abroad for many years, or indefinitely, you will need to consider foreign residency's effect on every area of your financial life. One area you shouldn't neglect, especially if you have children, is your estate plan. While many younger adults put off drafting a will or other estate planning documents, it is critical to resist this temptation if you live abroad. (For more about estate planning basics, see Chapter 12.) If you can, consult an estate planning attorney who has experience with expatriate clients.

Many concerns are easier to navigate if you take the time to address them before you leave the United States. For example, you will likely want to specify that U.S. law will govern the way your estate is executed — an important step to protect your beneficiaries' inheritance. You may find it more convenient to place some or all of your U.S. property in trust, to make the process of distributing it more straightforward. However, while trusts are a frequently used estate planning tool in common law countries such as the U.S., they are not as prevalent in civil law countries, such as Brazil. Trusts can therefore cause tax and transfer planning issues in these places.

If you are designating an American guardian for your child, you will want to be sure there is a plan in place for where your child will live and how he or she will get there in the absence of a living parent. You will need to take precautions to make sure your child does not inadvertently enter the foster or adoption system of the country where you reside due to the lack of an adult advocate nearby. If you plan to stay abroad at length or indefinitely, be sure to consult lawyers with experience in both U.S. law and the law of your new country.

Making your home in a new place, whether for years or for decades, can be an enriching and rewarding choice. Though living and working abroad pose extra complications, financial and otherwise, for many expatriates the benefits far outweigh these costs. If seeing the world appeals to you and you have the opportunity to pursue that dream, keep in mind the issues in this chapter — but do not let them hold you back.

CHAPTER 18

RETIREMENT PLANNING

Thomas Walsh, CFP® and Victoria Dubuc

In the early years of your working life, retirement can seem far away, a problem you have plenty of time to solve later. But one of the best moves you can make to prepare for retirement is to start as soon as possible. Even if your savings seem small at first, establishing the habit of saving will serve you well. A long timeline also gives you a better chance to let your invested savings work for you.

Once you have started to save, you may wonder: What next? How much will you need to save for your retirement and what is the best way to build that nest egg? While it is true that no one can look into the future and see exactly how much they will need, you can make educated guesses that will allow you to design a retirement savings plan that fits the resources you have available and the lifestyle you desire after your working life ends.

The first question to answer is how much you will need to save. These calculations can often be quite complicated — much more than, say, working out how much you need to save in an emergency fund. If you are approaching retirement from a big-picture perspective for the first time, you may want to meet with a financial planner who can walk you through the process of creating a long-term retirement savings plan.

Broadly speaking, deciding how much to save involves a few factors: estimating how long you are likely to live, estimating when you plan to stop working, and envisioning the lifestyle you intend to sustain as a retiree. It is easy to underestimate all three, especially how many years you will live after retirement. Health care continues to advance and grow more expensive, which together can mean you will need more retirement savings than you might expect.

A commonly cited rule of thumb is that most people can sustain their existing lifestyle on about 60% to 80% of their preretirement income. After all, work-related expenses such as commuting, eating lunch out several times a week and continuing education will no longer factor into your budget as a retiree. As with any rule of thumb, though, there are exceptions. Some retirees spend more in retirement. Without the 40 or more hours a week at work, they may fill their time with concerts, shopping, travel or various hobbies. Other retirees may find their spending drops even more dramatically than these estimates. Retirees who downsize their home or move to a lower-cost location could wind up with a significantly cheaper cost of living, stretching their savings. While you cannot anticipate everything about your retirement, be honest about your preferred lifestyle and how you expect to spend your time. This will help you set a realistic savings goal.

Once you have a general sense of how much to save overall, you can work backward to determine a baseline savings rate in the present. Consider your current assets and your projected time horizon, and remember that you do not need to save every dollar of your total. With a long time horizon, investing and compound interest can work to your benefit. You have likely heard that the sooner you can start saving the better; if you start at age 25, setting aside at least 10% of your gross (pretax) income should generate a comfortable nest egg in most circumstances. Getting started later means you will need to save a larger percentage of income to achieve the same end result. That said, don't feel discouraged if you don't start by 25. A 2019 survey from market-research company Morning Consult found that roughly 25% of workers start saving for retirement in their 30s and another 25% wait until their 40s or later. If you are getting started on the later side, you may want to take a close look at your budget so you can save more aggressively. But beginning in your 30s still gives you plenty of time to build and invest your savings before a traditional retirement age of 65 or so.

A small but growing segment of young adults want to retire much earlier than average. The "Financial Independence, Retire Early" movement, often abbreviated FIRE, represents an approach for individuals who hope to retire by age 40, or sometimes earlier. FIRE adherents try to spend as little as possible, saving and investing the rest in hopes of achieving a large enough nest egg to end the necessity to work at a traditional job. Most cite the figure of a net worth 25 times greater than an individual's annual expenses, though some want a bigger cushion to sustain a more comfortable lifestyle. It is unlikely that most people would be comfortable with the level of frugality necessary to pursue a FIRE plan, but as with any financial goal, it is a matter of balancing priorities and identifying what truly matters to you.

On the other end of the scale, a growing number of people are choosing to work longer than past generations. Many jobs require limited or no physical component, and the rise of remote work means that getting to and from a workplace is no longer necessarily a requirement, either. Whether it means extending their existing career or turning toward a "second-act" vocation, older workers are frequently delaying retirement. This trend may continue, or even accelerate, as technology continues to change how work happens and medical advances keep us healthy and active for longer.

Whatever your personal goals for a retirement age and a retirement lifestyle, you can use a variety of retirement saving vehicles to increase your chances of achieving those goals. As with any sort of investing, you will need to evaluate your risk tolerance. (For more on risk tolerance and other investing basics, see Chapter 5.) Even if your goal requires only a low return, you should invest at least some of your assets in equities, or stocks, so that future inflation doesn't eat away the value of your savings. Investing for retirement is a marathon, not a sprint, and setting your course carefully at the outset is critical.

SOCIAL SECURITY

If you pay attention to the news, you may be aware that the foundations of Social Security seem shaky. In 2018 the program tapped its trust fund to cover benefits for the first time since 1982. Unless Congress makes changes, Social Security's trust fund is likely to run out by 2033, according to a 2023 report from the plan's trustees. This doesn't mean Social Security will vanish by the 2030s, but if lawmakers don't act, the program will eventually need to cut promised benefits.

To understand why, it's important to know how Social Security works. Despite a common misconception, a worker does not pay money into a personal account through payroll taxes over the course of a career. Instead, those taxes pay today's retiree benefits. In turn, today's workers expect tomorrow's workers to pay their benefits, at least in theory. After earning 40 credits — about 10 years of full-time work — a worker becomes eligible for full program benefits. Workers who are at least 62 years old can elect to start taking benefits. Once you start taking benefits, you will receive them throughout the rest of your life.

When Congress passed the Social Security Act in 1935, it did not intend the program to fully fund retirement the way we understand it today. It was a safety net for workers who earned too little to effectively save, or who lost their savings due to misfortune (as many Americans had in the stock market crash six years prior). Social Security was intended to keep older Americans from becoming destitute if they lacked both savings and family willing to take care of them.

Today, the program faces additional stresses that Congress could not have anticipated in the 1930s. Medical advances have significantly increased the average American's life expectancy and are likely to keep doing so. At the same time, demographic shifts mean fewer young workers are available to support a top-heavy population as baby boomers continue to leave the workforce. Today's workers are having fewer children, and having them later, which means this problem is likely to persist.

Congress may act to reform or restructure Social Security. But lawmakers are often at odds as to how such reforms should look. Suggestions have included raising the full retirement age, raising payroll taxes or increasing means testing (that is, how benefits are tied to a beneficiary's financial situation) to make sure those most in need of benefits get priority. For now, young workers should expect that they may get less from Social Security than their parents did. This is why it is important to treat Social Security as merely one component of a larger plan for retirement.

TYPES OF RETIREMENT PLANS

Over the course of your career, you will likely encounter a variety of retirement plans, either through your employers or on your own. No one person is likely to participate in all of the plans we will discuss. But understanding the options available will help you make a sensible plan and, with luck, make the most of the saving methods you can access.

Qualified And Nonqualified Retirement Plans

Qualified and nonqualified plans are really umbrellas for many types of employer-sponsored retirement plans. Qualified plans meet certain criteria that allow them to receive income tax benefits not available to nonqualified plans. Funds in a qualified plan are generally only taxed when the owner withdraws them as distributions, not when employers make contributions or when invested plan assets grow within the account. Some qualified plans allow employees to take loans without triggering tax consequences as long as the borrower follows certain rules. And assets in qualified plans are protected from creditors by federal law.

Funds in a qualified retirement plan are generally only taxed when the owner withdraws them as distributions, not when employers make contributions or when invested plan assets grow within the account.

In order for a plan to be qualified, it must follow the rules laid out in the Employee Retirement Income Security Act, usually shortened as ERISA. Plan sponsors must submit detailed reports to the government and provide documents explaining the plan in detail to participants. They must follow rules governing how to fund the plan and how benefits accrue. Qualified plans also may not require more than one year of service for eligibility, and any employee 21 or older must be allowed to participate once that employee has worked for the required waiting period. For plans that are not 401(k)s, the waiting period may be extended to two years if employer contributions vest immediately. Qualified plans must offer at least two entrance dates per year, since they cannot make employees wait more than six months to enroll once they become eligible. Nonqualified plans may set eligibility requirements as they like, and employers may offer them only to particular staff members. They do not offer employees the tax deferral benefits of qualified plans, and employers generally may not deduct contributions on their business's income tax returns in the year that they are made.

Given the benefits of a qualified plan, it may not be immediately clear why any employers would offer a nonqualified plan. But there are good reasons. Qualified plans require keeping up with complex compliance requirements, which means they are not always cost-effective, especially for small employers. Nonqualified plans may also be used to supplement qualified plans. Unlike qualified plans, they need not be offered companywide, so some firms offer a plan aimed at top-level executives. Because these plans are not governed by ERISA's relatively strict rules, a company may tailor a nonqualified plan specifically to these employees' needs.

Note, too, that tax deferral isn't always the better option. If you expect your income tax rate to be higher in the future, whether because of changes to tax law or to your personal situation, you may be better off paying tax in the present and getting future distributions tax-free. This is the same logic underpinning a Roth IRA (individual retirement account), which we will discuss later in this chapter.

Defined Benefit And Defined Contribution Plans

Another way to differentiate between types of employer-sponsored plans is by whether the employer guarantees a particular level of benefits or a particular level of contributions. Defined benefit plans were once standard, but today defined contribution plans are much more common.

Defined Benefit Plans

In a defined benefit plan, annual funding amounts vary, with older employees typically receiving more as they approach retirement age. The employer promises that participants will receive a specified benefit once they retire, which makes these plans attractive to employees. The plan manages investments collectively, so the employer bears any risk related to bad decisions or market slumps. Plan participants are also spared the stress of managing their own accounts. Maybe the best-known type of defined benefit plan is the traditional pension; cash balance plans are also structured this way.

Defined benefit plans are quickly becoming an artifact of the past. The Congressional Research Service reports that the overall number of active participants in defined benefit plans fell by about 54% between 1975 and 2019. Today, defined benefit plans are mainly available to workers in the public sector, with only 15% of private sector workers taking part in them as of 2022, according to the Bureau of Labor Statistics. Employers found defined benefit plans difficult and costly to administer, in part because of years of low interest rates and increases in average life expectancies. Many companies have frozen their plans, meaning new workers cannot enroll and workers already in the plan cannot accrue more benefits. Other employers have offered lump-sum payouts to try to stem the plan's overall liabilities. In cases where these strategies aren't enough, plans have had to resort to cutting promised benefits for retirees.

Even if you do have access to a defined benefit plan as a private sector worker, you will likely want to supplement it, given the risk of your employer having to freeze the plan or cut benefits in the future. Public sector workers' pensions are backed by strong legal guarantees, which makes their position less precarious than their private-sector counterparts. But as states and municipalities face serious funding shortfalls, many are cutting back on hiring new staff as a result of pension obligations eating into their budgets. As with Social Security, a defined benefit plan is often more useful as a component of a larger retirement strategy than as a stand-alone approach.

While many employees like defined benefit plans because the employer promises a particular benefit level, these plans also have some drawbacks beyond the risk of underfunding. Savvy investors may forgo the opportunity for greater returns by giving up control of how the plan directs its assets. And, in contrast to many defined contribution plans, it is difficult (or sometimes impossible) to tap your funds prior to the plan's defined retirement age.

Defined Contribution Plans

In a defined contribution plan, each participant has a separate retirement account. The employer makes no promises about the ultimate benefit level, and it is up to the worker to invest the account's assets individually. In general, these plans include contribution limits for both employers and employees. The most common example is a 401(k) plan, but there are many variants. Other defined contribution plans include money purchase plans, profit-sharing plans, stock bonus plans, employee stock ownership plan (ESOPs), target benefit pension plans, savings/thrift plans, 403(b) plans and 457 plans.

Defined contribution plans generally favor younger employees, who have longer to invest before retirement. The funds in such plans are also portable, which makes it easy to transfer them to an IRA or other retirement account when the participant leaves a particular workplace. Many 401(k)s allow workers to borrow funds or make early withdrawals, subject to various rules and penalties. While taking funds out of your retirement savings has significant drawbacks, it can allow for greater flexibility than a defined benefit plan.

The obvious drawback for workers is that defined contribution plans leave the participants to bear investment risk. Employers may also reduce their matching contributions, leaving it up to the employee to fund the account. And in all retirement accounts, but especially in defined contribution employer plans, it is important to keep an eye on fees, which can easily eat into returns and even contributions.

Traditional And Roth IRAs

Individual retirement accounts, or IRAs, allow you to save for retirement with tax advantages outside the context of an employer-provided plan. Many people supplement employer retirement accounts with an IRA. Depending on your circumstances and goals, you typically have two IRA options: traditional and Roth IRAs.

Anyone who earns taxable income can contribute to a traditional IRA, up to $7,000 per year (as of 2024). However, to make the most of a traditional IRA's tax benefits, you must meet a few other requirements. If you do not have access to a retirement plan at work, you can deduct contributions fully up to the overall contribution limit. If you do have access to a workplace plan, you may only deduct your contribution if your modified adjusted gross income is $77,000 or less ($123,000 or less for married taxpayers filing jointly). Above that limit, the amount you can deduct phases out until your MAGI is $87,000 or more for single filers or $143,000 or more for married couples filing jointly. (For more on modified adjusted gross income, see Chapter 15.) Generally, nondeductible contributions to a traditional IRA have little upside.

If you meet the requirements, you can deduct traditional IRA contributions from your current taxable income, lowering your tax liability. Assets within the IRA are not taxed until you withdraw them. However, if you must withdraw funds before age 59 1/2, you will owe a 10% penalty. In this way, traditional IRAs are similar to qualified employer-provided plans. (Pressing needs such as medical expenses are sometimes an exception to the penalty, though preretirement distributions are still subject to tax.) Once you reach age 73, you will have to take required distributions at least annually or face harsh penalties.

QUICK NOTES

Comparing Traditional And Roth IRAs

Traditional IRA

- Anyone with taxable income can contribute.
- You can deduct contributions from current taxable income.
- Assets are subject to federal income tax when distributed, but not until then.
- You must take minimum distributions at least annually once you turn 73.
- Except for pressing needs like medical expenses, you cannot withdraw funds before age 59 1/2 without triggering a 10% penalty.

Roth IRA

- You can only contribute if your modified adjusted gross income (MAGI) is below a set threshold.
- You cannot deduct contributions.
- Distributions are generally excluded from the owner's gross income.
- No required distributions during the account owner's lifetime.
- You can withdraw contributions (though not earnings) tax-free and penalty-free at any time.

In contrast, Roth IRAs do not offer an immediate tax deduction. Instead, distributions are generally excluded from the Roth IRA owner's gross income. This means contributions, which savers make with after-tax dollars, grow tax-free instead of tax-deferred. In other words, while traditional IRAs give you a tax break in the present, Roth IRAs offer a tax break in the future. This can be a powerful approach, especially for younger savers whose contributions have plenty of time to grow. And, unlike traditional IRAs, Roth IRAs do not require distributions to be made during the owner's lifetime. Owners can also withdraw contributions (though not earnings) penalty-free at any time, even before age 59 1/2. Early withdrawals of earnings are subject to the same 10% penalty as traditional IRA withdrawals.

The annual contribution limit for Roth IRAs is the same as traditional IRAs ($7,000 for tax year 2024). However, you must stay below a certain level of MAGI to contribute directly to a Roth IRA at all. Single taxpayers with a MAGI below $146,000 may contribute the full amount; above that level, allowed contributions decrease until MAGI reaches $161,000, at which point taxpayers can no longer contribute directly to a Roth IRA. (For married couples filing jointly, these figures are $230,000 and $240,000, respectively.)

If you are eligible for both a traditional and a Roth IRA, which should you contribute to? First, consider how much your tax situation is likely to change. Many people expect to be in a lower income tax bracket in retirement, but this is not true of everyone. As a rule of thumb, if you think your tax bracket will be lower in retirement, it makes sense to defer taxes using a traditional IRA; if you think your tax bracket will be higher, the tax-free growth in a Roth IRA is more attractive. In some cases, you may lack a clear sense of whether your tax bracket will be lower or higher several decades in the future. If you are torn, consider that a Roth IRA offers tax diversification if you have a 401(k), which can give you more flexibility; similarly, Roth IRAs don't require you to take annual distributions past a certain age. This added flexibility can make Roth IRAs more appealing for savers who qualify. Note, too, that you may contribute to both a traditional IRA and a Roth IRA in the same year, as long as your total contributions don't exceed the annual limit. You can't contribute $7,000 to each separately in the same year, but you can contribute $4,000 to a Roth IRA and $3,000 to a traditional IRA if you wish.

Once you reach 50, the Internal Revenue Service allows you to make catch-up contributions to both sorts of IRAs. These may be as much as an additional $1,000 per year. You can also make catch-up contributions of up to $7,500 ($10,000 if you are between the ages 60 to 63, beginning in 2025) to certain qualified retirement plans, including 401(k)s. This rule is designed to help savers approaching retirement to beef up their tax-advantaged savings. However, if your income is above $145,000, a new provision set to take effect in 2026 requires that any catch-up contributions to a qualified retirement plan must be made on a Roth basis. This means that while you won't get an immediate tax deduction for these contributions, they will grow tax-free.

The government allows taxpayers of any income level to convert a traditional IRA into a Roth IRA. This strategy allows savers above the Roth IRA income limit to take advantage of the Roth IRA's distinctive features. The trade-off is that savers generally must pay income tax on the full amount of assets converted in the year the switch happens. However, if your traditional IRA consists entirely of after-tax contributions, a conversion to a Roth IRA is a tax-free event. (Note that if you have any pretax IRA contributions, even to a separate IRA, the conversion becomes even more complex, as you will need to calculate the pretax and after-tax contribution percentages when determining the tax owed.) For a large account, an IRA conversion can mean a significant tax bill — but also significant tax-free growth after the conversion is done. IRA conversions were once reversible within certain limits, but the 2017 tax reform package removed the ability to undo them. Conversions are still a useful tool but offer a smaller margin for error than they once did. For most taxpayers, it is a good idea to talk with a financial adviser or tax professional about when and how to perform a conversion if you decide to pursue this strategy.

Self-Employed Workers And Small Business Owners

If you are self-employed, whether or not your business has other employees, you have a few other retirement plan options at your disposal. These tools can help you to create more robust retirement savings in the absence of a traditional employer-provided plan.

A common choice for self-employed workers is a **Simplified Employee Pension**, or **SEP IRA**. It functions much like a traditional IRA but allows a freelancer to save much more. For tax year 2024, the contribution limit is 25% of compensation or $69,000, whichever is less. (The dollar amount is subject to cost-of-living adjustments from year to year.) Fees and administration requirements are generally low, making this an especially attractive plan for sole proprietors. Unlike some other small business plans, contributions to a SEP IRA are purely discretionary. If you have a lower-income year, you can reduce your contributions or skip them entirely. SEP IRA contributions are considered as coming from the business, not from you as an individual, which means you can also contribute to a Roth IRA in the same year you make a SEP IRA contribution. Furthermore, starting in 2023, both employer and employee contributions can now be treated according to Roth rules, allowing you to benefit from potential long-term, tax-free growth.

A **Savings Incentive Match Plan for Employees**, or **SIMPLE IRA**, is also relatively straightforward, if slightly more complex than a SEP IRA. A SIMPLE IRA is available to businesses with fewer than 100 employees, as long as the business has no other retirement plan in place. As a qualified plan, a SIMPLE IRA must allow all eligible employees to participate. Both employers and employees can make contributions, and employer contributions are tax deductible. Employers may either match employee contributions dollar-for-dollar, up to 3% of compensation, or contribute 2% of each employee's compensation directly. In either case, an employer must contribute each year, though employers that choose the matching option have some flexibility to adjust the matching level from year to year. Also, as with the new Roth benefits available for SEP IRAs, you can now make Roth contributions to your SIMPLE IRA.

Sole proprietors and freelancers may also want to consider a **Solo 401(k)**. In many ways, it works just like any other 401(k) plan. The main difference is that Solo 401(k)s are not subject to coverage testing and nondiscrimination rules (since there aren't any employees to discriminate among). While generally the plans are designed for just one participant, the "solo" in Solo 401(k) does have a little flexibility: You may also include your spouse if he or she earns income from your business. As both the employer and employee in a Solo 401(k), you can make two types of contributions. As the "employee," you can make elective deferrals up to 100% of compensation or the annual contribution limit, whichever is less. (This limit is $23,000 in 2024 for workers under age 50.) In addition, as the "employer," you may make nonelective contributions up to 25% of earned income. For the purposes of calculating these limits, earned income is net earnings from self-employment after deducting half of your self-employment tax and any plan contributions you made for yourself. A Solo 401(k) may allow for greater contributions than a SEP IRA, depending on your circumstances. While it generally involves more administration, it also offers other benefits, such as the ability to take a loan if needed.

You may occasionally hear a reference to **Keogh plans** in discussion of retirement plan options for small businesses or sole proprietors. These plans used to offer unincorporated businesses a way to sponsor qualified retirement plans for themselves or their employees. However, the law no longer distinguishes between corporate and noncorporate plan sponsors, so this term has begun to fall out of use.

MANAGING YOUR RETIREMENT PLAN

Maximizing Contributions

If all of your retirement savings are going into the same account, you may not need to give much thought to how to divide up the monthly amount you have decided to save. But in many cases, you will divide your retirement savings between an employer-sponsored plan, a traditional or Roth IRA, and even accounts not strictly designed for retirement alone, such as a taxable brokerage account or a health savings account. (For more on HSAs, consult Chapter 9.) When you have more than one account, your saving will be most effective if you prioritize your accounts thoughtfully.

If your workplace retirement plan offers an employer match, be sure to contribute enough to secure the full match if you can.

If your workplace retirement plan offers an employer match, be sure to contribute enough to secure the full match if you can. In most plans, an employer will match a percentage of your contributions, up to a certain portion of your total salary. In some cases, employers may match contributions up to a set dollar amount instead. Either way, an employer match is essentially free money and one of the best ways to make the most of your retirement savings. Getting the full extent of this match is always a smart first step in prioritizing retirement savings.

After doing that, evaluate your various accounts based on their tax benefits. In many cases, after your full match, your next priority will be a traditional IRA (for the immediate tax benefits) or a Roth IRA (to make the most of long-term, tax-free growth). Both IRA types generally provide access to a wider selection of investments, sometimes with lower fees, than you will find in an employer-sponsored 401(k) plan. Once you reach your IRA contribution limit, you may want to go back and maximize your 401(k) or other employer-sponsored plan contributions beyond your employer match. Additionally, employers can now make matching and nonelective contributions to employees' designated Roth accounts. Once you've made the most of your tax-advantaged options, you can spill into a standard brokerage account if you still have savings left over.

Avoiding Common Pitfalls

At this point, we hope you have avoided the biggest retirement pitfall: not saving anything. According to data from Northwestern Mutual's 2023 Planning & Progress Study, 13% of American adults have no retirement savings, and an additional 6% have saved $5,000 or less. As in many areas of personal finance, getting started is critical, even if you can only save modest amounts. Once you have started, however, there are still some traps to avoid.

One of the most common pitfalls of retirement saving is failing to leave your money alone to grow over time. While you can withdraw contributions (though not earnings) from a Roth IRA without penalty, you should avoid doing so except in true emergencies. Compound interest helps your money grow exponentially the longer you leave it invested. Dipping into your Roth IRA disrupts that process. Similarly, many retirement plans — including 401(k)s — allow account holders to borrow against the plan without triggering adverse tax consequences. Most 401(k)s let savers borrow up to 50% of their account balance or $50,000, whichever is less. Many financial planners insist that borrowing from a retirement account is never a good idea under any circumstances, since you can finance everything except retirement. In some situations, however, borrowing can be a sound strategy. For instance, using retirement funds to pay down high-interest private educational loans or to purchase a home can be reasonable approaches in certain circumstances. The problem arises when savers treat a 401(k) as a piggy bank. Borrowing from a workplace plan also presents risk, because if you lose or leave your job, you typically must pay back the balance in full within a 60- to 90-day grace period.

Another common pitfall is applying for Social Security benefits as soon as possible. This is not always a mistake, but applying without thinking about the ramifications certainly is. While you can start collecting at 62, your monthly benefits will be smaller than if you wait until 70. (It never makes sense to postpone benefits after age 70, as your benefit amount won't continue to increase.) Deciding when to take your benefits will involve weighing your life expectancy and your immediate need for the money. If you are married, your spouse's age and health will also play a role. The Social Security Administration offers an online calculator at ssa.gov/benefits/calculators, which can help you estimate. While you do not need to lock in this decision in advance, it is worth bearing in mind when you are planning for the big picture of your post-retirement income.

One hazard that is not specific to retirement accounts, but that can prove especially dangerous, is the temptation to panic in a market downturn. It is only human to grow anxious when the market drops. But if you stay invested, your portfolio will likely recover along with the market. If you cash in your investments, you lock in your losses.

Investing

Assuming that you direct the investments in some or all of your retirement accounts, you may feel overwhelmed at first. It is true that how you invest your retirement assets matters. We recommend reading Chapter 5 for a general overview of investing, which will outline some basic principles to get you started. You may also consider consulting with a professional, as even a one-time meeting may help you to form a useful "big picture" view of your various accounts. Whether you seek help or go it alone, remember that you shouldn't manage each account in isolation. Rather, view your portfolio as a whole as you make choices about diversification and asset allocation.

You may be familiar with the idea of asset allocation: the mix of bonds, stocks and other instruments that make up your portfolio. But with retirement savings especially, it is important to think carefully about asset location, too. By staying mindful of which accounts are tax-free, tax-deferred and fully taxable, you can make smart choices about how to protect asset growth. Different types of assets are taxed at different rates, so it makes sense to put assets that generate a lot of taxable income in tax-free or tax-deferred accounts, while assets that are taxed at lower capital gains rates are better choices for taxable accounts. Asset location is part of why it is important to consider your portfolio as a whole, rather than just managing each account in isolation.

Different types of assets are taxed at different rates, so it makes sense to put assets that generate a lot of taxable income in tax-free or tax-deferred accounts, while assets that are taxed at lower capital gains rates are better choices for taxable accounts.

Unrelated Business Taxable Income

While it is mostly true that traditional IRA assets are not taxed until you receive a distribution, there is an exception. Unrelated business taxable income, or UBTI, results when your account yields active business income. For example, you may own an oil drilling partnership in your IRA. If that partnership leases drilling equipment to another company, the rental income would be UBTI. If this income exceeds

$1,000 for the year, you must report it and pay excise tax. If you invest in limited partnerships or master limited partnerships, you should stay alert for potential UBTI and consult a tax professional if you think you may owe excise tax.

Planning For Distributions

It may feel early to consider how you will manage distributions in retirement, but beginning with the end in mind can be helpful as you save and invest. Some plans allow you to choose how to receive distributions, and the way you approach this choice can have significant consequences. You will also need to have a strategy in place for an employer-sponsored plan when you leave that job for a new position.

A plan may offer a lump-sum distribution, which is what it sounds like: You will receive the full contents of your retirement account all at once (or in a single calendar year). This can offer advantages if you need a big, upfront sum to purchase a home or start a post-retirement small business. It also provides protection if you fear an employer will not be able to meet its obligations in the future. A lump sum has a major downside, though, in the form of tax consequences. A retirement account's tax shelter ends if you withdraw the entire amount, meaning it is often smarter to forgo the lump sum unless you intend to roll it over into another qualified retirement account.

In many cases, it is more beneficial to roll over an existing plan into a new account. The IRS generally permits savers to roll over preretirement payments into another retirement plan or IRA within 60 days of the distribution. You can also direct your plan administrator or financial institution to transfer the payment directly, so the payout is never in your hands. A direct rollover is usually more beneficial, as otherwise your employer must withhold 20% for federal income tax; you won't get the withheld money until after you file your tax return the next year. A direct rollover also lets you avoid the chance of missing the 60-day window if something goes wrong on your end. Rolling over a retirement account lets you avoid paying immediate tax on a distribution. Your money can continue to grow tax-deferred without interruption.

When you reach retirement age, qualified plans and traditional IRAs have strict rules regarding required minimum distributions, or RMDs. For IRAs, you must start taking RMDs annually the year you turn 73 (the first distribution can be deferred until April 1 of the following calendar year, but in that case you need to take two years' distributions in that first year); for qualified retirement plans, RMDs begin the year you turn 73 or the year you retire, whichever is later. Note that, beginning in 2024, you are not required to take RMDs from qualified employer Roth plan accounts, including Roth 401(k)s. Failure to take RMDs can trigger steep penalties that seriously harm your overall nest egg, so it is important to plan for them, especially if you must make withdrawals from multiple accounts. As in investing, stay mindful of the different tax characteristics of your accounts when it comes time to make withdrawals. In most cases, it makes sense to leave assets in a Roth account as long as possible to make the most of tax-free growth. If you have charitable intentions, you can also use your RMDs as a charitable donation to make your gift stretch further, while reducing your own tax obligations. (For more on charitable giving, see Chapter 20.)

Also stay mindful of state laws on retirement accounts. You may not know where you ultimately plan to retire at this point, but it is worth familiarizing yourself with your state's rules to get a rough idea of how your state handles pension income, for example. For more on state taxes, see Chapter 15.

CONCLUSION

Saving for retirement is critical, but it also involves a lot of unknowns. You cannot control what the stock market will do over the decades to come. You cannot control inflation. For the most part, you can't control how long you will live or how much medical care you will need in later life. No one else can control these things either.

Yet there is no reason to throw your hands up in despair. Even though retirement involves circumstances beyond your control, it also involves things that are definitely up to you. You can control your discretionary spending, now and in the future. You can, at least to a point, control how much you earn. And you can control how you invest your savings in defined contribution plans and personal accounts. A mindful, methodical approach to retirement will serve you well in the future, even if your first few steps seem small.

CHAPTER 19

ASSISTING AGING PARENTS

Larry M. Elkin, CPA, CFP®

All of us enter the world completely dependent upon other people; we cannot survive on our own. One ironic reality of modern life is that many of us will again be forced to depend on others as our time on Earth draws toward a close.

If you are in your 20s, 30s, 40s or even your 50s, the frailty of old age is still a long way off. There is not much you can do about it anyway, other than to provide for your future financial needs, as discussed in Chapter 18. Your more pressing concerns about aging are apt to arise when parents or other family members are no longer able to get along without help. Although this chapter's title refers to aging parents, the material presented here should help you assist anyone whose capabilities are declining as their years advance.

The baby boom generation, born between 1946 and 1964, confronted the challenges of aging parents to an extent never before seen. Because lifespans increased rapidly through the 20th century and into the 21st, the boomers had parents who lived, on average, considerably longer than had ever been achieved in this country or almost anywhere else. At the same time, boomers tended to live farther away from their parents than had earlier generations. The boomers also married and had their children later than earlier generations of Americans. In fact, they were sometimes called "the sandwich generation" as they became involved in their parents' care even before their own offspring achieved adult independence.

Soon the shoe will be on the other foot — quite possibly your foot. As the 2020s began, an estimated 10,000 boomers were reaching their 65th birthday every day. As of the 2020 census, there were 55.8 million Americans age 65 or older, representing nearly 17% of the population. By 2050, the number of Americans 65 or older was forecast to reach nearly 86 million, about 22% of the population. Because the boomers tended to have fewer children than their parents did, and those children — the 1965-79 Generation X and the millennials born between roughly 1980 and 1995 — have started their families even later than the boomers did, they will likewise be sandwiched between child rearing and elder care.

HOW OLD IS 'OLD?'

People often say that age is just a number. When it comes to old age, however, this is untrue. Old age is a lot of numbers, and they each mean something different.

The customary definition for the start of old age is 65. This was the standard retirement age set when the United States established Social Security in the 1930s. The Great Depression was in full swing, and the program's founders wanted to encourage older workers to retire quickly in order to open jobs for younger workers. At the same time, they sought to portray the program as self-funding, on the premise that contributions from working-age participants would "earn" future benefits and presumably pay for those benefits, although this was impossible for those who retired just a few years after the program launched. Since most wage earners at the time were men, and men seldom lived past age 70 in those days, setting the retirement age at 65 kept the financial burden on younger workers relatively small.

Today's workers do not receive full Social Security retirement benefits until they are past age 66, and the threshold will reach age 67 in 2027. A reduced benefit for early retirement is still available at age 62. Medicare coverage becomes available at 65, however, and many tax-deferred retirement plans permit distributions without "early withdrawal" penalties after age 59 1/2. State and local governments, as well as private businesses such as cinemas and ski resorts, widely offer "senior citizen" benefits and discounts. The age requirements for such perks vary, but typically begin to apply between ages 60 and 65.

In the past several decades, demographers have come to view the older segment of the population as representing several strata. The "young old" are generally those who are 65 to 74, while the "old old" are 85 and over. Everyone in the middle is just "old." This reflects the reality that aging is not a single process, but instead many distinct, albeit often related, changes that occur at varying rates from one individual to another. Everyone ages in their own way, but we all pass through reasonably consistent stages.

For many people in their 60s and early 70s, retirement is an economic choice rather than a physical necessity. People at this age have often experienced only modest physical decline. Intellectual capacity is typically undiminished; the occasional difficulty remembering a word or a name is offset by the insight that comes with experience. Freed of the demands of raising children or caring for their own elderly relatives, individuals at this age may even have more energy or less stress than before. Grandchildren can enter the picture, and financial security may make increased leisure, travel or relocation practical. Couples can often enjoy these "golden years" together. This is a very good time for individuals to set their own affairs in order (because one never knows when an emergency might strike), and even to get involved in new activities and endeavors.

The physical and cognitive changes that accompany aging usually become more noticeable as people progress through their 70s and into their 80s. Chronic conditions such as diabetes, hypertension, cardiovascular disease, arthritis and osteoporosis may present themselves or produce more acute symptoms than before. Hearing and vision are often compromised, although modern eye surgery can do a great deal to restore the latter. Eventually, and especially beyond age 85, walking slows and gait changes to produce a characteristic shuffle sometimes described as walking on ice. Balance is impaired, and falls become a major threat to health and quality of life. The immune system declines. So does short-term memory and reasoning speed.

These changes usually happen gradually, with different hallmarks of aging appearing at different rates not only for different people, but within the same person. For one, hearing loss might be pronounced even though reasoning and memory is only minimally affected. Another might be physically strong enough to participate in golf or tennis, despite being in the early stages of dementia. When dealing with an older individual, be alert to the specifics of what has changed, but also pay attention to what has not. Don't focus only on capabilities that have been lost or diminished. Try to take full advantage of the abilities that are still present, while seeking ways to compensate for what is lost.

INDEPENDENCE

When we are in the prime of life, independence means having the ability to decide what we want to do and then do it. Everyone has constraints such as financial limitations, work and family obligations, and sometimes the conflicting priorities of a significant other. We may also have physical limitations. But within our limits, we find the freedom to be independent adults.

This does not necessarily have to change when we become elderly — not even for the oldest of the old.

Physical and cognitive decline will take their inevitable course, and we cannot ignore those changes. As we get older, we cannot do all the things that we used to do for ourselves. But we can do some things that we used to do. Usually there are many other things we can accomplish with a bit of help, or that we can direct someone else to do according to our instructions. As long as we are able to decide what will get done, when it will get done, how it will get done and by whom it will get done, we retain an adult level of autonomy rather than regressing to a childlike state of dependency.

I have had a lot of experience working with older people, both in my profession as a financial planner (in some cases as a trustee, a role discussed later in this chapter) and as a baby boomer who has gone through the process with my own relatives and in-laws. It has made me believe in the value of letting older individuals make all the decisions they are capable of making, even if they are not the same decisions I would have made on their behalf. Some restraint in imposing my opinions can make a huge difference in the older person's self-esteem and even slow the rate of cognitive decline. Just like a muscle, our minds stay stronger when we have the opportunity to exercise them. Besides, merely being younger and professionally trained in business matters does not make me the source of all wisdom when it comes to another person's welfare. A little humility and respect can go a long way.

Sometimes we have no choice but to intervene. A classic example is the elderly person whose abilities have deteriorated to the point where it is no longer safe to drive a car. Having a spouse or adult child demand the car keys can be traumatic and demoralizing, but it can also be necessary. Ideally, the soon-to-be-former operator can be persuaded to stop driving voluntarily. The high cost of maintaining and insuring a vehicle, especially one whose driver has a history of recent accidents, is one factor the family can raise. Another is the risk that an innocent child, young adult or parent could be killed or seriously injured in an avoidable accident. A more recent point of persuasion is the ready availability of ride-hailing and taxi services, which make owning a car superfluous today for many people of all ages. Perhaps rather than just taking away an older relative's car keys, the person intervening can swap those keys for a smartphone or tablet and some instructions on how to summon a vehicle and driver when one is needed. It is worth considering.

RIGHTS, POWERS AND CAPACITY

In the eyes of the law, a young child can do virtually nothing without permission from a parent or guardian. No matter how bright or grown-up a child happens to be, or how worthwhile and reasonable the proposed activity, young people are deemed to lack the legal capacity to make decisions for themselves. Gradually, the law makes provisions for the maturing individual to assume the privileges and responsibilities of adulthood: to sign up for a website, to enter into a binding contract, to vote, to enlist in the military, to open a bank account, to purchase cigarettes or alcoholic beverages, to make decisions about medical treatment, etc. For all of these things, an individual is presumed to have legal capacity upon attaining the required age, unless a court determines otherwise.

There are very few situations in which capacity expires merely because of advancing age. There are some, however. In the United States, the pilot of a commercial airliner must retire at age 65, and if a pilot over age 60 is on the flight deck of an international flight, that pilot must be paired with another pilot or co-pilot under age 60. On domestic flights, however, both pilots can be over 60 years of age. The illogic is obvious when you consider that a one-hour flight from Boston to Montreal is international while a six-hour flight from Boston to San Diego is domestic, but rules are rules. The rules are not set in stone, however. In response to a pilot shortage, at this writing Congress was considering raising the mandatory retirement age to 67.

With just a few exceptions, an individual who has legal capacity to make a decision or exercise some legal right also has the power to delegate that right or power to somebody else. (One of those exceptions is voting. You cannot have your spouse or parent sign over their voting privilege to you, nor can you use a power of attorney to cast a vote on their behalf. Don't even try.) It is also possible for an individual who has legal capacity to delegate decision-making power for someone else to use later, when needed. This power to plan for a future loss of capacity is the basis for many of the tools and techniques I will discuss in this chapter, some of which are also covered in the general estate-planning discussion in Chapter 12. Accident or illness can produce incapacity at any age, so this is an issue that should be addressed early in adulthood. It simply becomes more pressing, on average, later in life.

Without the proper documents, you might not be able to step in promptly to handle a medical or financial crisis on behalf of your parents or other elderly relatives.

What happens if an individual loses capacity to act but has not named someone else to take control in that situation? Sometimes the law provides a default answer. For example, a spouse can usually make medical decisions in an emergency, even without documents granting that power. Other times, lengthy and costly court actions are needed, and the outcome may be undesirable. Without the proper documents, you might not be able to step in promptly to handle a medical or financial crisis. Privacy protections written into the law might prevent you from learning all the facts you need to know to make informed decisions, or you may lack the power to direct providers to take such basic steps as paying overdue property taxes or other bills.

The time to plan for taking care of elderly relatives is now, before they need you to take care of them. This is primarily something they must do for themselves if they possess the mental capacity to arrange their affairs. Maybe they have already done so and have not told you what arrangements they have made or where to find their documents when needed. Ask them. There is no reason to be shy about raising topics that touch on their mortality; we are all human, and these are steps that everyone should take much earlier in adult life anyway. You can even use your own planning as a conversation starter: "I have made arrangements in case something happens and I can't make medical or financial decisions for myself. I am happy to tell you my plans — and by the way, have you done this too?"

THE BASIC TOOLKIT

Managing the financial and personal affairs of an elderly person could easily fill an entire book, and so it has (many times). There is also a professional discipline, elder law, devoted to this topic. If you want to get a broad yet solid overview of personal finance from the standpoint of an older person, without getting too deep into the technical underbrush, I recommend (shameless plug alert!) the book my colleagues and I wrote primarily for that audience, *Looking Ahead: Life, Family, Wealth and Business After 55*. The third edition was published in 2023, fully up-to-date as of early that year. It is available on Amazon, in paperback and as a Kindle-formatted e-book.

I will not go into as much detail here, because our focus in the later parts of this chapter will be on the specific issues that typically confront younger adults when seeking to help elderly parents or other relatives. But before you can do anything that is very helpful, you need to have the legal authority to do it. It is worth reviewing the basic tools and arrangements that can be useful in most families before we look a little bit beyond the basics to address more complex situations.

Joint Bank Accounts

One of the early signs that an older person is losing control over his or her affairs is a failure to pay bills accurately or on time, or paying for goods and services that are not needed and which have never been ordered. Like everyone else, senior citizens receive an astonishing amount of exploitative junk mail, but they are more vulnerable to that exploitation. You may be called upon to take control of checking and savings accounts.

Online and mobile-based bill payment has made it easier to handle this chore, even if the account is solely in your older relative's name. However, to be able to deal directly with financial institutions or to sign checks drawn on such an account, you will need a power of attorney or you must have your name on the account. The most common way to arrange this is to be named a "joint tenant," often abbreviated as JTWROS (joint tenants with right of survivorship). This calls attention to another advantage of this arrangement. When a bank learns a sole account holder has died, it will freeze that account and the funds will be unavailable until estate administration has commenced. This can be a real problem when making funeral and burial arrangements, or if you need to pay bills that are outstanding at the date of death. A joint tenant automatically becomes the owner of the account after the other tenant's death, and the funds remain available. Either joint tenant can deal directly with the bank about the account, even if only one owner is providing the funds.

Durable Power Of Attorney

A power of attorney (POA) is a legal document that delegates authority from one individual (the "principal" or "maker") to another individual (the "agent" or "attorney-in-fact") to act on the principal's behalf. It can be limited to a specific time and purpose, or it can be written so broadly that the agent can do almost anything the maker could do, for an indefinite period. It should therefore be given only in relationships of great trust. The agent need not be a licensed attorney, and usually is not, although if you want your attorney to handle a transaction for you, a POA can be used for that purpose.

A POA can be revoked at any time. A standard POA automatically lapses if the principal no longer has the legal capacity to revoke it (such as in cases of coma or dementia), and all powers of attorney become void immediately upon the principal's death. This is desirable in most business contexts. But it is a major problem when dealing with elderly family members, because their period of incapacity is exactly when you will have the greatest need to act on their behalf. A "durable" POA was developed to deal with this situation. Durable POAs remain in force despite the incapacity of their principals, although they also terminate upon death. A principal can revoke a durable POA at any time, as long as the maker retains legal capacity.

A durable POA may be signed many years before it is needed, when the principal is still relatively young and in full control of her or his affairs. This creates another problem. When the attorney-in-fact shows up years later, perhaps at a financial institution, and presents a durable POA that was signed long ago, how does the institution know that the POA has not been revoked in the interim? The principal may be unavailable or too incapacitated to vouch for the agent. Instead, many lawyers who draft durable POAs also provide a fill-in-the-blank form called an "affidavit of full force and effect." The attorney-in-fact completes and signs the form to attest that the POA has not been revoked since it was made. If you are the attorney-in-fact, you should make copies of this blank form and complete a new version each time one is needed, because you may be called upon to attest to the continuing validity of the POA many times over a period of years.

Many states have prescribed certain language and advisory notices for their durable powers of attorney. These forms are typically not mandatory, although they usually at least serve as the starting point for a POA drafted by an attorney. It is not required, although it is often advisable, that you hire an attorney to draft a POA. Practitioners will often provide a durable POA along with a will, a living will and a health care proxy (all discussed later in this chapter) as part of an overall estate planning project. Married individuals frequently name their spouse as the initial agent, but may also name adult children or other close relatives or professional advisers as co-agents or successor agents in case the spouse is unavailable to act.

A POA usually takes effect immediately. This means the agent could, theoretically, go forth and promptly sell the principal's house or close a bank account even if the principal is perfectly capable. This is one reason why the person nominated should always be someone who is entirely trusted. As a backstop, some principals will ask their attorneys to include provisions stating that the POA does not take effect unless the principal is determined by one or more doctors or a court to be incapable of acting for himself or herself. This is known as a "springing" durable POA. Springing durable POAs have their place, but this language adds another complication when the agent seeks to have an institution honor a POA. This technique should be used sparingly. In many cases, simply limiting the scope of powers delegated to an agent will be a better option.

QUICK NOTES

Durable Power of Attorney vs. Health Care Proxy vs. Living Will

Durable Power of Attorney (POA)	Health Care Proxy	Living Will
► Gives agent the power to act for the maker in an array of contexts, including legal and financial ► Must include provision to be "durable," and may or may not take immediate effect	► Gives agent the power to make medical decisions on the maker's behalf ► By design, comes into force when its maker is incapacitated	► Documents maker's desires for health interventions in a serious medical crisis where he or she cannot communicate ► Supplements, but does not replace, a health care proxy

Health Care Proxy

A durable POA is typically used to manage financial and business matters. Managing the health care of an elderly person is an equally important responsibility, and there is a similar tool available to address it. This tool is the health care proxy, sometimes also called a power of attorney. This can be combined in a single document with a durable POA, or it can be separated. The agent can be the same person or people named to handle financial affairs, or someone else.

There are a couple of important distinctions between a health care proxy and a financial POA. One is that, almost by definition, a health care proxy must remain in force when the maker is incapacitated; it does not need a special provision to make it "durable." In fact, most health care proxies state that they are only effective when the maker is unable to make medical decisions for himself or herself.

The proxy will almost always include a provision entitling the agent to receive confidential medical information about the maker; otherwise, it would be impractical for the agent to make decisions about treatment. The proxy may also provide authority for the agent to determine when to withhold or withdraw treatments including artificial nutrition and hydration. (These end-of-life issues are also typically addressed in a living will, discussed below.) A financial POA need not authorize the agent to receive confidential medical information, but this can create its own complication: If an issue arises concerning medical billing, the holder of the financial POA may need access to such information to deal with hospitals, doctors or other vendors. Some attorneys will, therefore, include such authorization in a durable POA for financial affairs. If the same person — an adult child, for example — holds both medical and financial powers, this problem does not arise.

Like durable POAs, health care proxies often have a prescribed statutory form, or attorneys will adopt statutory language for their state to ensure that the proxy is accepted by health care providers when needed.

Living Will

A living will, also called an advance directive, provides guidance to health care professionals and family members about an individual's desires concerning medical treatment in extreme circumstances. By default, many doctors and hospitals will take almost any measures necessary to prolong life, regardless of the quality of life that can realistically be achieved. This can lead to situations in which a patient who is unconscious, comatose or in significant pain is kept alive with artificial feeding, hydration and respiration when there is no hope of recovery. A living will is the place for an individual to express any preference for whether such treatment should be provided, continued or withdrawn under such circumstances.

As with a health care proxy, any instructions that the patient is capable of providing the attending physicians take precedence over the provisions of the patient's advance directive. Having a living will supplements a health care proxy but does not replace it, because there is no way for a single document to anticipate all the circumstances in a serious medical crisis. The living will merely provides guidance to the proxy holder and the medical team, so much so that some attorneys include the living will's instructions in the health care proxy itself to ensure they are not overlooked.

Wills And Trusts

At first blush, a last will and testament, while very important for other reasons, would seem to have little to do with assisting elderly parents while they are still alive. But this is not true, because it is rare for both members of a couple to die at the same time. When one spouse survives the other for an extended period of time, provisions in the first spouse's will can be extremely important in managing the financial affairs of the survivor.

Many couples, especially in first marriages, simply leave all their assets to the surviving spouse. This often works well enough for relatively uncomplicated financial situations, particularly if the survivor has good arrangements in place to manage her or his affairs in the event of incapacity or death. Sometimes, however, things can go very wrong. The surviving spouse may have poor financial-management skills to begin with, or those skills may have deteriorated with time and age. Heavy medical or long-term personal-care expenses can deplete assets quickly, as can uninsured exposure to legal claims for accidents or business setbacks. A survivor's remarriage without a strong prenuptial agreement may result in the diversion of assets from the first spouse's family, or it can expose the funds to the new partner's bad spending habits. There is also the threat that the surviving spouse can fall victim to undue influence from friends, relatives, caregivers or others. (I will discuss undue influence later in this chapter.)

To address these concerns, some couples' wills place some or all of the first decedent's assets in trust for the benefit of the surviving spouse and other family members, often but not always prioritizing the needs of the surviving spouse. The surviving spouse may serve as trustee, either alone or in conjunction with other individuals or an institution. The testator can also name successor trustees to serve when the initial trustee steps down or is otherwise unable to continue. Sometimes the trust is established while both spouses are still alive; this is a so-called "living trust" that avoids probate proceedings and expenses. The will can "pour over" any remaining assets to the living trust for management and eventual distribution.

Even if the first spouse's will has not established a trust, the surviving spouse can create a living trust for convenience and protection. I have occasionally served as trustee of such trusts. In that role, I have had the trust directly employ caregivers and other household help. Taking on the role of employer allows me to provide oversight of the quality of care the client receives, while placing responsibility for payroll and tax administration on my staff rather than on the elderly client. It also means that in the event of the client's death, I can retain the staff for a limited period to provide a smooth transition of the client's household to other family members.

BEYOND THE BASICS

Some people, including many of the clients our firm serves, have highly complex financial affairs. Often these include closely held businesses that may involve owners outside the family as well as within it, multiple real estate properties, or international holdings that require consideration of foreign as well as U.S. law. Ideally, the older generation has put clear and effective succession plans in place to handle the eventual transfer of control over those interests.

Life is not always arranged in the ideal manner, of course. The HBO television series "Succession," which aired from 2018 to 2023, portrayed a family-controlled (but publicly traded) business empire whose aging and declining founder was slow to name an heir apparent, leaving his patently underqualified offspring, their stepmother and various outsiders to jockey for position. Despite the necessary artistic license, many advisers saw all-too-familiar elements in the situation.

In theory, the holder of a durable power of attorney could step into the shoes of an incapacitated founder and make decisions in his place. In practice, however, there are many other structures that could limit this ability or make it impractical. Businesses are governed by bylaws, charters, partnership agreements, buy-sell restrictions, and many other contractual and legal obligations. Federal and state securities laws and state corporate law also create constraints.

Adult children who are not involved in a parent's business may need to ask about succession plans, especially if they are apt to need to help manage the parent's financial affairs at some point. It's better to address these questions in advance than to deal with the disposition of an ill-prepared business later.

Adult children who are involved in a parent's business will often have at least some idea about the succession plans that are in place, or the lack thereof. Those who are not involved may need to ask, especially if they are apt to need to help manage the parent's financial affairs at some point. It is far better to address these questions in advance than to deal with the disposition of an ill-prepared business later.

I have seen many unfortunate examples of the latter situation, but a particularly vivid one comes to mind. A local tax preparer had died, and his widow wanted to sell the business. A colleague and I were asked to assess its condition. When we visited the office in a Miami-area strip mall, we found hopelessly antiquated equipment and software, files in disarray, and a single bored-looking assistant who professed to know surprisingly little about what work remained unfinished. The assistant had no employment contract or noncompete agreement; if he wished, he could simply solicit the deceased practitioner's clients and walk away with most of what little value was present. The accountant's widow was not a tax practitioner herself and was in no position to take her late husband's place. We doubted that she would receive more than a token amount for her husband's lifetime of professional labor. If she depended on income from the business for her own support, we could only hope that he left her with adequate life insurance.

CAPACITY AND UNDUE INFLUENCE

I have referred several times in this chapter to the importance of an individual having capacity to make important decisions, and of having someone capable and trustworthy in place to make decisions when capacity is absent. This makes us ask: What is capacity, and who has the burden of showing it is or is not present?

The answer is both murky and complicated, except when the law declares that it is lacking at certain ages. Capacity is not a function of one specific level of cognitive or intellectual ability. A person can have capacity for one purpose but not for another. Also, because standards for determining capacity vary, a person might have capacity to make a certain decision in one jurisdiction, but lack it according to the standards that apply somewhere else.

As a very general rule, and at a minimum, a person must be able to understand what they are doing in order to have the legal capacity to do it. If someone is making a will, for example, they must be able to comprehend they are signing a will and not be under the delusion that they are a movie star signing an autograph for a fan. They need not understand all the legal nuances reflected in the will's language (and few nonattorneys do), but in most cases they should also be able to broadly identify the people they wish to benefit and the fiduciaries they wish to nominate to carry out their intent.

Most adults whose affairs are not under court supervision or who have not otherwise been found to be legally incapacitated are presumed to have capacity to make a will, even if they have some form of mental illness. The burden is on someone challenging the will to prove that the person making it lacked capacity, specifically at the time the will was made. A person suffering from schizophrenia, for instance, might lack capacity to make testamentary decisions during a delusional episode, but could be capable of doing so when stabilized and on medication.

The standard for determining capacity to enter into legally binding contracts can be somewhat higher. Some courts simply require that the contracting party be capable of understanding what the words in the contract mean, while others may set a higher standard that considers whether the individual is able to make a judgment about the merits of the agreement. Usually, a contract entered into by a party lacking capacity — including contracts entered into by minors — are voidable by that party, unless the contract is for necessities or if the person seeking to void a contract has already substantially benefited from it. In some cases, the other party must know or have reason to know that the individual lacked capacity before it can be voided.

A particularly sensitive issue involving capacity and the elderly is the question of when a person becomes unable to consent to sexual activity. In 2015, an Iowa jury acquitted 78-year-old Henry Rayhons of charges that he sexually abused his wife while she was in a nursing home with Alzheimer's disease. Prosecutors had said Rayhons engaged in sexual contact with his wife behind a privacy curtain in her room after nursing home staff told him she lacked capacity to consent. Rayhons' attorneys maintained that he viewed this as medical advice rather than a legal conclusion, and also that the wife's roommate was mistaken when she told staff she had heard the sounds of sexual activity on the date in question. The roommate later testified she could not be sure of what she heard.

It was unclear whether the jury concluded that prosecutors failed to prove the sexual activity occurred, or that it was not clear that even a woman institutionalized for Alzheimer's was incapable of consenting to have sex with her husband. Either way, the case highlighted the complexity of the issue, one that is likely to recur more often as the elderly population swells in decades to come. Even individuals with relatively advanced dementia can have interludes of clarity, during which they may be capable of some decisions that should be honored, unless a court has declared them incompetent.

We ordinarily expect the decisions of competent adults to be respected, even if those decisions are manifestly unfair or unwise. Courts will, in fact, usually honor such decisions unless they determine that the decision-maker has been subject to "undue influence." Often someone who challenges the gifts or bequests made by a person who has legal capacity will argue that the individual was subject to undue influence. This brings us to the next question: What constitutes undue influence?

As with capacity, there is no single standard of undue influence. In many places and contexts, it has never been defined in statute at all. In those situations it is a court-imposed demand, essentially saying that a transaction or agreement entered into under extreme duress will not be honored.

Let's use an example. Suppose an elderly but mentally competent homeowner has two children, a grown son and a grown daughter. One day the homeowner decides she no longer wishes to live in her home; rather, she wants to give the home to her daughter and use her savings and pension income to rent an apartment. The son gets nothing in this transaction. It may be unfair to the son, but does the homeowner have the power to carry out her plan, and will a court respect her wishes? Certainly, unless there is something else involved.

Now suppose this same individual makes the same decision, except that she does so only after her daughter has threatened to cut off all contact between her mother and the daughter's family, including the grandchildren. Can the son persuade a court to void the transaction because his mother has been subject to undue influence? Quite possibly. He might even be able to persuade a judge to appoint a legal guardian for his mother to shield her from such pressure in the future. I will discuss guardianship in the next section.

In 2014, California enacted a statutory definition of undue influence that effectively captures the way it is commonly applied. The statute summarizes undue influence as "excessive persuasion that causes another person to act or refrain from acting by overcoming that person's free will and results in inequity." The law goes on to list the following factors as indicative of undue influence:

1. The vulnerability of the victim. Evidence of vulnerability may include, but is not limited to, incapacity, illness, disability, injury, age, education, impaired cognitive function, emotional distress, isolation, or dependency, and whether the influencer knew or should have known of the alleged victim's vulnerability.

2. The influencer's apparent authority. Evidence of apparent authority may include, but is not limited to, status as a fiduciary, family member, care provider, health care professional, legal professional, spiritual adviser, expert, or other qualification.
3. The actions or tactics used by the influencer. Evidence of actions or tactics used may include, but is not limited to, all of the following:
   A. Controlling necessaries of life, medication, the victim's interactions with others, access to information, or sleep.
   B. Use of affection, intimidation, or coercion.
   C. Initiation of changes in personal or property rights, use of haste or secrecy in effecting those changes, effecting changes at inappropriate times and places, and claims of expertise in effecting changes.
4. The equity of the result. Evidence of the equity of the result may include, but is not limited to, the economic consequences to the victim, any divergence from the victim's prior intent or course of conduct or dealing, the relationship of the value conveyed to the value of any services or consideration received, or the appropriateness of the change in light of the length and nature of the relationship.

However, the law goes on to state that "Evidence of an inequitable result, without more, is not sufficient to prove undue influence."

GUARDIANSHIP

When a debilitated person of any age lives alone and without help, conditions can quickly deteriorate to life-threatening levels. Most elderly people ultimately rely on family members, friends, neighbors and others in the community to monitor their situation and provide support when needed. But not everyone has those resources. Sometimes outsiders, including the state, need to get involved.

Court-appointed guardians should be viewed as a last resort due to the potential for conflicts of interest and, in the worst cases, serious abuse.

A court-appointed guardian is an individual, or in some cases an organization, that is given decision-making power over a person when nobody else is in place to exercise it. A "guardian of the property" is granted complete discretion over the individual's assets and financial affairs, and is sometimes known as a conservator. A "guardian of the person" obtains authority over the individual's housing, medical care and other personal affairs. (The two roles are sometimes combined in one person.) These powers are similar to those voluntarily granted under a durable power of attorney and a health care proxy, but with one important difference: The individual has no power to revoke the guardianship or to replace the guardian with somebody else. Only the court can do that.

In many locales, any adult can ask a court to appoint a guardian for someone whom they believe to be in danger. Courts will usually schedule a hearing, but sometimes relatives or other interested parties are not notified, particularly if they live at considerable distance. We have seen instances in which attorneys have solicited elderly people and offered to have the client herself petition the court to appoint the lawyer as guardian, thus giving the attorney complete power over the client's assets and physical custody. Nursing homes will sometimes nominate clients to become the wards of affiliated organizations or friendly lawyers — who then ensure that the individual continues to be housed in the nursing home.

Many guardians are well-meaning and honest, but the arrangement is prone to conflicts of interest and, in the worst cases, serious abuse. Once a guardian is appointed, particularly one with whom a judge is familiar and has developed a degree of comfort, courts may be in no rush to respond to family members who belatedly seek to terminate the guardianship and make other arrangements.

Family members, too, can petition to become legal guardians. Sometimes this is the best outcome when the infirm relative has not previously delegated the necessary powers. Having a family member appointed as guardian can resolve conflicts within the family, and it will usually prevent the court from later appointing an outside party, provided the family member is diligent about looking after the person under their care.

Court-appointed guardians should otherwise be viewed as a last resort. Sometimes it is the best option, or the only option, and we can expect it to be used more often as the population ages. However, all of the planning steps we have considered in this chapter are geared toward making it unnecessary when there is a capable family member or trusted friend ready and willing to help.

LIVING ARRANGEMENTS

There are really only three types of places where an aging individual can live: in their own home, in somebody else's home or in some sort of institution. The right choice varies by person and stage of life.

I will address financial issues later in this chapter, but for many elderly people and their families, money is a key consideration, and often the most important one in determining which alternatives are feasible. Adult children with their own obligations are not always in a position to shoulder large costs associated with the maintenance of an aged parent, so the parent's resources must be stretched as far as they reasonably can go.

This is why it is useful to break down the bundle of services usually lumped together as "elder care" into their parts. Buying only the services the individual really needs is often the way to make money go furthest.

Staying Home

Most elderly people have spent decades in their own homes. Their home is typically where they are most comfortable and most independent, and this can lead to a higher quality of life. Also, a home that is paid for apart from taxes, utilities and maintenance, or a long-occupied apartment that may be rent-controlled, can be by far the most economical housing option available. Saving money on housing leaves more money for all the other things an elderly person will need.

But living at home, and especially living alone, can leave the elderly most vulnerable to sudden illness and accidents. It can also be the most isolating option. Loneliness can lead to depression and lack of good self-care; the individual may neglect nutritious meals, for example, if such meals must always be prepared for just one person and eaten alone.

With advancing age, many seniors will need at least some degree of in-home assistance. Changing bed linens and cleaning bathrooms and ovens may be nearly impossible for weakened bodies. Even routine dusting, vacuuming and laundry may be difficult and burdensome. Driving and shopping may be impractical without help. Someone may need to ensure that medications are taken at the proper times and in the proper dosages.

There is a wide array of resources available to meet all of these needs. Housekeeping services (excellent holiday and birthday gifts, by the way) or private domestic employees can keep homes neat and sanitary.

Home health aides and visiting-nurse services, and even doctors making house calls in some areas, can provide the necessary level of medical supervision. Taxis, ride-hailing services and online shopping can take people wherever they need to go, or bring supplies directly to them. There are dozens of monitoring services to summon help in the event of a fire, fall or other emergency. "Nanny cams" permit off-site relatives to monitor caregivers and conditions in the home. Many gated communities have community rooms and organized social activities that can prevent residents from becoming lonely and housebound. Some towns also have publicly run senior citizens centers — and the best of these provide supplemental services including transportation, help with taxes and vaccinations, and even overnight group excursions.

When an older relative needs the sort of services that an institutional setting can provide, we should not assume that the only choice is an institutional setting. Sometimes the same needs can be met, more economically and with a greater degree of privacy and autonomy, at home.

Nursing Homes

At first glance, a typical nursing home looks much like a hospital, minus the doctors. Patients are usually housed in private or semi-private rooms on floors that have a nursing station in a central location. Nurses, aides and orderlies enter the rooms at regular intervals to attend to the residents, who may or may not be referred to as patients.

But there are significant differences among nursing homes beneath the surface similarities. Facilities that provide **skilled nursing care** place heavy emphasis on recovery and rehabilitation after illness or injury. Frequently, an elderly patient who has spent substantial time in a hospital is released to a skilled nursing facility rather than being sent home. During a hospital stay, the patient's muscles may have atrophied. Difficulties with balance or other faculties may have been diagnosed (and may have contributed to the mishap that sent the patient to the hospital in the first place). The patient may have difficulties with speech, eating or other important functions. Skilled-care facilities have therapists on hand to help patients recover well enough to go home.

Custodial-care facilities are more like dormitories with a limited amount of on-site care, primarily for safety, housekeeping, monitoring and medicine administration. Residents typically remain in these facilities for extended periods of time. Private-pay institutions may be somewhat more upscale and generous with amenities; they do not participate in the government-run Medicaid program. Medicaid facilities will accept private-pay patients until their assets have been depleted to levels that qualify them for Medicaid coverage. These facilities, operating on limited budgets, can vary widely in quality. **Intermediate-care facilities** have more medical staff than custodial-care institutions, but are more limited in the rehabilitative services they offer.

Assisted Living

If a nursing home is something between a hospital and a dormitory, an assisted-living facility is analogous to an apartment or town house complex with concierge services tailored to the elderly. It provides a private room or a small apartment, with housekeeping and modest kitchen facilities (a sink and refrigerator, plus a microwave but less often a cooktop where fire could start); a dining room where collective meals are served at specified times; often a lounge or day room where residents gather for organized and casual social activities; and on-site health and nursing care to dispense medications, address minor issues and determine when other medical care is needed. The facility will often provide a segregated section for "memory care" where residents are much more closely supervised and often locked in to prevent dangerous wandering.

When an older relative needs the sort of services that an institutional setting can provide, don't assume that the only choice is an institutional setting. Sometimes the same needs can be met, more economically and with a greater degree of privacy and autonomy, at home.

These amenities can be quite nice and desirable, but also pricey. The basic rent for the apartment plus the limited housekeeping can range well into the thousands of dollars per month, plus the cost of meals and the necessary degree of medical supervision. Prices increase as the client requires more services, which can often be delivered without requiring the resident to relocate. Such a facility may be exactly what an elderly individual or pair (many establishments will take couples) wants, especially if they are in reasonably strong physical condition and value the convenience and social outlets of such group living.

But for others, these facilities can be excessively costly, anxiety-inducing or even dangerous. A socially introverted resident may not appreciate the group meals and activities. In fact, the atmosphere at some facilities has been compared to high school, with its in-crowds and outcasts.

Perhaps more importantly, standard arrangements in assisted-living facilities provide little protection against one of the biggest dangers that an older individual faces: falling, and the serious injuries that can come from a fall. A fall that is not discovered for hours can be life-threatening. Even when the fall is quickly addressed and medical attention is promptly delivered, brittle elderly bones are easy to break and slow to heal. Disabilities that result from a fall can leave a formerly active and busy individual confined to a wheelchair and house-bound.

Someone who is prone to falls, or who has fallen and is mobility-impaired, may require extensive in-home attention, or even round-the-clock care to prevent further injury. Private aides are welcome and commonly employed by individuals at many assisted-living facilities, but this cost stacks on top of the cost of the facility itself. It can be much more economical to arrange for such care in the senior's own home. Home health aides will often handle cooking and light housework, do the shopping, and accompany the individual to medical appointments or anywhere else they wish to go.

Senior Living Communities

A variant on the assisted-living concept, these communities may have larger, more fully equipped units and may be marketed to younger and somewhat more active couples. They can be rental apartments or condominiums that can be resold later at market prices to future occupants who meet the community's age requirements. Most offer on-site or on-campus assisted living to provide additional services as aging residents require them.

Continuing Care Retirement Communities

Another variant on the assisted-living concept, these developments require occupants to pay a substantial entry fee, plus typically large monthly rental charges. A portion of the entry fee may be refundable at the occupant's death or departure, but there is no ownership of the unit and no appreciation potential. In contrast to typical assisted-living facilities, these arrangements tie up significantly more of the resident's capital, and the portion of the entry fee that is not refundable is, in effect, a type of prepaid additional rent. The lure of most such developments is that they offer a range of care from independent living to full-scale memory care, all without leaving the residential complex. In some cases, the operators promise that rent (typically set at higher levels) will not change, no matter how much additional care is required.

We have seen clients consider some such communities before they have even been built. We cautioned that they have little opportunity to back out and receive their entry fee if they do not like the way the complex is ultimately built or staffed, or if they are not compatible with the other occupants. The large upfront cost also makes it more difficult to relocate to another area if, for example, they later choose to be closer to relatives.

Living With Relatives

Through most of American history until the decades after World War II, there was little need to discuss where elderly parents would live: They would live with adult children, or at least near enough so those children, usually a daughter or perhaps a daughter-in-law, would be primarily responsible for looking after them. When families were larger, expectations of personal privacy were smaller, life expectancies were shorter and relatively few women worked outside the home, the system worked well enough, apart from the burdens it placed on the caregivers.

Such arrangements are less common now, but they are not unknown. It is much less expensive to maintain one dwelling unit than two. Living with family members provides on-site help with chores, taking medications and dealing with emergencies. It allows grandparents and grandchildren more opportunity to enjoy one another, and when both parents work, having grandparents available to provide after-school transportation or child care can be a major benefit.

Sometimes an elderly relative can be installed in a vacant bedroom or other space. Other options include a separate apartment within the residence (often still archaically called a "mother-daughter" apartment) or purchasing a two-family home, sometimes jointly between parent and adult child. In the latter case, there should be some discussion about how the home will be titled and what will become of the parent's equity after the parent dies or moves out. If the surviving homeowner child has siblings, those siblings may receive a smaller inheritance as a result of the equity transferred to the surviving owner.

FINANCIAL CONSIDERATIONS

Older people, and especially affluent older people, tend to have relatively complicated financial issues. A lifetime of labor, saving and investments, along with the transition to retirement, the growing importance of estate planning, the availability and limitations of many government programs and the gradual decline of physical health raise so many difficult questions that it would take an entire book to address them. As I mentioned near the beginning of this chapter, my colleagues and I wrote that book. It is *Looking Ahead: Life, Family, Wealth and Business After 55*. You will probably find it helpful if these issues are important to you or your loved ones.

Here I will present only a very brief recap of things you should keep in mind if you are assisting an older person with their financial management.

Medicare is the primary source of medical insurance coverage for individuals over age 65 in the United States. The program provides benefits that cover hospitals, doctors and prescription drugs, with some significant limitations. It is usually advantageous to apply for Medicare three months before the individual reaches age 65; delay can result in higher premiums. "Medigap" insurance is private coverage designed to address some of the limitations of Medicare coverage. Medigap policies are standardized to allow easy price comparisons from one carrier to another.

Medicare generally does not cover the cost of staying in a nursing home or assisted-living facility. The major exception is for care in a skilled care facility for up to 100 days in a "benefit period." A benefit period starts after a three-day qualifying hospital stay. Once the individual has been out of a hospital or skilled-care facility for at least 60 consecutive days, a new benefit period can commence after another three-day qualifying hospital stay. Medicare does not pay the cost of room and board in the skilled nursing facility, and it does not pay for unskilled "custodial" care. Medicare covers certain in-home medical services as an alternative to care in a skilled nursing facility.

Medicaid is the joint federal-state program that provides medical insurance coverage for lower-income recipients and certain others who qualify. Unlike Medicare, it will cover custodial care in facilities that accept Medicaid reimbursement rates. However, there are relatively strict income and asset limits that govern eligibility for Medicaid. This means an individual may need to "spend down" other assets before qualifying. A look-back period, typically of 60 months, takes into account gifts that the Medicaid applicant or the applicant's spouse has made within that period, and will delay eligibility if the applicant has divested too much wealth. Certain assets, such as a home in which a spouse continues to reside, may be exempt from the limits, but some states may claim proceeds from a later disposition of the home to reimburse funds that were spent on an individual's custodial care.

Long-term care (LTC) insurance is a product whose purpose is to cover either institutional or in-home care for individuals who are no longer able to perform a certain number of "activities of daily living," such as feeding themselves, dressing or going to the toilet without assistance. Originally developed in the 1990s to help families avoid the Medicaid spend-down rules, and encouraged by some states to ease the strain Medicaid was placing on their budgets, LTC insurance has proved to be unexpectedly expensive because claims were more frequent, longer and more costly than actuaries first expected. At our firm, we generally advise against purchases of new LTC policies. However, if an individual has a policy in force and needs care, that policy should be examined carefully to see what may be covered and any available benefits should be claimed.

If your parent or certain other older relatives qualify as your dependent, you may be able to claim a credit of up to $500 against your federal income taxes. The parent's income must be below a specified amount, which was $5,050 for the 2024 tax year and is adjusted annually for inflation. You must have provided more than half of the parent's support or, if you did not because you split costs with other relatives, you and the other relatives must have entered into a multiple support agreement that is acceptable to the Internal Revenue Service. Nobody else must be able to claim the individual as a dependent (there are tiebreaker rules to determine who gets the credit if this is an issue), and the person being claimed must be a citizen, resident or national of the United States, or a resident of Canada or Mexico. These rules took effect in 2018 and, as of early 2024, are scheduled to be replaced by prior dependency rules after 2025.

HELPING FROM A DISTANCE

Ideally, we would all be able to keep our relatives close at hand (although not necessarily too close) so we can immediately know and respond when they need help. For many of us, that is simply not practical. We may live thousands of miles or hours of driving time away from the person who has asked us to serve as their trustee, health care or financial power holder, or for whom we are simply the most capable or closest available family member. Fortunately, there are many things we can do nowadays to keep an eye on elderly relatives even when they are far from sight.

In order to help effectively, it is important to understand their financial landscape. Where do they have their bank and brokerage accounts? Do they receive rents, pensions or other sources of income? How much, how often and how is it deposited? Who and where is the attorney, accountant or financial adviser they use? Where are their important papers kept? Do they have an off-site storage unit, a safe deposit box or both? Where are those depositories and where are the keys or combinations? Does somebody nearby have an emergency key to the elderly person's residence? Do you have an emergency key?

QUICK NOTES

Tips For Helping From A Distance

- ☑ Talk with your loved one to understand their financial landscape while they are still capable of handling their own affairs.
- ☑ At the first sign of compromised physical or mental capacity, arrange to receive logins to online accounts or duplicate statements sent to you.
- ☑ Investigate anything strange or unusual immediately.
- ☑ Encourage your loved one to wear a pendant to alert a local service of falls; if he or she lives alone, insist.
- ☑ Know who else has a key to your loved one's home, or set up a key code you can give remotely to a neighbor or first responder.
- ☑ Arrange for someone to be there, virtually or physically, if a repair person or other professional needs to visit your loved one's home.
- ☑ With permission, conduct or arrange for an inventory of the loved one's belongings.
- ☑ Make sure all tax obligations are being met.
- ☑ Check in often.

At the first sign that an individual's faculties or physical ability to manage his or her own affairs is compromised, try to step up your monitoring. Arrange for duplicate statements, utility bills and especially property tax bills to be sent to you, or set up logins so you can monitor these items online. If your parent does not use email, ask permission (or use your authority under a POA) to have notifications and correspondence sent to your email address. Pay especially close attention to property taxes, because if homeowners no longer have a mortgage, they are responsible for paying taxes themselves — and homes can eventually be lost through tax-lien sales if taxes go unpaid for too long.

Monitor bank statements and credit card bills closely. Unexplained and unusual charges, withdrawals or wire transfers can be signs of serious trouble. Investigate immediately. If an explanation from a parent does not make sense, something is probably amiss. Keep probing until you understand exactly what is happening.

Falls are a serious danger. There are many monitoring services that provide a pendant that can be activated, or which is self-activating, in case of a fall or other problem. These services will summon emergency help and notify you that there is a problem in the home. Particularly if the individual lives alone, insist on having such a service, and periodically check that the resident is wearing the pendant, at least while at home. Avoid services that make demands such as a three-year contract; there are many others that do not.

Know who has a key to the home. Having one or more people nearby with a key can be very helpful in an emergency, or just for peace of mind if the relative is temporarily out of touch. Another option is to install a keypad-controlled lockbox outside the relative's front door. Such boxes are often used by real estate agents and vacation-home rental managers. Having a key readily available means you can provide a code to neighbors or first responders so they can get inside in an emergency without breaking through the door. It is also useful for you or another relative should you arrive for a visit to find nobody home, or if the occupant is accidentally locked out.

Also try to know who is coming to the home and when. If an unknown tradesperson or inside delivery is expected, see if someone can be home with your relative when they arrive. Nanny cams or a video chat can allow you to monitor the proceedings remotely, or a phone call can allow you to discuss matters that are beyond the resident's expertise with the installer or repair person.

With the resident's permission, take a careful initial inventory of the home's contents, then update that inventory periodically. (When our firm does this for clients, we typically visit once or twice per year.) Pay particular attention to high-value items, of course, but even an unexpected change in the quantity of ordinary items on hand or the disappearance of less valuable belongings could be signs of problems like hoarding, forgetfulness or compulsive shopping. When items disappear, find out why and document the reason. "Gifts" to new friends, strangers or household employees could indicate undue influence.

Make sure tax returns are properly filed, especially if there is household help or if the resident has significant income. Nobody needs trouble with the IRS. Also, if household help is hired directly rather than through an agency, make sure that local laws governing workers' compensation, paid time off, overtime and tax withholding are observed, and that payroll tax forms are also properly filed. There are payroll services that specialize in handling the paperwork.

Finally, but perhaps most importantly, talk to your relative — often.

Some people, admittedly most of them mothers, contend that there is no such thing as calling your mother too frequently. That may be debatable as a general principle, but when you are looking after an aging relative from a distance, it is literally true. The more contact you have, the sooner and more easily you will notice that something may be wrong. It is more useful to have frequent short conversations than infrequent longer ones. Inquire what they are eating, what they are doing, whom they have seen or spoken with on the telephone. Ask if anything in the house needs repair. Try to be aware of medical appointments and ask about the results, especially about any changes in prescriptions. Keep a list available of all the prescriptions that your relative takes — in a medical emergency, doctors will need this information quickly. Be alert to changes in mood and memory.

One lesson I can share from experience is that certain kinds of illness, notably bladder or urinary tract infections, can cause confusion and disorientation so profound that it seems as if dementia has occurred overnight. Real dementia does not typically occur overnight, even in most cases of stroke. I have seen in multiple elderly people this pattern of sudden onset of confusion, which eventually resolves when the underlying infection is treated. But not all doctors, especially those who do not specialize in the elderly, immediately think to test for infection. Particularly in emergency rooms, the first protocol seems to be to consider stroke or some other vascular event. It was ambulance drivers, home health aides and others who frequently come in contact with the elderly who, on more than one occasion, raised the subject of a test for infection that later came back positive.

HOSPICE AND RESPITE CARE

At a certain point, conventional medical treatment stops serving to prolong life; it merely prolongs the process of dying. Often this comes at the price of considerable suffering for patients and families alike. Rather than spend anywhere from days to months in a hospital bed, tethered to tubes and technology and largely cut off from familiar faces and surroundings, many patients today choose to move to a hospice facility or to receive hospice care at home.

Medicare will pay for in-home hospice care for patients who are diagnosed with six months or less to live. Visiting nurses or other medical professionals generally deliver such care. They will do everything possible to relieve pain and otherwise make the patient comfortable, but cure or arrest of the terminal condition is no longer the goal, and treatments aimed at such results are typically suspended.

For brief periods of crisis, Medicare will pay for 24-hour continuous hospice care in the home.

Because hospice services are not routinely delivered on a 24-hour basis, family members or home health aides typically must provide considerable support to the dying patient. This can be physically and mentally exhausting. Medicare will also cover up to five consecutive days of occasional respite care, during which the patient will check into an inpatient hospice facility while the at-home caregiver has a chance to rest or attend to other matters. Hospice services have helped millions of Americans die a more peaceful and dignified death in the familiar surroundings of home, with loved ones close at hand. Countless survivors have expressed enormous gratitude and appreciation for these services and the people who deliver them.

THE FINAL ACTS (AND SOME FINAL THOUGHTS)

The last act most of us will perform for our parents is to say goodbye, whether this means laying them to rest, scattering their ashes or arranging a memorial service. When we execute their estate plans and settle their affairs, we are really acting for the benefit of the heirs who remain, not the person who has departed. In a sense this is true of funerals and burials as well, but many people have particular ideas about how they want to leave the world and be remembered.

Adult children are often reluctant to raise the subject of funeral and burial plans for fear of seeming morbid. Yet many professionals, myself included, have encountered little similar reluctance among older clients to discuss their own final arrangements. Trust and estate lawyers routinely ask older clients if they wish to include any instructions in their wills or in accompanying documents.

The death of a loved one, no matter how peaceful or painless or long-expected, is always stressful. It is a difficult time in which to make decisions about burial plots or funeral arrangements, yet many people have little choice. If the plans are not made well in advance, they must be made on the spot. While this is a highly unusual and difficult time for most of us, it is an everyday event for funeral directors, cemetery staff and clergy. These professionals deal with bereaved family members nearly every working day; they are almost invariably kind and supportive. Tell them what you want, and they will do everything within reason to accomplish it for you.

Funeral directors will usually gather the information that is required for the death certificate. They will ask relatives for basic biographical information such as the date and place of the decedent's birth and their marital status at the date of death. They will also ask how many copies of the certified death certificate you wish to have. While it is possible to obtain more copies later, it is more convenient to request them when the funeral arrangements are being made. You will need more copies than you think you do, for such matters as closing bank accounts and making life insurance claims. For most people I would ask for at least 10 copies; for someone with complex financial affairs including property holdings in more than one state, 15 or 20 copies would not be unreasonable.

It is possible to purchase a prepaid funeral plan through most funeral homes. In these arrangements, the individual might make the most significant choices of casket and burial plot, and either pay for these items immediately or set up a financing plan to set aside the funds over time. Problems can arise if the funeral home goes out of business or if the service must ultimately be delivered someplace else for some other reason. An alternative, often preferable, is for the elder relative to make some basic decisions about what type of service is desired and leave the relevant instructions in a readily accessible place, along with funds to pay for the arrangements.

I noted earlier that an individual's bank account will be frozen upon death pending probate proceedings. Setting up an account as joint tenants can work around the problem. Another option is to make the account a "pay on death" account, with a named beneficiary who automatically becomes the new owner upon the death of the one who set up the account. The trouble with this in the funeral context is that it may take a few days (at least) to obtain the death certificate, which the bank will need before it releases the account. In the meantime, the funeral parlor and other vendors need to be paid. It helps to have funds readily available that can be reimbursed later if necessary.

One more step that should be taken promptly after a relative's death is to cancel the deceased's credit cards. Note that if the deceased is the only person responsible for the account — even if duplicate cards were issued to enable relatives or household aides to make purchases on the relative's behalf — family members are not responsible for paying the outstanding balance on the card. Only the deceased's estate is legally responsible. When you call to cancel the account, the card issuer's representative is likely to read to you a script that makes it clear that family members are not liable for the decedent's balance. (This is not true, however, if another person still living co-signed to establish the account. That individual remains responsible.)

Most of us will eventually help someone make it through the last years of life. It is usually a labor borne out of love, or gratitude, or compassion, or all of the above. For financial and legal advisers, it can also be part of our professional duties.

Life has a trajectory not unlike that of an airplane's flight. We climb during our youth, cruise through most of our adulthood, then descend toward our final destination. We want that descent to be a smooth, gradual and comfortable one, ending in a touchdown so gentle we scarcely realize we have landed. We don't want to make a steep dive to the runway, and we especially don't want to crash.

Helping someone make that smooth final touchdown can be a long and demanding process. It is far from easy, but it is rewarding. Having done it for others, we can hope that someday, someone we love and trust will do it for us.

CHAPTER 20

GIVING BACK

Paul Jacobs, CFP®, EA

For many people, one of the greatest benefits of success is sharing with others. According to Giving USA, Americans collectively gave $319 billion to charitable causes in 2022. In addition, a study by the Corporation for National and Community Service and the U.S. Census Bureau found that 60.7 million Americans volunteered 4.1 billion hours in 2021, despite the lingering effects of the COVID-19 pandemic, and nearly one in four American adults formally volunteered between September 2020 and September 2021. That's a lot of generosity.

You may already be eager to give back but remain unsure about the best way to get started. Or maybe you want a more creative approach, or wonder how to balance giving with your other financial goals. Like all financial planning, the best approach will be tailored to your situation. But learning more about your options and identifying questions to ask yourself can help you create a customized approach that works for you.

GETTING STARTED

Before you decide how to give back, you should answer a few questions. Whom do you want to help, what do you want to give, and why is giving back important to you?

Most of us have a wide array of causes we support in the sense of being glad they exist and acknowledging that their work is important. But no one can give to every worthy organization out there. So the first step in an effective plan for charitable giving is identifying causes that spark your passion. Your answers will likely reflect your experiences, temperament and lifestyle. Some people find it rewarding to focus on one specific cause, funneling most or all their charitable and volunteer efforts in this direction. Others may prefer to contribute to larger charities that have the resources to reach many people with different needs.

A common conundrum is whether it is best to give a substantial amount to one or two organizations, or smaller amounts to more recipients. There is no single answer. It may help, however, to consider the pros and cons of each approach. Charitable gifts involve certain fixed handling costs and administrative expenses for the recipient. Smaller gifts necessarily devote more of the total to handling these upfront costs. However, this does not mean smaller gifts cannot do real good.

Consider three main criteria when evaluating a charitable organization: efficiency, effectiveness and innovation.

The nonprofit organization Bolder Giving suggested a 50-30-20 approach for charitable gifts. Focus 50% of your giving on one or two charities that mean the most to you. Set aside 30% for community organizations, such as your place of worship or your children's school.

The remaining 20% can go toward "impulse" donations, such as pledging to support a friend racing to raise awareness for a cause, or giving to support the victims of a natural disaster. This method is not the only way to split your donations; it is just one example. The important thing is to consider a holistic strategy, rather than giving to anyone who asks in the moment without a broader plan.

Timing your gift is also worth considering. Because of fixed processing fees, you may think it is better to give one large annual gift. Sometimes this is true, but not always. Many charities appreciate steady, monthly donations, since these can help with cash flow and planning. Recurring payments can also make it easy to fit your charitable contributions into your budget on a monthly basis, instead of setting aside funds in anticipation of a lump-sum gift. Many organizations even allow you to automate your gifts if you like.

If you don't already have an organization in mind, identifying one is an important step. If you want to support a particular cause, try to narrow the field by considering how you want your donations to be used. For instance, if you want to fight a particular disease, do you want your recipient to focus on research? Prevention? Advocacy? Any of these are fine answers, but they may point you to different organizations. You should also research potential recipients to get a sense of how they use donations. Even if you are already drawn to a certain charity, it is wise to take a closer look to make sure your organization of choice is operating effectively. At Palisades Hudson, we recommend three main criteria when evaluating a charitable organization: efficiency, effectiveness and innovation.

Efficiency is a measure of how well a given organization manages its donations. To evaluate how efficient a charity is, you may want to review its disclosure documents. The Internal Revenue Service requires tax-exempt organizations — as well as certain charitable trusts and political organizations — to file Form 990 each year. This form is generally available to the public. It includes information such as the organization's number of employees, level of contributions and annual expenses. Most of the time, the more an organization's money is devoted to program causes, the better. Note, though, that sometimes administrative expenses are higher for an organization just starting out or one that does a particular type of work. Websites like Charity Navigator and Candid (formerly GuideStar) can offer useful resources in evaluating a specific nonprofit organization, often including its Form 990. If you have any questions about what you see, reach out to the charity directly. Good nonprofit organizations are happy to answer donor questions.

Effectiveness is a bit less straightforward to measure than efficiency, but it is still important. Essentially, this quality measures how well a given organization addresses the cause it focuses on. For example, a charitable organization focused on increasing literacy might be very efficient in keeping its overhead low and devoting most of its funds to programming. But how many of its students learn to read, and how quickly? Effectiveness will be easier to gauge for some missions than others. You should consider the question of whether an organization has a track record of making a difference, as well as reasonable plans for future progress.

You may or may not find innovation a compelling attribute in evaluating an organization. Unlike the first two criteria, this third measurement is not always essential in identifying a strong organization. Many can do real good without reinventing the wheel. That said, it is worth asking whether an organization is tackling a problem in a novel way or generally doing the same work as other entities. If you are trying to decide between a few similar organizations, consider using innovation as a tiebreaker.

Beyond identifying the causes and organizations you hope to support, you should think about whether you have any secondary motivations for giving back. Charitable giving is often its own reward, but in some cases you can combine it with other goals. For example, you may want to carry on the philanthropic legacy of a parent or grandparent. Or you may want to ensure you are making the most of the potential tax benefits of your charitable gifts. Keeping any secondary motivations in mind can help you pursue charitable strategies that can put your gifts to work for both you and your recipients.

HOW TO GIVE

Monetary Gifts

Since this is a book about financial planning, you will likely not be surprised that the first method of support this chapter will discuss is making a monetary gift or donation. While this is far from the only way to help a cause you care about, it is a significant one. In fact, expanded philanthropy is a goal that shapes many people's long-term financial plans. Any thoughtful way you choose to display your generosity is a net positive. That said, there are strategies that can help you stretch your gifts further.

First, it is important to understand the basics of the charitable deduction available when filing federal income tax. Individuals can generally deduct up to 60% of their adjusted gross income (AGI) per tax year. (For more on AGI, see Chapter 15.) If you give appreciated property such as stock, this limit is 30% of AGI. These limits apply to gifts to "public charities" as the IRS defines them in Internal Revenue Code section 501(c)(3). This is why you sometimes hear people refer to charities as "501(c)(3) organizations," though private foundations may be 501(c)(3)s too. You can also deduct gifts to most private foundations, but the thresholds are lower: 30% of AGI for cash gifts and 20% of AGI for appreciated property.

To take the charitable income tax deduction, you will need to itemize your deductions rather than taking the standard deduction.

Given the current relatively high standard deduction, itemizing is not worthwhile for many people. But you cannot always know in advance exactly how a given year will develop. If you make gifts that exceed the AGI limits in a year you itemize, you can also carry forward the excess for up to five years. So it is wise to document any potentially deductible charitable gifts as you make them. Charitable organizations generally must provide a written disclosure statement for any gifts of $75 or more, and many organizations provide such statements for all gifts. This disclosure may be a PDF, an email or a physical document mailed to you. Whatever form it takes, be sure to keep your documents organized and to ask for documentation if the organization does not provide it to you proactively. Keep them in one central location, so you do not have to try to remember all your gifts and locate the documents at tax time.

If you make a major gift, especially in a year when you plan to itemize your deductions, you can often get more bang for your buck by donating appreciated assets directly to a charity, rather than selling them and donating the proceeds. Under normal circumstances, if you sell an asset that is worth more than it was worth when you acquired it (its "cost basis"), you will owe tax on the additional value (the capital gain). (For more details on capital gains taxes, consult Chapter 15.) Instead, you can give the asset directly to a charity. You can still take the charitable deduction — bearing in mind the lower limit relative to AGI — but because the charity is tax-exempt, it will not owe any tax on the gain when it eventually sells the asset. In many cases, this can allow you to effectively give a larger donation.

For instance, say you own shares of a stock you bought five years ago for $200 that are now worth $1,000. If you sold that stock to give the cash to charity, you would owe tax on the $800 of unrealized gain. If, on the other hand, you gave the shares directly to the charity, you can still take a $1,000 charitable deduction and avoid capital gains tax on the $800 of gains forever. On the other hand, if you hold assets with unrealized capital losses, it makes more sense to realize those losses, since you can use them to offset capital gains. In that case, sell the shares and then donate the proceeds. This strategy mainly works for tax-exempt public charities. When you give to a private foundation, certain gifts are only deductible up to the asset's cost basis, defeating the purpose of giving appreciated property.

Timing can also shape the tax impact of your gifts. If your current tax year will involve an unusually large amount of income, it is likely a good time for an especially generous charitable gift if you're inclined to make one. For example, you may end up with unusually high income due to a one-time windfall, which could push you into a higher tax bracket. To the extent you can, match high-income years with large deductible gifts. If you are not prepared to give a major gift to a particular organization, certain strategies can allow you to deduct a donation in the short term while taking more time to decide where you ultimately want to direct it.

Donor advised funds are a good option in a year where you know you want to make a charitable gift in part to offset high income tax, but do not have an organization in mind.

If your plans are flexible, you may want to proactively "bunch" major gifts together in the same tax year to secure the benefits of itemizing your deductions. This can be as easy as, for instance, moving a gift you'd usually give in December to January, and then switching back to December at the end of the year. Bunching is a multiyear strategy, so if you face significant financial uncertainty in the short term, it is not the most useful option. This technique is also best when you know that your gifts — alone or with other deductible expenses for the year — will put you well over the threshold where it makes sense to itemize.

Depending on your plans, you may find it useful to give to a donor-advised fund. Donor-advised funds are public charities that are often sponsored by financial institutions and mutual fund companies, as well as by philanthropic organizations. They are a good option in a year where you know you want to make a substantial charitable gift, but do not have an organization in mind. Donor-advised funds place contributions in an investment portfolio. The donor can offer advice on how to allocate the invested gift, and can eventually recommend distributions to qualified charitable organizations. You can take the charitable deduction the year you make the gift to the fund, regardless of when the distribution happens. Donor-advised funds also allow for anonymous gifts, if this is important to you. Before you make a gift, though, you should understand that recommendations to donor-advised funds are nonbinding, so you give up some control with this approach. Also, since the tax reform package that passed in late 2017 substantially raised the standard deduction, the tax benefits of small charitable contributions have essentially vanished for many taxpayers, whether direct or via donor-advised fund.

Some organizations let you determine how they will use your gift, especially if your proposed donation is large. While most charitable institutions prefer unrestricted gifts, offering donors access to restrictions can be a way to ensure that supporters feel their contributions are going to good use. If you want to give a gift with restrictions, discuss your intentions with the organization in advance. Once you agree on the specifics, you can either sign an explicit agreement or submit a letter outlining your intentions along with your gift. Some larger organizations also offer predetermined categories you can select when making your gift. For example, if you donate to your university, you may be able to direct your gift to a particular scholarship fund.

Generosity is wonderful, and it generally creates warm feelings. This is why it is sometimes challenging to decide how much you are comfortable giving. If you care about a cause or organization, you should try to give enough that you feel you are making a real difference. That said, make sure you don't give so much that you are harming your financial future. Make sure your gift is in line with your day-to-day budget and your long-term financial plan. (See Chapter 3 for more on budgeting and Chapter 5 for more on developing a long-term financial strategy.)

Other Ways Of Giving

Charitable trusts are a common choice for people who want to make large gifts. Two major types are a charitable remainder trust and a charitable lead trust. A charitable remainder trust provides a stream of income back to beneficiaries the grantor chooses, potentially the grantor him- or herself, for a set period. After that period, all remaining assets go to one or more selected charities. A charitable lead trust provides income to one or more charities for a certain amount of time before the trust assets revert to the grantor or to designated beneficiaries. In either case, a well-structured trust offers control over your gift and certain tax benefits. On the other hand, trusts can be costly to set up and administer. They are also subject to complex rules and regulations. If you think a trust may be a good fit for your goals, you should involve skilled counsel to make sure you set up and administer your trust correctly.

Life insurance may not intuitively seem like a vehicle for philanthropy, but there are several ways a life insurance policy can help you support a charitable institution. If your existing policy has outlived its primary purpose, you can give it to a charitable organization. You can potentially deduct the value of the policy at the time of the gift; if you still owe premiums on the policy, you can also choose to donate the value of the outstanding premiums to bolster the value of your donation. If it is more practical, you could also convert the policy to a paid-up policy of reduced value, so neither you nor the charity need to worry about ongoing premiums going forward. Note that for noncash charitable contributions, including life insurance policies, if the donation is worth more than $5,000 you will need to arrange for a third party to conduct a qualified appraisal of the gift.

Bequests are gifts an individual makes after death, usually through a will. Many people choose to recognize a school, faith community or other charitable organization in their estate. You may leave an organization a specific bequest (such as a piece of art); a general bequest (usually an amount of money); a demonstrative bequest (a certain amount from a designated source, like the sale of a certain stock); or a residuary bequest (the remaining value of the estate after all other bequests, taxes and expenses are provided for). Any of these bequests are reasonable ways to support a charitable organization in your estate planning. For more on bequests, wills and estate planning, see Chapter 12.

Private foundations are a popular means of establishing a long-lasting philanthropic legacy. Foundations are 501(c)(3) entities that, in most cases, focus on making grants to other nonprofit organizations. Later in this chapter, I will discuss setting up a nonprofit organization in more detail. But bear in mind that private foundations are subject to complex rules and can be expensive to run as well as to set up. You should expect to devote substantial capital and energy to getting a foundation off the ground. You can also make tax-deductible gifts to existing foundations, although remember that the IRS deduction limits are lower than for gifts to public charities. You may have connections to an existing family foundation, too. If you want to take an active role in a family foundation, the experience can offer perspective and a way to show that you value the philanthropic efforts of your parents, grandparents or other relatives.

Endowments most often apply to educational, religious or arts institutions, but in fact many nonprofit organizations can benefit from such gifts. Endowments are donations, usually in the form of investment funds or other property, which the donor intends for a specific purpose. For example, an endowment may underwrite an academic scholarship or support an arts organization's season of programming. In most cases, endowments are set up to preserve the gift's principal; the investment income supports the cause over many years, or sometimes indefinitely. You may want to support an existing endowment or set up a brand-new endowment. In either case, most organizations will happily work with you to determine the most productive way to set up your gift. Unlike trusts or foundations, endowments are generally administered by the recipient. This gives you less control, but also entails less ongoing responsibility.

Volunteering

While most organizations are grateful for monetary support, you should not undervalue your time and skill as potential contributions. In many cases, volunteers are essential to an organization's mission. And volunteering will often let you help people directly, while connecting you to others who are passionate about the same cause you value.

A charitable organization may also ask you to step into a leadership role. Your first instinct when asked to get involved may be to say no, either because you feel unqualified or because you worry about the amount of work involved. It is true that serving on a nonprofit board or taking on other leadership responsibilities can involve serious time commitments and responsibility. But think twice before you turn an offer down. Getting involved can be a great way to meet new people and make a difference at the same time. Before you join a board or a committee, make sure you understand what you will need to contribute, including the time commitment involved and any potential financial component. (Nonprofit board members are often expected to donate a particular amount each year.) Ask whether you will need to attend all meetings in person, or if people sometimes call in or join via Zoom. You may also want to ask if you can sit in on a meeting or two before agreeing to join, which will give you a better sense of how the organization runs.

If you take a leadership position, there are a few principles to bear in mind. First, be sure to read the room. Don't show up at your first meeting prepared to tell everyone how they should do things. Instead, concentrate on listening and learning for a while. Second, while you should be prepared to help when asked, understand that you will likely work your way up over time. Don't feel slighted if no one gives you major responsibilities right off the bat. Third, be mindful of your overall workload. Do not let your enthusiasm tempt you into taking on more than you can realistically achieve. You do more harm than good if you burn out quickly and leave others to pick up projects you drop. Finally, beware of potential conflicts of interest. The rules of the organization may dictate how you will need to handle potential conflicts, but it is important to remain alert to possible issues.

Before you join a nonprofit board or committee, make sure you understand what you will need to contribute, including the time commitment involved and any potential financial component.

Serving on boards and committees can be rewarding, but such commitments are not for everyone. If the recurring work or the time involved is too much for you to take on, investigate opportunities to help with particular projects instead. There may be a few big events where an organization needs extra hands for a few weeks, or even a few days, which will allow you to pitch in without an ongoing commitment.

Like many activities, volunteering is more enjoyable — and often more sustainable — with a friend. If you have found an organization you click with, consider inviting family and friends to participate, too. On the other hand, if you have not decided where you want to volunteer, ask around and see if you know someone who already regularly volunteers. In most cases, if you express interest in joining them, your friends will be happy to connect you with their organizations.

No volunteer commitment lasts forever. Once you find a way to volunteer, regularly reevaluate whether your volunteer activities remain a good fit. Don't be afraid to step away if your situation changes or if you realize that things are not going the way you originally hoped. Any charitable organization will be used to volunteers needing to leave for a variety of reasons. In most cases, they will be happy you were involved to begin with. As with a paid job, communicate your plans to leave in advance, especially if the organization will need to reassign your projects, and do what you can to help with a smooth transition. Know that good organizations do not bad-mouth former volunteers. They will simply wish you well and look for someone who can offer the enthusiasm or time you no longer can.

If your volunteer experience was not good, don't give up. Keep looking for other opportunities that will suit you better. No one will judge you if it takes a few tries to find the perfect fit.

Raising Awareness

A third option for supporting causes or organizations is serving as a booster within your network of family and friends. If a cause is important to you, you should not hesitate to let your loved ones know. You can also ask for their direct support, though be careful not to overdo it. Be mindful of your friends and family members' financial situations, and be sure not to unduly pressure people who may feel unable to say no, such as your subordinates at work. If you ask your network for support in a thoughtful and genuine way, many people will be happy to help.

Many nonprofits organize events that are specifically designed to raise awareness and funds, which can serve as an ideal entry point for sharing your passion. Consider participating in a marathon, walk-a-thon, dance-a-thon or other event if your organization offers such opportunities. Since the cause you are supporting is important to you, don't be afraid to share that emotional appeal with those around you. Asking for help in person is ideal, but do not discount the potential reach of your online networks as well. And remember to thank anyone who pitches in once your event is over.

STARTING YOUR OWN NONPROFIT

If you dream of starting a nonprofit organization of your own, the first thing you should do is identify why the idea is important to you. According to the National Council of Nonprofits, there are more than 1 million charitable nonprofits in the United States, and many struggle to attract funding and attention. Even a wildly successful nonprofit will require hard work to start and maintain. It is not a project to take on lightly.

That said, there are many reasons you may want to start your own nonprofit rather than support an existing one. You may see a particular need in your community that existing organizations are ill-equipped to meet. Or maybe you have an innovative approach to a problem that is substantially different than those pursued by existing organizations. Maybe you have an inherently entrepreneurial bent and want the emotional rewards that come with nonprofit work, as opposed to a for-profit startup. If you plan to start a private foundation, you may want to establish a family legacy and provide a way for your children to participate in your philanthropic work one day.

A note on terms: A 501(c)(3) organization, as discussed earlier in this chapter, is tax-exempt at the federal level and is eligible to receive tax-deductible contributions. Its status is determined by the IRS. The term "nonprofit" refers to an organization's incorporation status, which is governed by state law. Many organizations are both nonprofits and tax-exempt organizations, but the two terms are not interchangeable. In this section, I will assume you intend to secure tax-exempt status for your nonprofit.

Regardless of the type of nonprofit organization you intend to start, careful planning is critical. Take time to clearly define your goals, determine the source of your startup capital, and outline whom you envision running the organization once it is on its feet. All these factors will shape the way you proceed. You should also research existing organizations in your area to see if any have a similar or identical mission, which may influence whether or how you proceed. Take stock of your plans to finance the organization, both as it gets on its feet and once it is up and running. In many ways, starting a nonprofit is similar to starting a small business. You should honestly assess the demand for your proposed services and develop a detailed business plan as early as possible.

One small but important detail you should not neglect: Pick a name for your new nonprofit early. Before you start filing paperwork, check that your name is not already the domain name or trademark of another entity. Your secretary of state should offer a tool that will let you conduct a name search. A general internet search is also a good idea.

The two main structures for a nonprofit entity are corporations and charitable trusts. Some nonprofits are organized as limited liability corporations, unincorporated nonprofit associations or other types of entities, but such arrangements can create additional complications, which make them less popular choices. If you plan to set up your nonprofit as a corporation, you must file articles of incorporation with the state in which your nonprofit will be organized or based. Most states offer examples to work from. For a trust, you will need to create an irrevocable trust document, which will outline the organization's governance structure.

As you begin, gather a team. Among the most crucial people to recruit early are your board of directors (for a corporation) or trustees (for a charitable trust). Each state has different requirements for the number of directors a nonprofit organization should have, so be sure to investigate the rules when selecting your board. A state's minimum often falls between three and five directors. Some states require you to recruit your board before you file your articles of incorporation. In addition to people who will help you run the organization, you should secure the services of professionals who have experience working with nonprofits. At a minimum, consult an attorney and an accountant as you set up your organization. It is also wise to involve your financial adviser, who can offer perspective on how your new nonprofit fits into the bigger picture of your financial goals. Make sure everyone you recruit agrees about the organization's mission and core activities. You should also enlist your team's help in continuing to flesh out and refine your business plan.

If you set up your nonprofit as a corporation, you will need to draft and adopt bylaws. These are your nonprofit's operating manual, governing its internal management. In a trust, the trust document will cover many of the same topics. Many organizations offer sample nonprofit bylaws online, but be aware that specific rules for drafting bylaws vary from state to state. You and the board of directors should work together in the drafting process, along with your legal counsel. The particulars will depend on your organization's mission, but good bylaws should always cover a few basic points: the organization's purpose, the structure of both the organization and its board, and basic operational and administrative mechanisms. Include provisions for how the organization will be governed, the process for selecting new board members, requirements for meetings and conflict-of-interest policies. In a foundation, you may also want to lay out criteria for grants, which can minimize future disagreements between board members. Consider, too, how control of the organization will pass when you eventually depart, expectedly or otherwise. If you intend your organization to outlast your involvement, succession planning is essential.

QUICK NOTES

Points To Cover In Your Bylaws

- ☑ The organization's purpose
- ☑ How the organization will be governed, including the structure of its board
- ☑ The process for selecting new board members
- ☑ Meeting requirements
- ☑ Policies for avoiding potential conflicts of interest
- ☑ Succession plans

During this process you should identify your intended source or sources of revenue, as this decision will shape many of your choices about how your business is structured. Nonprofit organizations typically get revenue from private contributions (individual donors, corporate sponsors or both); government grants; fees for goods or services from the private sector (such as membership dues or event tickets); and fees for goods or services from the government. Some organizations focus on one of these revenue sources, while others rely on a combination of them. What makes most sense for your organization will depend on your mission and the goods or services you plan to provide. Nonprofits may also generate income in ways that aren't related to the main purpose of the entity. This income can be treated as unrelated business taxable income (UBTI) and subject to tax.

In setting up your organization, you will need to determine a compensation structure. By definition, a nonprofit essentially belongs to the community. Any profit goes back into the organization itself. An individual cannot profit from a tax-exempt organization except through his or her salary under IRS rules. Salaries in the nonprofit sector can vary widely, so it's worth doing some market research in advance. Remember that many donors want to see a nonprofit keep its operating expenses, including wages, relatively low. You should also be realistic about what your organization can support, especially at first.

Another important component of starting a nonprofit is a plan to deal with compliance. You should prepare and adopt a policy for dealing with potential conflicts of interest. This should ideally also cover document-retention practices and policies covering whistleblowers. Nonprofit organizations are subject to strict regulatory requirements. Nonprofits with tax-exempt status risk losing it if they participate in prohibited activities, such as political campaigns. Tax-exempt organizations also risk losing their exemption if they fail to fulfill recurring filing and recordkeeping requirements. It is important to create a plan from the outset to avoid these pitfalls.

If your charitable organization is a private foundation, employees and officers alike will need to be especially cautious to avoid self-dealing. This means insiders cannot buy property from or sell property to the organization, nor can they borrow foundation assets. Foundations also may not make investments that jeopardize their ability to fulfill their stated charitable mission. The consequences for violating these rules are generally serious financial penalties for anyone benefiting from the transactions, and sometimes for foundation managers overseeing those individuals as well.

Once your bylaws are drafted, hold an organizational meeting for the directors. They should review and approve the bylaws in their final form. This is also a good time for them to approve any initial resolutions, such as opening a dedicated bank account for the organization. Whether or not you plan to hire employees, your organization will also need a federal employer identification number (EIN). You will need this number to open a bank account, as well as to file federal tax returns.

Once you have incorporated at the state level, you can apply to become tax-exempt. To obtain tax-exempt status from the IRS, you will need to submit Form 1023, "Application for Recognition of Exemption." Certain organizations can file a simpler version of the form, 1023-EZ. In most cases, once your nonprofit becomes a 501(c)(3) organization, you will need to file IRS Form 990 annually. If you fall below the receipts threshold for this filing, you will still need to file either Form 990-EZ or Form 990-N to satisfy the organization's annual filing requirement.

You should also comply with state filing requirements. Once you receive tax-exempt status from the IRS, your state will likely allow you to apply for exemption from sales tax or other state-level taxes. You should also be sure to obtain any applicable licenses or permits you need to operate in your state. These vary depending not only on your location, but also the services you plan to provide or the types of clients you intend to serve. Certain states require specific periodic reporting, too; for example, some states mandate annual renewal of charitable registration forms. You should also set up a system to create acknowledgements to issue to donors, which will allow them to deduct contributions on their federal income taxes. If you receive funding from the government or foundations, you will face still more reporting requirements. Fundraising activities are also regulated by state law. Many states require charitable nonprofits to register with the state before soliciting donations from any state residents, and the rules can become even more complex if you plan to collect donations across state lines (a common practice in the internet era).

How much paperwork you will need to file, as well as the cost and the timeline, will vary from state to state. As just one example, say you plan to start a nonprofit organized as a corporation in Georgia. Documents you will need to prepare include:

- Articles of incorporation (state)
- Notice of incorporation (state)
- Georgia's Data Transmittal Form 227
- Initial "annual" registration (state)
- Bylaws
- Conflict of Interest Policy (if not included in bylaws)
- Charitable Organization Registration for solicitations (state Form C-100)
- "No Funds Received" statement (state)
- EIN application (IRS form SS-4)
- 501(c)(3) tax-exempt application (IRS form 1023)
- Georgia State Tax Exemption (after successful IRS application for 501(c)(3) status)

This list illustrates why it is important to assemble an experienced team to make sure you comply with all the various requirements your nonprofit organization may face.

Once your nonprofit is set up and you've fulfilled the requirements to operate in your state, you still have a lot to do. The specifics will depend on your organization's mission and goals, but there are a few things to consider early on. You will need to secure operating space and establish basic systems for accounting, fundraising and other operational activities. Set up a website or other online presence. If you plan to have volunteers, paid staff or both, determine the skills needed and how you will organize and oversee these workers. If you decide to hire paid staff, you will need to comply with a variety of requirements, such as quarterly reports of tax withholding. And if your nonprofit hopes to expand its reach to multiple states, you may need to complete additional requirements to comply with other states' regulations.

This section is meant as a broad overview of how to start a nonprofit, but you could easily write an entire book on this topic. (In fact, many people have.) While starting an organization of your own involves a lot of work and commitment, many people find it an especially rewarding way to give back to their communities.

BEYOND THE 501(C)(3)

While not every entity can offer tax-deductible donation opportunities, there are many ways to give back beyond traditional charitable institutions.

Although tax-exempt public charities cannot engage in political activity, there are plenty of nonprofit organizations with political goals. Some may be centered on one or more causes. For example, the American Civil Liberties Union (ACLU) is focused on protecting the civil rights of Americans; while it is a nonprofit organization, it is not a public charity. (Instead, it is what the IRS calls a "social welfare organization.") Other organizations support one or more candidates for office. If you are passionate about supporting political change and engaging in civic life, working with such organizations can be a great way to give back. You can volunteer your time or donate outright — just remember that you can't deduct these gifts when calculating your income tax.

Many people also volunteer for "fraternal societies" or "service clubs." These include the Elks Lodge, Kiwanis International, the Lions Club and many other organizations that often focus on community service. While these aren't charities, they often do a lot of good in their communities and receive support from donors and volunteers alike.

Depending on your talents, circumstances and passions, there are many ways to give back beyond those I've discussed so far. You could mentor a child in your life. You could give blood or plasma, assuming you are eligible, or register as an organ donor. And while most charitable organizations prefer monetary donations to goods, you can still reach out to local organizations to see if they need clothing, toiletries or other particular items; just be sure that what you give is in good condition and meets a real need.

No one person will adopt all the approaches in this chapter. But hopefully one or more of these sections has sparked your interest and pointed you toward a way to give back that suits you. However you choose to give, know that the people you are helping will appreciate your generosity. It is a cliché that "it is better to give than receive" — but even so, generations of philanthropists have found that the rewards of giving are very real.

INDEX

Page numbers in *italics* indicate a figure.

C

D

E

F

I

J

K

L

M

S

T

U

V

W

ABOUT THE AUTHORS

Photo by Chris Hedlund

Larry M. Elkin, CPA, CFP®, has provided personal financial and tax counseling to a sophisticated client base since 1986. After six years with Arthur Andersen, he founded his own firm, which would eventually become the Palisades Hudson organization, in 1992. The firm moved from its original New York base in Hastings-on-Hudson to Scarsdale, New York in 2002, and to Stamford, Connecticut 15 years later. In 2005 the firm expanded to Fort Lauderdale, Florida, a branch office that became the firm's official headquarters in 2017. The firm also expanded to Georgia in 2008, Oregon in 2012, and Texas in 2016. Its clients reside in more than 30 states, as well as in several foreign countries. The organization's investment advisory business currently manages more than $1.5 billion.

Larry is the author of *Financial Self-Defense for Unmarried Couples* (Currency Doubleday, 1995), the first comprehensive financial planning guide for unmarried couples. He was among the contributors to Palisades Hudson's first book, *Looking Ahead: Life, Family, Wealth and Business After 55* (currently in its third edition). Larry also serves as the editor and publisher of *Sentinel*, the firm's newsletter, and was the lead author of the firm's blog, "Current Commentary," during its run from 2009 to 2021. Larry received his B.A. in journalism from the University of Montana, and his MBA in accounting from New York University. He is a producer member of Film Florida and a past president of the Estate Planning Council of New York City, Inc., which gave him its first Lifetime Achievement Award in 2009.

Photo by Chris Hedlund

Brianna Aviles became part of the Palisades Hudson staff in 2022, joining the firm's Fort Lauderdale, Florida headquarters as a client service associate. She works on projects for clients across the company's practice areas, including investment, bookkeeping and tax projects. Brianna also provides support to the firm's Entertainment and Sports practice and is a contributor to the firm's *Sentinel* newsletter. A magna cum laude graduate of Florida Atlantic University, Brianna earned a bachelor's degree in finance. She currently resides in her hometown of Boca Raton, Florida.

Photo by Chris Hedlund

Anthony D. Criscuolo, CFP®, EA, has extensive experience in Palisades Hudson's investment, tax, estate planning and accounting practices. As chief investment officer and chairman of the firm's investment committee, Anthony led a team of portfolio managers and associates focused on finding the most efficient and cost-effective ways to implement client portfolio strategies. He oversaw more than $1.5 billion in client assets, including all aspects of investment strategy, portfolio management, due diligence and manager selection. Following an internship with the firm, Anthony began his career in the company's Fort Lauderdale, Florida office in 2008 and was a client service manager between 2011 and 2024. A native Floridian, Anthony worked out of the firm's Atlanta office, where he served clients around the country.

Anthony graduated summa cum laude from the University of Florida with a degree in finance and minors in leadership and entrepreneurship. He holds the CERTIFIED FINANCIAL PLANNER™ and IRS Enrolled Agent credentials and, during his time in Palisades Hudson's Florida office, completed the Fort Lauderdale Chamber of Commerce Leadership Fort Lauderdale program. Anthony was among the contributors to *Looking Ahead: Life, Family, Wealth and Business After 55* and authored many articles for the firm's *Sentinel* newsletter. He also appeared on the first season of the firm's podcast, "Something Personal." Anthony has been quoted as a financial expert by many leading publications, including Forbes, The Wall Street Journal and Reuters.

Photo by Chris Hedlund

Victoria Dubuc joined Palisades Hudson's staff in 2022 and is based in the firm's Fort Lauderdale, Florida headquarters. As an accountant, Victoria serves clients nationwide and across the company's practice areas. She contributes to tax, investment and bookkeeping projects in collaboration with her colleagues across the country. Victoria also contributed to the latest edition of the firm's book *Looking Ahead: Life, Family, Wealth and Business After 55.* She graduated cum laude with a bachelor's degree in accounting from Millennia Atlantic University and went on to earn an MBA in accounting from the same institution, graduating summa cum laude. A native of Venezuela, Victoria currently resides in the greater Fort Lauderdale area.

Photo by Chris Hedlund

Shomari D. Hearn, CFP®, EA, became Palisades Hudson's first-ever executive vice president and chief operating officer in 2023. As EVP and COO, Shomari holds executive responsibility for all of the firm's operations and for strategic initiatives such as the Entertainment and Sports Team. Shomari also continues to provide a wide range of services to Palisades Hudson's clients, including asset allocation programs, investment analyses, cash flow projections, retirement plans, tax strategies, income tax planning and compliance, accounting and estate administration. Though based in the firm's Fort Lauderdale, Florida headquarters, his client service and firmwide responsibilities regularly take him across the United States and abroad.

A New York City native, Shomari is a 1997 graduate of Duke University, where he obtained a B.A. in economics and a certificate in markets and management study. Since moving to Florida two decades ago, Shomari has become an integral part of Fort Lauderdale's business community, including the Greater Fort Lauderdale Chamber of Commerce. He has also become an active voice in the sports and entertainment community, and is a member of the industry group Diverse Representation. Shomari is a regular contributor to *Sentinel*, Palisades Hudson's newsletter, and was among the authors of the firm's book *Looking Ahead: Life, Family, Wealth and Business After 55*. He appeared on multiple episodes of the first season of the firm's podcast, "Something Personal." Shomari has also been quoted by financial columnists for The Wall Street Journal, CNN Money, Forbes Magazine and many other local and national publications.

Photo by Chris Hedlund

Paul Jacobs, CFP®, EA, assumed the role of managing vice president in 2023 after joining Palisades Hudson's executive team as a vice president in 2017. As managing vice president, Paul oversees the entirety of the firm's client service operations. He also continues to work with clients across the country to develop comprehensive personal financial plans, and he brings his significant experience to projects including charitable planning, dealing with concentrated stock positions, small business and family business planning, creating cash flow projections and retirement plans, and estate planning and administration. Paul formerly served as the chief investment officer for Palisades Hudson's investment advisory business, overseeing all aspects of investment strategy, portfolio management, due diligence and manager selection. He has been based in Atlanta since establishing Palisades Hudson's office there in 2008.

A frequently quoted expert for national publications, Paul's thoughts on financial topics have appeared in The Wall Street Journal, Forbes and Reuters, among many other outlets. During its run from 2009 to 2021, the firm's blog "Current Commentary" frequently featured Paul's writing. He is also the author or co-author of many articles for the firm's *Sentinel* newsletter and contributed to Palisades Hudson's book *Looking Ahead: Life, Family, Wealth and Business After 55,* as well as appearing on the firm's podcast, "Something Personal." A graduate of New York University's Stern School of Business, Paul holds degrees in finance and accounting.

Photo by Chris Hedlund

Melinda Kibler, CFP®, EA, serves Palisades Hudson's clients across the full range of the firm's services, including investment management and tax planning and preparation. She supervises the staff of client service professionals in the firm's Fort Lauderdale, Florida headquarters, where she is based. Melinda serves on the firm's investment committee, helping to oversee more than $1.5 billion in client assets, including all aspects of investment strategy, portfolio management, due diligence and manager selection. She is also a member of the firm's Entertainment and Sports Team. Melinda has direct experience in cross-border tax planning issues for international clients, estate planning reviews, accounting, bookkeeping and bill payment service administration, cash flow planning and insurance reviews.

A native of Wappingers Falls, New York, Melinda graduated cum laude from the University of Rochester, where she earned Bachelor of Arts degrees in economics and statistics, as well as a Certificate in Management in accounting and finance. She is also a graduate of the Lifework Leadership program. She was among the contributors to Palisades Hudson's book *Looking Ahead: Life, Family, Wealth and Business After 55* and her writing regularly appears in the firm's *Sentinel* newsletter. She appeared as a guest on the first season of the firm's podcast, "Something Personal," and a variety of national publications have quoted Melinda as an expert on financial topics, including Forbes, Fox Business and The Associated Press.

Photo by Chris Hedlund

Eric Meermann, CFP®, CVA, EA, is the senior client service executive in Palisades Hudson's Stamford, Connecticut office. As a vice president, he is also responsible for firmwide professional staff development, as well as serving clients in the Northeast and across the country. While he joined the executive team in 2017, Eric has long brought his extensive experience to the firm's investment management, retirement planning, estate planning and tax compliance practices. He is the lead executive for Palisades Hudson's business valuation practice and, along with Shomari Hearn, heads the Entertainment and Sports Team. He holds the Certified Valuation Analyst designation from the National Association of Certified Valuators and Analysts, of which he is a member. Eric is also a CERTIFIED FINANCIAL PLANNER™ certificant and an IRS Enrolled Agent.

Among the many leading publications in which Eric has been quoted as an expert are The New York Times, Forbes and The Pittsburgh Post-Gazette. He has also appeared on Ebru TV's *Fresh Outlook* program and can be heard as a guest in the first season of Palisades Hudson's podcast, "Something Personal." Eric regularly contributes to the firm's *Sentinel* newsletter and was among the authors of the book *Looking Ahead: Life, Family, Wealth and Business After 55.* A graduate of New York University's Stern School of Business, Eric holds a degree in finance and international business.

Photo by Chris Hedlund

ReKeithen Miller, CFP®, EA, supervises the staff of client service professionals in the Atlanta office, where he has been based since 2008. ReKeithen is fully involved in the broad range of services the firm offers to clients, from tax and financial planning to investment management and insurance consulting. His experience includes cross-border tax planning issues for international clients, estate tax preparation and planning, bookkeeping and bill payment services, and business acquisitions planning, among many other client services. He also serves as a member of the firm's investment committee and its Entertainment and Sports Team. He joined Palisades Hudson in the firm's Fort Lauderdale office in 2007.

ReKeithen has been quoted as an expert on financial planning topics by national publications, including Barron's, Bloomberg and NBC News. He has written on a variety of topics for the firm's *Sentinel* newsletter, contributed to the book *Looking Ahead: Life, Family, Wealth and Business After 55,* and appeared on the first season of the firm's podcast, "Something Personal." A native of Tallahassee, ReKeithen holds a B.S. in finance with a minor in entrepreneurship from the University of Florida, where he graduated with honors.

Photo by Shayna Image

Mamie Odom joined Palisades Hudson's staff as a client service associate in 2023, after having completed an internship with the firm in the summer of 2022. While she is based in the firm's Atlanta office, Mamie works on projects for clients across the country, including investment management, bookkeeping and tax preparation. She is also a contributor to the firm's *Sentinel* newsletter. A Tallahassee, Florida native, Mamie attended the University of Florida. She graduated cum laude with dual bachelor's and master's degrees in economics, along with a minor in family, youth and community sciences. Mamie currently resides in the greater Atlanta area.

Photo by Chris Hedlund

Rebecca Pavese, CPA, has worked extensively in Palisades Hudson's tax, financial accounting and estate planning and administration practices, and is a member of the firm's investment committee. Rebecca also supervises Palisades Hudson's accounting and administration services for estates and trusts. She has served as the principal supervisor of the firm's income tax planning and return preparation services and has overseen accounting services for a complex oil and gas investment partnership. A New Jersey native, Rebecca joined Palisades Hudson in New York and has been based in the firm's Atlanta office since 2008.

A recognized expert on tax and other financial topics, Rebecca has been quoted by leading publications including The Wall Street Journal, The New York Times and CBS MoneyWatch. She also appeared on the inaugural season of the firm's podcast, "Something Personal." Rebecca contributed three chapters to Palisades Hudson's book *Looking Ahead: Life, Family, Wealth and Business After 55,* and her writing regularly appears in the firm's *Sentinel* newsletter. Rebecca holds a B.S. in business administration from the University of Pittsburgh and a master's degree in accounting from Pace University.

Photo by Chris Hedlund

Kasey Radney joined Palisades Hudson in 2021 as a financial planning assistant and became a client service associate in 2022. A native of Dublin, Georgia, Kasey is based in the firm's Atlanta office. He contributes to projects for clients nationwide across the firm's practice areas, including bookkeeping, investment management and tax preparation. He is also a contributor to the firm's *Sentinel* newsletter and is among the authors of the most recent edition of the firm's book *Looking Ahead: Life, Family, Wealth and Business After 55*. A University of Georgia graduate, Kasey holds a bachelor's degree in consumer economics.

Photo by Chris Hedlund

Benjamin C. Sullivan, CFP®, CVA, EA, is extensively involved throughout the firm's asset management, personal financial planning, tax and valuation practices. He is also a member of Palisades Hudson's investment committee. In 2016, he established the firm's office in Austin, Texas, where he currently resides. As an Enrolled Agent eligible to practice before the Internal Revenue Service, Ben is authorized to represent his clients in tax disputes at all administrative levels. He is also a CERTIFIED FINANCIAL PLANNER™ certificant and holds the Certified Valuation Analyst designation from the National Association of Certified Valuators and Analysts.

Ben has been widely quoted in print, as well as interviewed in video and audio appearances, on personal financial planning and related topics in national media outlets including The Wall Street Journal, Money Magazine and USA Today. He can be heard as a guest on the first season of Palisades Hudson's podcast, "Something Personal." Ben has also written many articles for the firm's *Sentinel* newsletter and contributed two chapters to Palisades Hudson's book *Looking Ahead: Life, Family, Wealth and Business After 55.* A native of East Hanover, New Jersey, Ben graduated magna cum laude from Tulane University's Freeman School of Business with a degree in finance and legal studies in business.

Photo by Chris Hedlund

Thomas Walsh, CFP®, began his career in the firm's Atlanta office in 2011 and has been a client service manager since 2015. He is a CERTIFIED FINANCIAL PLANNER™ certificant and serves clients through his involvement in all areas of the practice, including financial planning, asset management and tax preparation. He is also a member of the firm's Entertainment and Sports Team.

Thomas is a regular contributor to Palisades Hudson's *Sentinel* newsletter and is among the authors of the firm's book *Looking Ahead: Life, Family, Wealth and Business After 55.* He also appeared as a guest on the first season of the firm's podcast, "Something Personal." His advice on financial topics has appeared in national publications including Investor's Business Daily, the Pittsburgh Post-Gazette and U.S. News & World Report. A native of Ormond Beach, Florida, Thomas graduated cum laude from the University of Florida with a B.S. in finance.

Photo by Chris Hedlund

David Walters, CPA, CFP®, has extensive experience in the firm's tax, investment planning, estate planning and accounting practices. He also serves as a member of the firm's investment committee and its Entertainment and Sports Team. David became a client service manager in 2006 and joined the executive team as a vice president in 2021. He transferred to Fort Lauderdale in 2007 before establishing the firm's West Coast presence in 2012. David practices in Hillsboro, Oregon, as well as serving nearby communities including Beaverton and the Portland metro area.

A Wisconsin native, David received his Bachelor of Science in finance and accounting from New York University's Stern School of Business. He has been quoted as an expert on financial topics by a variety of leading publications, including The Wall Street Journal, Money Magazine and The Portland Business Journal. He also appeared as a guest in the first season of Palisades Hudson's podcast, "Something Personal." David contributed a pair of chapters to the firm's book *Looking Ahead: Life, Family, Wealth and Business After 55*, and his writing regularly appears in the firm's newsletter, *Sentinel.*

ABOUT THE COMPANY

Palisades Hudson Financial Group LLC

Two principles have defined our firm since it was founded in 1992:

1. Effective financial advice must consider all the issues confronting affluent individuals. Investment, tax, accounting, estate planning, insurance, business management, retirement and philanthropic considerations — among others — must be addressed together, not in isolation. We accept the challenge to furnish knowledgeable guidance and excellent service in whatever areas our clients require.
2. Our loyalty lies only with our clients. We accept no compensation from anyone else. All charges to every client are clearly disclosed and agreed upon in advance.

Today we serve clients in more than 30 states, and as far away as Brazil, from our offices in Fort Lauderdale, Florida; Stamford, Connecticut; Atlanta, Georgia; Hillsboro, Oregon; and Austin, Texas. Our investment advisory affiliate has more than $1.5 billion in assets under management. Our services to clients range from providing tax returns and household financial management to operating sophisticated real estate and energy investment companies.

There is much more information about our firm, our staff and our work, including our newsletter and our podcast, available on our website at palisadeshudson.com.

WHAT'S NEXT?

LIFE'S BOTTOM LINE IS ABOUT MORE THAN THE BOTTOM LINE.

The previous book from the financial advisers of Palisades Hudson Financial Group, *Looking Ahead: Life, Family, Wealth and Business After 55*, reflects the reality that smart financial management begins with clear choices. Do we want to retire early or work as long as possible? Stay where we are or move to a new state, or perhaps abroad? Make our children financially independent or leave substantial legacies? Transition an existing business to new management, or maybe launch a new venture? What are our charitable intentions, and how do we best carry them out?

In our first book, currently in its third edition, we guide readers through how to identify priorities and use them to shape their finances at 55 and in the decades that follow. Get it from Amazon in paperback or as an e-book.